CTV

THE NETWORK THAT MEANS BUSINESS

CTV

THE NETWORK THAT MEANS BUSINESS

MICHAEL NOLAN

 The University of Alberta Press

Published by
The University of Alberta Press
Ring House 2
Edmonton, Alberta, Canada T6G 2E1

Copyright © The University of Alberta Press 2001

ISBN 0–88864–385–3 hardcover
      0–88864–384–5 paperback

NATIONAL LIBRARY OF CANADA CATALOGUING IN PUBLICATION DATA

Nolan, Michael, 1940–
    CTV, the network that means business

    Includes bibliographical references and index.
    ISBN 0–88864–385–3 (bound). — ISBN 0–88864–384–5 (pbk.)
    1. CTV Television Network—History. 2. Television broadcasting—Canada
—History.
I. Title. HE8700.9.C3N64 2001   384.55'4'06571   C 2001–911348–X

Printed on acid-free paper. ∞

Printed and bound in Canada by AGMV Marquis, Longueuil, Quebec.

The University of Alberta Press gratefully acknowledges the support received
for its publishing program from The Canada Council for the Arts. In addition,
we also gratefully acknowledge the financial support of the Government of
Canada through the Book Publishing Industry Development Program for our
publishing activities.

THE CANADA COUNCIL | LE CONSEIL DES ARTS
      FOR THE ARTS | DU CANADA
      SINCE 1957 | DEPUIS 1957

For my sisters
Eva Roche and Trudy Brown

CONTENTS

FOREWORD

by The Honourable Jim Edwards, P.C.

THERE IS NOT A LOT OF serious or scholarly writing about private broadcasting in Canada. Michael Nolan's *CTV—The Network That Means Business* goes a long way towards filling the gap. It is a timely book; wait a few years, and too many of the original players (or those who knew them) will be gone. Even today's survivors share the broadcaster's "deep-rooted aversion to paper."

Here are the giants who built Canada's first popular TV network: from extroverted Spencer Caldwell and John Bassett, to those who shunned the limelight, such as Murray Chercover and Dr. G.R.A. Rice, to today's media corporate players, John Cassaday and Ivan Fecan.

Here too are the programmers and news producers who rescued CTV News from near-abandonment and boosted it to Canada's most-watched service. CTV chose to offer news that "people are talking about." Michael Nolan documents the formula that made CTV programming successful—"it had to be sold before it was bought or launched." Thus the success and longevity of *Wide World of Sports*, originally with Johnny Esaw, *The Littlest Hobo*, and the nation's first network morning show, *Canada AM*, show the diversity of CTV's programming.

Nolan has a knack for the hilarious anecdote. John Bassett's famous temper becomes self-caricature as he grinds the front page of his own beloved *Telegram* into the carpet. The usually dour Dr. Andrew Stewart summons wary CTV executives to Ottawa on his last January 25th in office, slashes the air with a sword and then serves Robbie Burns Day scotch and haggis.

According to Nolan, CTV's history has four periods: for its first five years, an undercapitalized private company with two at-odds groups of shareholders; for the next 27 years, a cooperative; until 1997 a conventional company; then in rapid succession, the Baton—BCE—Bell Globemedia progression.

This is Michael Nolan's third book on Canadian media, although it should be his fourth. In the late eighties and early nineties, Michael and I tried in vain to persuade Dr. Dick Rice to tell his own story. Dr. Rice, my former boss at CFRN, was active in the industry for seventy-five years and was at his death viewed as the dean of world broadcasters. After four valiant pleas by Michael that the history not be lost, Dr. Rice closed the topic forever.

In its forty years, CTV has come to fulfill the policy purpose envisioned for Canadian broadcasting, decades before the launch of television. It had provided a popular Canadian alternative to the CBC and to the increasingly accessible US networks. If it did so by leading with imported American shows, so be it. Until the late eighties, so did the CBC. CTV came to have a reputation for Canadian broadcast excellence, be it W5, Olympics coverage, or sending the first TV journalist to Beijing. After all, in broadcasting as in politics, one must do well to do good.

PREFACE

THE HISTORY OF the CTV network is a subject that has interested me for a long time as a broadcaster, at an earlier stage, and more recently as an historian. Joining CTV News in the mid 1960s when the network became a co-operative following its founding in 1961, I encountered an interesting and energetic group of personalities eager to present an innovative television service to Canadians. My intention has been to trace the evolution of Canada's first national private television network to show how it has become a voice for Canadian populism. Looking back on its history, the survival of the CTV network was periodically in doubt given the internal struggles and external competition that it faced in an increasingly crowded broadcasting marketplace.

In general, the writing of Canadian broadcasting history has tended to show a bias towards the public sector. The origins of the Canadian Broadcasting Corporation, and its role as an electronic instrument of nationhood, have been well documented. For whatever reason, it could be argued that the private broadcasting industry has suffered from scholarly neglect. Indeed Canadian private television networks have been seen as ready importers of American programming and conveyors of low culture as they have tried to capture the widest possible audiences for their programming. Specifically, the CTV network seemed to have been a convenient whipping boy periodically for some of the challenges and problems faced by the Canadian broadcasting system as a whole, especially the preponderance of United States programming available to audiences.

Private broadcasters must assume a fair measure of the blame for scholars offering passing comment on their role in the Canadian broadcasting system which has often received an unflattering portrayal. The private owners have been inadequate custodians of their heritage, even though broadcaster-businessmen helped to establish the foundation for Canadian broadcasting between 1919 and 1932 during the radio era. With insufficient records and documents, historians face a handicap when they attempt to tell the story of Canadian private television.

T.J. "Jim" Allard, a one-time Executive Vice President of the Canadian Association of Broadcasters, has offered some insight in the Foreword to his book *Straight Up: Private Broadcasting in Canada: 1918–1958*: "Most of the decisions that really shaped broadcasting's development do not appear anywhere in the written record; nor flow from inquisitorial recommendations. All broadcasters have a singularly deep-rooted aversion to paper. Very few broadcasting stations in the so-called 'private sector' have made the least attempt to keep any records other than those strictly required by law."

Historians wishing to document the history of the CTV network face the stricture that Allard has cited. His warning should not go unheeded: "The cautious researcher must distrust most of the written record. It is wrong with distressing frequency." As an example, in his examination of the minutes of one House of Commons Broadcasting Committee, Allard eventually realized that a place in Saskatchewan referred to by a witness as "Community" was actually "Unity," the correct name.

With a meagre supply then of corporate records and documents, and a public record that has to be examined with some skepticism, the story of CTV clearly was a subject that demanded the use of oral history techniques. Whatever the shortcomings of such interviews, the insights of the knowledgeable personalities involved with the history of the network were crucial, if the evolution of CTV were to be chronicled in any systematic way. A number of the interviews focused on the early years of the network in the 1960s when CTV arrived and evolved soon after into a co-operative, the corporate structure it was to hold for almost 30 years. The 1960s and 1970s were building and growth years for CTV; the 1980s and 1990s could be described as years of consolidation and expansion.

The Board of Broadcast Governors licensed CTV in 1961 to serve as an alternative to the publicly owned CBC television established in 1952. Eventually the private network became the most watched general interest service in Canada. Throughout it all, the CTV story has included a colourful cast of boardroom robber barons, the appearance of vibrant on-air personalities and, often after much struggle, the development of innovative programming initiatives. Whatever its cultural impact as a broadcaster, there is no denying that CTV has provided a range of popular programming in news, sports and entertainment to which Canadians have responded.

Television, an entertainment medium, has attracted unconventional characters. The CTV saga is not without its distinctive personalities and lighter moments. While my general aim has been to keep the reader focused on the role that CTV has played in the Canadian broadcasting system, the circumstances that have involved somewhat unpredictable characters could not be discounted entirely in any account of the network's past. If CTV were launched in an atmosphere of uncertainty in the early 1960s, it surely seemed ready for a breakthrough as it celebrated its 40th anniversary in 2001 as part of the new Bell Globemedia Inc. In the end though, CTV has remained "the network that means business."

ACKNOWLEDGEMENTS

A GREAT MANY PEOPLE have made this book possible. I would like to thank John Cassaday, Arthur Weinthal and the Management Committee of CTV Television Network Ltd. for providing research funds. They recognized that the story of Canadian private broadcasting required further scholarly inquiry. The Graduate School of Journalism at the University of Western Ontario provided funding support as did the university's Social Sciences and Humanities Research Council (SSHRC) internal competition as well as the Ontario Arts Council and the Ontario Heritage Foundation.

The CTV story could not have been told without the co-operation of those individuals who were either participants in the network's history or were involved with the eventful circumstances surrounding its evolution. I am grateful to Johnny Esaw, the network's former Vice-President of Sports and a familiar national figure to Canadian sports fans, for allowing me access to his manuscript on his career, CFTO/CTV and his role in numerous backstage events. Similarly Michael Hind-Smith, the network's first National Program Director, kindly provided papers and a copy of his manuscript on his years in broadcasting including CTV. Gordon Keeble, Spencer Caldwell's partner and an early President of CTV, and Nancy Caldwell, Spencer Caldwell's wife, made available helpful documents. John Travers Coleman, a senior officer of CTV for 22 years, allowed me the use of a major paper he had written on broadcasting and provided network records. Peter O'Neill, a former Corporate Secretary and Director Public Affairs and Strategic Planning, provided corporate documents to aid in the telling of the story. Robert Henry Black was of assistance in allowing me the use of transcripts of early news and public affairs programming.

Without the following individuals who granted me personal interviews, the book could not have been written. I am grateful for their time and interest. They are: Douglas Bassett, Isabel Bassett, John Bassett, Matthew Bassett, Allan Beattie, John Beveridge, Robert Black, Bill Brady, Murray Brown, Tony Burman, Nancy Caldwell, Pierre Camu, John Cassaday, Tim Casey, Ken Cavanagh, Murray Chercover, Andrew Cochrane, John Coleman, Bill Cunningham, Hazel Desbarats, Fredrik Eaton, Johnny Esaw, Ivan Fecan, Jonathon Festinger, Ted Gardner, Eddie Goodman, John Grace, Ray Hazzan, Jim Hinds, Michael Hind-Smith, Doug Holtby, Gordon Keeble, Peter Kent, Nick Ketchum, Harvey Kirck, Tim Kotcheff, Finlay MacDonald, Andrew MacFarlane, Al MacKay, Michael Maclear, Peter Mansbridge, Gary Maavara, Bill McGregor, Trina McQueen, Eric Morrison, Greg Mudry, Don Newman, Kevin Newman, Jim Nicholl, Brian Nolan (no relation), Craig Oliver, Peter O'Neill, Ray Peters, Bruce Phillips, Valerie Pringle, Peter Rehak, Sandie Rinaldo, Lloyd Robertson, Mark Schneider, Fred Sherratt, Don Smith, Carole Taylor, Charles Templeton, Pamela Wallin, Allan Waters, Philip Wedge, Arthur Weinthal, and Don Willcox.

Chantal Bradshaw at the CRTC's Public Examination Room in Ottawa-Hull was of great assistance as was Lise Plouffe and Yves Larivière at the Commission. The staffs of the CRTC library in Ottawa-Hull, the Commission's documentation centre in Toronto, the National Archives of Canada, Public Archives of Nova Scotia, Centre for Newfoundland Studies in St. John's, Vancouver Public Library and London, Ontario Public Library responded promptly to requests. Representatives of the CTV affiliated stations were helpful in providing historical material on their stations.

Anne Gentleman and Linda Baier at CTV Television Network Ltd. helped uncover materials on the early history of the network. At Bell Globemedia Inc., I would like to thank Thomas Curzon, Jennifer Humphries, Jennifer Nelson, Leah-Anne Cameron and Carol Ashurst, Manager, CTV Archives and Sales, for responding promptly to queries. Annalee Ulsrud at Watt International also provided assistance. Dave Mills and Wendie Crouch at the University of Western Ontario's Graduate Journalism Program were of considerable help as were Judy La Forme and Joanna Hilchie. At Western I am grateful to Sid Noel, Roger Hall, Paul Nesbitt-Larking, Martin Westmacott and Hugh Mellon.

Sections of Chapters 2, 3 and 10 were based on my article "Case Study in Regulation: CTV and Canadian Broadcast Policy" in Martin W. Westmacott and Hugh P. Mellon eds., *Public Administration and Policy: Governing in Challenging Times* (Scarborough: Prentice-Hall Canada Inc., 1999) and are used with permission of Pearson Education Canada. Portions of the book have been presented before audiences at the following venues: Eighth Biennial Conference of the Midwest Association of Canadian Studies in Indianapolis, Indiana; Tenth Biennial International Conference of the Association for Canadian Studies in Killiney, Ireland; Association for Canadian Studies Annual Conference, part of the Congress of the Social Sciences and Humanities in Edmonton; and Public Broadcasting and the Public Interest Conference held at the University of Maine.

The two anonymous readers helped to clear up a number of problems and in general clarified the manuscript. Mary Mahoney-Robson, editor at The University of Alberta Press, has offered wise counsel throughout. Her able, editorial guidance has been much appreciated and has brought numerous improvements to the manuscript.

My wife, Carole, has remained a steadying influence during the research and writing. Any errors or omissions are my fault.

INTRODUCTION

THE CREATION OF THE privately owned CTV network ushered in a new age of Canadian broadcasting in 1961. For the first time in its history, the publicly owned Canadian Broadcasting Corporation (CBC) faced a major Canadian challenger. The birth of CTV raised the issue of the role of Canadian broadcasting that had been debated since the advent of publicly owned radio in the early 1930s. CTV as a popular television service challenged the notion that broadcasting should serve essentially as a vehicle for cultural uplift and as a vital instrument of nationhood.

CTV Television Network Ltd. was undeniably an entrepreneurial-minded operation reflecting the outlook of its founder. CTV promoted itself as "The Network That Means Business." The private, commercial television network put the issue of high culture versus low culture into sharp relief. CTV was to be a network for advertisers, which meant that it would be a popular, general interest service that would carry programming hoping to attract the widest viewing audience. Indeed Spencer Caldwell, CTV's founder, had marginal interest in broadcasting as a cultural vehicle. A consummate salesman, he envisaged the relatively new medium of television as a form of electronic communications that would sell consumer products and bring affluence. The concept of television as a vehicle to sell "soap" was in flat contradiction to the high-minded cultural role that the *Royal Commission on National Development in the Arts, Letters and Sciences* under the chairmanship of the Rt. Hon.

Vincent Massey, Chancellor of the University of Toronto, espoused for broadcasting a decade earlier.[1]

Beyond the question of the proper cultural role of television, Caldwell had capitalized on a fundamental realignment in the structure of the Canadian broadcasting system, a change that affected both the private and public sectors. *The Canadian Radio Broadcasting Act, 1932* had established the Canadian Radio Broadcasting Commission (CRBC); *The Canadian Broadcasting Act, 1936* had brought into existence the Canadian Broadcasting Corporation. Both the CRBC and the CBC were formed as broadcast operators with a mandate to provide a network broadcasting service. Significantly, they also regulated the private broadcasting sector. The private stations had lobbied vigorously for a separate, independent broadcast regulator. Their campaign eventually found fulfillment in the Board of Broadcast Governors (BBG) established in the *Broadcasting Act, 1958.*[2]

Canadian broadcasting had undergone a profound change. The private broadcasters were now legally co-equal with the CBC. They could no longer be perceived as secondary in the part-public, part-private Canadian broadcasting system. When it was licensed, CTV was a separate network of eight private stations parallel to the CBC and placed in a position to challenge the Corporation for viewing audiences.

The originator of the promotional slogan, "The Network That Means Business," was Ross McLean, who had joined Michael Hind-Smith, CTV's first National Program Director, as Executive Producer. Both had previously worked at the CBC.[3] McLean's five word call-sign touched the sensibilities of both the business community and Canadian viewers interested in an alternative, general-interest service that would broadcast popular fare. When CTV boasted that it "means business," the network obviously intended to attract advertisers to television. But if the network did not have programming, Canadian and American, to which Canadians responded in large numbers, the network would have nothing to sell to advertisers. In turn, advertisers would have insufficient audience reach to market their products. Programming, viewers and advertising were inextricably linked, if CTV were to mean business.

Given CTV's market driven approach, the network could not help but encounter at times a critical regulator whose chief concern was maintaining the integrity of the Canadian broadcasting system. The regulation of broadcasters demanded a delicate balance of ensuring a sufficient amount of Canadian programming was available in combination with the need to allow adequate freedom of choice in viewing behaviour. As in radio, from the beginning Canadian television had to compete with the popular fare that viewers have found irresistible originating in the United States.

In their analysis of the role of the Board of Broadcast Governors and Canadian television policy, Andrew Stewart and W.H.N. Hull noted: "The experience of the BBG, and of the CRTC since 1968, even with its vastly enhanced powers and resources, may provide evidence of the possibility that the Aird Royal Commission of 1929 and all such bodies since have based their recommendations on a false premise. Aird claimed to have found 'unanimity in one fundamental question—Canadian radio listeners want Canadian broadcasting.'" The authors concluded that "experience suggests that the Canadian public had developed an appetite for non-Canadian programs."[4] The ambivalence in broadcasting legislation, regulation and viewer behaviour was underlined earlier by T.J. Allard, a one-time General Manager and Chief Executive Officer of the Canadian Association of Broadcasters (CAB), who described officialdom's approach to broadcasting in these words: "Canadians want more Canadian broadcasting but let's so organize our affairs that we don't deprive them of American programs."[5]

Whatever the impact of successive broadcasting acts and regulatory rulings, the electronic media in Canada have been expected to play a leading cultural role. The demands on the broadcasting industry have been of such magnitude that the *Report of the Special Senate Committee on Mass Media* in 1970 described broadcasting as "The Beast of Burden": "Indeed, broadcasting is so much a beast of burden that we have saddled it with responsibility for holding the country and our Canadian culture intact. No other communications medium has this charge laid upon it by Act of Parliament: 'to safeguard, enrich and strengthen the cultural, political, social and economic fabric of Canada.' We rely for this on the same medium that is the principal advertising mainstay of the soap industry."[6]

There was a disconnect between CTV's intention to provide the public with mass entertainment and the findings of the Massey Commission. The commission's report had largely defined the notion of Canadian culture ten years prior to the arrival of CTV, Canada's first, national private TV network. In 1951, the Commission showed a deep suspicion of what had become known as popular culture or, in a more pejorative phraseology, low culture. In 1991, Paul Litt wrote at the time of the 40th anniversary of the Massey Commission: "Since the commissioners attributed mass culture almost exclusively to the United States, their highbrow cultural nationalism also served Canada's need to distinguish itself from its neighbour." Litt explained further, "Today the traditional high culture promoted by the commission is widely denounced as a facade for the ideological tyranny of Dead White European Males (DWEM)."[7] Recalling Vincent Massey's career, T.J. Allard had written even earlier: "Although he never realized it, Massey's idea of the ideal Canadian culture was basically aristocratic in nature, reflecting the best values of 19th century England. However admirable that kind of society might have been, it was long dead even in its homeland."[8]

Professor Frank Underhill took issue with Massey over the Commission's quest for a national Canadian culture and its description of American influences as "alien": "For we cannot escape the fact that we live on the same continent as the Americans, and that the longer we live here the more are we going to be affected by the same continental influences which affect them." Significantly Underhill noted that the Commission's hearings had drawn only a "minority of persons who are actively engaged in the arts, letters and sciences." The general population was hardly present: "The overwhelming majority of the people of Canada, or even of the radio listeners, were not there at all, because they were not interested enough."[9]

By the time CTV began broadcasting, the Massey version of Canadian culture was clearly out of date and inconsistent with the age of flower power. The somewhat artificial barrier between the notions of high and low culture had begun to crumble. During the first half of the 1960s, North American popular culture was in the ascendant as reflected in the writings of Susan Sontag. In calling for a "new sensibility" towards the notion of culture, Sontag wrote: "One important consequence of the new sensibility (with its abandonment of the Matthew Arnold idea of culture) has already been alluded to—namely, that the distinction between 'high' and 'low' culture seems less and less meaningful." In her essay "One Culture and the New Sensibility," Sontag concluded: "From the vantage point of this new sensibility, the beauty of a machine or of the solution to a mathematical problem, of a painting by Jasper Johns, of a film by Jean-Luc Godard, and of the personalities and music of the Beatles is equally accessible."[10]

FROM HUMBLE BEGINNINGS as a fledgling network in the early 1960s, CTV has grown to become 40 years later the most watched network in Canada as part of a major powerhouse of media convergence, the new Bell Globemedia Inc. CTV appeared to be successful, because it seemingly adhered to the spirit but not necessarily to the letter of the Aird Commission's notion that Canadians want Canadian broadcasting. The nationalistic tone to Aird's findings can be brought into question based on CTV's accomplishments as a privately owned national television service. Without the carriage of mass entertainment, much of it originating in the United States, CTV could hardly have survived as a network broadcaster especially in its formative years.

Canadians have shown that they will watch and enjoy quality, home grown programming, but they are not prepared to be denied access to American fare. Indeed over the years CTV has responded to the ambivalence shown by Canadians in their viewing behaviour. As Stewart and Hull noted, "In spite of the special interest groups which show up at royal commission hearings, parliamentary committee hearings and regulatory agency renewal hearings, the general public has historically demonstrated its preference for non-Canadian programming."[11] Given its market orientation and reliance on advertising for survival, CTV could not help but be aware of the ambivalence among Canadian viewers towards television broadcasting and had no choice but to take their viewing behaviour into account in devising network programming schedules.

The history of CTV can be divided conveniently into four distinct periods. From its founding in 1961 to 1966, the network operated as a private company. CTV Television Network Ltd. consisted of shareholders that included both broadcasters and nonbroadcasting investors. The early years were difficult for the network, which was undercapitalized and faced tensions between the two groups of shareholders.

The second and perhaps the most significant period in its history, from 1966 to 1993, saw the formation of the network as a co-operative when eleven stations in the mid 1960s bought out the shareholders of CTV Television Network Ltd. During these years, CTV expanded its network service but faced periodic boardroom struggles and dire circumstances in the early 1990s when an economic downturn occurred.

In the third period 1993 to 1997, the co-operative operation was realigned along the lines of a conventional company. Decisions were taken by a majority vote removing the need for unanimity among the network's Board of Directors on major issues. A new shareholders agreement opened the way for a single owner to emerge from the leading broadcasting groups in CTV.

The fourth period 1997 to 2001 saw extensive movement in the network's ownership. Baton Broadcasting Inc. (later renamed CTV Inc.) became the sole owner of CTV in November 1997. In December 2000, BCE Inc. received regulatory approval to take over the licensed broadcasting undertakings of CTV Inc. including the conventional CTV network. In January, 2001 a new company, Bell Globemedia Inc., was formed as a major undertaking in the age of media convergence. The company consisted of CTV, *The Globe and Mail* newspaper, Globe Interactive (an Internet content provider), and the Sympatico/Lycos Internet portal.[12]

Not surprisingly the operation of CTV throughout the various periods underwent changes to take into account the different corporate structures that governed the network and its relations with affiliated stations. Throughout the first two periods, CTV Television Network Ltd. had virtually no production capability at the network level. Like all television networks, CTV had arrangements with affiliated stations to carry programs that it sold to national advertisers. However unlike American television networks such as the National Broadcasting Company (NBC) and the Columbia Broadcasting System (CBS) or the publicly owned, Canadian Broadcasting Corporation, the Canadian private network owned no stations of its own in major markets. CTV was highly reliant on the eight affiliated stations that formed the network in 1961 to carry sponsored programming. CTV paid the affiliates for the time it rented on the stations.

For much of its history CTV was perhaps most comparable to the Mutual Broadcasting System (MBS), an early radio network, in the United States which began in 1934 when four stations came together as a group, none of them owned by Mutual. Instead as John R. Bittner noted, the stations in Newark, Detroit, Chicago and Cincinnati "agreed that Mutual would become the 'time broker' among the stations and pay them their regular advertising rate, first deducting a 5-percent sales commission and other expenses such as advertising-agency fees and line charges." The network functioned more "like a co-op than a profit-making network like NBC or CBS."[13] Recalling the history of CTV, John Bassett, a member of the first Board of Directors, remembered that "the old Mutual Broadcasting Company finally broke down in America" but CTV as a co-operative had continued to evolve for almost 30 years.[14]

To begin broadcasting, the CTV network under President Spencer Caldwell had reached an affiliation agreement with the stations it served in eight major cities across Canada. The time that the stations provided to CTV was referred to as the "network sales time" period. In the first affiliation agreement, 25 percent of the sale of the net advertising revenue in the network sales time period was allotted to the network management to operate CTV. The remaining 75 percent was distributed among the affiliates as payment for their air time used to distribute network programming. The "basis of payment to the [individual] station for broadcasting sponsored network programs" in the initial affiliation agreement was "75% of [the] applicable network rate for the station for the program period contracted for" after deduction of such items as "advertising agency commission."[15] The essential problem for the network during its formative years in the early 1960s was that, under the terms of the affiliation agreement, it lacked sufficient financial resources to provide the level of programming which the affiliated stations needed and were unable to produce themselves.

From a structural standpoint, the early years of the network's operations were complicated. The stations that would eventually be affiliates of the CTV network had come together as a group in 1960 as the Independent Television Organization (ITO). The seven stations were: CJCH, Halifax; CFCF, Montreal; CJOH, Ottawa; CFTO, Toronto; CJAY, Winnipeg; CFCN, Calgary; and CHAN, Vancouver. These stations along with CFRN, Edmonton, which had been licensed originally as a CBC affiliate, eventually formed what became CTV Television Network Ltd.[16] When ITO grew to eleven stations, the *Report of the Committee on Broadcasting* in 1965 noted that it was "not a network, but a means to mobilize the purchasing power of the eleven stations to compete with other potential buyers for programs—mainly American, and mainly light entertainment." ITO had a membership of stations "which largely overlaps that of CTV." They were "two interrelated and sometimes conflicting groups of private stations broadcasting in English."[17]

Beginning in 1966, the start of the second period in the network's history when it was reorganized as a co-operative, new shareholders and affiliation agreements were reached. The stations bought out the earlier investors and took ownership of CTV as a co-operative. At the same time, the new affiliation agreement arrived at in the mid 1960s introduced the notion of "station sales time" in addition to the earlier concept of "network sales time." "Station sales time" was a second category of network service to the stations. Under the affiliation agreement, CTV simply acted as a purchasing agent for the affiliates that paid the network to purchase additional programming and deliver it to the stations for use in their particular broadcast schedules where they could sell advertising. No money from "station sales time" was allotted to the network. In their own local markets as privately owned stations, the CTV affiliates provided "local time programming" for their viewers and kept whatever advertising revenues such programming generated.

A major structural realignment of the network in 1966 called for CTV to provide the stations with 30-odd hours of programming in "station sales time" for which the stations would pay the network. The amount of programming was in addition to more than 20 hours of "network sales time" programs for which the stations received compensation for their air time.[18] Thus the new affiliation agreement contained two major concepts: programming provided by CTV in "network sales time" on the affiliated stations and the additional programs bought by CTV and paid for by the stations in "station sales time." In combination, the two categories brought the total network service provided on the affiliated stations to about 60 hours. Separate payments had to be made by the network and the affiliates for the two program services.

In 1997 when Baton Broadcasting Inc. assumed 100 percent ownership of CTV, it no longer functioned as a co-operative as it was now under a single owner. Acquiring CTV had been a long-sought objective of Baton. BCE's acquisition of CTV Inc. (originally Baton Broadcasting Inc.), in December 2000 placed the private network under new ownership once again. Early in 2001, the formation of the company, Bell Globemedia Inc., followed the merger between AOL Online Inc. (American Online) and Time Warner Inc. in the United States and underlined the extent to which media convergence in North America had attempted to bring together content providers and communications carriers. The age of convergence brought a new media age with the potential to rival and even surpass the social and cultural impact that the introduction of radio and television brought to Canadian society earlier.

IF THE 1930S WAS A RADIO DECADE, then the 1960s surely belonged to television. When CTV presented its first broadcast on 1 October 1961, television had become the medium of national significance. The CBC broadcast the Progressive Conservative leadership convention that chose

John Diefenbaker as party leader in December, 1956. Four years later the presidential campaign of John Kennedy in the United States, and his skillful use of television, could not help but influence Canadian political behaviour. Television's extraordinary capacity to communicate experiences brought viewers political assassinations in the United States, the first moon walk and the arrival of Pierre Trudeau, Canada's first national, political TV hero. CTV did not seem to lack a sense of occasion.

CTV arrived as major questions were raised about the role of the CBC. A report by the House of Commons Broadcasting Committee in 1959 contained what Peter Dempson described as "startling information" that proved "what everyone in Canada had long suspected: the privilege of promoting Canadian talent and culture over CBC-TV is an expensive one." He outlined the report's findings for both English and French networks: "On the two networks, total production costs for 95 programs were almost $600,000 in a one-week period sampled. Of this, sponsors paid $215,000 for 40 programs and the taxpayers footed the bill for $382,000." Specifically the report showed, "On the English network, 'losing' programs outnumbered the profit-earners three to one. The gap between cost and revenue was over $80,000." A new era of competition between the private and public broadcasting sectors had begun with about 50 million dollars in advertising revenue up for grabs.[19]

The 1960s was a time of student anti-war protests and introduced the drug culture, mini-skirt and the pill. Society had begun to question established norms. At the end of the decade, the *Report of the Special Senate Committee on Mass Media* had warned that the media were "turning people off." The media, the report concluded, were involved "as participants" in the conflict of "people versus institutions."[20] From the start, CTV played to the tension in society with programming that could touch the sensibilities of Canadians. Peter Rehak, a former executive producer of the network's public affairs program W5, recalled the program's early fare: "There is newspaper magnate Roy Thomson, later Lord Thomson of Fleet, debating with a high school janitor who claimed Canada's social system favours the rich. Both are articulate and civilized. Neither convinces the other. Can anyone imagine Conrad Black doing the same thing today?"[21]

During the 1960s, CTV continued to extend its service to Canadians beyond the original eight television markets that established the network. Throughout the 1970s, the network's focus was placed heavily on developing its news service nationally and internationally. CTV sports remained a mainstay of the network for revenue especially during the first two decades. With prodding from the broadcast regulator in the 1980s, CTV was challenged to provide more quality Canadian drama. The network responded with the popular *Due South* in the early 1990s as it grappled with the expensive genre of programming. Later in the decade came CTV Signature presentations *Milgaard* and *The Sheldon Kennedy Story* as the network attempted to touch Canadian audiences with stories that have major social significance.

CTV frequently described its programming service as "populist." The network has aimed to satisfy mass audiences as opposed to the more intellectual fare that the public broadcaster was to offer. What did CTV mean by a "populist" television service? The question was addressed by network executives when they appeared at a licence renewal hearing in 1993. John Cassaday, then CTV President told the CRTC: "We really feel that we have much more of a populist approach, that we are much more 'main street' Canada, as opposed to the university halls of Canada....We like to think that we can touch people with our story-telling. We are not trying to educate them. We are trying to inform them—and it is more than a subtle difference to us."[22]

Similarly Eric Morrison, the Vice President of News, explained to the Commission: "To go back for a moment to the phrase 'populist', we view that not in a 'demogogic' sense, or not in a 'Hughey Long' sense, but in the sense of covering topics the Canadian public wants information on. Not perhaps what we feel they ought to know, but what is meaningful to them, and what in their daily lives is something that they want more information and understanding about, to help them comprehend the changes in the world."[23]

In contrast, Peter Mansbridge, anchor of *The National* on CBC English television, argued that the Corporation's flagship newscast is more interested in delivering the news that people should know about: "So you know, it's the age old argument. Is news what people are talking about or is news what people should know about?" Mansbridge maintained that the CBC's role is "to focus on what you know people should know about. And...quite often the story that people are talking about around the water cooler is the latest sort of tabloid television story out of the United States."[24]

Kevin Newman, a news correspondent for Global, CTV, CBC, and the American Broadcasting Company (ABC) in New York before returning to Canada to anchor a western based network newscast for CanWest Global Communications Corp., has described the *CTV National News* as more reflective of the country at times than the CBC: "I think CTV's strength is that it is more aggressive than the CBC in its news service. And I think it has a better understanding of what people are interested in than the CBC does. I think the CBC often thinks it is too clever by half and that CTV does not have that same kind of veneer of dare I say it 'intellectualism' attached to it....They approach everything on an intellectual level at the CBC often."[25]

The physical movement of CTV's corporate head office in Toronto reflected the different periods of the network's history and growth. CTV began its operations at 42 Charles Street East under Spencer Caldwell and Gordon Keeble and remained there during the years that Murray Chercover served as President. Under John Cassaday when CTV became a more streamlined broadcasting organization, the network occupied modern offices and studios at 250 Yonge Street in an imposing tower high above the Eaton Centre. When Baton Broadcasting Inc. assumed control of CTV, and later under Bell Globemedia Inc. with Ivan Fecan and Trina McQueen as leading executives, the network was consolidated in Scarborough where CFTO, the flagship station, was originally located. CTV boasts a major downtown Toronto presence with the Masonic Temple where productions such as *Open Mike with Mike Bullard* originate. While it has maintained a connection with its roots, CTV does not appear to have been governed by its past.

With the deep pockets of BCE behind it, the CTV network entered the new millennium in the healthiest economic position of its history. It was less reliant on public subsidy to assist with populist and mainstream programming initiatives. Trina McQueen, President and Chief Operating Officer of CTV Inc., saw the challenge that CTV faced was to ensure that the cultural impact of Canadian programming also met the requirements of private broadcasting as a business. The network, she said, had to free itself from "this welter of public subsidy and make sure that Canadian programming is in fact a good business decision as well as a good cultural decision. If we manage to do that, it will be an accomplishment that will, I believe, rival the creation of the CBC in terms of a contribution to Canadian culture."[26]

Throughout its history and especially in its formative years, CTV has come in for criticism from broadcast regulators and cultural nationalists for its importation of American fare or lack of Canadian programming.

Still the mass audience has shown a curious quiescence towards CTV. Seldom has there been a groundswell of public disapproval of the programming the network has provided. Indeed CTV has seemingly drawn protests or praise solely from interest groups such as Friends of Canadian Broadcasting and the Canadian Association of Broadcasters. Surprisingly, a network that "means business" has had generally little resonance in the public though it became the most watched television service in Canada.

Based on the attitude shown by Canadians, it could be concluded that they have enjoyed the range of American programming that CTV has presented and also have identified closely with the vibrant, local television news that the network's affiliates have provided in the regions they serve. Other forms of programming would appear to offer "diminishing returns" to the network's devoted viewers well satisfied with U.S. content and happily unconcerned with Canadian fare. In short, the quiescence of the mass television audience and a disinterested public have been CTV allies and have allowed the network latitude in interpreting its Canadian content commitments and designing its program schedules.

Whatever its contribution to the Canadian broadcasting system, there is no question that CTV's arrival brought a new broadcast era. The CBC recognized that it no longer was the only television game in town and would be challenged to remain the dominant Canadian broadcaster. Spencer Caldwell was ready to operate his network as a business and to provide programming for the masses. Clearly his was a network different from the "Holy Mother Corp.," the CBC's nickname.

Rae Corelli outlined the public versus private broadcasting tension that CTV had created: "Contrasting sharply with this [Caldwell's vision] is the viewpoint, widely shared among CBC personnel, that the mass taste is a myth and if you don't aim higher than westerns and private-eye-shoot-'em ups, people will never want anything more elevating than the rattle of six guns at the Longbranch saloon."[27] The creation of CTV—"The Network That Means Business"—set the country's broadcasting system on a new course.

CTV

THE NETWORK THAT MEANS BUSINESS

Spencer Caldwell—The CTV founder. Used with permission of the
Caldwell Estate.

ONE

The CTV Founder
1909–1961

SPENCER WOOD CALDWELL, entrepreneur par excellence and founder of the CTV network, was seldom restrained in his day to day business dealings. Typical of his boisterous style was when he set out in June, 1961 to hire Michael Hind-Smith away from the Canadian Broadcasting Corporation (CBC) as the first national program director of his fledgling private TV network. With his characteristic bombastic flare, Caldwell wooed Hind-Smith, who was later to become head of the Canadian Cable Television Association, with a gut-level, verbal flourish: "I hear you think you're pretty shit-hot. I wanna talk to you!" Somewhat astonished because he had never met Caldwell, Hind-Smith asked, "Now?" Caldwell who had just obtained a licence for Canada's first national private TV network responded: "Yeah, right now!" The CTV founder had mastered the art of persuasion. Some 14 hours later, Hind-Smith arrived home to regain his composure, shower and write his resignation letter to the CBC where he had worked for the past eight years.[1] Caldwell had his national programmer.

The recently licensed CTV network was only about three months away from its inaugural broadcast. Caldwell and the team he had assembled around him were on a break-neck schedule for what appeared to be almost mission impossible. Even the name of the network was a subject of some controversy. The CBC had seemed deeply concerned about its status as a national institution in the face of the new level of competition that Caldwell and his proposed network presented. With Caldwell, an avowed entrepreneur, who intended to operate the network as a business, CTV had the potential to erode the Corporation's mandate as a bulwark against Americanization in the cultural sphere. J. Alphonse Ouimet, President of the CBC, had lamented Caldwell's proposed use of the name "Canadian Television Network Limited" before the Board of Broadcast Governors (BBG). He questioned whether the name would lead Canadians to confuse the new, private network with the publicly-owned corporation: "You can imagine, just hearing this every night all across Canada on your screen—you can hear them saying 'This is the Canadian Television Network'—now the people cannot even differentiate between the CBC and the BBG after two years—you can imagine the confusion."[2]

Ross McLean, hired as CTV Executive Producer after leaving the CBC, recalled that the combination of the call letters really "stood for nothing," because CTV "didn't parse": "It was sometimes referred to as the Canadian Television Network. Should it have been CTN? In every way imaginable, CTV needed to make a name for itself." After he joined CTV, McLean explained that the following year was one of "hustle, hype, self-delusion, extravagant claims and countless assaults on corporate boardrooms, endlessly proclaiming the virtues of a new Canadian programming, seeking sponsors for 'revolutionary new concepts.'"[3]

McLean had built a solid reputation with a long list of programming credits produced in his years with the Corporation including *Close-Up*, *Tabloid* and *Midnight Zone*. With an annual salary of $17,500, the creative McLean admitted to *The Canadian* that he had taken a pay cut to join CTV, because the private sector proved interesting: "I would not have missed the CBC experience, but it *was* a little self-indulging. There was no obligation to *reach* anyone. I could operate a series like a hobby, for personal pleasure. Now I emerge from a subsidized cocoon to the Real World. I face the stimulating necessity to hit home with a program." With some prescience, McLean anticipated that CTV would not be "a critics' network" but rather "a people's network." CTV had to make a profit and no program was to be bought until it was sold. Caldwell had warned McLean: "Every show's gotta sell."[4]

Caldwell was prepared unabashedly to challenge the CBC. He was hardly restrained in his view that a commercial TV network could provide a valuable service to a mass audience in Canada. As a former CBC executive, Caldwell was a reluctant admirer of the Corporation and its mandate. Still he was essentially market oriented: "There's nothing wrong with the CBC and the millions the government gives it," Caldwell explained to the *Financial Post*. "It fills a minority-viewer need—though, I must say, rather expensively sometimes. But ours is going to be commercial TV, an advertisers' network."[5] Not by design but rather almost by accident, the pioneers and robber barons who built the CTV network 40-odd years ago managed to create a broadcasting entity that was surprisingly successful on the basis of the service that it has provided to Canada.

When the first broadcast in October, 1961 previewed several of the programs, CTV looked to be rich in quiz shows. Among the Canadian programs adapted from radio were *Take a Chance* hosted by Roy Ward Dixon; another quiz show *20 Questions* seen by viewers had also been heard on radio. Mitch Miller's *Sing Along With Mitch* and the western feature, *The Rifleman*, made up a portion of the American fare.[6] Critics were quick to contrast the market-place orientation of CTV, and its heavy reliance on American programs and advertising dollars, with the lofty, national mandate of the publicly-owned CBC. Dennis Braithwaite wrote at the time of CTV's launch: "None of the programs previewed last night appear to offer any competition to the CBC's quality news, documentary or drama programs. CTV is obviously stressing entertainment over information to capture the mass audience. Its shows will be entirely sponsored and one of them, *Take a Chance*, will offer cash prizes and expensive merchandise to contestants."[7] As an alternative to the long established CBC, the CTV network appeared to be on the defensive from the start. CTV could be seen as an electronic upstart in a country that had prided itself on the reputation of the public broadcaster with its noble and high-minded attitude toward broadcasting. Personalities undoubtedly played a major role in the genesis of CTV. The private broadcasting industry in Canada has been dominated by hard driving, often eccentric entrepreneurs who forever were seeking a pot of gold at the end of the proverbial rainbow. Clearly CTV owed its birth to a highly-motivated broadcasting personality, a steadfast adherent to the requirements of the market place and, above all, a skilled promoter.

SPENCER WOOD CALDWELL WAS the CTV network especially in its formative years. The tenacity of the network's founder could hardly be overestimated. Caldwell was the quintessential private broadcaster: entrepreneurial and adventuresome. He was described as "frank, enthusiastic, sentimental, charming, good-natured and tough."[8] Caldwell was also the typical alcoholic personality and he had a ferocious temper. When the pressures of business became too much, he would have drinking bouts lasting anywhere from a week to ten days culminating in a stay at a detoxification unit. Gordon Keeble, a former business partner of Caldwell's, recalled Caldwell's struggle with alcohol: "Every once in awhile, not too frequently, but every once in awhile things would get to be too much for him. He would be under too much stress and he would turn to the bottle. All you had to do was live through it if you could."[9] Senator Finlay MacDonald, the founder of CJCH-TV, Halifax, a CTV pioneer station, remembered that Caldwell was a "gregarious, engaging guy and a lovable guy, lovable particularly because of the problems he had with alcohol. He fought that all his life and it didn't seem to take anything away from our affection for the guy."[10]

Caldwell's wife, Nancy, observed that "he was incapacitated periodically" because of drinking, but beyond that was "a very likeable person, outgoing personality, a super salesman, quite innovative. He really would think up things." Caldwell had met his wife in Regina when he was selling radio transmitters for the Marconi company. An energetic individual, his wife remembered Caldwell's resilience in business should setbacks occur: "He was not a brooder, not at all."[11] Typical was Caldwell's resilience shown after he suffered a major reversal when he failed to get a Toronto private TV licence. The next year he applied successfully to operate the network.

Caldwell's business philosophy was based largely on that of Harold Carson, a member of the triumvirate of Taylor, Pearson and Carson, originally an automotive dealership based in western Canada. The firm entered the radio business in the 1920s recognizing that the radio industry represented a market for batteries both in the operation of local stations and listener receiving sets. Later the company established All-Canada Radio Facilities Ltd. that represented radio stations across Canada. At one time, Caldwell served as head of the syndicated programming division of All-Canada. Keeble, a former Vice President of S.W. Caldwell Limited, which served many facets of the broadcasting industry, recalled that Carson was "a nice man" but he was "not one inclined to excessive generosity as far as his people were concerned. He paid you what he had to pay you to get you. And essentially this was Spence too. He paid you what he had to but no more."[12] Caldwell's business outlook was to have lasting impact on the operation of CTV.

Keeble remembered Caldwell's complex personality in business affairs: "He had a notorious temper which didn't show very often but blew good [*sic*] when it went."[13] Above all, Caldwell was profit oriented; like many other entrepreneurial-minded private broadcasters, he anticipated that network television could become a lucrative business through the sale of air time to advertisers. He was decidedly on the side of those who would subscribe to the adage expressed by newspaper magnate Roy Thomson, who in describing a Scottish TV operation, said that owning a television station was "like having a licence to print your own money."[14] Caldwell seemed fascinated by television, a new form of communications where the integration of advertising, programming and electronics could be combined in a network of stations connected by microwave to provide a worthwhile service and produce healthy profits.

Caldwell's career paralleled closely the evolution of the early broadcasting industry in Canada. A Westerner, he was born in Winnipeg on 11 February 1909, only eight years after Guglielmo Marconi had conducted his successful radio experiments at Signal Hill, Newfoundland. Caldwell represented the fifth generation of his family; Spencer Wood Caldwell was the name of an earlier Irish ancestor. Caldwell's father worked as a department manager at Eaton's in Winnipeg; his mother was exceedingly religious and refused to ride public transportation on Sundays. From his parents, Caldwell acquired two notable qualities: an enormous capacity for work and integrity in business affairs.[15] His work was his life.

The family lived comfortably at 323 Vaughan Street in Winnipeg; Caldwell could have attended university, but he chose not to do so. Unlike Alan Butterworth Plaunt, the rich, Oxford educated founder of the CBC who envisaged a culturally independent Canada, Caldwell seemed eager to experience the business world; as a youth, he had acquired a keen interest in the technical aspects of radio and electronics.[16]

The Conservative government of R.B. Bennett established the Canadian Radio Broadcasting Commission (CRBC), forerunner to the CBC, in 1932; a full 13 years after the Canadian Marconi Company's XWA, Montreal (later CFCF), the country's first private radio station, was licensed in 1919. Throughout the roaring 1920s and for much of Caldwell's early life, broadcaster-businessmen dominated the Canadian radio industry. The CBC, the country's second public broadcasting agency, replaced the CRBC in 1936. Harry Boyle, a former CBC executive and Vice-Chairman of the Canadian Radio-television Commission, commented on how the early broadcasting environment shaped Caldwell's private enterprise bias: "Men like Spence grew up in the tradition that broadcasting is a money-making proposition."[17]

As entrepreneur, Caldwell possessed three qualities that are rarely combined: business acumen, salesmanship capability and technological foresight. Like many Canadian teenagers, Caldwell was fascinated by the "ham" radio craze of the 1920s. T.J. Allard, a former General Manager and Chief Executive Officer of the Canadian Association of Broadcasters, described how Caldwell attended the Kelvin Technical School in Winnipeg and "won first prize for persons under age 16 for originality, by putting together a crystal set in a walnut shell." Later Caldwell worked in the radio department of the T. Eaton Company, and "created a special crystal set, for Eaton executives, from a Benson and Hedges cigar box."[18] Not surprisingly he later sold crystal sets for both the Hudson's Bay and T. Eaton companies in Winnipeg. When the radio industry in Canada began to expand, Caldwell sold radio receiving sets for the Rogers Majestic Company; he succeeded in selling the distribution rights for the radio sets to Taylor, Pearson and Carson.[19]

Following a visit to England, Caldwell returned to Canada with the rights to sell a range of British sports equipment and component parts for radio sets. Thinking he had no duty to pay, he ended up in Montreal with his samples of British supplies and $500.00. However the duty turned out to be $487.00. With only $13.00 left, Caldwell began to sell hats and caps at Eaton's in Montreal. As he explained, "That was the extent of my French, too. I was a wow with Chapeaus et Casquettes."[20]

He did not rely on the sale of hats for long to make a living. Caldwell's interest in radio re-emerged and his technological know-how was turned to advantage. He assumed the position of sales engineer in western Canada for the Canadian Marconi Company. Ray Peters, a former Managing Director of CHAN-TV, Vancouver who was actively involved in the pioneer days of television, knew Caldwell during his Marconi days and remembered how he built up contacts throughout Canada especially in the west. This knowledge of the country was invaluable for Caldwell when he set out to build the CTV network. "Spence originally worked for Marconi and he sold radio transmitting equipment and he knew the country very well because he travelled across the country....Spence was quite a drinker in those years. He did a lot of business and then Spence ended up leaving Marconi and opening up his own...business of distributing syndicated radio programs."[21]

VIA Rail Canada
Name / Nom
SUGANTHA SAM

205 YORK ST.   LONDON, ON   ST

Itinerary / Itinéraire   VIA Préférence N°

From / De
LONDON ON   21Dec 15:49
To / À
ALDERSHOT ON   21Dec 17:10
Train VIA 076 Class / Classe COMFORTconfort

From / De

To / À

Train

Class / Classe

Receipt / Reçu   21Dec06 LNDNKV
Ex xxx8489 Total Amount: 26.50 CAD

Fare / Prix   25.00

G.S.T./T.P.S.   1.50   G.S.T. No / N° T.P.S. 105521785
H.S.T./T.V.H.

P.S.T./T.V.P.   0.00

Total   26.50

100669080   1/1

File / Dossier   FTR / ETF   21122006 11367

FTR / ETF FY2M080

VIA Rail Canada
Name / Nom

From / De

To / À

Train   Class / Classe & Services   VOID

Car / Voiture   Seat / Place

VOID

File / Dossier   FTR / ETF

2

Special needs / Questions ?! / Besoins spéciaux
www.viarail.ca / 1-888-VIA RAIL (1-888-842-7245)

TTY/ATS : 1-888-268-9503

Book online
www.viarail.ca
Réservez en ligne

Carry-on baggage - Maximum weight and size per article: 23 kg (50 lbs.) and 23 x 66 x 46 cm (9 x 26 x 18 in.). Maximum allotment: 2 articles (1 article on Renaissance trains). Extra articles must be checked where this service is available.

Baggages à main - Poids maximum et dimensions maximales par article : 23 kg (50 lb) et 23 x 66 x 46 cm (9 x 26 x 18 po). Nombre d'articles autorisés : deux articles (un article pour les trains Renaissance). Les articles supplémentaires peuvent être enregistrés lorsque ce service est offert.

Conditions of contract

1. Your rail ticket is not transferable and is valid only for travel on the train(s) and date(s) shown. You may exchange or refund your ticket up to one (1) year after purchase, subject to the conditions of the applicable fare plan. Please advise VIA Rail in advance of any travel cancellations.
2. Do not detach your coupon from the receipt or VIA Rail may refuse your travel, refund or credit.
3. Times shown in timetable or elsewhere are not guaranteed.
4. In case of necessity, VIA Rail may cancel a train or substitute alternate transportation without notice.
5. To ensure all passengers' safety, VIA Rail reserves the right to inspect all baggage.
6. You are responsible at all times for your carry-on baggage. VIA Rail assumes a limited liability for loss or damage to checked baggage. Ask VIA Rail personnel for more details.

Other conditions apply to your travel.

Conditions du contrat

1. Votre billet de train est non transférable et valable seulement pour un voyage à bord du ou des trains indiqués et à la ou aux dates indiquées. Votre billet est échangeable ou remboursable jusqu'à un (1) an après l'achat, sous réserve des conditions du tarif applicable. Veuillez aviser VIA Rail à l'avance en cas d'annulation de votre voyage.
2. VIA Rail peut refuser de vous accorder un voyage, un échange ou un remboursement si vous détachez le reçu de votre billet.
3. Les heures figurant à l'indicateur ou autrement ne sont pas garanties.
4. Si nécessaire et sans préavis, VIA Rail peut annuler tout voyage et le remplacer par un autre mode de transport.
5. Afin d'assurer la sécurité des voyageurs, VIA Rail se réserve le droit d'inspecter tous les bagages.
6. Vous êtes en tout temps responsable de vos bagages à main. VIA Rail assume une responsabilité limitée pour les bagages enregistrés perdus ou endommagés. Adressez-vous au personnel de VIA Rail pour de plus amples renseignements.

D'autres conditions s'appliquent à votre voyage
VIA 85-K5104 (02-03)

www.viarail.ca / 1-888-VIA RAIL (1-888-842-7245)
TTY/ATS : 1-888-268-9503

In 1936, the year the CBC was established, Caldwell broke his somewhat frenetic pace; he married Nancy Graham, a grey-eyed blonde from Regina with a Scottish and Welsh family background. When she met him, his future wife was not impressed with Caldwell's manner: "I didn't like him very much. He thought he was the big shot from Winnipeg. He was just too full of himself." Later on she recognized "a likeable side after all."[22] His new wife was somewhat bewildered by a seemingly endless supply of badminton birds and ping-pong balls that Caldwell had brought back from his year in Britain and which he later hoped to sell in Canada. Caldwell seemed to combine family life with business on a regular basis. His wife recalled: "For years, it seems to me, I was trying to palm off gifts of badminton birds and ping-pong balls."[23]

During the early years of the Second World War, Caldwell was on the move. He worked for both the private and public broadcasting sectors. In 1940, Caldwell was employed with the private station CKWX, Vancouver. Three years later, the CBC hired him to manage the publicly-owned radio station CJBC, Toronto and to launch the second CBC English language radio network known as "Dominion"; the other CBC network was called "Trans Canada." His wife, Nancy, encouraged him to take the position with CBC radio, because she thought it would be a notable advance in his career. A westerner, she was of the view that "everything happens in Toronto."[24] His experience with the CBC gave him an insight into radio programming and network broadcasting though his talents clearly were as a salesman and promoter, not as a programmer. Any notion of Caldwell launching a new era of Canadian programming in 1961 through CTV was improbable at best.

Whatever the BBG might have expected CTV to contribute to Canada's cultural experience, Caldwell was hardly one to initiate innovative Canadian programming. He was candid and not the slightest restrained about his programming capabilities. "If there ever was a guy not interested in programming, it was me," he recalled. "I've always been a salesman, a promoter." He had "promoted hell" out of CJBC, a talent that the CBC appeared to have recognized when the Corporation needed a skilfull promoter to launch their new "Dominion" network.[25] Caldwell was somewhat bewildered why the CBC would ever hire him because he was "just a salesman" and hardly interested in any notion of Canadian broadcasting as a cultural instrument of nationhood: "If ever there was a guy not interested in culture..."[26]

Not surprisingly, CTV was to be a network that meant business rather than a second TV network that was to nurture Canadian artists. Indeed Caldwell was hardly interested in programming concepts. A program was a commodity to be sold. Keeble, his business partner, observed that Caldwell was neither a program creator nor did he have any real sympathy for programming and programmers: "I could not say that he had any gut feel for the programming process. It was the necessary evil. It had to be there to give him something to sell."[27]

Similarly Caldwell saw the Canadian content regulations that the BBG had introduced for broadcasters in a similar way. In 1960 the broadcast regulator announced that a 55 percent Cancon requirement would apply to TV broadcasters on a weekly basis. When the private broadcasters objected, a four-week averaging period was applied and a phase-in time allowed for broadcasters to move from 45 percent to the 55 percent target by 1962.[28] Caldwell likened Cancon to the notion of "tariff protection": "It boosts the Canadian workforce. I don't say you should buy Canadian shows just to be patriotic. I say you should buy them because it is good business."[29] To Caldwell, broadcasting and culture were mutually exclusive concepts.

When Caldwell arrived in Toronto in 1943, he encountered Gordon Keeble who was "ensconced as his chief announcer at CBC up on good old Davenport Road."[30] The pair eventually established a working relationship that lasted for 20-odd years, including the early turbulent years of CTV. A few years after his arrival at the CBC, Caldwell returned to the private sector with All Canada Radio Facilities. He was placed in charge of transcription program sales for the company. At the same time, Keeble left the CBC to join Hayhurst Advertising as Radio Director and then went to CFCF radio, Montreal as Station Manager. The pair were reunited in 1950; Keeble joined Caldwell in S.W. Caldwell Ltd. The company of five divisions had over 100 employees and assets worth about a million dollars by the late 1950s. To Caldwell, it was "a very simple one-stop service to the broadcasting industry. It may look complicated from the outside, but from here, it's a simple and straight-forward set-up."[31] S.W. Caldwell Ltd. was to turn Spencer Caldwell into a millionaire and was the launch pad that eventually brought him CTV Television Network Ltd. in 1961.

The evolution of S.W. Caldwell Ltd. reflected Caldwell's integrated approach to business management that later found expression in the establishment of CTV. He envisaged providing TV stations linked by microwave with programming that could be sold to advertisers. S.W. Caldwell Ltd. foreshadowed the business philosophy that Caldwell brought to CTV: the integration of programming distribution, advertising sales and technological communication. Keeble explained the operation of the many facets of S.W. Caldwell Ltd. and how it embodied Caldwell's managerial style: "The characteristic was that they were all interconnected in that they supplied each other or they were logical offshoots of businesses we were doing. And that indicated as much as anything his spirit of developing and thinking."[32]

Caldwell was a conceptualizer, an idea man of the first order according to Keeble. "I can remember days when he would sit down with the American magazine called *Broadcasting* and he'd...just read through it and come up with ideas for half a dozen businesses." In Keeble's view, entrepreneurship was Caldwell's outstanding characteristic. He was able to envisage and begin "many business operations. But on the negative side, 'begin' is the operative word. Like most entrepreneurs that I know they are great on the concept...can get it going and the moment it is going they lose their interest in it and somebody else has to keep it going. So if there is a negative, that would be it."[33]

The company, S.W. Caldwell Ltd., had several divisions involved in various aspects of the communications business: the production and selling of radio and television programs, a film processing laboratory, an equipment division that provided specialized products for the electronic media, and TelePrompter of Canada Limited, the latter involved with the emerging field of closed circuit television.[34] Caldwell was a pacesetter in the Canadian broadcasting industry.

Launched on 11 February 1949, Caldwell's birthday, the company sold and distributed recorded radio programs to advertisers and stations; later it produced radio programs. Clearly the radio programs he obtained the world over for Canadian listeners were intended to provide entertainment to the widest audience and appeal to advertisers. Caldwell's own words underlined the enormous enthusiasm he showed for the radio product to be sold: "Remember Orson Welles in the *Lives of Harry Lime* series? And Michael Redgrave in *Horatio Hornblower*?" Still the radio program that Caldwell never forgot was the one that launched his company: "You might even remember the show that gave us our first big break in the radio business—remember that sultry-voiced young lady who used to breathe heavily through the late night schedule? *Lonesome Gal*?"[35]

During the early 1950s, radio in Canada was the medium of national attention. Television, in its infant stage, had yet to replace radio as the country's principal communications vehicle. In the first four years of operation, Caldwell's company had acquired 15,000 episodes of radio programs that were all aired in a series format. Ultimately as distributors of programming to stations, S.W. Caldwell Ltd. and the CBC, his former employer, divided the market for radio programs between them. In the sale of radio programs, Caldwell recognized a need for advertisers that he could fill: "All these programs were produced outside Canada. This means we had nothing to offer the advertiser who was interested in a purely Canadian show."[36] Clearly Caldwell marched to the beat of the advertisers' drummer as he was to do when he established CTV. His first priority was seemingly to serve advertisers, a reason for him later insisting at CTV that programs had to be sold first before they could be purchased.

To fill the void in Canadian shows, Caldwell bought The Academy of Radio Arts on Jarvis Street in Toronto operated by Lorne Greene. A one-time CBC announcer who later left Canada to become an internationally renown actor, Greene was perhaps most famous for his role on the TV program *Bonanza*. Caldwell began to produce Canadian radio programs from the academy. Without a private radio network, the programs had to be distributed on tape to stations. Gordon Keeble remembered the competition between S.W. Caldwell Ltd. and the CBC: "At one stage of the game, we had more commercial programming coming out of our little studio than they had on the CBC network."[37] Caldwell had taken on Holy Mother Corp. with a vengeance in radio as he was to do later with television.

When TV arrived in Canada in 1952, Caldwell simply adapted his already established business format to television by producing and selling films for TV stations. He obtained film productions from the United States and the United Kingdom when TV stations were in great need of programming; the shows he imported included *Gunsmoke, I Love Lucy, Liberace* and *War in the Air*.[38] These productions would have been chosen specifically for their broad audience appeal and for their potential to attract advertisers. Ray Peters, who became a leading executive with WIC Western International Communications Ltd., remembered how Caldwell was not one to lack a sense of occasion. Because of his early entry into the television program distribution business, "he convinced Westinghouse that he could produce their commercials for them." So in

1952 when the CBC signed on television stations in Toronto and Montreal, "Spence used to produce the Westinghouse 'live' commercials." In the early days of television, the production of live commercials was the accepted format in both Canada and the United States. "All of the stories that you heard about Betty Furness talking about the Westinghouse refrigerators and trying to open the door and it wouldn't open, and pulling the door open of the ice tray [compartment] and it coming off in her hand, and all of those things, were true."[39]

S.W. Caldwell Ltd. also owned a film processing laboratory strategically located on Jarvis Street across from the CBC. The 24-hour operation included the processing of all of the Corporation's news film. Keeble explained that "we used to do all the CBC's news footage for them, because we were right across the road from the CBC and their cameramen would go and shoot something on 16 millimeter film, bring it in, we'd run it through [the processor] and hand it back."[40]

The establishment of an equipment wing of S.W. Caldwell Ltd. was a logical development given the emphasis on the sale of radio and TV programs. Keeble noted the company's growth especially with the advent of television: "There was certain equipment that we needed for selling radio programs...the big, old six inch transcriptions and films and so on. So we set up an equipment division. We needed this equipment; somebody else must need this too! So we had Caldwell equipment company and it handled all kinds of ancillary products right from rewinds and white gloves...the whole bit for film."[41]

However the establishment of TelePrompter of Canada Limited was the clearest manifestation of Caldwell's entrepreneurial spirit and technological vision. When television began, announcers, TV performers, and any public speaker on television, had to learn to develop eye contact with viewers to capitalize on TV's advantage over radio. TV provided greater intimacy with the audience. They relied on a teleprompter situated below the lens of the studio camera that contained a 'rolling' script; this device enabled speakers on television to read and address viewers directly. Caldwell owned the Canadian rights to TelePrompter. He received a percentage of the rental fee every time a TelePrompter was used by the CBC or anyone else. Queen Elizabeth made use of a teleprompter when she spoke to a television audience estimated at 65,000,000 during a visit to Ottawa in the fall of 1957. Caldwell remarked after the event: "That's one machine that will never be used again. I think I'll have it gold-plated—at any rate, it's going to be retired and put in a special glass case on display."[42]

Murray Brown, a former President of CFPL Broadcasting Ltd., recalled the birth of CFPL television in London, Ontario, established by the Blackburn family in 1953, and the extent to which CFPL and other early TV stations relied on Caldwell. The mechanical device was not altogether satisfactory: "The thing I remember when we first went into television…in 1953 was he had a TelePrompter franchise for Canada which you could only get on a rental basis and it was quite a rental at the time. It was mechanical, it would quite consistently break down."[43]

TelePrompter of Canada was also an innovator in the development of closed-circuit television. A TV program was provided for a pre-selected audience similar to the way in which major world boxing events were later promoted. In the mid 1950s, Caldwell recognized the potential of this new form of communications for advertisers. In September, 1957 the British-American Oil Company promoted a new gasoline in Canada through the use of closed-circuit television. With the rights to closed-circuit telecasts, Caldwell was in a potentially lucrative position.[44]

By the late 1950s, Caldwell's business enterprise was housed in three Victorian mansions on Jarvis Street in Toronto near the CBC. The name of "S.W. Caldwell" appeared on each of the buildings. On the way to Jarvis Street and becoming a millionaire, Caldwell encountered prominent Toronto figures such as lawyer Joseph Sedgwick and businessman Jack Kent Cooke. He used office space provided by Sedgwick in the penthouse of the Victory Building on Richmond Street and later took over from Sedgwick when he left. When Cooke left Simcoe House, Caldwell succeeded him at that location. Cooke, who owned radio station CKEY, Toronto and who was to become a future owner of the Washington Redskins of the National Football League in the United States, left Caldwell a desk with no drawers. Cooke said he hoped that Caldwell would make as much money at the desk as he had accumulated. Cooke offered him a piece of lasting advice: "Don't have desks with drawers in them. Otherwise you put your problems in the drawers. When your problems are on top of your desk, you solve them."[45]

Like most entrepreneurs, Caldwell had some notable failures. He purchased a film studio from Rapid, Grip and Batten, a graphic design business, and hoped that it would become a successful film production house. The initiative, in Keeble's words, was "a big mistake" even though the purchase of the studio looked promising with the Canadian television industry at an early stage and TV stations in need of film: "It was a good idea…it was a good studio and we hired [film producer] Sid

Banks to run it for us and he did his very best with it. But...either we were too soon or too late, one or the other, I think probably too soon."[46]

In his private life, Caldwell enjoyed simple food and small parties with close friends. A Manitoban, he avoided Toronto night life and remained aloof from the city's corporate inner circle. He and his wife, Nancy, lived in Kensington Towers, an exclusive apartment building in Toronto; they had no children. When it came to food, Caldwell was the quintessential plain eater. "None of that guinea hen sous cloche for Spence," said Nancy. "He's a poached egg and ice cream type." Perhaps because work and his long days at the office seemed to define his life, Caldwell disliked large gatherings or socializing with the Toronto elite. He commented: "I keep thinking 'I could be back at the office. Why am I wasting time here being bored when I could be at the office where I'm not bored!'" Somewhat chauvinistically, Caldwell was of the view that women should stand by their man and men should stay out of the kitchen: "A young guy can learn a lot more at the office in the evening than he can at home drying the dishes. His wife may not like it at first, but she'll like it in the end because the young man who works harder gets further and ends up able to provide the things most wives want. His wife will be mad at him at one time or another, either because he's young and too busy or because he's old and too poor."[47]

Caldwell was inclined to shun exclusive clubs in Toronto and remained a lone outsider among the city's establishment. As Rae Corelli wrote shortly after Caldwell had established CTV, "Caldwell is a paid-up member of several exclusive haunts, such as Toronto's Granite Club, but he seldom puts in an appearance. If there is some special kinship among the wealthy, Spence Caldwell has yet to experience it. His wife's two oldest friends are working newspaper women."[48] Kay Kritzwiser was arts critic for *The Globe and Mail* and Helen Beattie Palmer was women's editor of *The Globe* and later joined *The Toronto Star*.[49]

Given the historic linkage between communications and transportation, it was hardly surprising that Caldwell should enjoy the sport of sailing to accompany his interest in television. "He liked to play sailor," said his wife Nancy. "He got a cruiser to go through the Trent canal." The couple had a summer cottage at Sturgeon Point in the Kawarthas in central Ontario. Their first major holiday was a cruise to the Caribbean, Jamaica and Cuba on the *Empress of Scotland*. Caldwell went around the world on the *Queen Elizabeth*. His death occurred in a tragic motor accident on 10 December 1983 before he could take another world cruise that the couple had planned.[50]

Nancy Caldwell was largely unsuccessful in getting her husband to experience warmer climes during the hard Canadian winter. "I hopefully try to promote a cruise each winter to keep him trapped away from a telephone," she said. "Once we went to Palm Springs for a holiday. After three days, Spence went to Hollywood on business." Still Caldwell thoroughly enjoyed the trivialities of life like barbecued steaks; he would prepare the meat on his portable barbecue with consummate care. Even when he relaxed, Caldwell's mind seemed to be in a business mode. He passed up golf and fishing. Instead he preferred to work on a daily schedule that would prevent raccoons from getting at the garbage on his summer property. Similarly he would try to devise some form of "closed circuit" on the property to combat poison ivy. "Everyone seems concerned about the life I live," explained the individualistic Caldwell. "People always give you advice on how to live, chiefly because they want you to live the way they do."[51]

Although an avowed private enterpriser, Caldwell drew considerable praise from several spokesmen for Canada's cultural community. They included Neil LeRoy, one time leader of the Actors' Union, and Mavor Moore, the noted Canadian actor and producer. LeRoy described Caldwell as helpful and generous: "If anyone in the industry had a run of bad luck and explained it to Caldwell, I believe Spence would help him. In all his dealings with my union, he is scrupulously fair." Similarly Moore drew attention to Caldwell's financial support for Canadian cultural initiatives. "One would have expected that a man whose basic business is to sell programs made outside of Canada would not be entirely sympathetic to Canadian projects in the same field," Moore explained. "But that's not true of him. Now I know that any worthwhile show business enterprise in Canada can be pretty well assured of Spence's support where it helps most—financially."[52]

Not surprisingly, Caldwell received praise from colleagues in the private broadcasting industry. Murray Chercover, President of the CTV network for more than two decades, described Caldwell as "one of the greatest innovators" over time in Canadian broadcasting: "He was a very bright, imaginative and convincing guy. A hell of a salesman."[53] John Bassett, publisher of the *Toronto Telegram*, who competed against Caldwell successfully for a private television licence, the present-day CFTO, Toronto, was also fond of the Manitoba native: "I liked Spence.

Spence Caldwell was, in my view, a first rate promoter."[54] In the short term, Caldwell and Bassett would be competitors when both sought the private television licence for the lucrative Toronto market in 1960. Bassett would be triumphant, but Caldwell's consolation prize was a licence for CTV. Bassett joined the network founded by his one time foe.

THE EVENTUAL AWARDING of a network TV licence to Caldwell by the Board of Broadcast Governors in 1961 was the culmination of a series of interrelated events that have defined the present-day Canadian private television broadcasting industry. They included a lengthy struggle on the part of private broadcasters to be placed on an equal legal footing with the publicly owned CBC, the BBG's awarding of licences for privately owned TV stations in major Canadian cities and finally Caldwell's winning of a network television licence after the BBG had denied his licence application for a Toronto TV station. The catalyst was the election of the Progressive Conservatives under John Diefenbaker in the 1957 federal election. The Tory electoral sweep the following year, when the party captured 208 seats, could not help but bring about a major change in both the political and broadcasting landscapes.

The new broadcasting legislation in 1958 reflected the extent to which broadcasting and politics have been entwined historically in Canada. The establishment of the BBG, a separate, independent regulator of broadcasting largely similar to the Federal Communications Commission (FCC) in the United States, followed the smashing election victory of John Diefenbaker in 1958. Diefenbaker had supported the private broadcasters and their call for a separate, independent broadcast regulator. He told a campaign rally in Kenora, Ontario on 18 March 1958: "The time is long overdue to assure private stations in competition with the publicly owned national organization that their cases shall be judged by an independent body. They should not be judged by those who are actually in national competition with them and are, in fact, their judge and jury."[55] The chairman of the BBG was Dr. Andrew Stewart, a former President of the University of Alberta. The new agency had three full-time and twelve part-time members.

The BBG appointed by the Tories could be perceived at first glance as a partisan body that favoured the private sector of Canadian broadcasting. John Bassett remembered the Board's appointment and the perception of the BBG as a pro Tory body: "The Tories were in power. Why the hell wouldn't it be? You don't think they were going to appoint a lot of Grits!"[56] Although he claimed to be unaware of Dr. Stewart's political leanings, Senator Eugene Forsey noted that the part-time appointments to the Board included Dr. Mabel Connell, John Diefenbaker's dentist from Saskatchewan. Forsey had been a long-time supporter of the Co-operative Commonwealth Federation (CCF), forerunner to the present day New Democratic Party (NDP), before he was appointed by Diefenbaker as a part-time member of the BBG. He had been on close terms with several leading Conservative politicians including the Prime Minister. Forsey underlined the political influence at work in the Board's makeup: "Most were patronage appointments, several were defeated Conservative candidates."[57]

Shortly after it was established, the BBG had decided to allow private broadcasters to apply for "second" TV licences in the major markets of the country beyond the service that CBC stations provided. Along with eight other applicants, Caldwell had applied for a private TV licence in Toronto in 1960. Caldwell and the other applicants lost out to John Bassett whose company Baton Aldred Rogers Broadcasting Ltd. was awarded the licence. With his capacity for salesmanship and technological understanding of electronic media, it was hardly surprising that Caldwell was exceedingly eager to own a television station. Still the *Broadcasting Act, 1958* had caught him off guard. He had spent about 15 years trying to ingratiate himself to the CBC Board of Governors, the broadcast regulator since 1936. Keeble concluded that the decision by the Diefenbaker government to favour a separate, independent broadcast regulator "was a body blow to him, because he felt that his history [ex CBC employee], his documentation that we had in our application and so on...would have suited the complexion of the CBC board."[58]

The BBG hearing held in Toronto during mid March, 1960 for the "second" TV licence was the highlight of the Board's licensing activity that also took it to the Canadian cities of Winnipeg, Vancouver, Montreal, Edmonton, Calgary, Halifax and Ottawa. Baton Aldred Rogers Broadcasting Ltd. emerged with the Toronto licence largely on the strength of its vibrant presentation before the Board. However Dr. Andrew Stewart, Chairman of the BBG, made it clear in his memoirs that he was against Bassett getting the Toronto licence. Stewart was of the view that because Bassett owned a newspaper, the *Telegram*, he should not be allowed to own a television station in the same market.[59] Still the Board was unanimous in its decision to award the Toronto TV

John Bassett, Andrew Stewart, Joel Aldred and Foster Hewitt (left to right) at the CFTO television studio. Photograph courtesy of Dr. Andrew Stewart from *Canadian Television Policy and the Board of Broadcast Governors.*

licence to Baton Aldred Rogers though Stewart, as Chairman, had voted against Baton's application. In Bassett's view, Stewart, a former university president who specialized in economics, was "a man of undoubted integrity but of limited intellectual capacity outside his own field" and possessed "a strong anti-American bias."[60] Bassett's outlook may have been influenced by the BBG's rejection of a transfer of shares held by broadcaster Joel Aldred in CFTO television, which had been proposed as part of a Baton reorganization, to American Broadcasting-Paramount Theatres Inc., a U.S. network conglomerate.[61]

The BBG hearings into applicants for the Toronto TV licence were held in the Oak Room of the Union Station building on Front Street. Channel 9 was the only remaining very high frequency (VHF) for Toronto.[62] Baton Aldred Rogers made its presentation before the BBG on 17 March 1960 at a morning session with E.A. "Eddie" Goodman, or "fast Eddie," as he was affectionately known in Tory circles, acting as counsel for the company. With Bassett, were his partners Joel Aldred, a well known TV commercial announcer and Foster Hewitt, renown for his legendary network hockey broadcasts in Canada. Rai Purdy, who was to become Director of Television Programming for the company, was also with the Baton group. Purdy had worked in a similar capacity for newspaper magnate Roy Thomson in Scotland in a Thomson-owned TV operation. "I don't like to boast," Bassett recalled, "but I gotta tell you, our application was a knockout!"[63]

Baton Aldred Rogers was the company formed by Bassett, publisher of the *Toronto Telegram* and John David Eaton, his partner, whose family business for generations was a retailing giant. Thus the name Baton. The company, Aldred Rogers, joined them. Joel Aldred's smooth delivery of television commercials in the early days of the medium soon made him a household name in Canada. Aldred was the on-air advertising personality for General Motors. He would travel to Los Angeles to appear as the commercial announcer on the Dinah Shore television show. Edward S. (Ted) Rogers was the son of Edward S. Rogers Sr., the inventor of the batteryless radio in 1925 during the infant age of the Canadian radio industry. Ted Rogers would later become a highly successful cable television entrepreneur.[64]

Bassett and Eaton joined forces in the early 1950s. When they purchased *The Toronto Telegram* newspaper in 1952, Eaton made it clear he wanted any profits from the venture to be separate from the family retail business and to go to his sons. In the end both Eaton and Bassett set up trusts for their families: the four sons of Eaton and Bassett's three sons. The equity interest was divided 70 percent for Eaton's family and 30 percent for Bassett's.[65] The estate freeze for succession duty purposes meant that the profits from the newspaper business fell to their children through the trusts and not to the two owners.

The trusts incorporated a holding company that eventually became Telegram Corporation Limited to hold the shares of *The Telegram* and *Sherbrooke Record*, the latter Bassett had "inherited" from his father. The trusts were to wind up and be distributed to the beneficiaries when the last of either Eaton or Bassett reached 65 years of age. Allan Beattie, Chairman of CTV Inc., and adviser to the Eaton family recalled the transaction earlier in his career as a lawyer for the firm of Osler, Hoskin & Harcourt: "John David really never did put any cash into the venture. What he did was he guaranteed a loan at the bank which was required to raise the purchase price for the paper they successfully bid for. My recollection is that it was something like four and a quarter million." The note that Eaton signed was eventually retired. Andrew MacFarlane, a former Managing Editor of *The Telegram*, recalled Bassett's announcement: "I remember...he came in one day and said, 'tear up the note.' That's it."[66] Bassett had a contract that allowed him to operate the newspaper and was paid a salary. "It was a reasonable enough salary," said Beattie, "it wasn't astronomical." Beattie characterized Bassett as a person who was not "totally consumed with having to make huge gobs of money. But he was at least equally if not more interested in having what he needed...to have a pretty handsome lifestyle which, of course, he was able to justify in this role as publisher and as a general increasingly public figure around Toronto."[67]

When Baton was created, the intention was for Bassett-Eaton and publishing magnate Roy Thomson to become involved in the application for the Toronto station. *The Telegram* publisher and his partner would own 51 percent of the common stock and Thomson 49 percent. But the BBG frowned on Thomson because of his extensive newspaper holdings and he withdrew. Bassett remembered Thomson's decision: "I wasn't present at the meeting, but Roy told me that Andrew Stewart [BBG chairman] made it very clear to him that any application of which he was an important part would be very unlikely to succeed." Bassett wanted Thomson to stay: "Roy quickly came out to see me...and my view was 'look Roy, we're pals, we're partners. Let them turn us down, if that's what they want to do.' But he said 'no, you'll lose the opportunity' and so he withdrew willingly which was very good of him."[68]

When Thomson stepped aside, Bassett was prepared to take in other partners to strengthen the application. "Foster Hewitt was a pal of mine," said Bassett. "I was chairman of the Gardens I think at that time. In any event, he came in for 10 per cent." Then Aldred Rogers made their move: "I had a call from Joel Aldred and they wanted a piece of the action. Well we had a good discussion and Aldred was very impressive fellow. And also at that time, he was the highest paid fella as an advertising instrument in the country. He was marvellous...tall, good looking and a great voice." Bassett saw Aldred as one who could give the application depth: "I was publisher of the *Telegram*. I knew nothing of broadcasting. He worked for General Motors as the on air advertising personality of the Dinah Shore show." Bassett then received a call from lawyer Paul Martin, a prominent Liberal, who represented Paul Nathanson who owned Sovereign Film Distributors Limited and whose father had been a friend of Bassett's father. Lawyers Eddie Goodman and Charles Dubin, counsel for *The Telegram*, represented by Heathcourt Blvd. Investments Ltd., also were involved in the application. *The Globe and Mail* reported the breakdown of investors and noted that Dubin and Goodman were to obtain their shares "in lieu of legal fees for setting up the company."[69] •

Bassett insisted on voting control in the company. Beattie outlined the voting stock arrangement that favored the *Telegram* publisher: "When Baton Aldred Rogers was set up, the *Telegram's* equity position was only 34 percent of the actual equity ownership. But they had another class of shares which they held...and those shares had enough additional votes to the 34 percent to give the *Telegram* voting control over the broadcaster, CFTO in effect. And that was part of the deal. Bassett said he had to have voting control." In the end, *The Telegram* had 51 percent of the voting stock.[70]

As legal counsel, Goodman orchestrated Baton's presentation. He had to exercise considerable control over Aldred. Goodman recalled: "Joel Aldred, if he had had his way, would have been the presentation and we would have lost. So I had to cut him to about one tenth of the time that he wanted to spend. And he had a couple of good ideas."[71]

Still the best laid plans at broadcast regulatory hearings can go awry. Despite Baton's well planned presentation, neither Goodman nor the company could have anticipated what would happen during their presentation. Gordon Keeble recalled a power failure that occurred during Baton's appearance before the BBG: "The presentation of it got screwed up by the fact that they were trying to move the snow off the tracks down below us. You could see them from the Oak Room and the power went out....Rai Purdy had produced this tape of the kinds of things they could do and they had to work around it, because they didn't have any power. They did get it in, because the power came back on and Eddie Goodman who was handling the presentation did a superlative job of ad libbing out of a terribly embarrassing situation." As for John Bassett, he "was boasting [and] was braggadocio all over the place about the fact that it was a locked up situation [for Baton]. But everybody proceeded including us on the basis of the fact that it's an open deal and may the best man win."[72] Since it was St. Patrick's Day, Goodman had seized the moment when the lights went out: "Mr. Chairman, if everybody would relax I am certain that the elves who come out every St. Patrick's Day will not harm a fellow Irishman like John Bassett, even if he is an Ulsterman. The lights will come back on."[73] Shortly after power was restored.

Despite Bassett's bravado, he firmly believed at the time that the licence would be awarded to another prominent company among the nine applicants: Rogers Radio Broadcasting Company Limited. The company's radio showpiece, station CFRB, Toronto, for many years the giant of the private broadcasting industry, was owned by Standard Radio. The control of Standard lay with Argus Corporation, which included several prominent names among the Canadian economic elite: E.P." Eddie" Taylor, Eric Phillips, John Angus "Bud" McDougald and Wallace McCutcheon, the group's chief spokesman at the hearing. "I was so convinced that they could get it that...as a matter of fact nobody at the time knew this, I secretly went to Bud McDougald and offered to make a deal with him; we'd go in 50–50. He turned me down," Bassett remembered. "He said, 'John, we're going to get it' and I thought they had a hell of a shot. But they blew it."[74] Goodman was also concerned about the application from Rogers Radio Broadcasting: "The reputation in broadcasting of CFRB had me afraid, but their presentation was not good. And they were arrogant. Joe Sedgwick who was a very good lawyer, instead of making a plus out of the contributions that Taylor, McCutcheon and Phillips had made to the community and philanthropic life of the country,...tried to steer around them and that was a huge mistake."[75]

When the BBG inquired at the Toronto hearing into the question of who held controlling interest in Standard Radio, the group's representatives showed a reluctance to admit that Argus was the controlling group, even though it was well known. Rogers Radio Broadcasting was dealing from a position of strength. The directors of Argus had a solid record of community service. The BBG had stipulated that a major factor in determining the awarding of the licence would be the "characteristics of the community and the nature of the available broadcasting service and the capacity of the applicant to provide the varied needs of the proposed service area."[76]

Bassett recalled the community accomplishments of the Argus group and how the *Report of the Royal Commission on National Development in the Arts, Letters and Sciences* (Massey Commission) had cited CFRB as the best example of a responsible private broadcaster: "Eddie Taylor had just run a successful capital campaign for Toronto General Hospital; Eric Phillips was chairman of the Board of Governors of the University of Toronto; McDougald, within a year past, had run a successful campaign for St. Michael's Hospital; McCutcheon was the chairman of the Toronto United Appeal. All they had to do was get up and give these names and give this record of community service and [refer to] the Massey Report and I think [they] would have got it."[77]

Still Baton Aldred Rogers put on an innovative presentation that clearly had an upbeat appeal to the BBG. Rai Purdy's idea to provide a visual production on the company's capacity for innovative programming was highly effective. "It was his suggestion which knocked everybody sideways," said Bassett, "that instead of getting up and speaking about our programming that we put it on tape, which was just brand new then, and we put little receivers for all the Board and big receivers in the audience and this is how we did it. Well it was just spectacular. But we went to enormous trouble."[78]

Prior to the Toronto hearing, Bassett had sent a TV camera crew to Montreal to shoot the BBG at the hearing in that city, the first item seen on the mock newscast. The second item involved Toronto's Mayor Nathan Phillips whom *The Telegram* had supported in his bid for the mayoralty. Bassett had Phillips "sign something or other of a news worthy nature" that was recorded on tape for the closed-circuit presentation before the story was reported elsewhere. "When the hearing ended at noon," said Bassett, "each member of the Board was handed a copy of the noon edition of the *Tely* and on the front page was this story that they'd seen." The members of the BBG took part in a narcissistic exercise at the Toronto hearing when they watched themselves at the Montreal hearing. Bassett remembered them looking at the monitors that had been installed and saying to each other, "There I am, There I am!"[79] Clearly the BBG was impressed with the glitzy style of Baton's presentation. Baton Aldred Rogers was awarded the licence. Bassett's group had taken full advantage of the superficial and impressionistic nature of television.

Senator Eugene Forsey, a Board member and a participant in the BBG hearing in Toronto, concluded that the Board awarded the licence to the company because its presentation was "unquestionably the best." The notion of Bassett getting the licence because of his Conservative party connections has to be weighed against the fact that there were several Tories among the Toronto applicants. In the end, Forsey recalled that the Bassett group was overly confident in its programming promises: "But this was true of everybody who got a TV licence. I suppose if we had known more we might have been skeptical about their promises; but we should probably have had to be skeptical about all the applicants."[80]

After Bassett's group was awarded the licence, Joseph Sedgwick, counsel for Standard Radio, argued angrily that Bassett's Conservative party ties had influenced the Tory board members. Keeble remembered that the Chairman of the BBG refused to tolerate his protests: "Dr. Stewart wouldn't let him get away with it. He just pursued him into every corner there was until he had to apologize. But Stewart had to defend the decision and he did it very capably."[81] CFTO, Channel 9 began broadcasting on 1 January 1961 and was to become the flagship station of the CTV network.

The inaugural broadcast of any station or network can be a harrowing experience for broadcasters. It is well known that the CBC television station CBLT, Toronto went on the air 8 September 1952 with its identification slide upside-down. There were anxious moments at CFTO prior to the first broadcast which was an 18-hour telethon for the Association for Retarded Children. Among the station executives awaiting the countdown on opening night were Murray Chercover who had been in the CBLT studio on a similar occasion, Rai Purdy and Johnny Esaw, the CFTO sports director.

Esaw recorded the anxious moments prior to sign-on: "I was waiting, sweating, with the knots, the nerves the dry throat, when producer Paul Kimberly asked for quiet on the set. Then, a horrified holler: 'My God, we've lost audio!'" But Esaw knew the countdown had to continue: "There was a sinking feeling but not time for any other reaction because the floor manager, Uncle Bobby Ash, was counting down...10...9...8. There was a shout 'Audio is back.' 3...2...1...'we're on.' What a beautiful sound that was, the greatest words ever spoken, it seemed to us at the time."[82]

In December, 1961 Baton Aldred Rogers Broadcasting Limited changed its name to Baton Broadcasting Limited. Baton was incorporated on 11 August 1971 and in late 1998 became CTV Inc. The company has remained one of the dominant television groups and a leading player in Canadian private television. "Spence Caldwell, if he were alive today, would tell you that...we won it on the presentation," said Bassett. "It was a hell of a presentation."[83]

CALDWELL'S APPLICATION FOR the Toronto licence was impressive but fell short as did seven others. Goodman who had attended a number of the BBG hearings when the "second" private TV licences were awarded thought that Caldwell lacked financial depth: "He and Keeble were both very good in that presentation and he [Caldwell] impressed the Board, but it was clear that they were not strong financially. Also I don't think their presentation was as broad as ours. The funny thing is everybody would come over to me and say 'it's going to be either you or us'."[84]

Caldwell was down; still he displayed a characteristic resilience. He was a persistent individual and chose to expand his horizons in response to the setback he had received in failing to get the Toronto TV licence. Drawing on his earlier experience, he recognized that the newly licenced private stations would need a supply of programming, especially if they could combine to form a "chain" or network of stations. Caldwell foresaw a potential for program sales to the stations. The BBG had envisaged that the private stations might showcase Canadian programming more effectively and economically by working as a group rather than as individual, distinctive operations.[85] The regulator favored a network controlled by nonbroadcasting interests, because it did not wish to see a "mutual company" established where the Toronto station would be in control.[86] A symbiotic relationship developed early between Caldwell, the broadcaster-promoter, and the broadcast regulator. Caldwell reapplied to the BBG not for another TV station but for a television network. After much effort, he was successful.

Keeble remembered their thinking and the potential both saw for some kind of programming exchange among the newly licensed private stations. "We had assumed," said Keeble, "that because of the shortage of Canadian programming and the commitments that everybody was making right, left and sideways that there would have to be some form of co-operative programming....So we had a fairly lengthy explanation or dissertation in the application about how this would work or how you could expect it to work and what the benefits would be thereof." The two broadcasters simply took the passage dealing with programming exchange from their original brief to the BBG for the Toronto licence, rewrote it, expanded the section and made an application for a network licence. Keeble explained that the particular circumstances at the time faced by the stations and the concerns of the BBG combined to give credence to their approach: "That particular presentation [for the network licence] I don't think ran 40 pages. Quite small because it's an idea. There's no practicalities to it at that stage. And I think also that the BBG realized there was a problem here. That these guys who had made all these commitments and built all these studios and so on were going to have a pretty tough time of it making their percentages and the percentages of Canadian content. So I think that when we dropped it on them [the BBG] they were very sympathetic to the need for this kind of service and I think they thought probably Spence and I...could run such a service, at least we'd get it going."[87]

Caldwell had to make two applications to the BBG to "form" and to "operate" a television network before he could establish CTV. The first hurdle was accomplished on 8 December 1960 when he received BBG approval to form a network. The BBG wanted to see, as Keeble recalled, "if you can work it out with these guys." In other words, Caldwell and Keeble had to show they could get the private stations on board before they could get approval to operate the network.[88]

The final BBG approval came after Caldwell's technological capacity to microwave or "link" the private stations merged with an ambitious scheme that John Bassett proposed for the television coverage of Canadian Football League (CFL) games in eastern Canada. The opportunity for lucrative profits through advertising brought the two earlier competitors together. Whatever the competition between them or the differences the pair might have in future, economic self interest was the motivator for their alliance. The origins of CTV were fundamentally different from the birth of CBC.

The CBC was born in 1936 and was intended to serve as an instrument of nationhood. Though it would eventually have wide appeal, the CTV network had a much simpler origin. Without the "Big Four" eastern conference of the CFL, CTV might never have emerged as a network. A curious series of developments over the televising of the eastern conference games proved to be the catalyst that prompted Bassett to join Caldwell's enterprise and brought the other newly licensed private TV stations into the network.

To the astonishment and dismay of the CBC, Bassett won the rights for the 1961 and 1962 seasons to televise the games of the eastern football conference. "In those days, the east sold their rights...and the west sold theirs," said Bassett. "There was no interlocking schedule then...so I didn't give a damn about the western rights. I never even bid on them."[89] The eastern teams were located in Toronto, Hamilton, Ottawa and Montreal. Bassett bid $375,000 a year for two years. He explained to the BBG on 13 April 1961: "This includes...broadly, all the television rights in Eastern Canada. It also includes the right of first refusal for the Grey Cup game in the same area."[90] As a backup measure, Bassett had appeared at the BBG hearing to seek a temporary licence to link stations CFTO, Toronto, CFCF-TV and CFTM-TV, the English and French language stations in Montreal, and CJOH, Ottawa. Still it was clear at the BBG hearing that Bassett had entered into agreement with Caldwell to join CTV and planned to broadcast the CFL games on Caldwell's proposed network.[91]

The alliance between Caldwell and Bassett was a straight business transaction. Bassett needed a network of TV stations to give the football games sufficient exposure for advertisers. Keeble had learned that Alphonse Ouimet, head of the CBC, had telephoned Bassett after the CBC's bid for the eastern rights was rejected. He wondered what Bassett was going to do now that he had the football rights. "John realized very quickly," said Keeble, "that he had three or four hundred thousand bucks in this apparently worthless property." Bassett became more reliant on Caldwell who had received permission from the BBG not only to form a network but also had arranged for the electronic capability to link the three eastern cities of Montreal, Toronto and Ottawa, as part of second microwave service, through negotiations with the communication companies.[92] CTV programming could be fed 'live' to the three cities. Until the second microwave was completed, CTV was able to use the existing facility for the electronic delivery of programs to the other five affiliated stations "in off-schedule hours" when the CBC was not transmitting programs.[93]

Caldwell had arranged for the transmission of programs by microwave to respond to the BBG's expressed interest in how CTV would distribute its programming. His ability to interconnect the stations afforded him advantage over the eight stations acting collectively as individual members of the Independent Television Organization (ITO) which did not have a similar technological capacity. When it came to technological vision, Caldwell was at his promotional best: "Our discussions with the communication companies have already led to a basic agreement to provide a second national microwave service which will be unique in itself since the direction of 'feed' will be reversible almost instantly and our network could, therefore, have programs appearing in succession from Toronto, Vancouver, Montreal, Winnipeg and so on."[94]

Bassett who was also chairman of the Toronto Argonauts football club and by his own admission, "a substantial shareholder in that football team" decided to join Caldwell's network to acquire a distribution system to televise the football games. Thereafter the newly-licensed stations in the remaining markets soon agreed to join the network. Murray Chercover recalled that when Baton "broke the logjam, as it were, all of the rest of them came in."[95]

Beyond the pressure of immediate circumstances created by the need for a football TV network, Caldwell and Keeble lobbied the private stations licensed from Halifax to Vancouver to persuade them to join the network they had been given approval to form. They received a generally favorable reception in six markets: Halifax, Montreal, Winnipeg, Edmonton, Calgary and Vancouver. The main dissidents were CJOH, Ottawa and CFTO, Toronto. Ernie Bushnell became irate at a meeting in the Chateau Laurier Hotel in Ottawa over a proposed programming schedule. "He got pretty vehement," said Keeble, "as was his habit about this situation, and he was just tearing strips off people me mostly because it was my schedule, I had drawn it."[96]

In the case of Toronto, Bassett's acquisition of the TV rights for football was most timely. Keeble remembered that he and Caldwell were summoned to the *Telegram*, "the old lady of Melinda Street," when the newspaper was located at Melinda and Bay streets in Toronto. Two days prior to the meeting with Bassett and Ted Rogers, Bassett had acquired the football rights. "When we got there," said Keeble, "Ted Rogers was also present. Now you may remember that the [Toronto licence] application was Baton Aldred Rogers. And...I certainly said this to Ted, I think he had been asked by John to be as obnoxious as he could. He was young, he had just completed his law training and so on." As the meeting progressed, Bassett "asked Ted to desist" and inquired as to when the stations were going to meet to consider joining together as a network.[97]

At a subsequent meeting chaired by Willard "Bud" Estey, who was to become a Supreme Court of Canada justice, the stations agreed to the network proposal but only after cooler heads prevailed. Estey had been asked to chair the meeting, because both Caldwell and Keeble would be principal participants and could have difficulty keeping order. The crucial meeting consisted of Caldwell, Keeble and representatives of seven stations. Bushnell was present but he was out in the hallway, because unlike the others he had not signed a letter dealing with the network concept prior to the meeting. Keeble remembered the unusual set of circumstances: "But we are facing a situation with the seven stations there and Bush out in the hall. I don't know who suggested that we ask him...to come in but that is what happened. Somebody went out and

said, 'look, come on in…you're part of this full exercise anyway.'" Bushnell entered the room and the stations reviewed the proposed network
application. Then Caldwell and Keeble were asked to leave to the room.
"They discussed it among themselves," said Keeble, "and when we came
back 15 minutes later Mr. Bassett was the one who said: 'We're going.
So that is how it all began.'"[98]

Caldwell applied to the BBG for permission to "operate" a private
network on 13 April 1961. He had managed to enlist eight stations as
affiliates and had formed a provisional Board of Directors for the proposed network. The Board consisted of Caldwell, Keeble and eight other
members, both broadcasters and nonbroadcasting businessmen, some of
whom had supported Caldwell's original application for the Toronto TV
licence. The six outside investors were: Kenneth B. Andras, a senior partner in the investment firm of Andras, Hatch & McCarthy; John A. Boyd
Jr., a partner in Andras, Hatch & McCarthy; James Cowan, a public relations consultant; Sydney Hermant, President of Imperial Optical Ltd.;
R.K. Martin, President of Martin Lucas and Co. Ltd., investment consultants; and William McLean, President of Canada Packers Ltd. Three
broadcasters were on the Board: John Bassett, the Board Chairman of
Baton Aldred Rogers Broadcasting Limited; E. Finlay MacDonald, President of CJCH Ltd., Halifax; and Lloyd B. Moffat, Vice-President of
Channel Seven Television Limited, owners of CJAY-TV Winnipeg.[99]

Clearly the nonbroadcasting businessmen who had invested in the
network were motivated ideologically and hoped to show that private
enterprise could rival the publicly owned CBC. Caldwell explained in
the preview issue of *The Canadian* that his supporters symbolized Canadian private enterprise: "Bill McLean of Canada Packers. Geoffrey
Phipps of Dominion Securities. Tim Lucas of Martin Lucas. Sydney Hermant of Imperial Optical. Ross Jenkins of Eatons.…Sure they are interested in making capital gains, but they are also interested in seeing that
this medium which talks to a man right in his own home is not a monopoly of government."[100]

The BBG approved Caldwell's application to "operate" CTV on 21
April 1961, only five months before the network went to air for the first
time.[101] CTV Television Network Ltd. owned no stations of its own and
had no production capability. Caldwell's emphasis was on the sponsored
programs, many originating in the United States, that the network as a
delivery system could provide to the stations rather than on the specific
Canadian program content that the affiliates would require.

Mr. Ernest L. Bushnell (left) and Dr. Andrew Stewart (right) at the official opening of CJOH-TV Ottawa, Ontario, 21 October 1961. Photograph by Herb Taylor. Used with permission of CJOH-TV, Ottawa from *Canadian Television Policy and the Board of Broadcast Governors*.

Still Caldwell faced a group of reluctant station affiliates unwilling to make major investments in the network. Originally Caldwell had envisaged that 49 percent of the common stock would be taken up by the stations. The shares were to have been divided proportionally among the various affiliates. In the end, only two of the private stations licensed earlier CJOH, Ottawa and CJCH, Halifax took up their full allotment of shares. Most of the stations subscribed to what Caldwell described as "a reasonable amount." Ernie Bushnell, President of the Independent Television Organization, the organization which purchased programs for the stations, maintained that the affiliates initially subscribed in total for only about 16 percent of the capital stock of the company.[102]

Significantly CHAN-TV, Vancouver never became a shareholder. Ray Peters, President Emeritus of WIC Western International Communications, recalled that CHAN was "up to its ears in financial difficulty" and reluctant to invest in a fledgling network: "We weren't going to put any money into the CTV network as a shareholder, because I wasn't convinced that Spence and Gordon knew how to run a network. I love Gordon dearly, he's a nice guy, but...at that time they didn't know what the hell they were doing. So we never became a shareholder. We did say we would carry some of their shows, some of their programs which meant that they could complete their network."[103]

Eddie Goodman suggested that perhaps the BBG moved too quickly to give Caldwell the network licence: "I think they looked upon the network as just something to connect up the stations. They weren't looking at a network as being a big player in Canadian programming and they gave it to him too quickly...instead of letting the stations jell and get established. However I'm not criticizing [the BBG] for that, they just wanted to get on with the job." Similarly Murray Chercover remembered the promises of performance that the stations had made: "Many commitments had been made by those new licensees and obviously those commitments were heavy duty in terms of expense in relation to potential revenue. No one knew exactly, because it was a brand new ball game."[104]

Critics would lament frequently the failure of CFTO and other private television broadcasters to live up to the lofty promises made at licence time before regulatory bodies. Robert Fulford was especially critical of John Bassett who promised a new era in Canadian programming: "They promised to broadcast the Toronto Symphony, the Canadian Opera Company, the Stratford Festival, the National Ballet....Above all, Bassett insisted, CFTO would *not* be a copy of the Buffalo stations that many Toronto viewers were watching—but that is more or less precisely what it has turned out to be." Fulford recalled how *Toronto Star* drama critic Nathan Cohen was exceedingly disturbed at the BBG and harshly critical of the newly licensed private stations when they made their applications: "Their submissions were hilarious fantasies to everyone except the Board of Broadcast Governors."[105] For much of its history, CTV which operated as a business and had to pay its affiliates to carry programs would face similar criticism.

Spencer Caldwell had spent three years and a sum of $200,000 in his unsuccessful effort to win a Toronto TV licence. He was forced to come up with another $250,000 to get the network licence. Ross McLean explained that when Caldwell decided to apply for a network, "Not another soul in the country came forward with a rival offer." When he got approval, many people believed at the time, that it was "a licence to burn money."[106] Caldwell's network would soon face major challenges given its uncertain financial status and the recalcitrant attitude shown by some affiliated stations. Still CTV Television Network Ltd. was ready to take on CBC. A new television era was upon the country. Spencer Caldwell, the determined Winnipeger, was not to be denied. His network was about to show Canadians that it meant business.

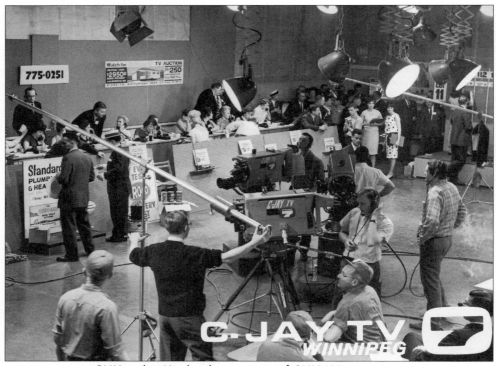

CJAY studio. Used with permission of CJAY, Winnipeg.

TWO

The Dominator
1961—1966

F ROM THE BEGINNING, John Bassett was the dominant figure on the CTV Board of Directors. Born with ink in his veins, the *Toronto Telegram* publisher was first and foremost a newspaper man. His second wife, Isabel, who was 24 years his junior when they married in 1967, recalled that "television wasn't as much his love as the newspaper was."[1] When the couple travelled, they would often visit world cities where the *Telegram* had foreign bureaus, which included London, Paris, Berlin, Moscow, Hong Kong, Washington and the United Nations in New York.[2]

Bassett's father, an Ulster immigrant, had published the *Montreal Gazette* in addition to owning the *Sherbrooke Record*. At one time, Bassett was on the editorial staff of the Toronto *Globe and Mail* but left to serve overseas in the army with the Black Watch regiment at the start of the Second World War. Not surprisingly, Bassett's roles as publisher of the *Telegram* and head of Baton Broadcasting Inc. made him a formidable public figure in both media and political circles. Despite his considerable financial success as a noted entrepreneur and sportsman, Bassett's political aspirations were thwarted on two separate occasions. Both times he was unsuccessful in his bid to win a seat in parliament.[3]

Still Bassett's superficial knowledge of television when CTV was in its infant era never seemed to prevent him from stating his position vigorously or even behaving in a bully-like manner. Finlay MacDonald, a member of the first CTV Board of Directors, characterized Bassett's attitude as a brash risk-taker: "'I'll fight this thing to the last God damn cent of John David Eaton's money.' You know that was the attitude. And he said this every time there was a lull in the conversation, didn't care who heard it." When asked about his long established reputation for being most assertive at CTV meetings, Bassett responded with uncharacteristic reservation, "I was."[4]

While Bassett's positions on vital network issues did not always go unchallenged by other directors and station representatives, his presence could not help but nurture heated and vibrant exchanges. John Coleman, a former Vice President, Government and Corporate Affairs and Corporate Secretary of CTV Television Network Ltd., recalled how meetings could become both acrimonious and humourous: "One of the tongue-in-cheek references to CTV board meetings was that while everyone had equal votes at the table, John Bassett's was always louder. And it was, literally and figuratively." Clearly Bassett's style was amusingly distinctive: "He had a delightful way of starting a meeting...saying 'I unilaterally oppose' such and such a motion. And at the end of the meeting saying, 'I unilaterally support' the same motion that he opposed going in." The obvious inconsistency would be dutifully noted at the meeting: "And someone would say, 'John, that's inconsistent with your going in position.' To which Bassett would reply that 'you don't get marks for consistency in this business.' And you don't. It's true. John was very flexible providing it was his way."[5]

Bassett's dominance of CTV and his behaviour at network meetings were reflective of his take charge approach towards life generally. "He was loud I suppose, he was impulsive," said Isabel Bassett, who has served as Ontario's Minister of Culture. "He was absolutely not moody at all. He looked at everything factually....Some people are that way and I think it allows you to be buoyant." The only time his wife remembered Bassett being downtrodden was when his oldest son from his first marriage was dying from cancer: "Very rarely did he get down except when Johnny was dying I would think. He would come home from the hospital and he would just be very quiet."[6]

Matthew, Bassett's son from his marriage to Isabel, was of the view that his mother helped to keep his father young in spirit: "I think that my mother added years to his life. He took up riding because she wanted to. I think that that was a great benefit to him." At home, Bassett was ever vigilant of the news on CFTO, his TV station: "He would watch the news every night," said Matthew. "That was his big thing. And if they screwed up then he'd call the producer directly, the CFTO news, and scream at them." Bassett took great pride in his local news beating other stations in the market. The three "low valleys" in Bassett's life were: the death of his son, the closure of the *Toronto Telegram* and his failure to win a seat in parliament.[7]

Andrew MacFarlane, a former Managing Editor of the *Telegram*, remembered that Bassett had one iron-clad editorial rule at the paper: "Don't mess with the Eatons." The reason was simple enough, said MacFarlane, "the Eatons were his partners." To get MacFarlane to become the Managing Editor, Bassett showed a characteristic persistence and determination to get his way, a behaviour that undoubtedly showed in CTV affairs. Bassett had asked MacFarlane, Assistant to the Publisher, to compile a list of prospective managing editors. After submitting the names, Bassett noted MacFarlane's name was not among them. Bassett inquired as to why not and learned that MacFarlane wanted to remain in his present position.

MacFarlane recalled that Bassett insisted: "Put your name on the list!" MacFarlane replied: "I don't want to be the Managing Editor." He remembered Bassett's retort: "Let me put it this way. Either you are the Managing Editor or you don't work for me anymore." MacFarlane responded: "What I would rather continue to be is Assistant to the Publisher." At this point, Bassett drew the bottom line. MacFarlane recalled the publisher's candid, terse summation: "Well I am very interested in that. There are two of us. There is the Assistant to the Publisher and there is the Publisher. The Assistant to the Publisher wants to continue the relationship. The Publisher doesn't. I win." Bassett's managerial approach in the naming of MacFarlane as Managing Editor of the *Telegram* "sort of gives you a flavour of what he was like."[8]

Perhaps no single incident manifested Bassett's capacity for self-deprecation more so than the publisher's memorable behaviour at *The Toronto Telegram* on the occasion when he questioned his newspaper's coverage compared to its competitor. Andrew MacFarlane related his eyewitness version of the happening when he delivered the Edward Clissold Lecture.

One day, Bassett's secretary summoned a gaggle—in our case, perhaps more like a giggle—of senior news executives to his office, where we found him pacing up and down on top of the first editions of the *Star* and *The Telegram* which were strewn around his floor.

"This is a fine newspaper," he said, pausing with his heel on the *Star's* front page. "And this line story," he said, grinding his heel into the splash, "epitomizes this fine paper's enterprise, journalistic vision and flair...."

"Whereas this," he said, tramping on the *Tely*, "this awful, travesty of an incompetent rag that I have the misfortune to own...but not for long, because I'm going to sell it and move to Nassau and I'll sit on the beach and think of you guys on the breadline up here, because you're all incompetents and you'll never get work again...

"This godawful newspaper doesn't have that fine story on its page one. It's not on any section page either. It's not on page two. It's not buried in the Bile Bean ads...It's not anywhere in this terrible, awful paper, which I took the appalling trouble to read right through and—"

At which point, I said: "We had it on Saturday."

"*What?*" said Bassett.

And J.D. MacFarlane, no relation, the editor-in-chief, replied: "He says we had it on Saturday."

Without pausing to draw breath, Bassett flashed his huge, Jack-Nicholson grin—shining like the entire ice surface of Maple Leaf Gardens—and said:

"Happiness, gentlemen, is when the publisher is full of shit! Meeting adjourned."[9]

Bassett kept his partner John David Eaton informed regularly on developments in the print and broadcasting industries. The two lived close to each other in Toronto's Forest Hill. Bassett was a constant visitor and would drop in unannounced at the Eaton home. Lawyer Allan Beattie, adviser to the Eaton family, remembered that Eaton was fascinated by the business: "John Bassett had a way, you really felt you were at the centre of all action that was going on in the whole town when you sat and listened to him. And I think John David found that very interesting, very compelling." However Eaton was not inclined to reciprocate in business affairs. He kept Bassett at arms length from the family retail business, even though his partner was prepared to offer advice periodically. "John of course, I suppose, would always have advice," Beattie recalled. "When the advice got a little intense, at about the three minute mark, [Eaton] would tell him 'it's none of your damn business John so let's talk about newspapers.'"[10]

The early days of CFTO, the CTV flagship station, were typical of the trials that the newly-licensed private station owners had experienced when their operations were trying to gain a foothold in a new industry. Baton Aldred Rogers Broadcasting lost money steadily for much of 1961, its first year of operation, before Bassett was forced to make major changes in personnel. Joel Aldred, the President, was bought out and a new management took over. In his recollection of the station's early years, Beattie recalled that for several months money was lost. Even though "Aldred had built a magnificent station," he said, "there probably was some question about his managerial experience....And they negotiated Aldred out and they brought in a fellow by the name of Bill Crampton to...tighten up the whole thing and get ruthless in cutting costs." Johnny Esaw, the CFTO Sports Director, has estimated that the station was losing something like $250,000 a month. The other personnel changes included the naming of Murray Chercover as Program Manager, Ted Delaney as General Manager in charge of sales and Larry Nichols from the accounting firm of Clarkson, Gordon as Comptroller.[11]

Given its dubious start and the fact that CFTO was losing large sums of money, the business was in urgent need of capital. At this point, the ABC network in the United States entered the Baton picture. Aldred's departure had prompted a corporate reorganization. The Telegram Publishing Company Limited, which published Bassett's *Telegram,* applied to the BBG to acquire the shares held by Aldred, Rogers Broadcasting. Ted Rogers was still to hold a small interest in the TV station. Extra capital was needed for the transaction especially given the losses that CFTO had suffered. American Broadcasting-Paramount Theatres Inc. (AB-PT) offered to invest in the station. The Telegram Publishing Company would maintain control in the operation of CFTO. As Stewart and Hull have noted, "The proposal was that AB-PT would buy some $300,000 worth of equity stock, and invest $2,000,000 in debentures. They would name three directors of the board of twelve."[12]

Ultimately the BBG denied the application for the corporate reorganization, because it would have given AB-PT an ownership interest of 25 percent in CFTO. The Board was "not prepared to recommend any transaction involving financial participation of American networks in Canadian television stations."[13] However an alternative arrangement was arrived at between CFTO and AB-PT that allowed the American company to invest in the Canadian station.

After the denial of the application, Allan Beattie described what took place: "And so what was worked out was ABC put up whatever the amount of capital was that would have given them their 25 percent of shares but instead of getting shares they got a form of debt that in value was the same as what the shares would have been worth." The debt arrangement had a number of interesting features, "one of which was that it would participate in the equity growth and in any dividends and that kind of thing in the same amounts as would have been paid had they been shares." The AB-PT investment was like a loan or a debenture that was described as "irredeemable." As Beattie noted, "So at no point...could the other shareholders of Baton just say that 'well, we'll get rid of ABC by redeeming the debenture and paying them off.' They couldn't do that. That was why the debenture was made irredeemable. So it would have all the characteristics of shares but not actually be shares."[14] Some years later, Bassett was able to announce that he had redeemed the debentures.[15]

CFTO had gone through a harrowing experience in its early months of operation. Over time, the station was to become a highly profitable enterprise and dominate the CTV network. Bassett's centralized view of the network and his insistence that Toronto was the linch-pin market could not help but raise the ire of other station owners in the regions of the country. "My view was that the Toronto market was the key market," said Bassett. "That unless that was recognized at all times in network policy, network programming and sales, we were off base....That view strongly asserted, as it was, did not get universal applause across the network. Quite understandable."[16]

IN THE FIRST YEAR of CTV's operation, it became clear early on that Spencer Caldwell's venture into network television was underfinanced. The network was unable to provide a level of programming service for the affiliates that would make their participation in CTV worthwhile. Michael Hind-Smith, the network's National Program Director, explained in a draft memorandum to the CTV Board of Directors: "A Network Affiliate 'pays' for a Network service by the share of time revenue which it is willing to return to the Network to pay for that service. The amount of his 'payment' is the measure of his regard for that service."[17]

In the first affiliation agreement that Caldwell had negotiated with the affiliated stations, the network maintained only 25 percent of the net advertising revenue from network sales time. The result was that this amount enabled the network to provide a limited service to its member stations. It was not long before network finances became strained leading to heated exchanges at meetings involving the network's management and station representatives.

Evidence of the extent to which Bassett exercised influence at CTV meetings can be found in a set of supplementary notes and impressions, which accompanied the official minutes of the affiliates meeting over a three-day period, 22–24 October 1962, a year after the network had begun operations: "The overall character of the meeting was, in everyone's opinion, its domination by John Bassett. He stampeded the rest of the affiliates, and controlled the meeting whenever he was present."[18] The result of the meeting's deliberations was that "some stations—such as Winnipeg and Moose Jaw—said absolutely nothing" during the three-day meeting and "in point of fact, nobody spoke out on behalf of the network except CTV people."[19]

Significantly, Bassett argued before the meeting that "with BBG approval, the Canadian Content restrictions be removed from CTV." The thrust of his argument was that CTV should not be held to Cancon quotas, because it had no owned and operated stations: "The network has no 'O&O' stations, it's in a completely unique position, it's ridiculous that it should be held to the Canadian Content policy." Still Bassett's bias towards seeking removal of the Cancon requirements was not shared by smaller and medium-sized affiliated stations outside of central Canada: "In discussion, it turned out that Halifax, Winnipeg, and CFRN, Edmonton, spoke out as being against the abandonment of the Canadian Content commitment on the part of the network."[20] Whatever Canadian programming the network could provide for these stations in the first year of its operation could not help but assist them in filling their program schedules.

Bassett also suggested to the meeting in October, 1962 several ideas pertaining to the revenue aspects and overall operation of the network. He had made a motion that was supported to reject a CTV proposal for an increase in compensation beyond the 25 percent of net revenue from network sales time. His argument was that CTV revenue could be increased without changing the original affiliation agreement. First, "his people had advised him that, if CTV would apply the same policies in selling as CFTO has regarding segmentation and discounts, we could increase our total revenue by 17%." Second, the notes of the meeting show that Bassett was of the view that "there had been an agreed-upon departure this year from the terms of the Affiliation Agreement by the stations accepting programming not fully sold. He also pointed out that the stations had given up the principle of a simultaneous sell-out in day and night, and said that it was important to note that the stations had shown co-operation when shown a need, and that we must realize that they do desire the further development of CTV." Bassett's third argument was that "we could go after the Bell Telephone Company for further relief—that it's ridiculous for us to pay for 35 hours of microwave when we don't use more than 22."[21]

Further, as a cost cutting measure, Bassett was prepared to go to great lengths and asserted boldly that the network should be prepared to drop the *CTV National News*, if it could not be sold to advertisers. He argued that "if we are providing extra services, we should eliminate them. The affiliates—by and large—do not need any management, promotion or extra programming help from the network. He stated further that if the CTV NATIONAL NEWS [*sic*] is a cost item to the network while unsold, it should be removed from the schedule." The notes of the meeting also recorded Bassett's endorsement of the financial status quo for CTV and a hint of the stations' desire to take over the network: "In final discussion Mr. Bassett asked if CTV is really concerned about the affiliates problems? Perhaps the real problem under discussion here is that the affiliates think they can run the network better. As far as he is concerned, the network position is good enough as it exists." On this aspect, "Ray Peters [CHAN] contributed the comment that CTV should cut its operating costs drastically—'as we did.'"[22]

Bassett outlined six major factors that caused the network's struggle prior to 1966 when CTV was restructured and the affiliated stations assumed ownership of the network as a co-operative. These several aspects were related to timing, structure and financing: the hasty establishment of CTV following the licensing of the original eight private TV stations; a naturally divisive network structure; the network's lack of owned and operated stations forcing it to rely on its affiliates for broadcast time to air network programs; an ensuing tension over payment to the affiliates for the network reserved time on the affiliated stations; a lack of stable financing for the network; and the Independent Television Organization's near elimination of CTV as a force in the buying of American programs.

First, the establishment of CTV in October, 1961 followed soon after the licensing of the private stations that eventually formed the network. The stations hardly had time to establish themselves in their own markets. Initially they were faced with large capital expenditures for TV studios and the technology that television demanded. For the most part, their interest in joining a network was subordinate to their preoccupation with immediate survival in their own markets.

Second, the network's structure could not help but cause tensions between the broadcast-owners and the nonbroadcasting investors in the network. Bassett explained that there was "a sort of natural conflict which became very apparent early between the desires and needs of the affiliates and those of the network shareholders."[23] The nonbroadcast members of the first CTV Board were in the majority. These members included Sydney Hermant, President of Imperial Optical Company Limited and lawyer Kenneth B. Andras, a partner with Andras, Hatch & McCarthy, a stock brokerage firm.[24] Most of the nonbroadcast members of the Board were shareholders and represented other shareholders and groups of capital. Throughout the Caldwell era of CTV, "it was never possible on a continuing basis really," said Bassett, "to bring the stations' and the network's needs together. And the fact that the network had no owned and operated stations of its own made it very difficult."[25]

Reminiscent of Bassett's assessment, Finlay MacDonald recalled divisions among Board members over the quality of programming that CTV could offer: "Sydney Hermant would have been the type of guy who would want to put the Toronto Symphony on....It had to be Spence or Keeble who would say, 'you know we can't do that. It costs too much money, we're not going to make any money'." MacDonald said that "outside of Keeble and Spence" none of the early CTV Board members "knew anything about a network." Eventually it became apparent that CTV in its original form could not survive as "a private network in which investors would expect a return for their money and would make a profit."[26]

The important question of how a delay centre would be financed for the network to take into account the time zones in the various regions and "delay" programming originating in Toronto touched off a board room squabble. "I can remember Spence Caldwell arguing with me very forcibly," said Bassett, "to set up in the west a delay centre which was essential. I mean you couldn't be showing [nightly] news at eight o'clock in the morning in Vancouver." Caldwell argued that the stations should establish the centre. Bassett disagreed and persuaded the nonbroadcasters on the Board that it was a network responsibility: "I said Spence, 'don't be ridiculous. That's a network function. You're sending out stuff.'" Bassett's recollection was that "on that occasion, the nonstation members of the board completely agreed with me. I can remember lawyer [Donald] Pringle saying 'well Spence...of course this is a network function'."[27]

Third, with CTV having no "O and O's" in major Canadian markets, unlike the three major American networks or the CBC, Caldwell was highly reliant on an adequate time allocation on the private affiliates to distribute the CTV programming. Inevitably intense struggles arose over the controversial issue of time payments to the stations, the amount of money the network had to provide to the affiliates to distribute CTV programming. What Caldwell needed to make the network a success, Bassett explained, was "an allocation of time." The problem was that "every time he took an hour away from the stations for network time, the stations would resist, because they would want that time for themselves to sell for the revenue."[28]

A fourth problem closely related to the question of time allocation was the recurring question throughout the network's history of time payments to affiliates. How was the network to compensate the affiliates for the time that it reserved on the individual affiliated stations? Unlike the arrangement between the CBC and its affiliates, the payments made by CTV to its affiliated stations were not guaranteed. The time that the network reserved on the CTV stations had to be sold first to advertisers. Only then could the pre-arranged payments be made to the CTV affiliates.

"What they [CTV and the affiliates] did was they took the time and they worked out a percentage deal," Bassett recalled. "They [the network] retained 25 percent of the sale, as I remember, and the stations then got 75 percent. But from the stations point of view, that time had to be sold first. It was not a guaranteed payment to the stations and then the 75 percent was split among all the stations so the [individual] station...would certainly not get what [it would get] if it could sell that time itself."[29]

A fifth problem for the network was its overall lack of stable financing. The network had informed the affiliates in October, 1962 of the perilous state of its financial condition: "Micro-wave, local loops, audition facilities for our national sales clients, promotion, staffing, offices in Montreal and New York and modern administrative, sales and operations facilities in Toronto all are a charge on the network dollar. But these cannot be maintained and expanded if the network's supply of dollars is siphoned off faster than it is replaced. If the money supply dries up, so must the flow of network services at the other end of the tape." The network forecast a loss of several hundred thousand dollars: "It is simple logic to conclude that rising loss figures (as of October 1 the projected known loss for 1962–63 was over $600,000) must soon be reversed and income and outgo brought more into balance or we will not have the legs to run from coast to coast. Without the muscle provided by adequate revenues your network's pace is slowed and our competitive stamina weakened."[30]

Finally, the ITO, a co-operative of the private stations and the same stations that eventually formed CTV, had preceded the formation of the network. At an early stage, ITO had served nearly to eliminate CTV as a force in the buying of American programs, the principal source of revenue to the stations in the early days of television. The private stations had realized that if they combined together in ITO, "economies of scale" dictated that they could be more effective collectively. In essence, ITO nearly became more relevant to the fledgling private stations than did CTV. The co-operative activity of the stations served to replace the vital network role of program buying which CTV later tried to assume.[31]

In a summary of the network's early years, Michael Hind-Smith underlined the destructive effect of three facets of the network's operation: the impact of early affiliation agreements, the network's limited finances and the threat presented by ITO: "The effect of limited revenues in our first three years, under the first Affiliation Agreement, was to limit our service in ever-diminishing ratios. As our service diminished, so therefore did our value. The second Affiliation Agreement, as a result, reduced our payments to match our reduced value, and we in turn reduced our service again to match our reduced revenues." He concluded that the net result was "we are being sucked inexorably into the vortex of a whirlpool in which we shall surely drown." Clearly ITO was seen as the network's principal enemy: "Our inability or our unwillingness to escape has had other important effects. Our inaction has served in part, to create a new force in television—ITO. This organization, which now seeks to destroy and replace us, has as one of its prime functions the very functions CTV was intended to fulfill—the pooling of resources for the creation of Canadian programming. Its member stations (our affiliates) are prepared now to pay ITO to do CTV's job." Hind-Smith recommended the creation of three separate programming funds to support the creation of more vibrant Canadian programming, the "overriding reason for CTV's birth and existence, and our one overwhelming opportunity to provide a unique and therefore valuable service."[32]

All of the factors cited by Bassett and Hind-Smith had considerable influence on network operations during the formative years of CTV. The extent of the level of tension between the network and its affiliates was illustrated in an internal memo sent to Spencer Caldwell on 17 June 1964. The document attempted to compare the revenue positions of the CBC television network and CTV. The memo noted: "*The CBC National English TV Network makes sales of some $11 million, a figure not unlike our target for 1964–65.*" A comparison between what the CBC paid to its network stations including those owned and operated by the Corporation, and the amount of CTV's payments to its affiliates, was also highlighted: "*The National English [CBC] TV Network makes station payments (including O&O's) of some $3 million, while li'l ole CTV is scheduled to make over $4 million next year.*" The memo explained: "*CBC spends 3% of total costs on affiliate payments; CTV is scheduled to spend 43%.*" At the end was the expletive: "It's a conspiracy."[33]

THE EARLY YEARS of the network's history established a pattern of struggle between the network and its affiliates that was to last for more than three decades. W.D. McGregor, a senior Vice-President of Electrohome Limited, owner of CKCO-TV, Kitchener, explained: "Caldwell didn't have enough financing really to do it in the grand manner and to survive an extended period of building, of the construction of that kind of an enterprise." McGregor recalled that "in the beginning, there was a big question of how many hours of each station's time he was going to use and how much he was going to pay for it." The question of affiliate time payments was a recurring issue that produced heated debate: "The problem is that a network, whether it is in Canada, the United States, Europe or wherever, a network uses a certain number of each station's hours, provides them with a program service, but in doing so the station looks at it and...tries to value what that's worth."[34]

A struggle between the network management and its affiliated stations began almost from day one. Gordon Keeble, Caldwell's associate, recalled that the affiliates "were in the driver's seat and they drove it for every inch it was worth."[35] Caldwell needed the affiliates a great deal more than they were reliant on him. Looking back on the network's evolution, Finlay MacDonald observed: "Fights were going on all the time; the language at the board table was shocking, it was just absolutely shocking."[36]

The rivalry between the network management and affiliates was so intense that Arthur Weinthal, CTV's Vice-President of Entertainment Programming, had second thoughts about his decision to join the network in early 1962, less than a year after it came into existence. As a programmer, Weinthal had considerable influence over the entertainment fare that Canadians were to watch on CTV for much of its history. A CTV meeting in March, 1962 erupted into a shouting match. Weinthal was bewildered: "There was a meeting of the stations and the network and it was just awful. It was just awful. I wondered what have I done, why have I come here, these people are yelling and screaming at each other."[37]

Weinthal arrived at CTV from Montreal where he had been a radio and television director of an advertising agency. He was the network's 33rd employee. "I was making $9,600 a year and they offered me $11,000 a year so I had obviously died and gone to heaven and I took my young family and hurled them into the back seat of my Chevrolet and drove down what was intermittently highway 2 and 401 and started at CTV." Weinthal joined Ross McLean and Michael Hind-Smith. He had come in contact with early CTV programming executives who were trying to develop programs for advertising clients. Weinthal had been responsible for Texaco and a number of other clients in his agency work. "The reason why they came to me," he remembered, "was all of the people who were the originally founding group of CTV were...ex CBC people. And there was nobody in the group who had any advertiser or advertiser agency background and they were billing themselves as the television service which would serve advertisers. So they had a notion that they had to develop daytime programming for advertisers which really didn't exist at the time and they came to me and would I do that."[38]

Weinthal's assessment of CTV was that Caldwell and Keeble had "cobbled together" the notion of a network after losing their bid for a

CFCF—Enjoy Channel 12. Used with permission of CFCF, Montreal.

The CJAY Girls. Used with permission of CJAY, Winnipeg.

Toronto licence and that the private stations had made unrealistic programming promises to the BBG to gain their individual licences: "But
essentially the station people were all interested in getting their own stations up and running and they had all made grandiose promises of huge
studios and great crews and credible productions in drama and music
and all kinds of things." Ultimately, the stations found it difficult and
costly to meet their programming promises and obligations. They were
focused primarily on their own local markets. The stations had under-
rated their costs and overrated their potential to attract advertising revenue. "Within the first year, they were all well on their way to going
broke," said Weinthal, "they built huge studios and there was nothing
in the economy that suggested that their grandiose schemes could have
been supported, certainly not by advertising revenue."[39]

The economics of Canadian broadcasting in the early 1960s were not
all that favorable to the network that was to mean business. The struggle
between the network and its affiliates over the sharing of advertising revenue was to remain a thorny issue. The crux of the issue was the desire
on the part of the stations to sell their own time. The *Financial Post* drew
attention to the tension point in the basic structure that had been created in 1961: "CTV's affiliates think they can earn more revenue by selling local spot announcements in prime viewing hours (evening hours)
than by sharing national advertising with the network."[40]

As early as October, 1962 only a year after the network had been
launched, the original affiliation agreement, which expired on 31
August 1964, appeared to network executives to be fundamentally
flawed. The CTV network management had sought a revised affiliation
agreement and an upward revision of the revenues allocated to the network. The tension between the network management and its stations
continued to mount. ›

A confidential report sent from CTV headquarters at 42 Charles St.
East in Toronto to the affiliates on 4 October 1962 drew attention to the
favourable economic positions the stations enjoyed collectively as CTV
members compared to other North American television networks. The
network reminded the stations that the CTV management had never envisaged the need to provide them with programming beyond the network
sales time period, in other words, unsponsored programs. The report to
the CTV affiliates explained: "Payments to the CBC affiliates range from
about 28% to 60% depending on the type of program provided. The
CBS network pays its affiliates a basic 30% of gross time charges less a

series of deductions which leaves some stations with a true net return of as little as 6%." The report noted that because CTV never intended "in its original planning to provide all the services offered by other networks it agreed to a much smaller share of revenue from time sales for itself, leaving 75% of such money for pay out to you as affiliates."[41]

The first year of the network's operation had underlined a major weakness in the original affiliation agreement relating to "sustainers" or unsponsored programs: "Experience has shown, however, that where service is concerned, we are expected to provide as many services as any other network—except, perhaps, regular sustaining shows. On occasion, we have done that, too—even to the point of allowing you to sell spots in such shows without any kind of revenue return to us. Sustainers on CTV? Certainly not something ever contemplated in the original concept of this network."[42] The CTV management believed that a new agreement between the network and its affiliates would have to be devised if the enterprise were to be viable.

Keeble underlined the problems CTV faced with two main aspects of its business operations: unsold programming and the nature of its advertiser buys. As the first affiliation agreement proved unworkable leading up to 1964, the need arose for "ad hoc" agreements between the network and its affiliated stations relating to unsold network time: "We weren't that great. We couldn't sell 100 percent of everything particularly since, and here's another bone of contention that arose, we made the advertiser buy Canadian." A network formula might stipulate three minutes, American, and two minutes, Canadian, would be sold to advertising clients so they could air their commercials in the programs they wanted. Advertisers could have their choice of the American and Canadian programming they purchased as long as they bought their commercial time in five minute blocs: three and two. "The [individual] stations weren't quite as ethical, shall we say, as this," said Keeble, "and frequently the advertiser could buy Yankee programming on the affiliates direct without any Canadian content requirement at all. Makes it tough for the network sales department."[43] In effect, the network policy on the purchase of commercial time was a stricture that placed CTV at a disadvantage when it had to compete with the private stations in the marketplace.

The distinctive relationship of the CTV network to its affiliates in Halifax and Ottawa reflected the financial strains and tensions that the network faced in its early years. The network tried to acquire the affiliates in the two markets to allow it to have owned and operated stations. CTV was successful in acquiring CJCH but failed in its attempt to purchase CJOH. Keeble dealt with this particular aspect of network operations when he reviewed the early history of the network for the BBG: "Since stations wouldn't or couldn't buy us, CTV tried to buy some of them. We were effective in the case of CJCH in Halifax, and ineffective in the case of CJOH in Ottawa....If we go back to 1960–61, we find that CTV began with really no body of experience upon which to build. There was, in my opinion, no original error—nobody knew what would happen because this particular phenomenon had never happened in Canada before, a private network."[44]

Eventually, in August 1964, CTV acquired the controlling interest in CJCH Limited whose President Finlay MacDonald was a prominent name in Tory circles and later became a Canadian Senator. The acquisition established CTV Atlantic Ltd. as the majority shareholder, a company with joint ownership between CTV and the MacLean-Hunter Publishing Company Ltd. MacDonald explained to the *Halifax Mail-Star* at the time: "For all practical purposes our organization will become a CTV owned-and-operated station and we are delighted to be the first such operation." He stressed that both the network and CJCH had "interdependent plans for expansion" and such a close relationship was essential "for the improvement and extension of program service to the Maritime region."[45] On 15 September 1963, CJCH had been linked by microwave to the CTV network, a development that ushered in a new age of broadcasting for the maritime area. MacDonald informed viewers that the technological advance would mean enhanced programming such as "Canadian Football, Wednesday night NHL Hockey, a nightly National News Report from Ottawa and a glittering array of new season programs, from the major networks of America and the United Kingdom." The new television era was made possible because of "reversible instantaneous telecasting from coast to coast. Nova Scotians will have another window on the nation and the world."[46]

Still CTV's relationship with CJCH, and the network's attempt to gain a foothold on the east coast, eventually raised questions from other affiliates notably CJOH, Ottawa. Stuart Griffiths, Managing Director of CJOH, contacted Keeble and was curious about the deal with Maclean-Hunter involving CJCH. Griffiths, a former CBC executive, also questioned the network's attempt to buy his own station. Keeble wrote to Caldwell telling of Griffiths's inquiries: "Stuart wanted to know what our deal was in CTV Atlantic with Maclean-Hunter since he wanted to know how we could sell off our interest in the station. I frankly couldn't remember…so I was able to tell him only the things which he already knew—that CTV Network has no shares in its name in CJCH Limited but that it owns exactly 50% of the company which is the registered shareholder."[47]

In the exchange with Keeble, Griffiths probed the nature of the network's initiative to buy the Halifax and Ottawa affiliates: "Our brief discussion of this purchase [Halifax] led to some wry comments from Stuart that our bid to buy Ottawa was made in small part with Ottawa's money which they had paid us as part of their share subscription. He also wanted to know if we had had to turn to the bank for the money necessary to complete the Halifax purchase. This came up because the purchase was not completed at the time of the audited statement but the money has since been paid over."[48] CTV's structural problems and the business outlook of its top management could not help but affect the capacity of the network to improve its programming service to the stations.

TO UNDERSTAND CTV's early struggles to provide meaningful Canadian programming, the kind of fare the network's affiliates would value beyond game and cooking shows, it is important to grasp Spencer Caldwell's notions of programming and sales. Indeed Caldwell would have to accept some responsibility for the network's failure to air more innovative programming. The president's reluctance tended to exacerbate tensions with the stations looking for programming they could not produce themselves. Michael Hind-Smith explained that "one of the problems that dogged the five years or so in which he was the president of the network was that he was really quite reluctant to invest in programs."[49]

The first purchase that Hind-Smith made on behalf of CTV was from the firm of Hanna-Barbera, the company that was to later create the *Flintstones*. In recalling his early years with CTV, Hind-Smith wrote: "Steve Krantz (husband of, and later Executive Producer of his wife Judith's spectacular television novels) had a deal for me. Screen Gems represented the very successful Hanna-Barbera, Hollywood-based creators of animated cartoons….They had a new one, *Top Cat*. Throwing caution to the winds, I bought it sight unseen." When he learned that Hind-Smith had broken his golden rule, "never buy until you've sold,"

Caldwell went ballistic. "He just about had a catfit," said Hind-Smith. "The notion of actually owning something you hadn't presold to some-body, it was quite foreign. And I think that impeded the whole relation-ship with the affiliates over the years." Caldwell's reluctance to invest in programming tended to confine the network. "He well understood if the advertiser brings you the *Rifleman* or whatever the…names of programs are, well fine," said Hind-Smith. "If they bring you that, it's sold then the margin is there. But to actually invest in a program or a program series or a program concept and then go out and sell it made him very, very uncomfortable."[50]

Caldwell's attitude towards the interdependent concepts of program-ming and sales was a natural outgrowth of his background as an origi-nal distributor. "He represented CBS," said Hind-Smith, "and it was to him quite normal if you bring in a property and once you've sold it in Canada, then the money would flow back to whoever owned the prop-erty. I guess Liberace's transcriptions were a pretty good case in point. Once you've sold it, then the rights' holders would get a piece of it." Still Caldwell had nothing to do with the creation of such transcriptions or programs. "He was essentially a distributor." Moreover Caldwell appeared to have little sense of public obligation that pertained to the notion of a television network licence as public property. As Hind-Smith explained, "He was shrewd enough to know that he had to make a cer-tain obeisance, if you like, to that [public obligation] but, if he were to get the licence or whatever he wanted, it was certainly nothing that he would ever seriously consider, I think."[51]

Though Caldwell was a skilled salesman and a promoter, a discon-nect eventually occurred between CTV's management and its affiliates over programming, the essence of broadcasting. Caldwell's reluctance could stymie innovation. The stations dominated by the irrepressible Bassett continued to assert their position in the marketplace. Hind-Smith concluded that "the stations became increasingly restive over the notion that the network was not prepared to advance some major recap-italization." In addition, by 1965 the ITO headed by CFTO's Murray Chercover had continued to buy competitively against the network. "We would go to Hollywood for the buying sprees which took place in May-June," said Hind-Smith, "and we found ourselves in direct compe-tition with the Independent Television Organization and so it donned on them that they didn't really need to deal with the network any-more."[52]

Despite Caldwell's reluctance towards programming innovations until the marketplace was tested and they were sold to advertisers, as a general interest service CTV took several initiatives to provide Canadians with a national news service, attractive sports programming and mass entertainment fare. Hind-Smith claimed to have brought two principal innovations to CTV in its early stages: the establishment of the *CTV National News* in 1962 and the launch of *W5* in 1966, the network's flagship public affairs show. By 1966, as he explained to *The Globe and Mail,* CFTO, Toronto was the originating station for the network's news and public affairs programs with the exception of the program *Insight* which came from Ottawa. "He had been responsible for them and had largely initiated them."[53]

The CTV news at first had been produced at CJOH, Ottawa; *W5* originated at CFTO, Toronto. "But the problem underlying both those programs," Hind-Smith remembered, "was that the network had to plead with the affiliates to produce them for a fee." The staffs of both the *CTV National News* and *W5* were hired at the request of the network by CJOH, in the case of the former, and CFTO, as to the latter. The long running *W5* launched in 1966 was produced "entirely on staff that CFTO had supplied under our editorial direction." Hind-Smith said, "I think that sort of demonstrates the weakness of the position, the hand that CTV was playing at the time."[54]

A keen rivalry developed in the early 1960s over where the *CTV National News,* a major network program, would be produced. There were two main reasons why CJOH, Ottawa was chosen as the initial site for the newscast as opposed to CFTO, Toronto, the city where the CBC network news originated. First, Caldwell, Keeble and Hind-Smith believed that CFTO would emerge as the strong man of the network, as it became in the late 1990s when Baton Broadcasting Inc., later known as CTV Inc., achieved control of CTV. The principal reason why the network chose Ottawa to produce the national news on a shared cost basis was to counter the influence of CFTO in the network and provide a counterweight of sorts or another option.[55]

A second reason for CTV's action was to draw a stark contrast with the CBC. By originating its news in Ottawa and not Toronto, the private network would not appear to duplicate the public broadcaster's news reporting efforts. CTV also started its newscast a half hour earlier. To gain a leg up on the CBC news presented at 11 P.M., the CTV news in the fall of 1962 was aired at 10:30 P.M. But CTV paid a price for trying to differentiate its news presentation from the Corporation. "It didn't make awfully good commercial sense," said Hind-Smith, "CTV news got clobbered at 10:30 because it was running against action adventure programs starting at 10 o'clock. And it required people to drop those programs. So it wasn't a very good business decision."[56]

At CJOH, Stuart Griffiths, "a very tough and wily negotiator," had arranged with Hind-Smith for the production of the original newscast in Ottawa on a contract basis with the network. CTV paid CJOH to originate the newscast. As National Program Director, Hind-Smith said he had "considerable suasion over the casting of the news" but did not have "direct control over it." As for the original news anchors, Griffiths had expressed a preference for Peter Stursberg, a former CBC World War Two correspondent. "Now he already had arrangements with Charlie Lynch [newspaper columnist] which suited us fine," said Hind-Smith, "they were in the 10:30 slot." Hind-Smith had worked for Griffiths earlier at the CBC. "We were immensely helped by the talents that existed at CJOH," said Hind-Smith, "particularly the commitment that Stuart Griffiths who really was an outstanding person had towards news and he really contributed an enormous amount to it beyond what he was just paid for it."[57]

Murray Chercover has maintained that "CTV news was initially created by the ITO group." His recollection of the origins of the newscast is that "from the time CTV news came into being until the takeover of the network [by the stations] in 1966, it was run by the stations not by the network." There was "no editorial responsibility at the network." The stations as members of ITO were used as "stringers or if not as stringers as bureaus" and they "paid for it collectively on a collaborative basis." Indeed initiatives taken by Hind-Smith on behalf of CTV and Chercover, as head of ITO, were often interrelated. Harvey Kirck wrote that Hind-Smith negotiated with him when he left CFTO to join the network news in Ottawa.[58] At the same time, Chercover recalled: "I was Chairman of ITO. We got together and agreed amongst the stations that the most acceptable personality to front the newscast as our anchor was Harvey Kirck who was working as our managing editor at CFTO. And he moved to Ottawa and Stuart's [Griffiths] news department simply took on the editorial responsibility."[59]

Still Baton's John Bassett was furious about the news originating in Ottawa and not at CFTO in the early 1960s. "Now all of this absolutely rotted John Bassett's socks," said Hind-Smith. "As the publisher of the

Telegram at that point, as a major figure in his own right in public affairs, he was just aggravated beyond words that that network jewel, if you like, should originate in any other place other than CFTO." Hind-Smith's recollection was that Bassett threatened "directly and indirectly to simply withdraw from any involvement in CTV news, unless it was eventually brought to his station which of course is exactly what happened." The *CTV National News* was moved to Toronto in the fall of 1966. "I think that the threats were not to be taken idly. He was determined to have it and he was in a position to insist on it."[60]

W5 (Who, Where, When, What, Why) in name and concept was cleared through Hind-Smith's office. His editorial direction as national programmer was more evident on W5: "More so than probably at *CTV [National] News* which required…judgements made every seven seconds whereas W5 was a weekly magazine program. I had much more suasion over it in terms of the content of it." Another program that originated in Toronto during the early CTV days was the predecessor to *Canada AM*, a show called *Bright and Early* originated by Gordon Farr, Hind-Smith's executive assistant and "a very bright young fellow."[61]

The program *Network* starred Bill Brady, a young morning radio personality at CKEY, Toronto and Denyse Angé, a Quebec City songstress with a French bistro style. The show, which was on the air about a year, featured both leading American talent and Canadian performers. The program was one of Canadian television's first forays into late night talk and entertainment and faced considerable American competition.

Brady remembered the telephone call from the CBC that brought him to CTV: "I was cutting my grass one day in Willowdale and my wife said Ross McLean wants to talk to you. And I thought it was a gag. You know we were younger then and we did stupid things…sometimes cruel things to each other. It would be the equivalent now of an actor getting a call from someone who said it was Steven Spielberg." McLean said, "you probably don't think it's Ross McLean….Here's my number at the CBC, will you call me?" Brady telephoned the CBC to hear McLean explain: "This isn't for public knowledge but I'm going to be going over to CTV and that will be announced in a few days. I've got an idea for a late night television show." *Network* featured guest interviews with prominent entertainers such as Phyllis Diller, Tony Bennett and Janet Leigh, music under the direction of Peter Appleyard and comedic "blackout" sketches reminiscent of the Sid Caesar show.[62]

Denyse Angé occasionally did interviews with French performers in their own language in an attempt "to bilingualize" the program especially since CFCF, Montreal was a network affiliate. To emphasize the national aspect of the program and to ensure it was not focused entirely on Toronto, taped inserts were provided from the affiliated stations in Calgary and Vancouver. "We would have pieces from Montreal," said Brady, "and they would try to be bilingual by having Denyse speak some French." He recalled CTV's meagre financial resources that were provided for the show: "It was low budget and...they had the perfect baby sitter of the moneybag and his name was Oliver Babirad. And Oliver wouldn't let you spend any money. If the cast needed a breakaway chair for a barroom fight, you'd get one chair. You couldn't use it in rehearsal, because it would break...and Oliver wouldn't release the money."[63]

Still Brady saw the arrival of CTV in the dissident 1960s as a timely moment in Canadian television: "I think the public was...at a point where they found some of the CBC stuff tiresome and boring...when all sorts of crazy stuff was happening and there was wild television and here was CBC plodding along and CTV provided that interesting alternative." In his view, the CTV network "gave gifted people a platform, a venue, an opportunity and gave them a freedom....I have a hunch that there was far less freedom and flexibility [given] to the planners and to the doers at CBC and I think CTV said, 'you are going to do this on a shoestring.' So their imagination ran with them."[64]

To acquire audiences for its programming, CTV had adopted an early strategy that avoided direct competition with the CBC. As Shirley Mair explained in *Maclean's*: "CTV is airing some of its strongest shows at times when CBC audiences are likely to be either small or lukewarm. For instance, CTV is matching *Maigret*, an hour-long British detective series, against two so-so CBC half hours—*Live a Borrowed Life*, a Canadian panel show, and the *Bob Cummings Show*, a U.S. situation comedy." At the same time, CTV planned "to get more audience for 20 *Questions*, a half-hour parlor game, than CBC is meanwhile getting for two fifteen-minute programs, *The Nation's Business* (free political talks) and *Mr. Fixit* (how-to instruction for handy-men)."[65]

CTV PROVIDED CANADIAN sports enthusiasts with a lively alternative to the CBC and much controversy especially when Bassett's station CFTO and CTV had acquired the broadcasting rights to the Grey Cup football classic in 1962. A major brouhaha occurred involving CTV, CBC and the BBG.[66] The privately-owned network brought a new dimension to sports programming through the efforts of Johnny Esaw, an aggressive and cost-conscious broadcaster, who joined CFTO in 1960 from western Canada. Esaw lived by the theory that "if you don't take the first one, the second one may never arrive." That outlook was in harmony with the entrepreneurial spirit of broadcaster-businessmen such as Caldwell and Bassett. Foster Hewitt, the legendary play-by-play announcer for the Toronto Maple Leafs and a principal in Baton Aldred Rogers Broadcasting Ltd. had contacted Esaw on behalf of Bassett. The *Telegram* publisher was curious as to why Esaw who was then in Winnipeg had not applied for the position of sports director at CFTO. "It was the hottest thing going," Esaw recalled. Eventually he took the position and had to fly back and forth across the country for a period to audition a potential sports staff in Toronto and also fulfill commitments to Winnipeg radio station, CKRC, and Regina radio, CKRM. Esaw was the play-by-play broadcaster for both the Winnipeg Blue Bombers and the Saskatchewan Rough Riders of the Western Football Conference.[67]

Between 1961 and 1966, a range of vibrant, sports programming was presented to Canadians that went beyond the CBC's established practice of broadcasting the familiar National Hockey League games. Illustrative of the new sports style seen on CFTO and then on CTV were: *Wide World of Sports*, *Sports Hot Seat*, Canadian and World Figure Skating Championships and the Olympics. Esaw's acquiring of *Wide World of Sports* was in direct response to an earlier initiative he had taken on behalf of the American Broadcasting Company (ABC). Shortly after the 1960 Olympics in Squaw Valley, California, Esaw received a phone call from Roone Arledge, President of ABC, who inquired if he would buy the North American rights to the World Figure Skating Championships to be held in Vancouver, the first time the event was held in the same year as the Olympics. Esaw remembered that Arledge was concerned that "if an American network shows up on the scene, they'll ask a ton!" Esaw bought the rights to the figure skating championships for $10,000 and turned them over to Arledge.[68]

When ABC went on the air with the popular *Wide World of Sports* in 1961, Esaw saw his opportunity: "So he [Arledge] owed me a big favour. And I said, ok, I want *Wide World of Sports!*" Esaw got the program at the end of 1961, and by following year, as he recalled, "we were heavy" with the sports show. "We would take the best of their programming and we would add some Canadian." The network's sports coverage increased steadily with the expansion of microwave facilities. In 1963, CTV broadcast the Canadian Figure Skating Championships from Edmonton. The following year after Esaw had bought the Canadian rights to the winter Olympics in Innsbruck, Austria for $5,000, CTV was able to air a Canada-Russia hockey game. In an era without satellite delivery, Esaw did the play-by-play of the game on videotape which was then flown back to Toronto to be aired on the network.

CTV network documents showed how sports specials such as the Olympics could draw large audiences. In attempting to impress its affiliates with the impact of *Wide World of Sports*, CTV drew attention to the ratings such programming had measured: "a special Elliott-Haynes survey, conducted to determine the audience of the Canada-Russia Olympic game on CTV, shows 725,000 homes in CTV's ten markets were tuned to this special late-night event (10:00-11:30 P.M. Toronto time). Elliott-Haynes adds that CTV viewers in some 1,225,000 homes watched one or more telecasts of the 1964 Winter Olympics." A business oriented network such as CTV could not avoid highlighting the notion, "Television sports franchises in Canada have established themselves as particularly effective advertising tools."[69]

CTV was able to capture Petra Burka's triple Salchow when she won the Women's World Figure Skating Championship in 1965. Indeed CTV sports was a major component of the network's early programming. "So much so in fact" said Esaw, "that in an early licence renewal application" for CTV, the broadcast regulator set two conditions: "You must keep *Wide World of Sports* and W5 on the air. So sport was certainly recognized" when it was made a condition of licence.[70]

WHATEVER THE STRUGGLES or accomplishments of CTV in its pioneer years, the *Report of the Committee on Broadcasting in 1965*, under the chairmanship of Robert Fowler, was not flattering to the network. Caldwell was intent on challenging the CBC. However CTV appeared to be some distance from showing signs of being able to compete with its critics' view of the relevant national programming that network television should provide. Clearly, the Fowler Committee seemed oriented to the notion of cultural enlightenment and skeptical of the programming for mass audiences that CTV had tried to produce: "The programs provided by CTV are dominated by light entertainment and programs of mass-appeal. It has produced an adequate national news service, and has a relatively inexpensive weekly Sunday-afternoon program called *Telepoll*, reporting the opinions of Canadians; for the rest, there are few programs of any real value or substance."[71]

Fowler had appeared to show a bias towards high culture in its assessment of CTV's programming during the network's early years when limited budgets were the order of the day. Predictably the committee contrasted the mass entertainment or low culture of CTV with the cultural uplift mandate of the CBC. The reaction to CBC television programs was "generally favourable." The committee noted that "many programs produced by the CBC—especially information programs, drama, and special reports—compare to advantage with programs produced anywhere in the world." But there had been "a flood of criticisms of the quality of programs produced by private stations."[72]

Fowler's study concluded that a major dilemma had resulted from CTV's original structure as it related to the day-to-day operations of the network and the programming that it could provide: "The station operators admit, quite frankly, that CTV is a private company organized to make money, and that most of the investment in it is held by people not in the broadcasting business. If there are to be any profits from private broadcasting, the stations want the profits themselves and are unwilling to let outsiders make money out of it."[73]

CTV had a dubious beginning largely because of a curious structure and ill-conceived financing. The network's capacity to survive and contribute to the cultural goals of Canadian broadcasting appeared highly questionable by the mid 1960s. In the end, a solution had to be found, if CTV were to serve as an alternative to the CBC. The stations hoped to assume ownership of the network and pay off the private investors who originally had endorsed Caldwell's bold initiative when he took on the CBC with an "advertisers' network."

By the time of a public hearing before the Board of Broadcast Governors in February, 1966 when eleven affiliated stations applied to the BBG to assume control of the network, CTV was insolvent. William Jones, a Vice-President of ITO, explained to the hearing in Ottawa: "The annual statement of the CTV Television Network 1964-65 shows a capital deficit of $856,000—the budget projections of 1965-66 indicate a further loss of $328,000, giving a total deficit, as of September 1966, of $1,184,000."[74] The lack of financing had meant that throughout its early years CTV's programming initiatives were seen to be marginal. Ray Peters recalled that in the network's early years CTV relied heavily on game shows and was characterized steadfastly as the "Quiz Show" network or a "game try," as newspaper columnist Jack Miller called it.[75]

Following the release of the Fowler Committee's report, the stations had a major task ahead to convince the BBG that they should assume control of the network. Fowler was not in favour of the stations getting control of CTV.[76] The stage was set for a crucial regulatory hearing in February, 1966 that would decide if Canadians would be able to continue to watch a second TV network that would be owned by its affiliated stations. The day-long regulatory hearing would be perhaps the most significant in CTV's history.

Spencer Caldwell would not appear before the BBG again. He had resigned on 1 October 1965 to be succeeded by Gordon F. Keeble as President and Chief Executive Officer. Keeble, originally Executive Vice-President and a director of the network since its inception, had a wide range of experience in both Canadian private and public broadcasting. Caldwell remained as a director of CTV and was to be available to the network as a consultant.

A CTV press release quoted Caldwell who had made known his decision to the network's directors: "I've spent forty years of my life in Canadian broadcasting—the last six devoted day and night to the creation of CTV. The time has come when I'd like to relax a bit. The basic structure of the Network is now well established. The architect's job is over, and I don't have to stay to set every brick and finish every room. I'm happy to step back now while others continue the development and expansion of CTV in the future."[77] In early 1966, CTV appeared to have dim prospects before it could have any glimmer of hope to perform as the network that could mean business for advertisers and offer enhanced programming to Canadian viewers.

CTV Board of Directors: Key figures are Spencer Caldwell, CTV President (centre, end of the table), Gordon Keeble (left centre) and John Bassett, with glasses, examining documents (foreground). Photograph courtesy of CTV.

THREE

Power Struggles Within the Co-operative

1966–1970

THE DAY LONG hearing before the Board of Broadcast Governors on 23 February 1966 was a decisive event in the history of the CTV network. The broadcaster-businessmen who represented the eleven stations that belonged to the network had arrived in Ottawa hopeful that the BBG would allow them to assume control of CTV as a co-operative. Their takeover plan involved a buy-out of the shares of the existing investors who had been involved with Spencer Caldwell. The three classes of shareholders in CTV Television Network Ltd. included private investors, most of the affiliated stations and Caldwell. The nonbroadcasting, private investors held the majority position, over 42 percent of the common shares of the company valued at $95,234 and 70 percent of the preferred shares estimated at $868,500. The total of the CTV stock held by the three shareholding groups in February, 1965 had been estimated at $1,463,396.[1]

Clearly the BBG hearing ushered in a new age for CTV. In the end, the broadcast regulator acted against the Fowler Committee and approved the stations' initiative. The private network functioned as a co-operative for some 30-odd years. Fowler specifically declared: "The necessary private television network must not be allowed to fall under the exclusive control of the private stations, and steps must be taken to ensure adequate program performance by them, both individually and collectively."[2] John Bassett was of the view that by deciding to allow the stations to assume control of the network against the wishes of Fowler, "Andrew Stewart and the Board of Broadcast Governors showed great guts!"[3]

By the time of the Ottawa hearing, three new TV stations representing widely different regions of the country had become CTV affiliates in addition to the eight founding members of the network. CHRE-CHAB, Regina-Moose Jaw, joined the network in September, 1962; CKCO, Kitchener and CJON, St. John's were added to the network in September, 1963 and in the fall period of 1964 respectively.[4] The BBG hearing in 1966 was the end result of extensive backstage activity at the eleventh hour by both the stations and the network management.

Stuart Griffiths representing CJOH, Ottawa and Larry Nichols of CFTO, Toronto had been instrumental in getting the stations together to structure a new arrangement for the operation of the network that involved both shareholders' and affiliation agreements. "There had been some talk with Spence," lawyer Eddie Goodman remembered, about the possibility of his eagerness to sell "because he was in dire financial need at the time. So my partner Lionel Schipper and I...took the instructions and we drafted an agreement." Goodman appeared for the applicant, CTV Television Network Ltd., which sought permission to transfer shares of its capital stock to the participating stations. John Bassett was enough of a realist to be "very amenable to sections which didn't give him control," because he knew that he would never get the licence or the consent to buy the network: "They didn't want Baton to control it," said Goodman, "Now those days are gone." Bassett agreed with Goodman's assessment of his chances of owning the network in the mid 1960s. He said that it was questionable "as to whether they [BBG] would have approved it. I don't know. Questionable, I don't think they would have."[5]

Bassett's unpredictable personality again was revealed in his refusal to go to an all important meeting in Winnipeg where the affiliated stations' representatives gathered before the BBG hearing in Ottawa. He pulled a sudden about-face at Malton airport when the plane that was to take himself, Goodman and Schipper to Winnipeg was delayed. Goodman recalled Bassett's argument that he was not going to wait around hours "to go and freeze myself in Winnipeg. He said 'you got my proxy, you vote for Baton.'" Goodman was taken aback: "I said 'John you got to be there. I mean you've been the driving force.'" Bassett steadfastly refused and predicted that the stations would agree and off he went. Schipper saw Bassett's decision as helping to solve the problem of a cost sharing formula. He amusingly remarked: "Well, that's 25 percent of the problem solved." As Goodman noted in his memoirs, "CFTO was to pay 25 percent of the expenses under the formula."[6]

The stations wanted the network, but Spencer Caldwell's group was ever vigilant. The behind-the-scenes activity among the individual stations had been paralleled by the determined attempts of Caldwell and his associates to hold on to CTV. An internal memo from Gordon Keeble to Caldwell on 6 May 1965 underlined the extent to which Caldwell had tried to explore several options to rescue the network. Specifically the memo listed six items that touched on the structure of CTV, the network's strained relations with the affiliated stations, its finances and strategies for survival. A committee of the network's directors was to give consideration to the matters that were addressed.

The first item suggested, "Giving management authority to open serious negotiations with CHCH-TV, Hamilton, with view to establishment of joint company to be flagship station and production centre for CTV." Clearly the intent was to have CHCH, whose owner Kenneth Soble appeared at the BBG hearing in Ottawa, replace CFTO as the network flagship. The second and third items addressed the issue of informing CFTO of such a move and the possible repercussions that might follow: "Manner of notice to CFTO since the above item—if agreed—really is recognition of the fact that we cannot proceed with this station beyond the current agreement." Thirdly, "The determination of the counter-action to be taken if CFTO fights back or attempts to enlist support among the other affiliates. Or, put another way, the devising of a method to drive a wedge into the T-O-M [Toronto, Ottawa, Montreal] accord."[7]

The internal memo also outlined three other possible strategies for Caldwell's group. The fourth item urged, "The serious continuation of negotiations for the acquisition in whole or in part of CKVR-TV Barrie, in association with the partners in CTV Central." Significantly, the fifth matter addressed the issue of Canadian content and raised two possible forms of financial assistance: "Can an appeal be made for Government aid and, if so, what form should it take? A subsidy of our distribution costs, supported by the license fees now paid by our affiliates, is one possibility. A revision in Canadian Content requirement or a re-shaping of this into something more practical is another. These are direct forms of help."[8]

Still Keeble suggested another course of action involving the broadcast regulator: "A simple and indirect assist would be a statement from the BBG re-affirming their belief (as expressed in proposed regulations in 1960) that a co-operative station-owned network is not desirable and would not be licensed." Finally, "The determination of a public line to be taken by CTV in answer to much recent unjustified criticism, since the stations complaining the most are those who deliberately enforced an [affiliation] agreement which makes it impossible for CTV to do the things they now demand, as part of network service."[9] The buildup in tension between the CTV management and its affiliates was palpable prior to the BBG hearing.

Despite the Fowler Committee's reluctance to see the stations get control of the network, Goodman recalled that two important factors had a potential influence at the BBG hearing: "CTV was broke. And secondly, I said 'look, if I'm going to take this hearing, I got to have a commitment from the stations that none of those guys are going to get up and speak.'" To present a uniform position to the BBG, Goodman insisted that Murray Chercover, later President of the network, would be the sole representative of the affiliated stations: "I said now the stations are going to be represented by Chercover....He was bright and he knew broadcasting. So we sat down and Chercover and I and Stu Griffiths...put together what we were doing and how we were going to do it and how we were to finance it."[10]

THE ELEVEN STATIONS in the various regions of Canada that formed CTV emerged from a range of media backgrounds that included newspapers, the radio industry and other media, notably the film industry. Their growth would see the emergence of powerful broadcasting entities such as Baton Broadcast Inc., WIC Western International Communications Ltd., Electrohome Ltd., and Moffat Communications Limited. The application to transfer ownership of CTV to the stations involved prominent personalities in the Canadian private broadcasting industry.

The CTV affiliate in British Columbia was CHAN, Vancouver represented at the BBG hearing by Ray Peters, President of British Columbia Broadcasting System Ltd.[11] The licence for CHAN originally had been awarded to film-maker Art Jones who had established a company under the name Vantel Broadcasting Company Ltd.[12] Jones's short stay in the broadcasting business was illustrative of the extent of the risk taken by early private TV broadcasters.

CHAN's first broadcast was on Halloween, 31 October 1960 at 4:30 P.M. By early 1961, Jones was gone, a victim of financial difficulties. He was succeeded by Peters whom Jones had hired as head of station marketing. At the time of CHAN's 30th anniversary, Peters recalled: "They appointed me Managing Director in February of 1961 and at that point we didn't have any audience, we had very poor programming, no money and our signal was very poor."[13]

Peters teamed up with Frank Griffiths, a noted regional media figure and owner of CKNW radio, Vancouver to purchase CHEK-TV, Victoria in 1963 and provide CHAN with greater financial resources. CHEK, originally a CBC affiliate, joined the CTV network in 1981. With two markets that could be sold in combination, suddenly BCTV, as CHAN became known, was more enticing to advertisers. Peters recognized that CHAN should be part of a Canadian network to gain programming that would help to fill the Canadian content for television stations. Looking back at the 30-year history of CHAN he explained: "So very early in 1964 I was responsible for putting a group of stations together that ended up purchasing the [CTV] network."[14]

Peters's view [WIC Western International Communications Ltd.] of CTV was in sharp contrast to John Bassett's idea of how the network should operate. Bassett [Baton Broadcasting Inc.] was strongly assertive of the view that production from Toronto should dominate on the network. Peters favored productions from all regions of the country, especially British Columbia.[15]

CFRN-TV, Edmonton and CFCN-TV, Calgary were represented at the hearing by G.R.A. Rice, President of Sunwapta Broadcasting Co. Limited, and Gordon Carter, General Manager of CFCN Television Limited, respectively.[16] The two television outlets were examples of how private television ownership evolved from early radio operations. The transition from family owned radio operations to television was common to a number of regions.

CFRN-TV, Edmonton, originally licensed as an affiliate of the CBC aired its first broadcast on 17 October 1954. The pioneer behind the establishment of the television station was Dick Rice, later to become "Dr." Dick after the University of Alberta awarded him an honorary law degree.[17] Rice, a broadcasting pioneer, was born in England, became a student of electronics and later joined the admiralty service of the Marconi Company. According to Barbara A. Moes, "In this capacity he went to sea with the Navy, was torpedoed in the Mediterranean in the First World War, rescued by an Italian destroyer and returned to England."[18]

Rice managed CJCA radio, Edmonton in the early 1920s. Later in partnership with grocer Hans Nielsen, Rice purchased CFRN radio,

G.R.A. Rice, President,
Sunwapta Broadcasting Co.,
CFRN, Edmonton.
Photograph courtesy of
CFRN, Edmonton.

Edmonton and eventually established CFRN-TV. Sunwapta Broadcasting Co. Limited owned and operated both CFRN radio and television operations. CFRN-TV passed to Baton Broadcasting in the 1990s in a strategic merger between Electrohome Limited, which acquired the station from Rice, and Baton. The CRTC approved the merger in August, 1997, an initiative taken by Baton on its way to gaining effective control of the CTV network.[19]

The ambience of Broadcast House on Stony Plain Road in Edmonton, home of CFRN, has an unmistakable sense of Canadian history with emphasis on its Indian past. The name "Sunwapta" is an Indian word meaning "radiating waves" named after Sunwapta Falls and Sunwapta Pass in the Rocky Mountains. Under Rice, the company boasted: "We at CFRN are proud of this original Canadian name, and our Indian motif will be evident throughout all Radio and Television promotion."[20]

CFCN television had its radio origins with W.W. Grant, another Canadian radio pioneer. After early experiments with radio at Morley and High River in Alberta, Grant, a veteran of World War One, made an arrangement with the *Calgary Albertan,* a local newspaper, to locate his station in Calgary. CFCN radio eventually became the Voice of the Prairies.[21]

The predecessor of CFCN television was CHCT-TV, the first Calgary television station established in 1954. The TV operation under the presidency of Gordon Love, another western radio pioneer, was formed after radio operations CFCN, CFAC and CKXL joined together. CFCN withdrew from the arrangement in 1958, the year the BBG succeeded the CBC as the broadcast regulator. Two years later CFCN received the second TV licence in Calgary. CFCN-TV's first broadcast was on 9 September 1960 when a news and public affairs program called *Pulse* was aired and hosted by broadcaster Larry Langley.[22]

Maclean-Hunter Limited purchased CFCN-AM radio and television in 1966 in what the *Report of the Special Senate Committee on Mass Media* described as the publishing company's move "into the broadcasting field in a major way." The Report explained: "In order to comply with a Board of Broadcast Governors requirement that no person might have an interest in more than one station on the CTV television network, Maclean-Hunter sold a minority interest in CJCH-TV Halifax."[23] Gary Bobrovitz noted in a *Broadcaster* article in June, 1985 the achievements of CFCN-TV since airing its first broadcast in 1960: "Since then, CFCN-TV produced the first Canadian Football League game on CTV, used instant replay for the first time in Canada and became the first station in the West to transmit in color."[24]

The Moffat family was another prominent western Canadian name in private broadcasting. Two members, Jack Moffat and R.L. (Randall) Moffat, the brother and son of Lloyd Moffat whose name had been identified closely with the evolution of private radio broadcasting in western Canada represented CHAB Ltd., Regina-Moose Jaw and Channel Seven Television Ltd., owner of CJAY-TV, Winnipeg at the BBG hearing. With them was Jack Davidson, General Manager of Channel Seven, and also present in his capacity as treasurer of the Independent Television Organization (ITO).

Moffat Communications Limited, a company whose shares were first listed on the Toronto Stock Exchange in 1972, had its beginning shortly after the Second World War. Lloyd Moffat obtained the licence for

CKY-AM radio, Winnipeg in 1949, an initiative that marked the official birth of the company. CJAY-TV became CKY-TV in 1973.[25] Following the death of Lloyd Moffat in 1964, his son, Randall Moffat, became head of the company.[26]

A relatively new member of the CTV network was CKCO, Kitchener represented at the Ottawa hearing by Eugene Fitzgibbons, Executive Director of Central Ontario Television Limited. The company had been established in 1953 largely through the initiative of a single individual and two media organizations representing broadcasting and the film industry. The principal figure, Carl A. Pollock, was the President of Electrohome Limited and later became President of Central Ontario Television Limited. The two companies instrumental in establishing the TV company were Kitchener-Waterloo Broadcasting Limited, owner of radio station CKCR, Kitchener and Famous Players Canadian Corporation Limited. CKCO-TV aired its first program on 31 March 1954 as a CBC affiliate.[27]

The reason that CKCO-TV joined the CTV network in September, 1963 was for its survival and to provide viewers with a network alternative. The station had found itself in competition with two powerful CBC affiliates in Toronto and London. Stations CBLT-TV, Toronto to the east and CFPL-TV, London to the west both spilled over into the Kitchener-Waterloo market. CKCO management underlined for advertisers the destructive economic impact of this early broadcasting environment and the rationale for joining CTV: "Advertisers would buy CFPL-TV London and CBLT-TV Toronto and reach the Kitchener-Waterloo area through spill from both stations."[28]

William McGregor, a former President of CAP Communications Limited, was instrumental in the Kitchener station joining the CTV network. He foresaw that CKCO had little choice but to link up to the new private network: "As I looked at our station's positioning in those days...I could see CBC in Toronto expanding their coverage to push further into the territory that we had been trying to stake out and CFPL had applied and received permission to push their signal out again from the other side." McGregor concluded that "there really wasn't a place for us to live. So I could see that our best future lay with...CTV."[29]

John Bassett, as owner of CFTO-TV, Toronto was in a position to prevent CKCO, from joining the network. Bassett recalled that the nearest affiliate "had the right of a veto" over any new entrant to the network under the terms of the first affiliation agreement. Still he steadfastly refused to oppose Kitchener's entry and countered those who argued that new members of the network, beyond the original eight, should have to pay to join CTV: "I said you're nuts! We want the network to cover the whole of Canada. We got to get into these markets; let's make it as easy as we can!"[30]

Along with the presence of such notables as Bassett, Keeble and Chercover, another leading spokesman for CTV at the BBG hearing was Ernie Bushnell. His extensive career had involved both the public and private broadcasting sectors. Bushnell was born on 19 November 1900 just a year before Marconi had completed his successful experiments in radio communication at Signal Hill in St. John's, Newfoundland.[31]

CJOH, Ottawa had been licensed to Bushnell TV Company Limited. Bushnell had been involved in almost every facet of the broadcasting industry. Among his achievements was his founding of the first radio advertising agency in Canada in January 1927, Broadcasting Services Ltd. The following year he became Manager of the private radio station CKNC, Toronto owned by the Canadian National Carbon Company Ltd. In 1933, Bushnell joined the Canadian Radio Broadcasting Commission (CRBC), forerunner to the CBC as Program Director of English Language Programs. CJOH-TV went on the air on 12 March 1961.[32]

Bushnell explained to the hearing that the original Caldwell scheme for a private TV network was not suited to Canadian needs. The crux of the problem was that the shareholders wanted a quick return on their investment that could be attained more readily if the network relied on American programming as opposed to the production of Canadian programs that would aid the fledgling private stations: "The original motivation of the stations was based on a desire for...good Canadian programs. Unfortunately, the revenues which would make the network commercially profitable for its shareholders were more easily available from the sale of United States program properties. The result was that in the field of Canadian productions, the network for very good commercial reasons was very cautious—perhaps too cautious."[33]

Another pioneer, radio broadcaster, W.V. "Vic" George, President of Canadian Marconi Company, led a three-member delegation representing CFCF-TV, Montreal to the BBG hearing. George also had watched the evolution of the Canadian broadcasting industry from its earliest days when private stations dominated throughout the 1920s and the Canadian National Railways entered the radio business. He had been employed with CNRO, the Canadian National Railways radio station in Ottawa, before moving to CFCF, Canada's first radio station, as manager in the early 1930s. CFCF radio had begun broadcasting regular programs in December, 1919.[34]

CFCF-TV went to air on 20 January 1961. The TV station later became part of CFCF Inc., a diverse company that focused on conventional television and cable-TV. The establishment of the television operation followed the founding of CFCF-AM radio and CFQR-FM, which started broadcasting in 1947, all owned by the Marconi company. Multiple Access Limited, a publicly-owned Canadian company, purchased Canadian Marconi in 1972.[35]

E. Finlay MacDonald, President of CJCH Limited, Halifax and Donald Jamieson, Vice-President of Newfoundland Broadcasting Company, St. John's represented CTV's easternmost stations at the BBG hearing. By the late 1960s, Jamieson had entered the federal cabinet in the Liberal government led by Pierre Trudeau and would eventually serve as Canada's External Affairs Minister. MacDonald had seen the growth of CTV from its earliest days and experienced the struggles that had ensued between the affiliated stations and the nonbroadcasting private investors. The development of both eastern TV stations had followed the establishment of their earlier radio operations with the same call letters: CJCH, Halifax and CJON, St. John's.

When MacDonald appeared before the BBG in June 1960 at the Lord Nelson Hotel in Halifax to apply for the television licence for CJCH, he felt compelled to engage in some histrionics to make his case. The first day of the hearing had been a mild disaster for MacDonald. He had tried to follow procedures that the Board had laid down and avoided reading aloud his programming plans that were contained in briefs presented to the regulatory body. The lone competing application for the Halifax licence was a company to be incorporated as CHAL Limited. The principal owners were Mitchell Franklin and Peter Herschorn, inheritors of a movie chain in the Maritimes known as The Franklin Herschorn Theatre Company Limited.[36]

"But my opponents did the exact opposite of what the procedures required," said MacDonald. "They read...all of their programming plans and so on which left me standing there bereft of any programming thing which I was told not to do." Don Jamieson who had attended the hearing remarked to MacDonald after the first day, "we've blown it!"[37] MacDonald and Jamieson stayed up all night, rewrote much of the next day's presentation, and prepared to impress the board in round two. The next day MacDonald came on with a stylish vengeance.

He charged that his opponent had clearly breached the procedures that the BBG had established for the hearing. He demanded the same privilege that had been granted to the Franklin-Herschorn application: "I said, you want to talk about programming and I opened this book and ripped out the pages one by one and read every one of them!" Clearly MacDonald's flamboyance had impact on the media covering the hearing: "The press reporting on the thing said all they could see was the fluttering pages going down...about 80 pages of programming notes." MacDonald did not finish until he had created grave doubts in the minds of the BBG members about the financial implications of his opponent's application: "Then...we ripped apart the financial brief of the other fellows and the fact that they couldn't possibly get a dolly in the size of the studios they were planning...and such and such. So I was convinced that we won it fair and square."[38]

MacDonald said he took nothing for granted in the licence application to the BBG despite the perception that the Board was a pro Tory broadcast regulator. As the BBG hearings progressed, "I got the distinct impression," said MacDonald, "that the people who were appointed to the board were getting increasingly irritated and nervous about the 'nudge-wink' kind of thing. And I wasn't going to get caught in that kind of trap."[39] For this reason, MacDonald lobbied the bureaucracy of the BBG but not the board members themselves.

In Newfoundland, CJON-TV grew out of the radio operation established in October, 1951 by Jamieson and Geoff Stirling, two colorful Newfoundlanders. Like many recipients of broadcasting licences in Canada, Jamieson and Stirling came to learn the value of political connections. Jamieson, originally an opponent of Confederation and who favoured economic union with the United States, explained in his memoirs, No Place for Fools, that Newfoundland's Premier Joey Smallwood had assisted the pair in winning the radio licence: "We acquired a license for a radio station [CJON] only after we had discovered the hard way, through two unsuccessful attempts, that without a signal of the Premier's support, the licensing authority was not especially impressed by the other merits of our application."[40]

Subsequently, the awarding of a private television licence to Jamieson and Stirling in 1955 was some commentary on the interplay between politicians and broadcasters in the acquisition of television licences in

Canada. E. Austin Weir, a public broadcasting enthusiast, wrote that the CBC had attempted to obtain a TV licence for St. John's the previous year and establish its own station so that the public broadcaster would have an owned and operated outlet in the province. Like Quebec, Newfoundland with its distinctive culture and the fact that it was the last province to join Confederation in 1949 was "of prime importance to the CBC."[41] Still Jamieson and Stirling won the licence for a privately operated station even while the CBC was the broadcast regulator. Weir concluded in his examination of national broadcasting that patronage was an influential factor in the awarding of the TV licence to CJON's owners: "This award was not inconsistent with the general system of political patronage all too prevalent in this country. The CBC swallowed its disappointment, extended its microwave service to St. John's, and put CJON on the national network."[42] CJON, the only TV outlet in Newfoundland, remained a CBC affiliate until October, 1964 when the Corporation established a broadcasting transmitter in the province. CJON then joined CTV.

Jamieson's career took him from employment as bellhop at the Newfoundland Hotel in the 1930s to Canada's High Commissioner to London, England before his death on 19 November 1986 while jogging near his Swift Current home. In a retrospective on his active life, Pat Doyle wrote in the St. John's *Evening Telegram*: "He...went on to become one of the most popular provincial and federal politicians and represented Newfoundland in the federal cabinet for 11 years, including a period as external affairs minister and while in...that post served briefly as chairman of the United Nations Security Council."[43]

Still it was through broadcasting that Jamieson became widely recognized, especially on a suppertime news program called *News Cavalcade*, a half hour of news, weather and interviews. The show became enormously popular throughout Newfoundland. The news format served as a vehicle to give Jamieson a high profile and catapult him to national prominence as President of the Canadian Association of Broadcasters (CAB).

In both broadcasting and politics, Jamieson possessed a capacity to ad-lib and improvise. He became renown as a multi-task broadcaster on *News Cavalcade* where he performed without a script and presented the news, announced the commercials live and interviewed prominent guests in the studio. Ted Gardner, who became Director of Sales at NTV, as CJON later was known, was a 16-year-old boy when he began to work at the station in 1961 and watched Jamieson broadcast the news.

"This was a totally ad-libbed newscast," said Gardner, "and the stories would be prepared during the day at which time around four or four-thirty in the afternoon the scripts would be given to Mr. Jamieson and he would spend probably a half hour, 45 minutes in his office going over them." Gardner recalled Jamieson's photographic memory: "He would memorize these scripts word for word. And at that time as well, he would do the commercials live....Then he would beat it back to the other end of the studio...and do the weather forecast live and probably do another commercial." Still Jamieson was not finished: "Then they'd play a bridge of music for 15 or 20 seconds and he would go over and sit down and interview a person, a live interview for some notable person who had made some headlines or was a visiting dignitary who might have been into the province."[44] Jamieson appeared on *News Cavalcade* between 1955 and 1962, ten months of the year, five days a week but not in the summer months. He left the program in the early 1960s when he became involved with the CAB and later entered federal politics. Jamieson's news program received an award for the best daily news show on any Canadian private station in 1957–58.[45]

Geoff Stirling, Jamieson's business associate, had a most eccentric reputation in Canadian private broadcasting. Stirling seldom granted interviews to journalists and claimed on one occasion that he had been on the end of too many "hatchet jobs."[46] However he explained to Alexander Ross the nature of his personality and what motivated him in life. By age 50, Stirling was a multi-millionaire through his media holdings in radio, television and *The Herald* newspaper in St. John's. As Ross wrote, "Altogether, he is worth something like $20 million. But, when you meet him, he somehow conveys the impression of owning nothing but his body and the clothes on his back."[47]

After his mother died when he was 14 years old, Stirling prayed that he would become wealthy so that he would have freedom throughout his life. A world traveller, he became interested in the psychedelic culture of the 1960s and later his enthusiasm for Eastern mysticism prompted him to import "this and that swami from India," in part as a gimmick for his radio stations but also because he was curious about their lifestyle. Still Stirling's behaviour and his "cosmic insights" could not trivialize the considerable success he enjoyed as a media owner. "The man is like a shortwave radio," Ross explained, "fading in and out from one frequency to another. One minute he sounds like John Bassett, the next like William Blake."[48]

Ross's assessment of Stirling was that he had much in common with other noted entrepreneurs such as Edwin Land of Polaroid, Thayer Lindsley, a founder of the Rio Tinto mining group, venture capitalist Ben Webster and the late Ralph Farris who built the Northern and Central Gas energy conglomerate. Such individuals "took an almost existential approach to the process of risk-taking, all of them professed to be disinterested in money, except as a means of keeping score, and all of them have struck me as highly developed human beings. None of them could be described as money grubbers. They are artists of action, these entrepreneurs, and their goal is to transcend themselves."[49]

Stirling had lofty objectives for network television in Canada. "Taking the highest possible aim," he said, "it would certainly be to expose all the known knowledge of the world to the audience on all levels of art, religion, crafts and to maximize entertainment, sports and public affairs information." Private broadcasters had to be realistic financially and should go "beyond the sheer aim of making money but to present also meaningful programs in the national interest."[50]

Despite his noble vision for network broadcasting, Stirling seldom attended CTV Board of Directors' meetings. Still he was a critic of network operations. John Coleman recalled his frequent absence: "All of the time that I was at board meetings, which was 15 years or so, I think Geoff appeared at three board meetings. So he was not an active player. He spent a lot of time on the telephone with various different people in the organization, principally Murray [Chercover], and with other directors and he wrote a lot of letters, largely acrimonious letters, about issues that he didn't agree with having read the minutes of the meeting." The response from the network generally was, "Well Geoff, if you felt that strongly you should have attended the meeting. You didn't and so that's what happened."[51]

WITH THE CAST OF CHARACTERS present at the BBG hearing, it was hardly surprising that lighter moments occasionally prevailed. A highly memorable and terse statement came from Jamieson when the Board members had attempted to learn whether microwave capability could be made available to the east coast province of Newfoundland for simultaneous delivery of programming. When questioned on the subject, Jamieson's humorous retort underlined the tensions in CTV between the "have" stations and the "have-not" affiliates that characterized much of the network's history: "Mr. Chairman and members of the Board, I want to say that I am going to get simultaneous delivery out of this network, even if it takes every cent that John Bassett has." Jamieson confessed to having the advantage "of being able to reconcile a completely and thoroughly subjective and selfish objective with what I think is an essential national object, and that is to establish a coast-to-coast network in this country."[52]

Andrew Stewart had remained Chairman of the BBG; the Vice-Chairman was Pierre Juneau who would head the Canadian Radio-television Commission (CRTC), successor to the BBG, two years later. At the hearing, Eddie Goodman analyzed four major aspects of the CTV application: the present shareholdings of the network; the relevant factors dealing with the proposed purchase by the stations of the nonstation shareholders' interests; CTV's proposal for a new share structure after the reconversion of the network shares; and the nature of a new affiliates' agreement.[53]

The existing CTV share structure consisted of 228,516 common shares, issued and outstanding, with a par value of one dollar each. The stations making the application to take over the network owned 45,203 of the common shares and 2,219 preferred shares. Goodman explained to the BBG: "Now that works out to slightly under 20 per cent of both the common and the preferred that are presently outstanding. The balance, of course, are owned by the non-station shareholders and we are buying from them 183,313 common shares and 10,438 preferred."[54]

The most relevant factor relating to the purchase of the shares by the stations was the formation of a holding company called Canet. The eleven CTV stations seeking to buy out the nonstation shareholders proposed to pay in cash $444,313 for the 183,313 common shares and for another 2,610 of the preferred shares. Canet Holdings Limited, a company controlled equally by the eleven CTV stations, was to purchase the remaining 7,828 preferred shares. This would be done by issuing to the sellers of shares interest-bearing debentures "in the aggregate principal amount of $782,800, which is the par value of the shares so purchased." The 7,828 preferred shares held by Canet were increased ten times to 78,280 and the par value of the shares was changed from $100.00 to $10.00. Goodman explained to the BBG that Canet eventually would take the money it received from CTV and then "it pays off the debentures that are held by the non-station former shareholders...." The debentures were guaranteed by CTV and eight of the eleven stations and were able to be redeemed over approximately a five-year period.[55] John Bassett recalled the circumstances surrounding the change of ownership of CTV which saw the network pass from Caldwell's group to the affiliates: "We bought out all the private shareholders including me. They bought my shares. We bought them out on the basis of the money they had put in. They got no profit, but they suffered no loss....In any event, Baton and all the other shareholders, the affiliates, put the money in to buy them out dollar for dollar."[56]

Gordon Keeble maintained that the stations were "going for the jugular" in 1966 and after recovering their earlier losses "they were in a pretty healthy financial shape." The stations decided "this was something they were going to have and nobody else was going to make any money out of their efforts. That's really what it comes down to." Keeble was appointed President of CTV and he negotiated with Goodman, "a co-operative deal," which essentially gave the original investors back their money: "No interest, no dividends, no nothing, they got back exactly what they put in over a period of time from a company called Canet which was formed by Eddie Goodman's firm and they issued these bonds and they were paid off I think over a period of three or four years. So...the original shareholders, and they were a good group, didn't suffer too much. Money tied up that didn't do anything....the original investment but nothing else."[57]

Goodman's presentation also dealt with the provisions of the separate agreements covering both the new shareholdings in CTV and the affiliates' operations. He explained that "in coming to the decisions...on the terms of this [shareholders'] agreement and the affiliates' agreement, the stations proved beyond any doubt whatsoever that they are capable of working together in harmony and co-operating to provide the public service that is required by a network and to meet their responsibilities as broadcasters."[58] The stations were required to make immediate additional investments of money in CTV.

In future, the costs of operating the network would be divided proportionately as they related to the "additional capital or advances" that the stations had to provide to finance CTV. The proportions were based "on the current highest national 60-second spot rate published by each of the stations."[59] The rate cards for each individual affiliate in the CTV network (highest national 60-second spot rate) were added together. A percentage of the total rate cards was calculated for individual affiliates to determine the proportion of each station's share of costs in the eleven markets.

Goodman cited a specific case for the BBG: "For example, if the total of Montreal—of the total rate card, of the spot rate card, turns out to be 15.41 per cent...Canadian Marconi Company will have to contribute on that amount. On the other hand Regina is 3.95 per cent so they contribute 3.95 per cent of the amount. The stations themselves have felt that their own rate cards indicate their own financial capabilities."[60]

The shareholders' agreement also outlined the structure of the CTV Board of Directors which was to consist of 12 members, one from each of the eleven stations in the network along with the CTV President. Each station had one representative on the Board of Directors and each had a single vote.[61] The principle of equality of ownership was to be applied throughout much of the network's history, regardless of the number of television stations an individual owner held. The provision eventually led to considerable internal wrangling and tension.

Along with the shareholders' accord, the CTV stations had also reached a new affiliation agreement. The arrangement represented a sharp break with established practice. Specifically, the affiliates agreed to pay for programs beyond those originally provided by CTV in the category known as the "network sales time" period.

In the past, the eleven stations had made available to CTV in network sales time a total of 23 3/4 hours each week for the network to provide sponsored programs. In return CTV paid the affiliated stations, in Goodman's words, "a varying proportion of these monies that it received from the advertisers."[62] The amount of "network sales time" was maintained in the 1966 affiliates' agreement. A new time category was also created known as "station time" or "station sales time" when the network would provide additional programming to the stations which they purchased. The two categories—network sales time and station time which amounted to 36 1/4 hours—brought the total network service to 60 hours.[63]

Murray Chercover recalled that in the new affiliation agreement "we simply folded the ITO and CTV activities together." The program time that the stations had provided as members of ITO was brought into the network. Goodman explained that for the classification of network sales time, CTV was to pay "in the aggregate to the affiliated stations 75 per cent of the gross revenue in accordance with the network rate card which has been settled, less an amount equal to the percentage or—such percentage of the revenue as the Board of Directors may determine which the network may retain for programming and delivery."[64]

The amount of the payments by the stations to CTV for "station time" would be "such sum as in the opinion of the Board of Directors of the network is necessary in addition to the normal revenue of the network, to enable the network to finance all its obligations both operating and capital." Goodman summarized the affiliation agreement by concluding that "while the stations get on the one hand a certain amount of money from their time, they have really issued a blank cheque to meet the needs of the network for program delivery and all other expenses."[65]

However all did not go as planned at the BBG hearing even though Goodman and the stations had left little to chance. Goodman's uncle, Kenneth Soble, owner of CHCH television in Hamilton, intervened at the hearing. He urged the Board to postpone its decision on the future of CTV, until he could make application to either purchase the outstanding shares of the existing network or, if unsuccessful, form a new company to take over the network. Soble appeared with 36-year-old Maurice Strong, President of the Power Corporation of Canada Limited, which by the mid 1970s was "the most powerful corporate complex in Canada," according to Wallace Clement.[66]

Strong who was to have a wide ranging career in the Canadian corporate world, and with international bodies, was a director of several other Canadian companies including Canada Steamship Lines, Consolidated Paper Corporation and International Utilities Corporation. With the backing of the Power Corporation, Soble told the Board that he and his associates were prepared to establish a company with authorized capital of eleven and a half million dollars. Dennis Braithwaite, a *Globe and Mail* columnist who attended the hearing, wrote that Strong, "a 36-year-old millionaire industrialist...seems to have a holy mission to save CTV from the Bassett group."[67]

To counter the impression given by the stations about the urgent need to rescue CTV, Soble produced a letter from Ralph Draper, Chairman of the media review board with the advertising agency, Vickers and Benson Ltd. Draper saw no problem on the horizon that would necessitate "a rush answer on such an important item" on the future of Canadian television and heaped praised on Gordon Keeble, Michael Hind-Smith and Arthur Weinthal, three members of the Caldwell group: "In regard to programming, we have never had anything except the highest regard for the abilities of Gordon Keeble, Michael Hind-Smith and Arthur Windfall [sic]. As long as they are with the network, we are sure Fall programming plans can be conducted."[68]

Indeed the future prospects of Caldwell's associates had arisen during a line of questioning by the Board's special counsel John Nelligan to Goodman, an exchange that seemed to foreshadow a power struggle that ensued later within the co-operative. Nelligan wanted to know "to what extent the present personnel of the network will be retained and to what extent you contemplate changes." In his reply, Goodman referred specifically to Keeble but made no mention of Hind-Smith or Weinthal: "First of all we say now that the president of the network [Keeble], in whom we have confidence and for whom we have affection, will stay on as president of the network....We are going to...let it continue for a while, evaluate the potential of various persons, like anybody else who goes into a company in which they are going to be spending many millions of dollars [and we] will evaluate it."[69] In the end, Soble did not get his wish. The stations took over the network. As for the Caldwell group, Hind-Smith was fired at the end of 1966 and Keeble was gone by October, 1969. Weinthal stayed on with CTV for 30-odd years before stepping down in the mid 1990s.

The BBG approved the application for the ownership transfer on 4 March 1966. Media watchers focused on the extent to which the BBG had gone to ensure that John Bassett was unable to assume control of CTV by inserting several clauses to the document approving the network's takeover. In the *Toronto Daily Star*, Roy Shields argued that the Board showed a curious naivete in its decision: "This apparent determination to keep Mr. Bassett from dominating the network is a bit naive, because as CFTO goes, so goes the network. His is the only station (apart from CFCF in Montreal) with the facilities for bigtime production. Inevitably it will be in a commanding position when decisions are made on whether to undertake programs of major scope."[70]

FOLLOWING THE BBG'S DECISION, extensive backstage manoeuvring took place that was to produce board room tensions and firings and had a lasting impact on the network's future. It was an intense period of rivalries. The Caldwell holdovers in CTV, Hind-Smith and Keeble, now had to work with the affiliates who had been part of ITO, in reality a competitor to the network. The potential for major differences was apparent. The uneven interplay between personalities and circumstances soon began to tear at the newly formed co-operative.

When the affiliates assumed control of CTV in 1966, they kept Keeble as President. He undertook two major initiatives. First he gave Hind-Smith a working contract for his position as Vice President, Programming. Keeble recalled that Hind-Smith was more concerned "about the intricacies of a takeover because, that is what this is, than I was." The new CTV Board composed of the affiliates, as Keeble remembered, "didn't like the idea that I had given him a contract." Hind-Smith offered a similar interpretation of the circumstances at the time: "They [affiliates] didn't like me particularly, but they liked Gordon." Second, Keeble hired Murray Chercover from Baton as his Executive Vice-President who moved to the network's headquarters at 42 Charles Street East in Toronto. His initiative was aimed partly at winding down ITO: "I said to myself I need someone to fill my ex position which was executive VP and Murray is certainly capable...and he knows all the fellows in the group. And further, if I leave him alone, he will continue to run ITO in competition to the network. And I think that is kind of a silly idea so I hired him. I never regretted it, but I sure got rid of ITO too."[71] The stations' annoyance at the contract given to Hind-Smith, and the arrival of Chercover who had the affiliates' support, provided a potentially, uneasy relationship between both men.

Still it was a Board of Directors meeting in Vancouver on 24–25 November, during Grey Cup weekend, that was a major turning point for the CTV network. In the 1966 Grey Cup, Saskatchewan beat Ottawa 29–14 after Saskatchewan's Al Ford was able to grab a deflected pass by Ron Lancaster in the end zone that shifted the momentum of the game in the west's favour.[72] Momentum also shifted in the CTV Board room towards the affiliated stations now the owners of the network. The CTV meeting produced a fundamental change in the senior management, a realignment that could not help but exacerbate tensions. Any chance of reconciliation between the Caldwell group and the stations was irretrievably lost.

An internal memo from Keeble to Hind-Smith in early December 1966 after the Grey Cup weekend underlined the major changes that had occurred in the structure of the network's management. Clearly the stations were in charge. They had not taken long to assert themselves by realigning the duties of senior network management. Not surprisingly, Keeble and Hind-Smith found themselves operating in a new context.

With reference to the CTV directors' gathering, Keeble noted that "many serious items were discussed at the meeting of our Directors in

Vancouver last week, some of them reflecting a less than satisfactory performance on our part in some areas." The crux of the central issue decided by the directors was that Keeble as President was to be removed from the day-to-day operations of the network and be responsible only for future policy and planning. He would have no operational responsibility which the directors handed to Chercover. Keeble explained the managerial change that had taken place with its sweeping implications: "As a result of their concern in both areas of operation, the affiliates gave me at the Vancouver meeting a directive recommending, first, that I divorce myself 'as quickly as possible from the physical operation of the network and concentrate on the operation of the network at the policy and board level' and, second, that Murray Chercover 'be given immediately full and total responsibility for the operation of the network and the institution of policy as directed by the President, with all personnel of the executive level being responsible and reporting directly to him.'"[73] The change meant that Hind-Smith would have to report to Chercover, a reorganization that represented a potentially explosive situation.

His working relationship with Chercover was, in Hind-Smith's terminology, "scabrous." As he put it, "I don't think we ever saw eye-to-eye on anything." As for how he related to Hind-Smith, Chercover's characterization was "not badly in any social sense." However workwise, said Chercover, "not at all." It was an "old fashioned power struggle," Hind-Smith maintained. "Murray and I began in television at the same time. He worked in the studio beginning just as I did. He was the one who put the first slide upside down [CBLT, Toronto]; in the same week, I was a freelance host at CBC television. So the years go by and I became really the operational honcho of CTV in both programming and sales and I think...egged on by John Bassett it became an intolerable situation that I rather than he [Chercover] should be the one calling the shots in the network."[74]

After the stations assumed control of the network, CTV underwent a period of severe austerity when Hind-Smith was forced to watch a sharp reduction in programming initiatives that he had undertaken under Caldwell. An internal memo from Chercover to Hind-Smith following the affiliates' meeting on Grey Cup weekend referred to a programming "cut-back" and realignment of the network schedule that affected programming in which Hind-Smith had been involved. Chercover explained, "There is a possibility that *Bright & Early* will be terminated either in January or March, at which time the *University of the Air* program would be delivered adjacent to a later transmission period." In retrospect, Hind-Smith argued that "Murray Chercover is fond of saying he invented morning television, *Canada AM*. In fact I invented it with *Bright and Early* which didn't go anywhere."[75] The program which aired at 7:30 A.M. had as its newscaster Jim Fleming, a Toronto broadcaster, later to become a federal Liberal cabinet minister. *Canada AM* was first seen by Canadians in September 1972.

The crunch finally came on 5 December 1966 not long after Grey Cup weekend. Chercover fired Hind-Smith after the affiliates had decided upon major managerial changes in the network. "Well that decision was no sooner said than done," said Hind-Smith, "and I was presented with a request for my resignation on the 5th of December 1966 which I refused....And I was out of there in the space of two hours that fateful day." Hind-Smith admitted to having "independent views on things" and saw his firing as "authorized by the board and executed directly by Murray Chercover." To Hind-Smith his "wilfull dismissal" was a breach of a two-year contract with the network that still had 16 months to run. In a recap of events, Hind-Smith was to write later: "Gone for broke: the affiliates get rid of Caldwell; and Chercover gets rid of me."[76]

Part of the stations' disenchantment stemmed from the contract that Keeble had given Hind-Smith. In Keeble's words, "The board didn't like the fact that I had given him a contract. They had to buy him out."[77] Hind-Smith claimed he had been assured by Keeble earlier that his performance was satisfactory. Following the Vancouver meeting of the affiliates, Keeble's capacity to honour the contract was in grave doubt, because as President he had been removed from operational responsibility for CTV.[78]

The new CTV Board of Directors had presented Chercover, the executive to whom the stations had given authority for day-to-day operation of the network, with a list of the Caldwell holdovers who were to be dismissed. Aside from Hind-Smith, Chercover said he responded to the Board's directive by saying "whoa!" He called for the Board to provide at least "a six-month interregnum" during which time he would "give clear direction and get results," or not, at which time he would take action. Chercover explained his position to the Board this way: "As soon as I see that X or Y does not understand or respond to the direction I've given, they'll be gone. But if they do respond, then you have to acknowledge it was the supervision, the senior management people, who put them in the jackpot."[79]

The upheaval at CTV drew considerable attention from newspaper columnists. Bob Blackburn writing in the *Toronto Telegram* commented on the rise of Chercover and the firing of Hind-Smith who had been seen as the number two man in the network before the stations took over: "Chercover was deftly slipped in between Keeble and Hind-Smith, as Executive Vice-President, and Hind Smith's responsibilities were limited to programming. Some observers felt at that time that Hind-Smith would either resign or be squeezed out, but there were effusive denials of this possibility by all three, who at press conferences stressed with almost sinister insistence that there were no grounds for such speculation." With some prescience, Roy Shields wondered about the future of Keeble, another Caldwell holdover: "Hind-Smith was hired by former CTV President Spence Caldwell who repeatedly clashed with [John] Bassett. CTV's current president, Gordon Keeble, was also a Caldwell man. Will he then be the next to go? Would this not seem a distinct possibility, especially since Murray Chercover, CTV's number two man and Bassett's former program chief at CFTO, appeared to have new power within CTV?"[80]

IN 1968, CHERCOVER BECAME President of CTV, a position he was to hold for more than two decades. Keeble was made the network Chairman. As head of CTV, Chercover cultivated perhaps the lowest public profile of any major network executive in North America. A Canadian Press story in the *Vancouver Province* highlighted his avoidance of the limelight: "If you don't work for the country's private television network or do business with it, it's likely you know little about Chercover. That's because the former small-town radio station employee and CBC executive doesn't grant interviews."[81] Chercover explained why he stayed below the radar screen: "I know as someone who started out in the entertainment industry in the theatre, in film and television in the United States that everybody has a press agent. I never had a press agent."[82]

Still his reluctance towards public exposure could not conceal either Chercover's knowledge of the broadcasting industry or his drive to succeed. Bassett, who agreed with Robert Fowler that programming is the "whole story" in broadcasting and the rest is merely "housekeeping," recognized Chercover's programming capabilities and ambition:

"Murray Chercover was a very talented programmer and he came in as Vice President under Gordon Keeble and I think there was a certain amount of conflict between the two of them. Murray was very ambitious, no question about it."[83]

Chercover was born in Montreal and moved to Port Arthur, Ontario when he was three and a half years old. His family was in the horse business through successive generations: "The family business started after my grandfather emigrated to Canada from Russia. He was in the horse business in Russia." He remembered that prior to World War Two his father "was the largest horse dealer in all of Canada. He had about 4000 head a year."[84] Businesses such as the pulp and paper industry could hardly function without the animals. As a youngster, Chercover shovelled out horse stalls as his father would negotiate horse deals with corporate officials such as the President of Abitibi.

The horse story helps to explain two aspects of Chercover's character known mainly to network insiders. He was willing to get his hands dirty and would arrive in the CTV screening room at four o'clock in the morning to examine a documentary scheduled to be broadcast. He also displayed hypochondriac tendencies attributable to the fact that he broke horses for his father and experienced numerous physical injuries. He did not realize how sore a shoulder could be until his children would jump to him playfully. Between riding horses and playing football, Chercover has broken his nose and several ribs. His family had a history of heart problems on his mother's side. Chercover had a quadruple by-pass in 1990. He has a regular supply of medication at all times. "I have always got a anti-histamine or decongestant," said Chercover, "I carry headache tablets. I get headaches occasionally but I don't have migraine, I'm not incapacitated....I'm a complainer."[85]

Senator Finlay MacDonald maintained that Chercover "had no sense of humour, at all. Life was serious and he was a hypochondriac. He had pills to meet any kind of situation." In addition, Chercover "was always convinced he was going." MacDonald recalled speaking at a dinner in Chercover's honour and underlined his admiration for the network president's Jewish ancestry: "I said on the one side of their head was the dreamer and visionary and the poet and so on and the other side was the cost accountant. I said 'no other race has this that I have seen.' There is always a dreamer who falls on his ass...who comes a cropper. But I said 'the Jews seem to have the ability to be able to dream it and implement it' and I said 'this is Chercover.'"[86]

Bruce Phillips recalled an amusing happening in Chercover's office at 42 Charles Street East in Toronto when he joined CTV as Ottawa bureau chief in 1969. A meeting with Chercover, network executives Tom Gould and Don MacPherson was reminiscent of one of "Ernie Kovacs' parodies on television." Phillips experienced a sense of déjà vu when he entered Chercover's office which had "four or five monitors all blasting away with signals coming in from one place or another." There was also "a huge wall with a fish tank and all kinds of tropical fish floating around in it." Phillips, a newspaper correspondent for Southam News Services, was introduced to television land in startling fashion: "Murray was doing deep breathing exercises with an exercise belt, one of those weighted belts, breathing in and out deeply and we all sat there for what seemed to me like a day and a half, but I'm sure was only a minute and a half, waiting to be recognized by himself."[87]

The first five or ten minutes of the meeting was taken up with a friendly discussion about Chercover's exercise belt culminating in MacPherson insisting that he must try on the distinctive apparel. For Phillips accustomed to the conventional, reliable print medium, his introduction to television indeed was a memorable occasion. "I thought, I've read about this kind of thing somewhere! This is television, show bizz and he [Chercover] talked for awhile about his latest program buying trip to Hollywood and all that kind of thing, dropping names as he went and I was absolutely dazzled by all this stuff."[88] Ron Base wrote in *Maclean's* magazine about Chercover: "He is, by turns, emotional, overwrought, sensitive and a hypochondriac, the kind of man who keeps a drawer full of pills and sometimes wanders relentlessly into the office at 2 A.M. to look at a piece of film."[89]

As a teenager, Chercover left northern Ontario when he won a scholarship to Lorne Greene's academy of radio and television arts in Toronto. There he won another scholarship to the Neighbourhood Playhouse in New York, the dominant school of theatre arts in North America in the late 1940s. When he was in New York, the Dumont organization started the first television network in North America. Chercover produced the first drama series on the new network where he built both personal contacts and gained an understanding of the television medium. In March, 1952 Stuart Griffiths, manager of CBLT, Toronto offered Chercover a contract as a drama producer/director. By then, he had met his future wife, Barbara Ann Holleran, an Atlanta, Georgia actress and writer. Later Chercover would join Baton's CFTO television.[90]

WHEN HE WAS the CRTC CHAIRMAN, André Bureau, no doubt aware of the internal tensions in CTV that Chercover faced, inquired how he managed as President of the network co-operative. Chercover responded: "In order to relate to this I think I should first say that when you enter a swamp to drain it it is very difficult when you find that you are up to your hips in alligators." As to the notion of his function "as that of walking a tight-wire down the centre of the boardroom table," Chercover explained: "The question is who is on which side of the board table and which pit I am going to fall into."[91]

When he was President, Chercover had to contend with fundamental disagreements. The discord at CTV meetings that occurred between John Bassett and Ray Peters was directly related to two different visions of how the network should operate. Bassett's position steadfastly was central Canada oriented and stressed the dominant role of Toronto in network programming. "My view was that...I believed that Toronto was the key market in the country," said Bassett. "There could be no argument about that. The fact is that there is no comparable market in the United States. Toronto is by far more dominant in the Canadian market than any single city in the United States. New York is not as dominant across America as Toronto is in Canada. There's no Chicago in Canada. There's no Los Angeles in Canada. There's no Detroit in Canada." Bassett remembered the boardroom rancour: "Peters would scream and yell and I'd scream and yell back. I'd say, 'well Christ you can't produce a national show out in the sticks for Christ sakes Ray!' You know he'd roar and I'd roar back at him."[92]

Peters's concept of how CTV should operate was in flat contradiction to Bassett's centralized position. "We weren't running it very long before we ran into a lot of disagreement....Everybody thought it was personal," said Peters. "The newspapers used to talk about the feud between Peters and Bassett, but John and I never...[could] really figure it out." The differences between the pair revolved largely around network philosophy: "Anyway he used to insist that all of the production of the network be done by CFTO," said Peters. "He wasn't happy at the end of each year in the spring setting up the program schedule both for station sales time and the schedule of CTV sales time, if he didn't occupy all of the programs and produce them all." Peters thought Bassett to be too clever by half: "Now if he ever sat down with a pencil and figured out what it was costing him to produce all those programs, what he was charging for them, he would soon figure out that he was winning the battle but losing the war. At any rate he used to make me furious about this!"[93]

Peters envisioned a more decentralized CTV. He preferred the network to broadcast programs that would reflect the regional variation of the country. "My vision really of the network," said Peters, "was that we should be producing some programs out of Montreal reflecting the areas of Quebec...some programs out of the Atlantic provinces, out of Halifax...some programs out of Toronto reflecting Ontario, we should be producing programs out of Winnipeg, Calgary and...out of British Columbia."[94] In the two contending positions, CTV was a microcosm of the historic tensions in Canadian federalism.

Another western broadcaster, Dr. Dick Rice of Edmonton, could also be an active boardroom player though his participation drew less media attention. Rice did not always take kindly to Bassett's bombastic outbursts and his penchant for dominating board meetings. Amidst some of what Chercover described as the "outrageous dialogues," Rice was inclined to put Bassett in his place. Dr. Rice was "the only person I have known," said Chercover, "to cause John Bassett to walk out of the room in high dudgeon. He would say, 'alright John, stop trying to control this.'" Following Rice's stricture, "John got up and tore out of the room! Now Ray Peters never did that. Arguing but not to the point where either one of them walked out." Later Allan Waters, head of the CHUM Group, joined the CTV Board. Chercover recalled that Waters "would go instantly" with Baton.[95]

The relationship between Bassett and Chercover was a crucial aspect of network operations. Bassett insisted that the network had to grow and he recognized Chercover's abilities as a programmer: "I was very strong for the network and I felt that if we were going to develop the network which I was very keen to do...they had to have some good leadership and they had to have somebody who really was very talented in the whole programming area." Still Bassett argued that he controlled CTV over time: "Well I say...through the years by and large I controlled it anyway. You ask Murray Chercover and he'll laugh and say 'that isn't true.'"[96]

Chercover remembered Bassett's support for CTV and his eagerness for control: "In the long term, John was very supportive of the network in the generality. The only thing that concerned him was that he didn't have total control....I respected him and he respected me. We got along fine. Maybe we've shouted at each other from time to time." Still

Chercover seemed to be fighting a kind of rearguard action periodically given Bassett's dominance in network affairs. On one occasion Charles Templeton, Director of News and Public Affairs, contacted the network president about the content of a *W5* program. Bassett apparently had tried to influence Templeton's judgement. Chercover insisted to Templeton that he should stand firm and not accommodate such initiatives. The CTV President said that when disagreements arose over a specific program to be carried on the network, "John carried it, every time, every time."[97]

Perhaps no other matter could be more illustrative of the tensions within CTV than the issue of how much Canadian football the network could afford to carry. As network coverage of football evolved, CBC and CTV shared TV coverage and later would bid for the broadcasting rights. The winner acquired the national rights and could then sell back to the other party to share some broadcasts.[98] On one occasion when CTV had managed to win the bidding, "Bassett came to a board meeting charged...on fire," said Chercover. He boldly asserted that "now that we have the rights clearly to ourselves, let's dump the CBC!" Upon hearing Bassett's sudden pronouncement, Chercover felt compelled to respond. He said, "excuse me!" as he tried to capture the board's attention to explain the implications of what had been proposed: "I spent at least 25 minutes trying to communicate to the board what the costs of having all of the football would be and how it would impact on our schedule and our revenue and all the rest of it. Nobody wanted to hear it."[99] Bassett demanded the vote to be called, the Board Chairman sitting beside Chercover concurred and Bassett's motion to have all games on CTV passed.

Chercover waited for two days and then phoned Bassett and said, "John I have to talk to you. You understand this is going to cost CTV and Baton so can I see you?" Bassett answered: "yeah!" When Chercover arrived at Bassett's office, he had two of his executives with him: Joe Garwood and Ted Delaney. Chercover recalled the thrust of his comments when he informed Bassett why the network could not carry all CFL football games: "Look John! This is the pre-emption pattern. It will destroy the launch of our fall schedule. There is absolutely no way either the network or CFTO can afford to have this much football. It's disrupting the launch of our...public affairs programs, it's disrupting the launch of all of the new series we have acquired. It's disrupting the revenue to this extent, it will disrupt the revenue to that extent." After he heard Chercover's cogent lament, Bassett responded instantly: "Call another board meeting!" Some three weeks later, Bassett reversed himself and made a motion before the Board of Directors to return to the status quo and have the CBC involved in football coverage.[100]

THE NEW, CO-OPERATIVE STRUCTURE of CTV experienced ongoing power struggles throughout the late 1960s. A year after Chercover became President, Gordon Keeble was gone. "It became apparent as time went on," said Keeble, "that they really wanted me out." Indeed the tensions between the affiliates and the network management personnel from the Caldwell days were not eased readily. Nowhere was this more apparent than in an exchange of letters involving the network management and the directors. Ray Peters, President of British Columbia Television Broadcasting System Ltd., had written to Murray Chercover in September, 1967 and urged him to start "to describe in detail the dramatic improvement in CTV programming since it has been owned and operated by the stations." CTV had shown "a drastic improvement in general program quality in one short season" but in Peters's view, the network was still "plagued with the old Spence Caldwell image."[101] A carbon copy of the letter went to Keeble, and the CTV directors, and prompted a sharp rejoinder from Caldwell's former associate.

Keeble too shared "pride in the accomplishments of the past year" but scoffed at Peters's reference to Caldwell: "Spence hardly needs me to defend him but I was around in those days too, just as you were and it's simply ridiculous—particularly in an internal communication—to pretend that the shortcomings of the old CTV were solely the responsibility of Spence Caldwell."[102] From the early days of CTV, Peters had referred to the major shareholders in CTV Television Network Ltd. with Caldwell as "the Bay Street investors."[103] In his response to Peters, Keeble recalled the position adopted by the affiliated stations during the Caldwell era, specifically in the second affiliation agreement: "You were one of the negotiators of and signatories to the second Affiliation Agreement—a document which, it is now admitted, was designed to drive the old CTV out of business as quickly as possible. Therefore, if the old image was cheap and dirty, you and the rest of the station people have to bear the major responsibility for it since you have absolutely no evidence to indicate that Spence was walking away with the money to pay it out to his baronial friends on Bay St."[104]

In his letter to Peters, Keeble could not help but blame the affiliates for the earlier bankruptcy of CTV: "I hope that it will be apparent to you that I am not criticizing the action or actions which the stations took in past years. The old Affiliation Agreement was entered into with no compulsion on either side and you were, therefore, entitled to specify the conditions under which you were prepared to affiliate. If those conditions were such as to drive the Network Company into bankruptcy, that was the choice for the old CTV to make. However, if the application of those stringent conditions brought about a diminution in the quality and quantity of the service, it seems most unfair to blame the old network for it." Keeble did not mince words over the reasons why CTV was able to have a fresh start: "The bold, new CTV has come about by the willingness of the stations to surrender to their own company privileges and percentages and time they were not prepared to give to the old one. That's fine— that's your right—but it is not your right to blame the old company for shortcomings created by you and the other stations."[105] Clearly Keeble's relationship to the new owners appeared to be strained.

"I found at a board meeting of October '69," said Keeble, "that I was being offered an alternative. I was then Chairman and Murray was President. I could stay on on a five-year contract with a substantial raise, but I would be answerable to the President of the company, Mr. Chercover. And I don't know what I was supposed to do during this period. That wasn't spelled out. So what it was ultimately, obviously, was a buyout. They would keep me going for five more years at a very handsome salary and I won't do anything which is an alternative not acceptable to me. So I resigned." In five years time, Keeble would have been 58 years old. "I didn't want any part of it," he said.[106]

Finlay MacDonald, owner of CJCH, Halifax, recalled a directors' meeting where John Bassett had become most irate at Keeble: "At one particular stage, Gordon Keeble did something or said something or was the cause of something, some decision, and Bassett got completely out of control...I mean [he] practically had to be restrained in anger. And it was pretty clear after that, that Gordon's days were numbered. Gordon was the perfect gentleman, just a perfect gentleman. But unfortunately the perfect gentleman personality wouldn't work with someone like Bassett."[107] Keeble attributed his tenuous position to the circumstances that frequently accompany business takeovers: "The people who are doing the takeover like to have their own people. And I have seen this happen many times; it happened once to me in the cable business....And somebody was telling the board that there was this conflict between Murray and me. I don't know who that would be. It wasn't me. But they got this story in their heads. And it reached a point in '69 where I gathered later, not at the time but later, that they had appointed two or three members of the board into a committee to discuss Murray's future and mine. They may have formed such a committee, but if they did, they never talked to me. They talked to Murray though."[108]

Chercover offered his version of the circumstances involving Keeble's departure from the network after the stations had assumed control of CTV. He maintained that Keeble had extended himself and went beyond his role as President as directed by the Board of Directors. Chercover recalled he told Keeble that he had "challenged the Board and the share-holders in respect to what they had decided to do." In the end, the Board decided it was a "severance package, good bye!" Still throughout the period of intricate backstage manoeuvring at CTV, Chercover main-tained the relationship between him and Keeble had been steady for the most part: "Look, I like Gordon Keeble. I had a nice relationship with him, I had no reservation about staying in the background and just doing it, but Gordon couldn't take the fact that he was president titu-larly but he didn't have the authority."[109]

With Keeble's departure, the Caldwell era for the network that was to mean business had truly ended. Whatever the future of CTV, the new, co-operative corporate structure soon began to look like a recipe for countless boardroom squabbles and inter-regional rivalries. At the same time, CTV would be challenged in future years to present the style of programming that the broadcast regulator would demand.

THE CTV AFFILIATES were hard pressed to impress critics when they had unveiled their programming plans before the BBG. A program called *Omnibus* was to be aired each month consisting of specialized drama, ballet and documentaries. Other programs planned for the fall schedule of 1966 included the *Sports Hot Seat*, *National Women's Mag-azine* and a morning program, *The A.M. Show*, which was to provide news, sports and weather. Roy Shields was hardly restrained in his criticism: "That's fine until you note *Omnibus* will include 'the best productions of Great Britain and the United States and elsewhere.' At one *Omnibus* a month, that doesn't leave much room for Canadian production." In a broader context, Shields was sharply critical of CTV's lack of a credible news service which would provide the fledgling network with a clear identity: "What the network desperately needs is an expanded news service that can provide viewers with more than the present stultified nightly telecast of announcers reading wire copy."[110]

Still the network had begun to have some impact. The production of the *CTV National News* had been moved in 1966 from CJOH, Ottawa to CFTO, Toronto, the network's flagship station, where it was to remain. A glimmer of hope for CTV had been its impressive televised coverage of three major events in the late 1960s: the 1967 Progressive Conservative party leadership convention where Robert Stanfield was chosen to succeed John Diefenbaker, the 1968 Liberal leadership convention which chose Pierre Trudeau as party leader and the landing of the first man on the moon in 1969 when Neil Armstrong took "a giant leap for mankind." A major innovation in public affairs programming on the network was the introduction of the long running *W5*, in September 1966.

CTV had acquired the talents of the newscaster who was to become the network's most nationally recognized news anchor based on longevity of performance. Canadians had been introduced to Harvey Kirck on 3 December 1963. His 20-odd-year stay on the anchor desk, which paralleled Pierre Trudeau's reign as Prime Minister, was to make him a mainstay of the private network. Kirck read his last newscast on 27 April 1984.[111]

To compete with the CBC and to provide the network with a true identification, CTV news required a more clearly defined Canadian presence. A team of credible and reliable news correspondents had to be developed. In its sports and entertainment programming, the network had to appear as a television organization with some form of popular, cultural impact that would be an alternative to the CBC. As a national private network, critics had viewed CTV as an electronic carrier of American programs and home grown quiz shows. The first task then in the 1970s was to establish a solid foundation for the growth of the *CTV National News*.

THE DAYS OF THE BBG, which had licensed the CTV network, came to end in the late 1960s. The *Broadcasting Act, 1968* brought into being a new broadcast regulator, the Canadian Radio-television Commission, under the chairmanship of Pierre Juneau. While the BBG with its chairman, Andrew Stewart, had introduced Canadian content regulations and had kept a watchful eye on the legalistic aspects of broadcasting developments, Stewart's relationship with the private broadcasters was not without its comedic moments. Indeed Stewart, a Scot, was a former university president with a decided sense of humour.

Robbie Burns Day on 25 January 1968 was highly memorable for a vibrant gathering of BBG members including the Chairman and Dave Sim, a full-time member, and the CTV Board of Directors at BBG headquarters in Ottawa. Among those at the event was Finlay MacDonald who recalled the concern when they were hurriedly called to the afternoon meeting in Ottawa. Fearful that the heavy hand of the broadcast regulator was about to come down on them, they attended dutifully. "It was mysterious," MacDonald remembered. "We were suddenly summoned to Ottawa by Andrew Stewart to a meeting and we wondered what in the name of God it was about! What's happening, are we going to lose our licence, go to jail, what's happening?"[112]

The directors including MacDonald and Bassett were in for a surprise: "So we walked in and sat around the table not knowing what the hell is going on. And suddenly Stewart leaps up, hauls a sword out and starts screaming a Gaelic curse! It was...[Burns's] day and he invited us all down there and the door opened, in came one of the girls carrying about five quarts of scotch, and another one carrying a haggis....And haggis is not everybody's cup of tea." As Stewart waved the sword, he was offering a toast with a characteristic Scottish brogue, "Here a za to us!" and, with the sword, "scaring the shit out of all of us!"[113]

The event received only passing comment in Stewart's memoirs: "The Chairman ordered a haggis and Sim provided the appropriate liquid for a toast. At the time that coffee would have been served, the haggis was marched in, copies of Burns' *Ode to the Haggis* were distributed and the verses were read by Dave Sim."[114]

The broadcasters including Bassett, reluctant consumers of haggis, were mindful of adhering to the dictates of the regulator in charge of renewing their licences. So they participated in the Scottish happening and ate the haggis with a fair measure of recalcitrance. The CRTC under Pierre Juneau too would be a watchful regulator though special liquid gatherings for haggis were surely a rarity in the history of Canada's distinctive broadcasting system.

CTV
NATIONAL
NEWS

From Ottawa, the nation's capital, CTV National News presents a crisp, authoritative, immediate picture of happenings from around the world at the people-to-people level every evening. The news from around the world as it affects Canadians...responsible...personable... graphic...and warm. CTV National News ...Canada's national television news. Call us now for '64-'65 availabilities.

CTV TELEVISION NETWORK LIMITED

MONTREAL	TORONTO	NEW YORK/CHICAGO
849-8021	924-5454	Enterprise 6868 (no toll charge)

AB DOUGLAS

PETER JENNINGS

HARVEY KIRCK

LARRY HENDERSON

CTV National News with Ab Douglas, Peter Jennings, Harvey Kirck and Larry Henderson (top to bottom). Photograph courtesy of CTV.

FOUR

"In Colour, the *CTV National News*"

1962–1972

A PRIVATE CANADIAN television network seeking to be an alternative to the CBC had no choice but to have a credible news operation to sustain itself as a business. The expansion of the *CTV National News* was consistent with the approach to news programming that Murray Chercover, the network's President, had adopted. He was of the view that "the first fundamental element that a network must present in order to be a viable alternative is a viable news service as a foundation stone."[1] Still any network news service must inevitably be a major cost item. The level of news programming that CTV could provide would depend heavily on the affiliated stations' willingness to finance the network news operation.

Bruce Phillips, a former Ottawa Parliamentary bureau chief, underlined the inevitable internal conflicts that arose over the fundamental notion that "every dollar that stayed with the network was a dollar they [affiliates] didn't get." Clearly Phillips perceived that the network's structure presented its management with major challenges in programming areas: "It was the only network around that carried the seeds of its own destruction within its corporate structure. You know a...network director who also was the owner of a television station had difficult choices to make, because I think it could be fairly argued that there is an inherent conflict of interest for a director of a company making decisions that work to the disadvantage of the company of which he well may be an owner or a major shareholder." Phillips credited Chercover "who was caught in that particular situation" for being "a master negotiator and manager to have kept that whole thing together."[2]

From 1968 to 1990, Chercover had the onerous task of reconciling the various interests within the CTV co-operative at a time when competing conventional television services and specialty channels introduced a new age of television to Canada. As the TV market in Canada continued to evolve, it began to break in two directions. At one end of the spectrum were long time, general interest networks such as CTV and CBC; at the other end were the new "niche" services with the potential to erode traditional audiences and cause a major audience fragmentation.

Chercover had to attempt to steer an even course among the CTV directors in the corporate boardroom while ensuring the overall business health of the network. At times, his presidential role was a supreme challenge. Still the need for a credible network news operation was one area where CTV management and the network's Board could find common ground. The affiliated stations' attitude towards network news was an extension of the importance they had placed on the coverage of news developments in their own local and regional broadcast markets to build close identification with viewers. The fact that a number of TV affiliates had grown from earlier local radio operations that served their communities with news and information reinforced the importance of a network news service.

In its early years, CTV had managed to establish its news and information programming with a network newscast that originated in Ottawa. By building on the reputation of the public affairs program *W5*, which originally aired on 11 September 1966, CTV introduced *Canada AM*, a morning news and information program, first seen on 11 September 1972. The CTV news service began to expand its national bureaus and develop its own team of foreign correspondents during the 1970s. The growth culminated in a major breakthrough in 1979 when CTV became the first broadcaster in North America to establish a bureau in China, six years after Prime Minister Pierre Trudeau's historic mission there in the fall of 1973.[3] Through its news programming, CTV would become eventually a formidable competitor to the CBC.

Clearly John Bassett had wanted the network news moved from Ottawa to CFTO, Toronto. Bassett acquired the operation of the flagship newscast for his station in 1966 after the stations took over CTV but not before the news service had gone through an early period of struggle. By the year 1970, the *Report of the Special Senate Committee on Mass Media* concluded that the network provided "a very creditable national news programme every evening."[4] Still for most of its early life, the network had struggled to deliver its news service with limited resources, a small staff and amidst recurring boardroom struggles and managerial changes.

The original CTV network news from Ottawa on 24 September 1962 was presented at the unusual time of 10:30 P.M. Charles Lynch, a national newspaper columnist, and Peter Stursberg whose reports had been heard on CBC radio during World War Two, read the newscast.[5] At the time, television news had moved beyond the notion of "radio with pictures" but still functioned without sophisticated electronic delivery that it later enjoyed. Canada's first TV network news anchorman Larry Henderson had appeared on the CBC in January, 1954 and joined CTV in the early 1960s. He recalled the technological limitations during the pioneer days of CBC network news: "There was no television reporter outside of Canada at that time. So as anchorman, I took the cameras abroad. We didn't have satellites so...there would be a 48-hour delay in your stuff and it was flown back and I took it to Russia, the Middle East and the Far East, Korean War and Vietnam and so on at its early days."[6]

When CTV News began, the network was at a decided disadvantage in competition with the CBC and its larger staff and superior resources as well as the Corporation's long tradition of reliable, credible news gathering. The CBC's reputation had been greatly enhanced during the Second World War when Canadians heard their own correspondents, such as Matthew Halton and Peter Stursberg, bring them 'live' reports on war developments and analysis of the principal international happenings. Clearly the news coverage of World War Two had underlined the advantage the immediacy of radio reports enjoyed over the print industry. The electronic media had come of age. By 1970, television undoubtedly had replaced radio as the medium of national significance and attention.

The third volume of the *Report of the Special Senate Committee on Mass Media* drew attention to the new media hierarchy: "Television is the most believed and most important medium for international news and for Canadian news of national importance. Newspapers are identified as the most believable and important for local news. The written word is believed especially when it is local. Radio is not far behind newspapers in satisfying local news needs."[7]

From the beginning, CTV stressed a personalized style of news coverage reminiscent of American networks to compensate for its limited resources. CTV News was introduced to Canadians amidst a changing media environment when the television medium moved to a new level. TV news became intensely visual in the 1960s and a communications' vehicle which had an extraordinary capacity to communicate experiences. By July, 1963, CTV had a new on-air news team and provided Canadians with a market-oriented, personality-driven newscast at the more conventional time of 11 P.M. By exploiting news personalities, CTV tried to counter the advantage the CBC held with its greater news gathering resources.

A youthful Peter Jennings, who later would become the TV network news anchor for the American Broadcasting Company (ABC) in the United States on *World News Tonight with Peter Jennings* teamed up with Baden Langton, who also departed subsequently for ABC radio in New York. The Americanization of Canadian TV news formats had begun. Jennings arrived on Canada's national media stage without any previous journalistic training on newspapers or wire services. He had begun his radio career in Brockville, Ontario at a small private station, CFJR, owned by Jack Radford, a colleague of Jennings's father, Charles. Radford had been the Director of Station Relations at the CBC and later obtained a private licence to operate the Brockville radio station. Charles Jennings had been employed at CKGW, Toronto, a private radio station, during the pioneer days of the medium. He had the distinction of being the first network newscaster heard over the CRBC, the country's first public broadcasting agency, established in 1932. The CRBC was the forerunner of the CBC established four years later. Charles Jennings later became a CBC executive.[8]

"It was a kind of little club in those days," Murray Brown, a former President of CFPL Broadcasting Ltd. in London, Ontario recalled. Brown, who represented CFPL television, a CBC affiliate at the time, became a friend of Charles Jennings and remembered offering some fatherly advice to his son Peter in the mid 1950s. "One day I was in Ottawa and he said, 'Murray...I've got a son Peter, he's working in the bank here in Ottawa. I'd like to see him get into broadcasting but I don't want to put him in the CBC. Could you have a talk with him?'" Brown had a discussion with the younger Jennings in his hotel room for about an hour and advised him to get a position at a small radio station which he did when he went to CFJR. Jennings later joined CJOH television in

Ottawa when it went on the air. "Then the CTV thing came up," Brown recalled, "and you know the story from there."⁹

CJOH, Ottawa where Jennings was introduced to television, was owned by Ernest Bushnell who also belonged to the Corporation's 'old boys' network. Jennings became popular as host of a teenage dance program known as "Club 13." Thereafter he joined CTV News and was immediately perceived by *Time* magazine to be as "healthy as a hint of mint."¹⁰ Indeed the Jennings-Langton team on CTV was reminiscent of the newscast format introduced to Americans in the early 1950s when Chet Huntley and David Brinkley ushered in a new era of American TV journalism. The similarity was not lost on *Time's* assessment of the CTV newscast: "The CTV show is produced with a shoe-string budget of less than $500,000 by station CJOH-TV in Ottawa. Hunger has given it inventiveness. Shorter to allow for commercials, the CTV newscast is played for the eye, while the CBC plays for the ear. It makes indulgent use of film, and brings on two newscasters, in the Huntley-Brinkley fashion, rather than one."¹¹

Still CTV had to struggle for market share against Earl Cameron, the solid TV newscaster on the CBC, whose demeanour was a model of neutrality. A shift in the time slot for CTV news from 10:30 P.M. to 11 P.M. meant that it faced overwhelming competition from the CBC, which took continued pride in its reputation for objective news presentation free of personalization and technical gimmickry. *Time* outlined the uphill battle that CTV faced: "Pitted against such minority audience CBC shows as *Quest* at 10:30, CTV drew a larger news audience than CBC in two of three eastern cities where the two networks compete. But at 11 P.M. CTV is outgunned."¹²

The CTV network's promotional material for the 1962–63 television season had underlined the advantages that advertisers could enjoy with their messages seen on a network newscast delivered on a new microwave system: "FIRST across-Canada television news service available for sponsorship. CTV plans a late evening national network broadcast supplemented by an early evening edition for Central Canada, both utilizing the new CTV multi-million dollar microwave and originating from central CTV news studios in Ottawa."¹³ By the 1964–65 television season, the network had undertaken an even more personalized form of promotion for its national news.

The on-air news personalities of the fledgling network had changed. Near the end of 1963, Harvey Kirck, formerly the news director at

CFTO, Toronto had replaced Baden Langton who had gone to ABC. Reviewer Pierre Maple writing in *TV Guide* noted that Kirck was "fitting in well with Peter Jennings on CTV's national news."[14] Ab Douglas, formerly of CFRN-TV in Edmonton, a network affiliate, remained as one of the four newscasters along with Larry Henderson who had joined the network. CTV had no choice but to present itself as a clear alternative to the public broadcaster with a style of presentation markedly different from the Corporation. In a sense, the personalities of the news messengers were to be made as prominent to viewers as some content of the news that they reported.

As a private network, CTV tried to draw a sharp contrast between the warmth and unpretentious manner of its news presentation when compared to the dispassion and detachment of the CBC national news. The distinction was stressed in the network's message to advertisers for the 1964–65 season: "From Ottawa, the nation's capital, *CTV National News* presents a crisp, authoritative, immediate picture of happenings from around the world at the people-to-people level every evening. The news from around the world as it affects Canadians...responsible...personable...graphic...and warm."[15]

STILL THE HISTORIC STRUGGLE between the network and its affiliates stemming from internal rivalries could not help but find its way into the daily news operation. The location of CJOH in Canada's capital had been a major determinant in the final decision to originate the news in Ottawa rather than Toronto. Since CFTO, Toronto appeared to be the dominant station in the network, Spencer Caldwell's team had decided to produce the news at CJOH, Ottawa to create a second network force. Still internal rivalries prevailed. Brian Nolan, a producer who later went on to ABC television after his involvement with the CBC program, *This Hour Has Seven Days*, and with CTV News, recalled his early experience at CJOH. The Montreal and Toronto stations often "would not send us material on a big story or they would send the outs of an edited piece. So this was really very frustrating." The net result was that it was "difficult to produce that newscast."[16]

Not only were there structural tensions among the network's affiliates but also the CTV nightly news originally was produced in a stressful newsroom atmosphere. Jean Pouliot, the CJOH News Director and his assistant, Joe Gibson, managed a newsroom which consisted of a staff of veteran journalists and eager youngsters. The younger, inexperienced journalists ranged in age from their late twenties to early thirties and were new to television. They worked alongside veteran journalists Charles Lynch and Peter Stursberg, experienced war correspondents, in an often uneasy relationship. Nolan recalled the tense atmosphere: "There was a lot of tension in that newsroom." Peter Jennings found himself in uncomfortable surroundings as an inexperienced newcomer amidst journalistic heavies: "Peter...came from an afternoon dance show and he was also very difficult. He was very defensive of his inexperience and took criticism very hard and there were a lot of battles. So that first year really was very difficult and very tense." The tendency of Stuart Griffiths, the General Manager of CJOH, to intervene regularly in the operation of the newsroom added to the anxiety: "Stu Griffiths, I liked him personally, he was a very cultured guy, very erudite, charming to talk to, go to a party discuss Picasso, or something, but he was awful to work for, because he interfered in every decision in the newsroom." Nolan remembered the impact of Griffiths: "He drove Pouliot nuts, literally sent him into the hospital with these incredible migraine headaches. And then Pouliot left CJOH and Joe Gibson became the News Director. So it was a very difficult time. The atmosphere was not conducive to really creative endeavours."[17]

Griffiths had returned to Canada from Britain where he had been in charge of the program department at Granada Television in London.[18] He was a dominant force at CJOH and had been employed earlier at the CBC. He was regarded by knowledgeable insiders as a skilled broadcaster. Mavor Moore explained in *The Globe and Mail*: "Griffiths was already a dirty old capitalist pillar of CTV (the private network) when Judy LaMarsh, on the advice of many in the industry, nominated him for the CBC presidency in 1966. But the left-wing shadow still adhered and half the Liberal Cabinet would have none of him."[19]

Despite the early struggles of CTV to produce a network newscast, the inexperience of its young television journalists, inadequate resources and managerial distractions, the news operation in Ottawa took great delight in beating their public broadcasting competitor. From the beginning, the CJOH newsroom was united in the single-minded determination to gain supremacy over the Corporation and its long established reputation. With limited facilities, CTV resorted to journalistic techniques such as a skilful structuring of news copy with two-day old film to give the appearance of immediacy. The introductions to news stories would be written in the present tense before the visual material, with older information, was shown to the viewer. Nolan remembered the trials of CTV News during its formative years and how the network had to cope with a lack of adequate resources: "CTV has always had an image that it looked better than it was, even today by...smoke and mirrors, by some osmosis you know, it always looked better than it was. But we had very few facilities in those very first days."[20]

IN ADDITION TO THE NEWS, CTV's public affairs programming, which was influenced too by the American model, tried to provide innovative alternatives to the CBC. The network showed Canadians a new form of political broadcasting on 27 January 1963 with a half-hour public affairs program called *Platform* produced by Robert Henry Black. He had introduced several programs at CJOH including *Encounter*, a series of weekly discussions on leading issues, and also had directed the *CTV National News*. The program *Platform* was carried weekly on most of the CTV affiliates.[21]

Platform featured spokespersons for the four political parties: Liberals, Conservatives, the New Democratic Party and Social Credit. Each participating member of parliament was isolated in a sound-proof booth and faced a series of pointed questions from the program's moderator Ab Douglas. The strength of the format was that the audience's attention was focused on the specific reply of each isolated member of parliament. The program allowed for a fast-paced question and answer session with each participant on a variety of issues. Towards the end of the program each week, the participants left their isolated booths for a head-to-head encounter. Douglas would focus the give-and-take part of the program on the central issues raised earlier in the broadcast and on the most controversial answers provided by the participants.[22]

The CTV network's expressed purpose of the program format was to enliven political broadcasting on television at a time when Canadians were struggling to elect a majority government. In three elections, 1962, 1963 and 1965, voters chose minority federal governments. Political broadcasting on television was unimaginative. The visual medium of television had just begun to break free of the constraints governing political broadcast formats that had been applied to radio for almost three decades dating back to the *Broadcasting Act, 1936*. Politicians, broadcasters and the Board of Broadcast Governors, the broadcasting regulator, ultimately recognized that a more exciting style of presentation was required.

A news release from CJOH, Ottawa on 11 January 1963 announced the new format for *Platform* and underlined both the uncertain political climate in Canada and the need for a new approach to political broadcasts: "One single fact emerged with startling clarity from the last federal election. Canadians are confused about which of the four political parties they want as the government of their country." At the same time, the station's announcement explained that political broadcasting needed "a shot in the arm" and the program *Platform* would provide a new form of political communication and information: "This confusion was fostered in part by the watered-down soap-commercial type of political broadcasting the voters have been subjected to since the beginning of television. Differences between the parties have become obscured and their aims are hazy at best to most Canadian voters."[23] Clearly CTV had hoped to overcome the legislative constraints that had held back innovative political broadcasting for more than two decades.

Platform was another example of the extent to which the CTV network had been influenced by U.S. models. Specifically, the network hoped to create the same enthusiasm among the electorate in Canada that the televised political debates between Senator John Kennedy and Vice-President Richard Nixon had nurtured in the American electorate in the 1960 presidential election. A network news release that announced the introduction of *Platform* on 30 January 1963 was hardly restrained in its enthusiasm for American formats: "Political debates made world history in the last election in the US when Kennedy and Nixon faced each other before the cameras. The same format will be followed on *Platform*."[24] The program was moved to prime time on 14 April 1963 after the federal election of 8 April that year to replace *Telepoll*, a public opinion program that left the network for the summer season. CTV noted that the move "takes advantage of stimulated interest in Canadians affairs, kindled by the federal election."[25] The private network had hoped to build audience with American style formats during a time of political uncertainty in Canada.

Another programming initiative—a preview of plans for Canada's Centennial in 1967—was seemingly designed to project CTV as a network with a national perspective, even though the broadcast was presented well ahead of the actual event. The program was aired four years before the historic occasion on 1 July 1963. The broadcast, which originated at CJOH was hosted by Peter Jennings and dealt with the preparations for the forthcoming Centennial year. Jennings asked at the beginning of the program: "Is this idea for a national birthday party a mature, sensible one or an expensive way to 'wallow in national pride' as someone has put it."[26] The program included an interview with John Fisher, the Head of National Planning for the celebration of Confederation, who had become known as "Mr. Canada." Several CTV affiliates including CFRN, Edmonton, CFTO, Toronto and CFCF, Montreal contributed reports on the extent of planning for Centennial celebrations in Alberta, Ontario and Quebec.[27]

THE YEAR BEFORE Canada's Centennial saw the *CTV National News* undergo a major transformation. The network moved the entire news operation to CFTO, Toronto from CJOH, in the fall of 1966 after a difficult early period in CTV's history. The move not long after the affiliates had taken over the network was some solace for John Bassett who had wanted the newscast produced at his station. As Nolan explained, suddenly CTV started "to look like a network" especially with its "large Toronto presence."[28] The move of the national newscast to Toronto in 1966, where it has remained, represented a sharp break with the past. Previously the CTV news had been produced at CJOH on a contractual basis with the network. The CJOH news department had editorial responsibility for the network news and relied on the member stations to provide material from the various regions of the country. Under a new arrangement in 1966 when the newscast was moved to CFTO, the network was to be in charge of the nightly news program with more centralized editorial control. A CTV network staff would be hired specifically for that purpose.[29]

The CTV news operation at CFTO was situated at one end of a long newsroom where the more extensive local news staff was also located. The network had a new beginning but it still had a skeleton staff. Nolan produced the nightly newscast from Monday to Friday for about four months before departing for the ABC network in December, 1966. He was supported by two strong writers: Mike Finlan, a colorful Irishman, and Gordon Penny who both wrote news copy that was lucid and imaginative. Harvey Kirck who anchored the newscast from Toronto could also serve as a news writer. In 1966 Terry Brown was a weekend producer with Al Parks as a writer and mainstay of the weekend package.

A "chroma-key" of Nancy Greene during Michael Nolan's 10 February 1968 newscast. Photograph courtesy of CTV.

"A CTV News and Public Affairs Production" credit from the 10 February 1968 newscast, with Michael Nolan. Photograph courtesy of CTV.

Michael Nolan succeeded Vic Phillips, who had a short-lived stay at CTV, as weekend news anchor. Wally Macht was the network's lone correspondent to cover western Canada.

The CTV network news produced in Toronto was billed as a clear alternative to the CBC especially in the style of presentation. The network was not at all hesitant to boast that its newscast was in colour. The new format in the fall of 1966 called for Harvey Kirck, anchor of the news in Toronto, to be linked with correspondent Ab Douglas at CJOH, Ottawa in a fast-paced newscast where visuals were exploited to the fullest. Excitement was expected to fill the air with the brash introduction of CTV news to Canadian households. At eleven o'clock, the viewer would see Kirck announce "Harvey Kirck in Toronto" with a sharp cut to Ottawa live for "Ab Douglas in Ottawa." Then the viewer was taken back to Toronto where Kirck, explaining the origins of the day's news, would announce, "and tonight's reports are from Washington, Halifax and Vancouver." Then came a loud thundering voice: "In colour, the *CTV National News*" before a commercial was inserted into the newscast. The first real information that viewers received on the private network was an advertising message.

Brian Nolan's production sense and instinct for the medium of television were apparent in the style of presentation to which Canadians were introduced. The newscast had a fast-paced rhythm. CTV hoped to appear as a sassy upstart when compared to the CBC. The Corporation had been watching the private network and was prepared to rejuvenate *The National*, its flagship newscast. Knowlton Nash commented that "with a brash new kid on the block in the form of *CTV National News*, it was inevitable that something would change."[30] In its attempt to appear to be on the cutting edge, CTV used most effectively three visual techniques: cold "video" rolls, freeze "film" frames and an electronic innovation called "chroma-key."

Given the electronic interaction between Toronto and Ottawa during the CTV news, it was possible to begin a story visually in either city. Nolan enjoyed taking the viewer directly out of an Ottawa story to Toronto and rolling "cold" a film or video tape of a news story with Kirck reading a voice-over but not seen himself immediately by the viewer. The technique made for a vibrant package and accentuated television's strength as an intensely visual medium.

Kirck found the production technique to be unsettling and even confusing to the viewer, because it could appear to be an abrupt change of venue. Still CTV was prepared to reach for any advantage to streamline its presentation and project a new form of TV newscast to capture market share. Kirck remained uncomfortable with some of Nolan's innovative production techniques: "As a producer he wanted to do a real flashy, fast cut, fast paced program. And it worked up to a point. Didn't fit with me for one thing as the presenter, as the anchor. Sloppy Harve and all these fast, fast, fast things happening all around him, he wasn't fast himself. But we toned it down....I am really proud of those times. We made it on chewing our shoe laces. And we put out a creditable program."[31]

Nolan's use of film could be eye-catching. When a frame of a television news film was "frozen" on the screen for the viewer, the visual impact was sudden and dramatic. The device would be used frequently to introduce stories and helped to vary the pace of the newscast. Rather than having only the anchorman on camera to read an introduction to allow for a seven or ten second rollup of a film before the viewer actually saw the visual content, the CTV audience instantly could see the frame of film "frozen" on the screen. The viewer's curiosity was aroused immediately.

The use of "chroma-key" was a major innovation in the fall of 1966. The electronic technique, as Kirck and Rowland noted, "could project or 'key' a picture shot by one camera, as a backdrop for the picture of another."[32] "Chroma-key" made for a visually exciting package; because it gave the viewer a sense of almost participating in the actual news events. The electronic innovation was a major visual accompaniment to the news anchor.

On occasion, CTV would freeze the first frame of a film to a news story and then roll it for the viewer accompanied by the "chroma-key." Nolan remembered that "if the image on the first frames of the film worked in perspective to the anchor, we would roll it in the 'chroma-key.' But you couldn't always use that because the first shot...might have been a guy's nostril or something and there's the anchor sitting there with this big nose behind him. So it had to be in perspective so it worked."[33]

BEYOND THE MOVE OF CTV News to Toronto from Ottawa, the 1966–67 television season was generally an exciting one for the network. The first CTV broadcast in colour was on 31 August 1966 when the network promoted a new schedule of programs for the fall.

Regularly scheduled programming in colour began on 1 September of that same year. Hosted by Kirck, the hour-long broadcast in August featured speeches and congratulatory statements from Judy LaMarsh, the federal Secretary of State, Andrew Stewart, Chairman of the Board of Broadcast Governors, and Gordon F. Keeble, the President of CTV.[34]

The colour broadcast included a preview of W5, a new network public affairs program. Peter Reilly, executive producer of the public affairs show, outlined some of the provocative stories that the program would examine. The first issue seen on W5 dealt with the politically-sensitive issue of gun controls. Peter Rehak, who became Executive Producer of the popular show, recalled its early impact when the initial program presented an up-front style of journalism: "The program sent a teenager to buy a rifle, then sent him to the top of the Toronto's newly-built city hall and had him aim the sights at the pedestrians below. The view through the gunsight's hairs became a television classic. But the story was more than sensationalism. It sharply contrasted Canada's lax gun laws with its stringent puritan legislation governing alcohol."[35] As it turned out, Reilly, a former CBC news correspondent, had a brief relationship with CTV. He became embroiled in a controversy with John Bassett allegedly over the question of access to a top news story in the mid 1960s that involved a teenager by the name of Steven Truscott as the central figure.

The 14-year-old boy who had been tried in adult court for the rape and murder of a Clinton, Ontario girl, Lynne Harper in June 1959, was sentenced to hang. Later he had his sentence commuted to life imprisonment. Author Isabel LeBourdais, a lawyer's daughter, believed that Truscott was innocent and wrote a book about his trial entitled *The Trial of Steven Truscott* published in 1966.[36] The following year the Supreme Court reviewed Truscott's case, but to the author's surprise the court agreed with the initial legal decision in the case. Truscott was found to be guilty.

A dispute between CTV and Bassett arose over the question of whether the network or *The Telegram* had rights to the reporting of the Steven Truscott hearing by Isabel LeBourdais. Wilfred Kesterton writing in the *Canadian Annual Review* at the time explained the struggle between the CTV Executive Producer and the newspaper publisher, an issue that appeared to underline a potential conflict of interest for Bassett: "Reilly said that CTV had exclusive rights to Isabel LeBourdais' reporting of the Steven Truscott hearing, but that Bassett had demanded that Mrs. LeBourdais write for his Toronto *Telegram*, and had threatened to take

W_5 off his television station unless CTV allowed her to do so."[37] Ken Cavanagh, who also hosted W_5, said that Reilly had "signed a contract with Isabel LeBourdais....Peter locked her up on a contract for CTV."[38]

After hosting only the first show of W_5 in the fall of 1966, Reilly quit abruptly and joined CBC television as host of a new program *Sunday*. Michael Hind-Smith, the network's National Program Director, was astonished when he heard the news: "Reilly was a loose canon. And whether he invented the scrap with Bassett or for what particular reason, whether interference existed or didn't exist, it certainly existed in his mind. And I was in Montreal the day that he blew up, but I was accosted in the press club in Montreal with 'what do you say about Peter Reilly's resignation?' My mouth dropped. I said, what, what, what? He hadn't bothered to tell me. And I didn't know what the problem was, but that was it. He was gone."[39]

Reilly's departure was unexpected and a setback for CTV. Hind-Smith had sought out the CBC correspondent who was recognized for his aggressive, no-nonsense approach to journalism. In June, 1966 just a few months before its first broadcast, CTV had not yet named its new public affairs show which had the potential to fill a void left after *This Hour Has Seven Days* on the CBC was taken off the air in May of the same year.[40]

The precise genesis of the name W_5 was an open question. The name for the program was cleared through the office of Michael Hind-Smith, who approved it. Cavanagh whom Hind-Smith had hired about the same time as Reilly, and who succeeded him as host of the program, remembered a discussion among producers and writers in the CFTO cafeteria. "I would say to you that I was one of the first people who mentioned the 5 Ws. I don't think anybody could take specific credit." Cavanagh recalled the flavour of the conversation among the participants over coffee: "What about 5Ws? Then 5W and eventually W_5!" Cavanagh said the name "got cleared and that was it. Michael, as a senior executive, would have been the one who cleared the name." At the time, some concern was expressed over how many of CTV's affiliates, or more importantly CBC stations, would have been seen on Channel 5 in their local markets. A question arose, said Cavanagh, "are we going to run into some sort of cross identification they wouldn't want?"[41]

Clearly Reilly had seemed eager to join the private network. He told Bruce Lawson of *The Globe and Mail*: "They really mean business. It's

a heartening thing to behold. I've been given no strictures on me at all."
Reilly was to oversee both news and public affairs at CTV. Lawson
noted that he had a budget of about $1,500,000 with about $600,000
allotted for news. The Sunday public affairs show that became W5 was
estimated to cost about $13,000 a program. Hind-Smith described
Reilly as "prickly and dynamic and opinionated and all those things we
value."[42]

Bill Cunningham, a former Executive Producer of the CBC news who
coined the name, *The National*, described Reilly as "one of the most talented of all of us." Still another side to Reilly was unpredictable. "He
was terribly undisciplined," said Cunningham. "He got into a hell of a
fight with Bassett. And of course he quit over it. So W5 was just
launched...and bang he's out looking for another job. And the guy was
so talented he'd just pick himself up, dust himself off and somebody else
would give him a job." Cunningham remembered the celebratory mood
on the opening night of W5 when he and Don Cameron, who both later
joined CTV, watched the first program: "We were up in the green room
and then Peter and a gang of us all went out and got hammered."[43]

Cavanagh described Reilly as "a great guy to work with": "You could
fight with him. He would encourage you to and you felt quite free in
doing it." The cash strapped CTV did not prevent Reilly from sending
Cavanagh on a foray to London, England in 1966: "We established the
system of W5 shooting. You went out and you shot the shit out of anything that moved, squacked, talked, bitched, had an idea, you just shot
it all! It became the routine. You were expected to come back, whatever
your basic assignment would have been, with at least three or four other
stories. You know, amortize the cost....So you worked your little buns
off."[44]

Still after several months, Reilly walked off *Sunday* on the CBC network in still another dispute involving network administration. This
time his resignation arose over an interview he had planned to do with
Walter Gordon, a one-time Liberal Finance Minister. At the time, Jon
Ruddy explained that Reilly stomped off the TV set "in as fine a display
of TV ego as has been seen since last fall" when he had left CTV: "Reilly
had set up the interview and fully expected to conduct it himself, only
to be informed that the city editor of the *Toronto Star* was being called
in to handle the job."[45]

Bassett offered his own interpretation of the imbroglio between him
and CTV over the reporting by Isabel LeBourdais on the Steven Truscott

story. He never talked to Reilly but had dealt solely with Gordon Keeble, President of CTV: "What I wanted was a release on the story, which the network had, for use in *The Telegram*....And I had a great shouting match. Peter Reilly was not involved at all." Still Bassett came up empty in a heated exchange with Keeble: "Gordon Keeble was the President of the network. And Gordon Keeble in effect told me to 'go to hell!' He said, 'you're not going to have it!' Well I said 'okay, that's your view, you're entitled, forget it.'" Bassett said he never spoke to Reilly, because he wanted to deal with the network president who was "very good" and also "very tough": "I mean I didn't deal with the employees. I dealt with the top guy. I was a director of the network. But Gordon was absolutely adamant."[46]

The day that Reilly resigned from CTV, Bassett and his wife Isabel had flown to Ottawa to dine with Georges Vanier, the Governor General. "I was in my room in the Chateau changing into my evening clothes when the phone rang," said Bassett. "And it was Canadian Press I think or somebody saying Peter Reilly just resigned...because he says you are trying to dominate the news." Bassett expressed surprise: "Well I said 'you ought to check with Keeble.' I said 'dominate the news.' I said Keeble told me 'to go to hell!' I said I don't understand what Peter Reilly is upset about. He's president, he's won the argument. I said I've got to run. I am going out to dinner. And that was it." Bassett argued that Reilly "had a private agenda" and his behaviour had "generated a lot of publicity for him." *The Telegram* publisher maintained that throughout his life he had been "a good target for others who felt there was some benefit for them attacking me. That's normal and that's part of the act."[47]

Reilly who displayed a quixotic life style died in 1977 at the relatively young age of 44.[48] In 1969, he married his fourth wife, Hazel Snowsill, with whom he worked on the program *Sunday* at the CBC following his departure from *W5*. "I think he was somebody who was very resourceful," said Hazel now married to journalist Peter Desbarats. "He certainly wrote well." Reilly was a regular contributor to *Saturday Night* magazine. She recalled his election as a Conservative Member of Parliament for Ottawa West in the 1972 federal election: "He was very good with people and had a great sensitivity about people down on their luck, people in difficult circumstances."[49]

At the time of Reilly's death, Robert Fulford wrote in his *Saturday Night* magazine notebook: "In the spring of 1975, when *Saturday*

Night's first 'new' issue came out, there was a party at a hotel in Ottawa. Reilly showed up, and after a good many drinks he asked me to autograph a copy of the magazine for him. I wrote on it 'For Peter Reilly, who always gets me in trouble.' He looked at it in mock dismay: 'Oh come on, it's not that bad.' I took my pen and added, 'though it's always worth it.' And it was, too."[50]

REILLY'S DEPARTURE CREATED an opening for Charles Templeton who assumed the position of Director of News and Public Affairs for the next three years. Templeton had been a man in motion throughout a career that had involved evangelism, politics, broadcasting and the print media, notably *The Toronto Star*. Murray Chercover approached Templeton to take the position. However the furor over Reilly's lament about Bassett's interference in network operations apparently gave Templeton pause. That Templeton felt obliged to contact Bassett, and to ask if he were in favour of his appointment, was some measure of the extent of Bassett's influence as a CTV Director.

While Templeton was negotiating with CTV, he called Bassett to ensure that he would have sufficient freedom in the position: "I made it crystal clear if I was coming that we have a clear understanding....So I called John in advance of it all and told him and he in his bluff, and sometimes pompous way, although I like John, [said] 'well of course Charles, I want you to do a great job over there and so on'" On at least one occasion, Bassett sought to influence Templeton's editorial judgement: "One time...he called me about a story...and asked me something which I was not willing to do. And I said no. But what it was I can't recall. And John took it in good grace." Templeton was acutely aware of Bassett's assertive manner: "If you would let him, John would interfere not infrequently and quite bluntly. I had the same experience you see with Beland Honderich when I was Managing Editor of *The Star*....They are both very strong willed minds."[51]

Templeton had never worked for a newspaper when he joined *The Star* and admitted that he knew virtually nothing about television when he was hired at CTV. "I went to *The Star* and I had never worked for a newspaper and they hired me as a features editor." He was a journalist of limited experience having drawn cartoons for *The Globe*: "And I didn't know what the hell I was doing. Scared to death. And in walks this guy with no experience, so they plunk him down and he is fully in charge of page seven, which was our features page. And the resentment was very, very strong as you can imagine." Similarly Templeton had worked as a freelancer for the CBC, but realized that he was unfamiliar with a great deal about the intricacies of television. Still Templeton saw himself as "a ready talker" and was of the view that CTV "looked like it needed leadership."[52]

A man with no formal education beyond grade eight, Templeton was not one to lack a sense of occasion and was prepared to put his own stamp on CTV. Besides, two important political leadership conventions were in the offing where CTV would be front and centre ready to challenge the CBC. Above all, Templeton was prepared to show innovation and insisted that the network break with established practice: "One of the things I required if I went to CTV was a free hand to do it my way. That is not just naked ego. It's the fact that I don't like to do things the traditional way, never have. I knew that I would want to do things that are not commonly done. Not simply to be different from CBC but simply to do the job well."[53]

An upheaval of sorts followed not long after Templeton's arrival in 1966 as Reilly's successor. Templeton made his presence felt: "I clashed with John [Bassett]...and I clashed with Murray [Chercover] once. Harvey [Kirck] and I, yes." He attributed his differences with Kirck to a collision of egos, a not uncommon occurrence in network television: "I think it was. I had come in from the outside. And Harvey was an old pro. And there were things about the broadcast [newscast] I didn't like. And I wanted it to be better than it was. And Harvey resented being told to change. And I can understand that. He was a pro. But nonetheless I am responsible....He is responsible to me. I am responsible to the network."[54]

When Templeton arrived, the small CTV news team included Kirck as managing editor and anchorman. Don Cumming, his assistant, had helped to organize the realigned news operation in Toronto. Wally Macht remained the western correspondent and Henry Champ who would later join the National Broadcasting Company (NBC) and the CBC reported from Quebec where the Quiet Revolution had produced major social change. Peter Kent, who became a much travelled newsman, would soon join CTV and later in his career move on to the CBC, NBC and Global television. In Ottawa, Max Keeping handled weekend on-air duties backing up Ab Douglas in the coverage of national politics in the parliamentary press gallery. On the weekend, Terry Brown was the producer/lineup editor; Al Parks was a mainstay as a writer for the weekend network news. Later lineup editor-writers Errol Weaver and Martin Dewey joined the CTV news department.

Templeton's arrival had immediate impact. Both Cumming and Brown departed CTV and went to the CBC. For a period, Brown had served as network assignment editor. Cumming's departure, in particular, was not entirely unexpected. Harvey Kirck recalled a blowup between Cumming and Templeton over "a few frames of film of a nude woman that we'd aired in a newscast—but that was only a pretext." A clash between the pair was inevitable: "Behind the confrontation was Don's ill-concealed contempt for Charles, and Templeton's readiness to return the sentiment."[55]

Kirck too did not escape Templeton's determination to streamline the network news operation regardless of the extent of his previous television experience. Templeton relieved Kirck of his duties as managing editor to allow him to focus his full energies on his role as network anchorman. John Must, a producer with the network's W5 show, assumed Kirck's editorial duties. Kirck was incensed but grew more sanguine as time passed: "You see I ran the newsroom for two or three years. And then Templeton said, 'you're doing too much. You're going to burn yourself out. Just do the newscast.' And he put John Must in charge of the newsroom. That smarted a little bit, but it was the right move in the long run....There again, that's Templeton. I would be mad as hell at him for doing that. But in the long run, it was the right thing to do." Kirck maintained a respect for Templeton while he was at CTV: "We had arguments every day, everything, how the newsroom operates, what's the show going to be, how are we going to do this, how we were going to do that....I guess all the time we were arguing and fighting I still had a great respect for him....I don't like some of the things he does, but he never does anything that he doesn't make it work for Charles."[56]

Still for the impressionistic television viewer, Templeton appeared to be a respectable front man. The fledgling CTV network had sought credibility for its news operation and turned to the former evangelist and political leadership aspirant at a crucial time in the history of the country. Canadian politics was in the midst of profound change at the mid-twentieth century. Two major political conventions in 1967 and 1968 would see the Progressive Conservatives and the Liberal party of Canada select new leaders to succeed John Diefenbaker and Lester Pearson.

Television live and in colour would communicate those two major political experiences to Canadians. Templeton would be front and centre for CTV at both Tory and Liberal conventions in Toronto and Ottawa. In the final analysis, political conventions are a straight numbers game for competing television networks; the networks can use such major occasions to build audiences. CTV saw the political season of the late 1960s as an opportunity for audience growth, credibility and image enhancement that hopefully would move the private network beyond the age of the "quiz show." Canadian political leadership conventions were modelled after their American counterparts. Television eventually came to shape such political events.

THE 1967 TORY LEADERSHIP CONVENTION turned out to be a watershed in the history of the development of CTV News. The young network showed that it was a formidable rival to the CBC. Since that political happening, CTV has never looked back. Peter Kent, a floor correspondent for CTV, remembered a pep talk at the Westbury Hotel near Maple Leaf Gardens, home of the convention, and the determination on the part of the private network to beat the CBC's coverage: "I remember...our pep talk and those who had never done a convention before having Tom Gould and Charles Templeton, Don MacPherson...[say] 'you guys better spend this money right. We have to be competitive. This is the first time that we stuck our neck out.' And of course John Bassett senior had sprung a lot of the technical wherewithall to actually get down there and run the cables and put the cameras on the floor." A major debate was who was going to be the first over the boards at the Gardens to be on the convention floor when it counted. Before the balloting, television correspondents were constrained and were to be on the floor only during the controlled demonstrations of the leadership candidates which lasted about half an hour. As Kent recalled, Henry Champ shattered the dictates of convention organizers: "I remember Henry Champ saying, 'don't worry boss, I'll be the first over the boards' and he was. He broke a lot of the rules of the electronic media there that it became standard after that that journalists had a right on the floor."[57]

Unlike CBC, the telecast of the Conservative convention on CTV was in colour, a decided advantage for the private network. CTV ever ready to compensate for limited resources looked more technologically upbeat with its mobile "peepie-creepie," a portable television camera, and its chroma-key set. Significantly, CTV scored a major "scoop" when Pierre Berton managed to report the results of a crucial ballot on CTV before the convention had even learned of the results. "I hired Pierre simply because I wanted to beat the bloody CBC and do the best possible job," said Templeton. "I knew that Pierre was immediately recognizable...also so tall that he could get to a candidate when other people couldn't."[58] The interest among Canadians in the convention had continued to build. Bruce Lawson wrote in *The Globe and Mail*: "The Tory convention next week is going to be one of the Canadian TV events of the year. To TV buffs, rivalry of the networks may be almost as interesting as the rivalry on the convention floor at Maple Leaf Gardens."[59]

Templeton had a single purpose at the convention: trounce the CBC. Don MacPherson, a CTV Vice-President, gave Templeton considerable technical assistance in organizing the network's coverage. Throughout his career, MacPherson held various administrative positions with the CBC, Global Television and First Choice Pay Television. In 1967, Templeton credited MacPherson for his considerable contribution: "Don MacPherson was extraordinarily good technically....It may have been Don who thought of the 'peepie-creepie.' As a matter of fact I am almost sure it was and to him should go the credit. Don was a genuine expert in terms of electronic transmission....And Don saw to it that...even the quality of our pictures were better than the CBC. And much of that credit must go to Don. Technically I was an amateur."[60]

CTV stole the television show with its electronic "peepie-creepie" which took the convention and the CBC by surprise. Templeton remembered the strategy devised by the network prior to the convention: "One of the things we did was pull a surprise by building a stage about 15 feet high with a camera on it and on wheels. We got the permission of the Gardens to build it and store it in back and then when the time came we brought it in so we could come in on a close-up of the person we were interviewing. And more than that, it let you know we were there. And we got a number of breaks in terms of the people we could interview. Anyone could go where they were, but this thing moves in on you and this camera is looking down at you, it's going to get your attention and we did."[61]

The response of *The Globe and Mail* columnist Dennis Braithwaite was typical of the reaction that CTV received after its coverage of the convention: "Two of the most exciting moments in the television coverage of the Conservative convention occurred exclusively on CTV. One was John Diefenbaker's 11th hour press conference on Saturday, the other was Pierre Berton's pirating the first ballot results and getting them on the air ahead of the official announcement." Braithwaite concluded that CTV had arrived as a national news network: "CTV showed itself capable of matching or topping the best that the CBC can do; the corporation exhibited serious deficiencies in the area of political journalism."[62]

Still even when CTV had triumphed, not all went well internally at the network. Harvey Kirck, the national news anchorman, had suffered a national humiliation during the convention coverage that Templeton had dominated on camera. Kirck was effectively cut out of the broadcast and relegated to the role of visible, booth announcer performing station breaks while Templeton held forth along with CTV's guest pundits Berton, writer Scott Young, Parliament Hill watchers, Douglas Fisher and Charles Lynch, and pollster Peter Regenstreif. Kirck almost resigned from the network following the convention. He burst into the executive office of Murray Chercover and lamented Templeton's behaviour which had effectively eliminated him from the national broadcast: "You saw what happened, Murray. I'm finished. I quit. I will not be put in that position. What the hell does that man think he's doing."[63] As a national news personality, Kirck's ego was bruised badly.

As justification for his action, Templeton argued that Kirck was a solid newscaster but questioned his news judgement: "I think Harvey had one of the best reading voices of anybody in international television and was delighted to have him on the eleven o'clock news. But he was not a newsman and had no really good news sense." Moreover Templeton did not see Kirck as a political commentator: "Harvey...was not a great spur of the moment commentator. And we had gone into that convention absolutely determined to beat the pants off the CBC."[64]

For his part, Kirck felt Templeton had demeaned him during the broadcast and was inclined to want "to tear at somebody's throat." He was surprised because that kind of behaviour was out of character for Templeton: "I think it was partly Charles' ego. He had Berton down on the floor and I think when Charles gets in a situation like that he wants to control all of it. And in his terms, when you are on live television, you control by talking. And he didn't want to give anything away, give away to the floor....I tried. It wasn't like Charles to do that kind of thing. But he really shafted me real good. I made station breaks all night."[65]

In the end, Kirck stayed on with the network and lived to smile another day during the Liberal leadership convention. Though he was not part of the CTV news team at the convention when the Liberals met in Ottawa 4–6 April 1968, through circumstances Kirck managed to regain some stature at Templeton's expense. Martin Luther King, the prominent Negro leader, was assassinated on 4 April 1968 in Memphis, Tennessee and a wave of black rioting followed in American cities. CTV's convention coverage of the Liberal leadership convention was interrupted. This time Templeton was reliant on the Toronto newsroom which received American network news feeds and the latest reports on the riots. Kirck had stayed in Toronto and was called upon to provide running commentary and to put into context the developments that had erupted suddenly in the United States. At an early stage of the Liberal convention, the King assassination had superseded developments surrounding the choice of Lester Pearson's successor. During this initial phase, the CTV emphasis was on Kirck in Toronto rather than Templeton in Ottawa on CTV.[66]

Kirck felt mildly vindicated with the exposure he received and the story he was able to report during the Liberal convention. "I suppose somewhere in the back of my head there was a little satisfaction there. It's interesting the kind of thing that I was working on that day was my kind of thing.…You know solid things that were happening, dynamic. I could never get involved in politics that way. One of the conventions I was out on the floor and I just hated it. I wasn't good at pushing in front of everybody else."[67] Pierre Trudeau was chosen on the fourth ballot at the Liberal leadership convention as Lester Pearson's successor. In June, 2001 Templeton whom Warren Gerard described in *The Toronto Star* as "a man of many parts" died at the age of 85 after living with Alzheimer's disease.[68]

Kirck and CTV News also gained wide audience acceptance with its Apollo mission telecasts between 1968 and 1970. In 1969 Neil Armstrong made history when he became the first man to set foot on the moon, the culmination of the Apollo program. These "special" broadcasts represented a new style of programming for the network through an innovative advertising arrangement with Texaco Canada Ltd. and NBC in the United States.[69] The new advertising format was a further indication of the influence of U.S. models on CTV and showed the extent to which the network would go to accommodate particular sponsors.

Under the agreement with Texaco, the company was given the first opportunity to advertise on special news programmes. Texaco had agreed to commit a specific, minimum budget for such programming. When CTV wanted to run a news special, the network would simply inform Texaco that the program was to be aired. Texaco could agree to sponsor the broadcast or refuse. The notion of "instant commitment to TV sponsorship," an American practice, had not been tried before in network Canadian television. The innovation replaced the earlier arrangement whereby sponsors would purchase their spot advertising for predetermined time slots.[70]

DESPITE SUCH OBVIOUS ADVANCES in its programming during the late 1960s including the coverage of political conventions and the moon landing, CTV remained a network that was under financial duress. Perhaps no single incident represents the financial constraints of CTV in 1970 more so than the coverage it attempted to provide on the occasion of the one hundredth anniversary of Manitoba's entry into Confederation. To mark the event, Prime Minister Pierre Trudeau, then a bachelor, had invited singer Barbra Streisand to a gala event at the National Arts Centre in Ottawa. The singing sensation had also caused an uproar when she appeared in the Canadian House of Commons. She and the Prime Minister had made eyes at each other to the chagrin of the official opposition.

As CTV's Ottawa bureau chief, Bruce Phillips functioned at the time without a network cameraman. The Ottawa bureau was reliant on the camera personnel of CJOH, the network's Ottawa affiliate. The formidable handicap gave rise to the need for CTV to improvise. On the night that the Prime Minister appeared at the Arts Centre with Miss Streisand, Phillips received a call from Geoff Scott, parliamentary correspondent for CHCH, Hamilton.

Phillips recalled the circumstances: "Geoff Scott...had his cameraman down there and he shot these pictures and Miss Streisand was garbed in what I can only describe as the absolute, irreducible minimum and she waltzed into the Arts Centre on the arm of the Prime Minister who in those days, of course, was a bachelor and a pretty spectacular figure himself. And it caused a near riot! So Geoff's cameraman shot all this fabulous footage." Neither CTV nor CBC had shot film footage of the spectacular occasion. Phillips quickly saw an opportunity to upstage Holy Mother Corp. Scott wanted about $125 for the film footage to cover the cost of his cameraman's time and the film stock. Phillips did not have authority to spend the amount of money in those days and was unable to get budgetary clearance from his immediate superior in Toronto. The amount of money was seen as an "excessive charge" for Scott's film. In the end Phillips paid Scott out of his own money and put the film on the air to "the great embarrassment of the CBC as well."[71]

BY 1970, CTV WAS ALMOST a decade old. Phillips remembered the increasing rivalry between the private network and the CBC nurtured in part by the CRTC, the broadcast regulator and successor to the Board of Broadcast Governors which had licensed CTV: "And as the years went on,...we did expand the reach of the network, the ratings continued to grow, the revenues continued to improve and the CRTC I think was a help to us, because they kept enough of an eye on news and network operations...to ensure that some at least minimal proportion of the revenues were invested in news and public affairs coverage."[72]

Television news continued to grow in influence. The October crisis of 1970 was the major domestic news story of a new decade. The Front de libération du Québec, a leading separatist group, kidnapped James Cross, a senior British trade commissioner and murdered Pierre Laporte, a provincial cabinet minister. Laporte's murder occurred after the government of Pierre Trudeau had invoked the *War Measures Act*, the first time the legislation had been introduced in peacetime. Peter Kent, the CTV Quebec correspondent at the time, recalled one incident that clearly showed the influence of TV news and the extent of Canadians' reliance on the medium.

Tom Gould who anchored the CTV coverage in Toronto asked Henry Champ in Montreal to describe the personality of Robert Lemieux, the lawyer who had represented the FLQ at numerous news conferences. Kent remembered a sharp audience reaction: "Tom Gould in the anchor chair in Toronto [said] 'Henry, a lot of people are wondering what this Robert Lemieux is like'....And Henry came back and said something like 'Tom, I got to tell you he's the kind of guy you'd like to sit down and have a beer with. He's a very fascinating personality.' And the phones across the country went nuts!" Kent who had taken a short respite from the story received a phone call at home to get back to the station promptly: "When I did get back, they said 'tell Henry that he's got to go on the air and explain himself, apologize,' because people thought that Henry was saying 'this FLQ lawyer was a nice guy' and here a Minister of the Quebec government had just been murdered and Cross was still missing and the *War Measures Act* had been declared....That was probably the first time that I had been part of something that really stimulated the audience."[73]

In the early 1970s as CTV News began to have still a greater reach, CBC network executives continued a close watch on the growth and impact of the private network. The positive reviews that the private network had drawn for its coverage of the Tory leadership convention in 1967 provided the CBC with a wake-up call. In short, CTV was no longer a young electronic upstart but a more credible force in Canadian journalism. CTV had become a serious competitor for advertising dollars with an audience built on the foundation of its news service. The CBC network relied on advertising for a portion of its revenues beyond the accustomed annual parliamentary appropriation for the Corporation's radio and television services. Internal correspondence among CBC executives underlined the serious attention that the CBC paid to the Nielsen ratings of both *The National* and the *CTV National News*. The days of the public Corporation maintaining a casual attitude towards audience ratings were over. CTV could not help but focus the Corporation's attention on the need to remain relevant to a majority of Canadians, if the Corporation expected to receive a healthy parliamentary appropriation.

Knowlton Nash, Director, Information Programs, explained to CBC executives in February, 1970 the need for CBC to maintain its profile in the event that CTV decided to expand its network newscast to a half hour: "In view of the new CRTC proposed regulations allowing news to be sponsored, it is probable that CTV would go to a half-hour National News in order to pick up revenue. It would be critically disadvantageous from a competitive point of view if CTV made a major publicity campaign about its new half-hour news while CBC remained at 18 minutes."[74]

Later in 1970, Nash drew attention to the results of a Nielsen audience survey of both network newscasts: "The average audience for the August 10–23 period was 1,782,000 for *The National*. The *CTV National News* audience averaged 782,000." He also underlined the results showing the CBC also dominant in the category of number of homes in which television was in use: "The above is on the basis of viewers, but also interesting is the number of homes using television. These figures show 942,000 homes were turned to CBC on the average night in August for *The National*, compared to 430,000 homes for CTV. In March 1970 the CBC average was 949,000 homes and the CTV average 438,000 homes."[75] Ratings had become a matter of the highest priority for the CBC.

Significantly CBC executives also observed the style of the CTV news presentation. The faster-paced and more upbeat newscast that CTV presented contrasted with the more traditionally upright CBC news. Canadian audiences seemed to grow accustomed to the more visually exciting newscast on the private network. Nash had heard criticism of CBC's presentation when compared to the private network and asked Peter Trueman Head, Daily News & Information—TV for his reaction.[76]

Trueman who would later join Global television, a new private Ontario TV network, as a news anchorman responded to Nash and in the process underlined CTV's Americanized style of presentation. He compared Harvey Kirck, CTV's news anchor, to David Brinkley whose career as a broadcast journalist was spent with both NBC and ABC: "Kirk's [sic] personality is quite different from any of the announcer personalities we have used traditionally in *The National*. He has a fast, clipped, almost sardonic, kind of delivery—very much in the Brinkley manner—to which CTV's writers cater. A combination of the writing and his delivery tend to make the CTV show more wry and at the same time more vulgar (in the broad sense of the word) than *The National*."[77]

EVEN THOUGH THE public broadcaster was aware of the new level of news competition that privately owned CTV presented, Trueman was reluctant to break with established CBC practice. He clung to CBC's reputation for respectability and questioned the CBC's critics: "I think it is very important that we preserve the qualities on *The National* which the casual critic might be tempted to label stodgy because I suspect that really what they are talking about is responsibility, reliability and a straight-forward un-hoked presentation."[78]

By the early 1970s, the CBC had again undergone internal struggles between its News and Current Affairs divisions and had to deal with the question of regional sensitivities to programs that were broadcast outside Toronto. Tensions could arise at CBC regional stations when journalists from central Canada were parachuted in to report national stories on CBC. With CTV News a formidable opponent, the Corporation faced a new external threat. Early in 1973, Nash wrote to Denis Harvey,

Chief News Editor-TV, and argued that it was no time for internecine rivalries: "We have enough of a challenge in fighting CTV and I don't want to see us get into an internal hassle."[79] Clearly CBC, the country's public broadcaster wanted to be dominant and was not prepared to ignore its competition or the dictates of the marketplace.

CTV had gained respectability for its news coverage. Still a greater expansion of CTV News was about to occur. The network expanded, the co-operative became more profitable as a business and additional advertising revenue followed. A greater number of news bureaus were soon to open nationally and internationally. An innovative morning show *Canada AM*, which was to become a Canadian institution, began in September 1972. The growth period at CTV was to culminate with the arrival of Lloyd Robertson from the CBC in 1976. His nightly presence and capacity to communicate the days news to Canadians brought a new sense of reassurance to viewers of CTV.

The news team of Kirck and Robertson combined the two notions of trust and tradition. In ten years CTV had gone from what was essentially a newscast produced on a shoe string at CJOH to a network news division that provided a distinctive, populist style of coverage. Whatever its shortcomings, CTV News had shown that it could truly touch Canadians and challenged the public broadcaster. Clearly Canadian viewers had a news alternative and a network that had no choice but to ensure that as a business it remained a profitable enterprise.

Cassius Clay taking his best hold after the panel threw a fast one at him.

ON THE HOT SEAT

Johnny Esaw doing telecast of a Canadian Football League game for CFTO. Right, on hot seat, Rocky Marciano, undefeated retired heavyweight champ.

"On the Hot Seat." Cassius Clay (later to be known as Muhammad Ali) is featured in the top photograph. Photograph courtesy of Johnny Esaw.

FIVE

Telepoll, Laugh-In and Wide World of Sports

1962–1972

BESIDES ITS NEWS SERVICE, CTV relied on sports programming, the importation of American fare and low cost Canadian entertainment productions to build audience during its first decade. Programs such as *Telepoll* and the *Sports Hot Seat* helped the network to respond to the Canadian content quotas stipulated by the BBG. From the beginning with its emphasis on the business aspect of broadcasting, CTV emphasized mass entertainment or what could be considered low culture in its programming to differentiate itself from the CBC whose mandate steered the Corporation's broadcast schedule towards fare that was to educate and enlighten. Still the CBC also provided a range of both Canadian and American programming. Clearly with the arrival of the private network and the programming it provided, Canadians were given a voice for populism.

The program content of a television network is largely what defines its style of service and contribution as a cultural industry. CTV's early years of programming to a mass audience were uneven for three reasons. First, it should be remembered that the entrepreneurial Spencer Caldwell, the network's founder, by his own admission was hardly interested in network television as a cultural vehicle. CTV was to be an alternative service to the CBC, a network for advertisers. Second, his insistence that programming concepts be sold first to advertisers, before they could be developed, placed heavy constraints on network programmers. Third, many technical aspects of the network's operation including extension of service, rather than programming, preoccupied management in the early years.

Throughout much of the 1960s, emphasis had been placed on extending the reach of the network and expanding its transmission system. By the early 1970s, CTV had spread its television service across Canada with a streamlined delivery system. The network had taken the initiative to provide coast-to-coast transmission in direct response to prodding by the CRTC. The CRTC had noted in a public announcement on 22 January 1973 that it wished "to encourage as high a proportion of Canadian production as possible on the CTV Network and also to make the CTV Network available as alternate viewing to an increasing number of Canadians in the more sparsely settled areas."[1] CTV had expanded its coverage from 79 percent to 87 percent of the population by 1973, the year the CRTC renewed the network's licence for three years.[2] The following year the network service was extended to approximately 90 percent of Canadians through an expanded microwave system.

CTV was able to announce that a nine-year contract had been signed with CN Telecommunications to connect CJON-TV in St. John's, Newfoundland with CJCB-TV, the network's affiliate in Sydney, Nova Scotia. The establishment of the two-way transmission arrangement ensured that CTV would have fully operational microwave facilities from Newfoundland to British Columbia for the first time. The CTV network consisted of 16 affiliated stations across Canada. They were located in the original eight cities of Vancouver, Edmonton, Calgary, Winnipeg, Toronto, Ottawa, Montreal, and Halifax in addition to eight other private TV operations located in St. John's, Sydney, Moncton, Kitchener, Sudbury, Thunder Bay, Regina and Saskatoon.[3] In the network's first decade, the technological infrastructure had become developed. CTV had the potential to be a major network force in Canadian broadcasting. Still a stiff challenge for the network was the need to parallel its streamlined delivery system with an improved programming performance.

The earliest years had been difficult as the network found its legs. But by the mid 1960s, there were signs CTV was attempting to move beyond its infant programming age as a "quiz show" network with some fare that was to have lasting impact. The five-year-old network offered viewers a montage of morning news, courtroom drama and gospel rock music. However sitcoms, westerns and variety shows produced in the United States remained a mainstay of CTV programming. As is still true today in Canadian broadcasting, the importation of American programming helped to produce the revenue that supported Canadian productions, a fundamental, historical dichotomy of the country's broadcasting system.

ON THE NIGHT of 31 August 1966, when Harvey Kirck had previewed a new fall season he interviewed Terri Clark and Pat Murray, hosts of the CTV's first morning show *Bright & Early*, which aired Monday to Friday on the network. Royce Frith, later a Canadian Senator and High Commissioner to Great Britain, acted as host of the program *This Land Is People*. Earlier Frith had hosted a popular show called *Telepoll* that surveyed Canadians on leading issues of the day. The CTV produced programs for the 1966–67 season included, in the words of Arthur Weinthal, the network's Vice President of Programming, "an innocent little group of program hours in the first few years of our life."[4] Three such programs were *Brand New Scene*, a musical variety and talent discovery program featuring country folk music, *A Singin,* a gospel rock show, and *Magistrate's Court*, a CTV daytime courtroom drama.

Popular U.S. programming was a major component of the CTV prime time hours in the fall of 1966. *The Monkees* was a U.S. musical sitcom starring Mike Nesmith, Peter Tork, Mickey Dolenz and Davey Jones. *Pistols & Petticoats* was a situation comedy on a western theme starring Anne Sheridan. Other popular American shows were *Batman* starring Adam West; the U.S. drama programs *Run For Your Life* with Ben Gazzara, *Sea Hunt* with Lloyd Bridges, and *I Spy* with Robert Culp and Bill Cosby; and the long running U.S. drama series *Mission Impossible* with Martin Landau, Barbara Bain, Greg Morris and Peter Graves. Popular musical varieties seen on CTV in the mid 1960s included shows with marquee entertainers: Jackie Gleason, Andy Williams and Dean Martin.[5]

CTV would be called upon to balance its American programming with a range of Canadian fare to meet the expectations of the broadcast regulator. The BBG and later the CRTC expected CTV to be a principal player in the country's broadcasting system and to provide a meaningful programming alternative to the CBC. Still it would be some time before the private network could meet the broadcast regulator's expectations forcing CTV to withstand periodic criticism of its meagre contribution to the noble goals of Canadian broadcasting as articulated by officialdom in Ottawa.

The program *Telepoll* was illustrative of CTV's attempt to provide home grown offerings during the early 1960s. The program touched Canadians' sensibilities, because it had an interactive quality, a programming genre that was to come later in the evolution of Canadian television. Otherwise the network had little noticeable to offer viewers or the Canadian cultural experience beyond its news service. Beyond *Telepoll*, CTV programming had hardly impressed Robert Fowler and the committee he headed that examined the state of the Canadian broadcasting system.[6] As host of *Telepoll*, lawyer Royce Frith had an authoritative presence on a program that provided polling data on national issues in the days before a more sophisticated polling of public opinion was to become commonplace in the Canadian media.

Telepoll was CTV's first major foray into public affairs programming. Its findings were often quoted in newspaper stories dealing with leading public issues. The program sponsored by CN-CP Telecommunications was fully funded for the network. By sponsoring *Telepoll*, CN-CP had attempted to direct its advertising message toward the business community.[7] A frequent contributor to the program was Peter Jennings who was then a news anchor for the network at CJOH, Ottawa.

Telepoll cost about $3,500 for each half hour of programming making it probably the most expensive CTV produced show at that time. The cost of other CTV entertainment programming on a per half hour basis, in the musical and game show categories, was less expensive: *West Coast* at $3,400; *Showdown*, $2,500; *Try for Ten*, $2,200 and *A-Kin-To-Win*, $2,500. When it began as a network, CTV spent $800 per quarter hour, or $3200 each hour, to provide a national news service.[8]

Regardless of their quality or suitability, programs such as *Telepoll* helped CTV to respond to the Cancon quotas. On 1 June 1959, the BBG had proposed that the "Canadian content of the programs of any station shall not be less than 55% of the total program content during any week."[9] Although the Cancon regulations have been amended periodically and have drawn controversy, they were a central component of the regulatory system in Canadian broadcasting. Generally private broadcasters accepted such regulation reluctantly.

CN-CP TELECOMMUNICATIONS was one of a number of the early advertisers who recognized the potential of television advertising. The private network soon proved attractive to major advertisers such as American Home Products. As Weinthal explained, "Packaged goods people were the ones who were looking for more space on the air, because they had many brands."[10] Other well known advertisers who began to sponsor programs on the CTV network in the early years included: Aluminum Co. of Canada Ltd.; Benson & Hedges Canada Ltd.; Bristol-Myers Co. of Canada Ltd.; Bulova Watch Co. Ltd.; Colgate-Palmolive Ltd.; General Motors Products of Canada Ltd.; Lever Bros. Ltd.; Procter & Gamble Co. of Canada Ltd.; Molson's Brewery Ltd.; Timex of Canada Ltd.; and Weston Bakeries Limited.[11]

CTV's arrival as a competitor to the CBC had the potential to alter the earlier relationship that the Corporation had with advertisers. Unlike the CBC which enjoyed a parliamentary grant from the Canadian taxpayers, CTV was solely reliant on advertising dollars. From the beginning, the private network emphasized its business orientation and offered national advertisers Canadian news, sports, variety and, "the entertainment makers of Hollywood and New York."[12] Not surprisingly CTV attempted to be as "user friendly" as possible to advertisers and nurtured any sign of enthusiasm shown by ad agencies such as MacLaren Advertising for television as an advertising medium. At an early stage in CTV's history, MacLaren bought network shows for advertisers who recognized the potential of the television medium.[13]

The arrival of a competing private network and its "user friendly" approach could not help but have considerable impact. CTV argued that the CBC was able to attract advertisers by charging them something less than the actual cost of sponsored programs. With no form of subsidy, CTV did not enjoy such an advantage. The private network was forced to charge advertisers the full cost of programs. With the introduction of the CTV network, two schools of thought emerged over the question of the role of television advertising as it related to the costs of programming. CTV was entirely reliant on the marketplace; CBC was not.

"As soon as private [television] broadcasting got going, we quite clearly saw that the public broadcaster was subsidizing the advertiser by not charging the full amount of money for what programs actually cost," Weinthal explained. "That argument actually still goes on. CBC takes the view that they are putting out a program service and any contribution they get from the advertising community helps the cause." The two viewpoints, private versus public broadcasting, on the question of advertising amounted to, in Weinthal's words, "the difference between having to address yourself to a bottom line and not having to address yourself to the bottom line."[14]

When Trina McQueen was an executive with the CBC, she challenged Weinthal's notion about the public network undercutting the market. McQueen, who became the President and COO of CTV Inc. in 2001, told a House of Commons committee that the accusation was unfounded: "So in every case where there has been a detailed investigation of our supposed undercutting of the market, we have come up clean. We do not do it, not because we are good little girls and boys, although we are good girls and boys, but because it is just not in our interest. We want to charge the highest price we can get for every piece of our inventory."[15]

Whatever the early controversy over advertising practices on the part of the two networks, by the 1970s television advertising had gained a new credibility. Any reluctance that national advertisers might have had toward the new TV medium, in comparison to radio or print, had been largely overcome. Weinthal explained that advertisers came to recognize that television was a growth industry: "People were buying television sets like fury, television signals were expanding, there was talk that maybe some day in the future this could all be in colour and an aggressive business position was being taken by people in the broadcasting business."[16]

ANOTHER CONTENTIOUS ISSUE related to the costs involved in the importation of American programming, the lifeblood of the Canadian broadcasting system. The popular American program, *Rowan & Martin's Laugh-In*, that was aired first on CTV and captivated North American audiences in the late 1960s, was typical of the extent to which the CBC chose to compete in the marketplace for American fare. CTV introduced the popular American production which featured comics Dan Rowan and Dick Martin and helped to launch the career of Goldie Hawn. Perhaps *Laugh-In* was best known for the well known phrase "Sock it to Me" which swept North America at the height of the program's popularity. Even United States President Richard Nixon appeared on the program.[17]

Philip "Pip" Wedge, who spent 28 years with CTV, and was responsible for purchasing American programming, recalled how *Laugh-In* was brought to Canada by CTV and how the CBC took it away from the private network. The program was produced by George Schlatter and Ed Friendly, a team who had produced many American shows. Wedge remembered the distributor of the program telling him how the CBC wanted the successful show: "The distributor, and I forget who it was, said to me 'look, the CBC wants it. George Schlatter is saying to me, I don't care who has been with you all this time. I don't know how long this phenomenon is going to last. Get the maximum dollar you can out of Canada.' So we lost it to the CBC."[18]

Following the 1968–69 season when *Laugh-In* had been aired on CTV, the CBC outbid the private network for the show and paid nearly twice the price. According to Alex Barris, author of *The Pierce-Arrow Showroom Is Leaking: An Insider's View of the CBC*, CTV had paid the NBC some eight thousand dollars a week for the program. The cost for the CBC was nearly double that of CTV, an estimated fifteen thousand dollars weekly to broadcast the fast paced U.S. program with wide appeal in 1969–70. Barris raised an important question about the behaviour of the public broadcaster. The issue he touched has recurred throughout Canadian broadcasting history and underlined the dichotomous nature of the role played by the public broadcaster: "But does it make sense that the CBC should be paying so much to import an American program which was already available to many Canadians—and to do so at a time when the CBC itself is cutting back on Canadian light entertainment programs largely because of lack of funds to produce them?"[19]

About the same time as the Canadian competition occurred over *Laugh-In*, Wedge recalled another example of how the CBC sought to regain an American program that the network had discarded earlier. "*The Carol Burnett Show* was on CBC. CBC dropped it. They weren't happy about it. We took it over. I don't know whether we paid more or less than CBC did. I know CBC didn't want it, because in those days if CBC wanted something they got it. We had it for a year, built the numbers up tremendously and suddenly the CBC decided they wanted it back." The popular program returned to the CBC.[20]

By the early 1970s, the CBC's TV schedule seemed to aim at programming all things to all people as opposed to a sharp focus on the twin public broadcasting goals of cultural enlightenment and educational uplift. The Corporation appeared to view CTV not as an alternative to its public broadcasting mandate which was intended to explain Canada to Canadians. Rather the CTV network was seen as an outright competitor. The CBC appeared ready to challenge CTV in the marketplace, even if the public broadcaster were forced to air mass entertainment from the U.S.

The CBC weekly program schedule for the 1972–73 season in prime time showed popular American programs such as *Mary Tyler Moore*, *The Partridge Family*, *The Carol Burnett Show*, *All in the Family* and *MASH*. Unlike a later era when the CBC would Canadianize its prime time schedule to try to appear as a more distinctive public broadcaster in the multi-channel universe, American shows were a dominant feature in the early 1970s. The Canadian fare included *The Nature of Things*, *Front Page Challenge*, and *The Tommy Hunter Show*. The CBC also held to its established practice with the segment, *Tuesday Night,* at 10 P.M. which was a time period devoted to high culture. As Sandy Stewart wrote, "From almost the beginning of television, there has been a prestige slot for classical or at least high-brow productions."[21]

Long before *Laugh-In*, the American influence on Canadian broadcasters had been immense and could not help but affect the behaviour of both private and public TV networks in Canada. Canadians reached eagerly to hear and watch popular American programs whether it was *Amos n' Andy* on radio or *I Love Lucy* on television. From the standpoint of both Canadian TV networks, the competition south of the border remained formidable. CTV and CBC had no choice but to take into account Canadian response to American television.

Canadian listeners and viewers could not help but be influenced by the American programming formats that have always been available to them. Throughout their history, Canadians have shown that they will never be denied access to popular, entertaining programs originating in the United States. Just as American programs influenced the listening patterns of Canadians in the early days of radio, so too did U.S. programming models such as *Laugh-In* affect the attitude of Canadians toward television. By the time CTV began broadcasting, Canadians' insistence on being able to have a wide choice of American programming was long established. Indeed the notion of freedom of choice had been a main concern of the members of the Royal Commission on Radio

Broadcasting in 1929, the first federal inquiry into Canadian radio under the chairmanship of Sir John Aird.

Given this backdrop and the economics of the Canadian broadcasting industry, private broadcasters such as CTV have had to know their audiences to survive. They have been inclined to question the cultural objectives of broadcasting articulated by broadcast regulators when confronted with the commercial imperatives of the marketplace. Indeed Canadian programming has always faced major competition from Canada's southern neighbour whether it was news, sports and especially entertainment fare in the drama genre. In the mid 1990s, Arthur Weinthal singled out the two salient factors of geography and population as major determinants in the behaviour of CTV, as a national private network: "You have 19 million English speaking people in this [small] country [and], as I always characterize it, 70 per cent of them are facing the back of the auditorium....We lie next door not to another country but to *the* other country. They invented entertainment, they boxed it, packaged it, created it and make it work."[22]

DESPITE THE FORMIDABLE American competition facing Canadian broadcasters at all programming levels, the CTV network proved to be an innovator in sports broadcasting from its founding in 1961. The CBC had enjoyed a near monopoly on the television coverage of Canadian sports, a component of Canadian culture. As in its news broadcasting, the notion of the CBC as a public broadcasting institution tended to supersede the personality of any individual sportscaster with the exception perhaps of Danny Gallivan and Foster and Bill Hewitt, whose broadcasting longevity overrode the CBC's no star system. Canadians had grown accustomed to the carefully balanced presentations by sports broadcasters Steve Douglas, Fred Sgambati and Jim Coleman on the CBC, just as they had become attuned to the controlled news presentation of the stoic Earl Cameron.

No longer would the CBC have the sporting field to itself. CTV introduced Canadians to a vibrant style of coverage that played to the dictates and constraints of the television medium and touched the sensibilities of sports fans looking for an alternative to the CBC. Not only the content of the programs but the style of the sports broadcaster changed. A more personal, opinionated and "in your face" form of sportscasting

Johnny Esaw broadcast position at the 1988 Olympics in Calgary. Photograph courtesy of Johnny Esaw.

emerged on the private network in the 1960s, a decade when television was able to capture outstanding performances and communicate experiences in sports like never before.

The personality most closely identified with CTV sports and who was responsible for its early major coverage became well known to Canadian fans, first on radio in western Canada and later nationally on television. Johnny Esaw joined CFTO-TV in Toronto in 1960, as Sports Director, and became CTV's Vice-President of Sports in 1974. He was a shrewd, aggressive promoter of sports broadcasting in the early years of television. Two programs, the *Wide World of Sports* obtained through an arrangement with the ABC and the *Sports Hot Seat* were major initiatives in the 1960s. Within a decade, Esaw's efforts had helped to build the international reputation of CTV sports programming especially through Olympics coverage. Many Canadians came to know Esaw as a broadcasting performer and sports personality. They were less familiar with his distinctive family background and backstage activity on behalf of CTV to obtain the broadcasting rights to memorable sports events nationally and internationally.

Esaw's family lineage was Assyrian. As Esaw wrote, "When I say Assyrian, most people think I mean Syrian, Armenian or even Lebanese. Assyrian is the oldest race in the world. It's in the bible. But where's Assyria?" He learned from his family the location of Assyria where his parents and eldest sister were born: "They lived in the region of Urmia, Persia in the town of Mosul, squeezed between Ottoman Turkey and Persia—now known as Iran. Our people enjoyed the status of being a privileged Christian minority, a minority which greatly angered the Muslim population." In the first decade of the 20th century, when Sir Wilfrid Laurier and Clifford Sifton, Minister of the Interior, were opening the prairie west to new settlers, Esaw's parents chose an area outside North Battleford, Saskatchewan. The Canadian Pacific Railway offered immigrants free parcels of land, if they would work for the railway. Later his parents moved into North Battleford. In Esaw's words, "For several years the Assyrians found North Battleford a comfortable place in which to live. Many farmed while others worked on the railway or began small businesses."[23]

Born in 1925 at Notre Dame Hospital in the small community of about 5,000, Esaw soon became a hockey enthusiast. He had two close friends in North Battleford, both of them hockey notables. Emile "The Cat" Francis became a star goaltender in the National Hockey League with the Chicago Black Hawks and the New York Rangers. Later he coached and managed the Rangers, St. Louis Blues and was a builder and director of the Hartford Whalers. A second friend, Ken McKenzie, was named the NHL's first Publicity Director joining the league in 1946 when the memorable Clarence Campbell became the league's President. Esaw recalled that McKenzie eventually "took his entire savings, $365, out of the bank and launched *Hockey News*—which would become hockey's bible." McKenzie was an avowed promoter of the sport of hockey which made it easier to sell advertising space in the hockey publication. Esaw noted the success of McKenzie's approach: "'Write something flattering and you can't miss,' was Ken's philosophy. When he left the NHL, the *News* kept growing and after thirty years of success with the paper, he sold it to the Whitney's [*sic*] of New York for $4 million. Ken was quite a salesman."[24] So was Esaw.

After becoming a well-known radio personality on station CKRM, Regina, Esaw moved on to CKRC, Winnipeg. "The first person I met in

Winnipeg was [sportscaster] 'Cactus' Jack Wells, the man whom I was replacing and also the man with whom I'd be competing on another station [CKY]." But Wells hardly saw Esaw as a competitor. Cactus Jack wanted to make sure Esaw had adequate transportation following his arrival: "He roared in his hearty way: 'Welcome to Winnipeg,' and in a gesture that tipped off the generous and thoughtful man that created part of the Wells legend, tossed me the keys. 'You'll need a little transportation until you're settled, then you can send the keys back.'"[25]

At CKRM, Regina he had received a starting salary of $235 a month. His annual starting salary in Toronto was about $15,000 not including talent fees for such events as broadcasting Canadian football games for which he could be paid about $300 a game.[26] The sports director's job at CFTO was to bring Esaw national recognition and provide him with a broad field of action, much of it partaken behind the scenes, to catapult the station owned by Baton Aldred Rogers Broadcasting Ltd., and the CTV network, into a major television franchise in sports broadcasting.

Esaw and his wife, June, enjoyed Winnipeg, which prevented him from applying directly for the Toronto position. Still John Bassett, Joel Aldred and Foster Hewitt sought him out, perhaps because of his connection to western Canada. A well-known Sports Director from the west could be an asset especially if CFTO were to become part of a private TV network. Hewitt told Esaw: "If you say yes, our search is over and the job is yours."[27]

After Esaw agreed to take the job at CFTO, he was suddenly inundated with other offers from eastern Canada. First off the mark was Wes McKnight, Head of Sports at radio station CFRB Toronto, for many years the giant of the private radio broadcasting industry. Referring to Hewitt's offer McKnight told Esaw: "Whatever he agreed to pay you, we'll increase the amount substantially if you break the agreement." Esaw said he could not do that but recommended Bill Stephenson at Vancouver radio station CKWX for the position at CFRB. The next offer came from Terry Kielty at CFRA radio in Ottawa. Kielty asked if Esaw were available and when he received a negative answer also inquired if he could recommend a sportscaster. Esaw again recommended Stephenson with the qualifier that he may already have been contacted by McKnight. As an alternative, he recommended Don Chevrier, a young sportscaster at CJCA, Edmonton.[28] That is how three noted western sports broadcasters familiar to Canadians moved east for fame and fortune. The East had money, people and recognition.

Esaw became well known nationally when CTV won the rights to broadcast Canadian football league games, but two other sports were to make him a true innovator in television coverage: car racing and skating. "Remember, in the dawn of television, everyone was trying to play crystal ball in deciding what would create good TV in terms of production and viewer-appeal." Esaw became convinced that "skating and car racing were 'naturals' for TV." In 1961 he was able to act on his conviction. Imperial Tobacco Ltd. was responsible for the first major international car race in Canada featuring the charismatic Stirling Moss as the major attraction. The timing for television was important, because the Mosport Raceway had just opened near Bowmanville, Ontario.[29]

The Player's Ltd. "200" was to be a major showcase for racing talent. Esaw had worked closely with Stan Houston of Public Relations Services Ltd. who handled the Imperial Tobacco account. Houston later founded what became The Edelman-Houston Group. CFTO covered races involving Player's Ltd. ranging from Formula One to the Player's Ltd./GM Series, the Formula-Atlantic and the Trans-AM. The coverage captured the career of the noted driver Gilles Villeneuve, although at the time of his tragic death, the broadcast rights to the Formula One had gone to the CBC. Significantly, Imperial Tobacco, the sponsor of the car racing events on CFTO, paid for the production costs. As Esaw noted that, "With the birth of CTV, motorsport coverage and Player's Ltd. gained vast new exposure. When we had our agreement with ABC to carry *Wide World of Sports*, the package included part ABC material and part local production so our racing fit in very well....it was more than 30 years of good relationship and the astonishing part is that the price remained the same to CTV—ZERO!" Racing enthusiasm increased in Canada especially when Player's Ltd. was able to manage a date on the Formula One Grand Prix schedule. "That was in 1967 and another major event to celebrate Canada's Centennial and CTV was at Mosport for it. Soon we had the rights to all Grand Prix races around the world so that there was televised continuity."[30]

Esaw's belief that skating competitions would be attractive to Canadian television audiences stemmed in part from his experiences as a youth in North Battleford when he would sneak into the Empress Theatre to watch on film Norwegian skater Sonja Henie, a three-time

Olympic champion. As he remembered, she would "make some Holly-wood lothario fall all over himself while she did a wild two-turn spin that caused her skirt to rise up almost over her ankles. (There was a certain Victorian modesty in vogue throughout the world then, the long skirts being retained for such active pursuits as skating, tennis and even horseback riding)." Henie was a remarkable athlete whose lifetime earnings, according to the *Guiness Book of Records*, was an estimated $50 million. CTV's gaining access to ABC's *Wide World of Sports* in the early 1960s was timely in that interest in the World Figure Skating Championships and the Olympics was growing in Canada. From 1953 to 1960, the skating pairs of Norris Bowden and Francis Dafoe and Barbara Wagner and Bob Paul had captured silver and gold medals that could hardly go unnoticed.[31]

THE YEAR 1962 BROUGHT MAJOR CHANGES in Canadian televised sports. An important development took place when an arrangement was made with ABC to carry *Wide World of Sports* in time for the program to broadcast outstanding performances by several Canadian skaters in Prague, Czechoslovakia at the world figure skating championships. Otto and Maria Jelinek captured the gold in world pairs. For Esaw, it was a highlight of his 40-odd years of sports broadcasting: "They [Jelineks] set the tone for Canada. Wendy Griner followed with the silver medal. Virginia Thompson and [William] McLachlan were draped with the bronze for dance but the great moment was yet to come."[32]

Esaw's words recalled the moment when Canada's Donald Jackson made an outstanding comeback: "Baby-faced Donald Jackson went into the men's final trailing the hometown favorite Karol Divin by 47 points. The lead, especially under the old rules, appeared insurmountable but the slim and elegant Jackson came on the ice and stood the figure skating world on its ear." It was, as Esaw explained, a situation of high drama: "Pumped up by the music of Carmen he flew from jump to jump magnificently, landed the world's first triple lutz and had the crowd in the palm of his hands by the time his routine finished. The judges admitted the perfection and inspiration of it all and the result was seven perfect sixes. He was world champion. What a comeback! What history!" Throughout the 1960s other noted names were made famous through televised coverage including skaters Don MacPherson, Petra Burka, the pairs team of Debbi Wilkes and Guy Revell and Karen Magnussen.[33]

After Esaw had arranged the contract with Roone Arledge at ABC to acquire *Wide World of Sports,* the backstage deal-making seemed to accelerate. Skating became more popular and CTV increased its coverage. Esaw recalled: "The more television we delivered, the more saleable it became. As a result, more time was devoted to the sport as CTV produced specials rather than inserts for *Wide World of Sports.* And inevitably as the economics of the figure skating and television escalated, there was an increase in wheeling and dealing behind the scenes." Dick Button, a five-time United States world champion, became an influential broker in the negotiations over the rights to figure skating telecasts in North America. In Esaw's words, "He'd buy the North American rights to skating and then sell the Canadian rights to me for CTV. He had such a strong position and influence with the governing International Skating Union that I was prepared to go along with it and CTV was guaranteed world rights."[34]

Not only did Button have impact on the structure of the negotiations for broadcast rights but also the former U.S. world champion influenced Esaw's broadcasting style that stressed partisanship. Esaw was an avowed "homer" when he attended international skating events, a practice that was based partly on the American penchant for extolling the virtues of U.S. skating performers. With Esaw in the broadcast booth, CTV was nearly a participant rather than just an observer in the coverage of sports. He explained his approach in these words: "After all, politics—both external and internal—raged in the sport so you fight the system and try to help your own. For instance, following a good performance by a Canadian skater, I'd immediately stand up with my headset and microphone and applaud as loudly as possible. When one person stands in a seated crowd, others follow automatically and one person can usually work up a standing ovation. The hope was that the judges might be impressed and possibly bump up their marks a fraction, maybe enough to move a Canadian skater up a notch or two."[35]

American models had considerable influence on the CTV sportscaster. Esaw had watched Dick Button's behaviour as a sports interviewer. In 1971, at the World Championships in Lyon, France, Button skillfully improvised during coverage on the ABC network after the American hopeful, Janet Lynn, finished out of the medals. Austria's Trixi Schuba had won the gold and Canada's Karen Magnussen had captured

Johnny Esaw and Canada's Karen Magnussen in Bratislava, Czechoslovakia in 1973. Magnussen won the gold medal in the Ladies' Singles Competition in the World Figure Skating Championships. Photograph courtesy of Johnny Esaw.

the bronze with Lynn finishing fourth. When the skaters were on the podium, ABC, which employed unilateral cameras that allowed "cutaways" from the world feed, broadcast an interview between Button and Lynn. Button had controlled the American skater's media environment and orchestrated nearly a pseudo-event. While the world watched the medal ceremonies, American audiences saw only the Lynn interview with the skater stealing the spotlight.[36]

Whatever CTV's accomplishments in broadcasting international skating competitions, John Bassett, owner of the network flagship station, was hardly impressed with the extent of programming devoted to skating that the network aired. As Esaw explained to Curtis Stock in a *TV Times* retrospective look at figure skating, Bassett laughed at the idea of broadcasting skating events: "He thought it was a joke. I remember he kept calling it that 'fancy' skating. We still laugh at that. Bassett was a football and hockey man. They were the only things that mattered. Nobody got hit in skating, so Bassett was never too impressed. But he was impressed by the ratings and the revenue." Events such as Skate Canada and other skating championships on CTV have attracted 1.4 million viewers for each program.[37]

Throughout the 1960s, CTV remained highly influenced by U.S. models and the behaviour of American audiences towards sports broadcasting. The *Wide World of Sports* was intended "to provide advertisers with week-after-week impact in Canada's major markets." CTV blended Canadian sporting events with American and International competitions. The *Wide World of Sports* seen on CTV during the 1964–65 season featured 34 sports specials pre-released by the ABC network; ten top Canadian sporting events which were live or on videotape and eight international sporting events either on tape or film. CTV underlined the structure of the sports package for its member stations which had to meet the Canadian content quotas: "Self-Balancing Canadian Content." The program was expected to deliver "the younger, larger, higher-income families in CTV's ten vital marketing areas."[38]

Clearly the network recognized that, if the American model could be adapted to Canada successfully, sports programming would make CTV highly profitable as a business. The participation rate schedule for sponsors or network "rate card," as it was described, for 1965–66 showed that a sponsor had to pay $1,050 for a 60-second spot announcement during 26 consecutive weeks of CTV's *Wide World of Sports*; $1,000 for 39 weeks and $950 for the full 52-week schedule. The prices included charges for broadcast time, distribution and origination of programming.[39]

To appeal to viewers, CTV could not help but stress sports coverage given the favorable reception that such programming had received in the United States. At an early stage, the private network began to challenge the CBC with its concentration on sports, a programming category that would become increasingly controversial. A serious debate arose as to whether the publicly owned CBC should be engaged in sports programming to the extent that it was. The issue became more acute in the late 1980s and early 1990s as the CBC faced financial cutbacks and private broadcasters showed that they could provide sports coverage that would rival that of the public broadcaster.

CTV had informed its stations and advertisers prior to the 1964–65 season, "The hottest item in U.S. network programming today is SPORTS!" As a new private TV network, CTV intended to copy the American format and buttressed its case with the backing of American TV executives: "ABC Sports Program's Vice President Chet Simmons says the public is insatiable in its demand for sports and adds that his biggest problem is finding time to carry it all. NBC sports Vice President Carl Lindeman predicts it won't be too long before major sports make a move to invade prime time hours."[40]

Nothing persuades network affiliated stations to adopt specific programming formats more than raw audience numbers, the lifeblood of the private broadcaster. Not surprisingly, CTV was at its persuasive best when the network attempted to have its Canadian affiliates accept the American sports product: "Take a look at the record of ABC's *Wide World of Sports*: Nielsen's U-S NTI report for January, 1964 shows ABC's *Wide World of Sports* with a 19.9 rating compared with an 11.1 rating for NBC's *Bing Crosby Golf Tournament* and 9.0 for the CBS *Golf Classic* the same Saturday afternoon." CTV explained to member stations: "Resultant audience shares were 28.4% for ABC's *Wide World of Sports*, 19.6% for NBC and 17.7% for CBS."[41]

Naturally a new Canadian network could not ignore the sport of hockey as a vehicle to attract advertisers. Canadians had grown accustomed to Foster Hewitt, and his son Bill, on Saturday night over CBC television. Still CTV had begun to build ratings with its Wednesday night telecasts of National Hockey League games: "This broadcast season [1963–64], CTV's Wednesday night NHL Hockey attained a per game audience total of 1,014,000 homes according to Nielsen's November NTI report. And this same survey shows CTV's football with a per game audience total of 839,000 homes."[42]

CTV emphasized the universal appeal of sports programming, as well as its indigenous quality. *Wide World of Sports* would allow advertisers

to construct "a network television campaign utilizing the lively, imaginative action-packed programming which makes *Wide World of Sports*
unique in Canadian television." Advertisers could also "reach millions
of prime prospects among the younger, growing, higher-income homes
in CTV's ten major markets…with maximum impact." In addition sponsors could "expand the impact of network television by conducting
aggressive and exciting merchandising and promotion campaigns
nationally, regionally or locally."[43]

The 1964–65 season of *Wide World of Sports* on CTV showed the
programming mix that occurred when Canadian material was included
with the American product. Viewers had a range of sports events from
which to choose including water skiing, softball, horse shows, wrestling,
car racing, golf, soccer and tennis. The Canadian component included
the International Jumping and Horse Show Royal Winter Fair and Canadian Intercollegiate Football Championships in November, 1964; the
Tournament of Champions curling event and the track and field Maple
Leaf-Telegram Indoor Games in January, 1965; the following month in
skiing, the Canadian Beehive Championship in Banff, Alberta; later in
June car racing, the Player's "200" at Mosport, Ontario; and in September from Vancouver, a tennis event, the Canadian Davis Cup Trials.[44]

SPORTS FANS LOVE to argue. The simple concept was behind the origination of the CTV program that distinguished the private network's
approach to sports broadcasting and drew a stark comparison with the
more quiescent fare seen on the public broadcaster. In 1962, Esaw introduced the colorful and provocative *Sports Hot Seat* on CFTO. The popular program was to last for eight seasons. A sports broadcast that featured an opinionated panel of questioners and a strong guest from the
sporting world to respond to a controversial, topical issue could not help
but stimulate interest among viewers. Esaw's instincts proved to be accurate given the interest the program generated: "I thought the best thing
about sport is the sports fans in argument. So I sort of boiled this down
to getting, as it turned out, a key figure in sport and then a panel of three
guys, writers or broadcasters or whoever and I was the host of it."[45]

In the early 1960s, Canada was having great difficulty in international hockey. The first guest on the *Sports Hot Seat* was Jack Roxbor-
ough, President of the Canadian Amateur Hockey Association (CAHA),

Swimming great Johnny Weissmuller, who never lost a race in competition, appears on the *Sports Hot Seat.*

The great Yankee slugger Mickey Mantle is questioned on the *Sports Hot Seat.*

Tennis star Arthur Ashe is seen on the *Sports Hot Seat.*

Jack Nicklaus, Johnny Esaw and Arnold Palmer on the 17th Fairway
at the Canadian Open Golf Championship in Mississauga in 1965.

Johnny Esaw and the
great boxer Joe Louis.

Photographs courtesy
of Johnny Esaw.

and the question to be addressed was the following: "Should Canada get out of World Hockey?" Esaw remembered the format and the role played by Milt Dunnell, a *Toronto Star* columnist: "As it turned out...the quietest, the most intelligent, the most courteous person in the world turned out to be the star of that show, because once he got on the show, he became the opposite. And that was Milt Dunnell. There wasn't a thing Milt didn't know about sport. He had a photographic memory, it was incredible. Milt would just challenge these people and he was always right."[46]

Given the popularity of the *Sports Hot Seat*, sponsors soon saw the marketing advantage to be gained from the program. As Esaw explained, "We went ahead with it with confidence but even those of us involved were a little stunned at the response. Suddenly I had the hottest sports show in Canada and there was no shortage of interested sponsors. Wally Beaupre, President of Dow Brewery in Toronto, was the first to appreciate the show's potential and his company supported the show for many years." The timing of the program was an important factor, because it was launched in the early 1960s when a new style of boxer appeared who boasted that he could "float like a butterfly, sting like a bee." Esaw wrote that Cassius Clay who became Muhammed Ali in 1964, when he announced he had embraced the Muslim faith changed his name because he considered Clay to be the name of a white man.[47]

Clay was a mainstay of the *Sports Hot Seat*. The boxer received $1500 for his first appearance on the program and turned out to be a sensation. Esaw who recognized that such a sports personality could build ratings went back to him again; this time Clay, as he was then known, wanted the $1500 in advance. Esaw refused and told him he would have to do the show first. Then the money would be turned over. Clay could be unpredictable. Esaw remembered the boxer walking off the set during the taping of the program: "Jack Koffman, of the *Ottawa Citizen*, was on the panel for that show and Jack could be pretty out-spoken. I always encouraged the panel to strike nerves and Jack succeeded so admirably that an enraged Clay stomped off the set. Jack had stared directly at Clay and sneered that the fighter hadn't proved anything yet and wouldn't be able to knock out a sick welter-weight."[48]

As moderator, Esaw had to improvise: "We immediately went to commercial and I went chasing after Clay/Ali. I reminded him that I still had his bundle of money in my pocket and there it would stay if he didn't come back to the set and finish the show." Esaw finally persuaded the boxer to return: "It's wonderful the way money could dissipate Clay's anger. He came back and put on another wonderful show biz performance for us." Throughout the eight seasons that the *Sports Hot Seat* was on CTV when many well-known sports personalities were seen on the show, two notable guests were never able to appear. Golfer Jack Nicklaus always had too many conflicts in his schedule and Vince Lombardi, coach of the Green Bay Packers of the National Football League, became ill with cancer and could not make an appearance.[49]

TWO FACTORS THAT enabled Esaw to build and develop CTV into a major sports network were the entry he enjoyed to corporate offices and the CBC's somewhat tentative approach to sports broadcasting that was related to its bureaucratic culture. Esaw's presence as an on-air sports broadcaster served him well when he sought access to the heads of companies as possible sponsors as in the case of Wally Beaupre and Dow Brewery: "I had the advantage of being on the air and I could go through doors that other people couldn't get to. A salesman from the sales department, he would have to go through the routine, secretaries and appointments and so on, where I'd pick up the phone and I'd say 'Wally I've go something to talk to you about....'"[50]

A similar advantage Esaw enjoyed with two other sponsors, Carling O'Keefe and Labatt breweries: "John Labatt was a very good friend of mine, because he ran the Labatts in Winnipeg when I was there. They had breweries all across the west. Well John was coming up the ladder in the Labatt family. So he was running the Winnipeg plant and we got together. Winnipeg is a great party town....He then moved back to London and in the Toronto area so I got with him in football and away we went for years. Those connections made a great, great difference."[51]

Still the CBC in the 1960s and into the 1970s had left Esaw and CTV with a broad field of action. "They were like the Italian government," he remembered. "They were changing, every six months or every year they had a new director of sports. And they would just be getting their feet wet and he's moved along and somebody else would come in...." In the meantime, a wide gap was left for an aggressive promoter such as Esaw: "So the CBC was reluctantly getting involved in sport, but they were leaving it open....I went into all these areas, the figure skating people and hockey."[52]

Again in 1962, CFTO was able to capitalize by televising hockey
games in the Junior Ontario Hockey Association league, the only hockey
that was available for the private station in Toronto to telecast. For
many years, games in the National Hockey League were seen only on the
CBC on *Hockey Night in Canada*. Coincidentally, Bobby Orr, a young
defenceman from Parry Sound, Ontario arrived in the junior league with
the Oshawa Generals. Orr was a special kind of defenceman, a remarkable talent and was to become a leader of future Boston Bruins Stanley
Cup teams. He changed the role of the defenceman in much the same
way that Paul Coffey was to emulate later with the Edmonton Oilers.
The hockey that CFTO could telecast was the Sunday afternoon dou-
bleheader at Maple Leaf Gardens. Esaw recalled John Bassett's role in
the arrangement of the telecasts with Stafford Smythe: "John Bassett, of
course, was the chairman of the Gardens. So John actually made the deal
and I went down and finalized it. And so we started doing Sunday afternoon junior hockey and that was when they were getting about 2,000 a
game. We wound up filling that place Sundays with 15,000 people after
a period of three or four years." CFTO interviewed Orr every Sunday
during the telecasts, because "we arranged that the Gardens would have
the Oshawa Generals in the game that was to be televised."[53]

In the year 1967, Canada's centennial, it could be argued that CTV
sports came of age in a manner reminiscent of the network's news division when it scored a major triumph in its telecast of the Progressive
Conservative leadership convention held at Maple Leaf Gardens that
same year. The Centennial hockey tournament in Winnipeg was perhaps
the first major event covered by the network that showed the extent to
which CTV sports was in the ascendant. Canadians could not help but
notice the viewing alternative to the CBC available to them. The Centennial Tournament in 1967 seem to foreshadow the dominant role that
CTV was to play in 1988 as domestic and host broadcaster at the 1988
Winter Olympic Games in Calgary.

Esaw observed that the CTV's style of broadcasting had impact, as
he recalled the 1967 event which had a format involving six international teams: "While CTV had been on the air as a Network for years
at that point [since 1961], the Centennial Tournament was the first event
that really caused Canadians to sit up and play closer...[attention] to the
fine sports coverage we had been generating. It was a form of force feeding because all Canada wanted to watch this tournament." Esaw saw
the Centennial Tournament as a watershed event: "In doing so, many

Canadians were getting their first serious exposure to our network and they liked what they saw—not just the hockey, but on-air people, production values, style and all the other elements that win viewers." Canada was victorious in the tournament, a sort of prelude to the historic encounter between Canada and Russia in 1972. The response of fans and viewers "was exceptional."[54]

Canada has numerous talented female athletes that CTV sports brought to public attention perhaps none more than skier Nancy Greene Raine who was named Canada's female athlete of the 20th century by editors and broadcasters of the Canadian Press and Broadcast News. CTV Sports captured one of her greatest moments in 1968 when she defended successfully her World Cup Title won the previous year. At Rossland, British Columbia, Greene who in the same year won gold and silver medals at the Winter Olympics in Grenoble, France ended her competitive career in triumphant fashion.

Johnny Esaw remembered "The Tiger," as she was known, and how CTV was involved in broadcasting her World Cup defence: "For once, she had a small edge beyond her own determination and talent. The final and deciding race would be on home turf, Red Mountain in Rossland, B.C. This, of course, was a 'must' for CTV Sports and we would do anything to get the rights to the race. We succeeded. There were certain logistics involved and to have the facilities we needed we immediately hired CFCN-TV's Calgary mobile unit and dispatched it to Rossland. CTV was set to deliver Nancy's great moment to all of Canada." Greene had even persuaded the outstanding skier from France, Jean-Claude Killy, to come to British Columbia to watch the final race of her sensational career. "Killy confided to me later," wrote Esaw, "that he initially had no plans or intention of going to Red Mountain but had a complete change of heart when Nancy telephoned and turned on a flood [of] tears. Killy being there was appropriate too, because CTV had arranged to have Austrian Toni Sailer—the first triple gold medal skier in Olympic history (Cortina, 1956)—to be there as well." After defending her World Cup crown, Greene retired at the age of 24. She married her coach Al Raine. Greene had continued the tradition of noted female Canadian skiers who included Lucille Wheeler and Anne Heggtveit, with whom Greene had roomed at the Squaw Valley, California Winter Olympics.[55]

Early sports broadcasting on radio and television in Canada in the private sector has had a range of personalities from the free wheeling and down home play-by-play style of "Cactus" Jack Wells to the erudite

analysis of Tom Foley whose "Sports at Six" Commentary on radio station CFRA, Ottawa enlightened fans through his writing, interpretation
and humour. CFTO, Toronto over the years employed several sports-
casters who became well-known network commentators and were
involved periodically in memorable happenings. The sports department
headed by Johnny Esaw included Tim Ryan, who went on to CBS sports
in the United States, and Brian McFarlane renown for his *Hockey Night
in Canada* appearances and numerous books on hockey. The names of
Tom McKee, Pat Marsden, Bernie Pascal and Fergie Oliver were also
familiar to viewers.

Two notable incidents that occurred at CFTO served to underline
how curious backstage developments can alter the careers of talented
individuals. In McKee's case, the night of 27 October 1967 at CFTO
brought a sudden change. The date was significant, because McKee was
to meet his wife for dinner to celebrate their wedding anniversary
according to Esaw. McKee was in a rush to leave the station after finishing his sportscast. A woman caller kept him on the phone following
his sportscast inquiring about an item that he had broadcast. In the heat
of the moment and anxious to move on, the frustrated McKee told the
woman impolitely, "go blow your nose." Unfortunately for McKee, the
woman caller knew John Bassett who fired McKee almost on the spot
before Esaw could plead his case.[56]

When he learned what had happened, Esaw went to see Bassett who
refused to change his mind. Perhaps aware of Bassett's tendency to be
impetuous, Ted Delaney, the station's General Manager, suggested to
Esaw he should persist with Bassett: "Ted Delaney called me and said I
should give it one more shot. I did and Mr. Bassett relented. I called Tom
and told him what I had achieved and he said he appreciated the effort
but he had taken a job with the CBC. He stayed there until he joined TV
Labatt to promote Blue Jays' baseball, working under former CBC colleague John Hudson."[57]

Aside from his firing, according to Esaw, the most memorable event
for McKee was when he covered the arrival of the Voyageurs who had
canoed from the Northwest Territories to Expo '67 in Montreal for the
official opening of the Centennial year extravaganza. "We had the rights
to Expo," Esaw explained, "and this was to be a big moment....What
was memorable to Tom is that he had a canoe expert sitting on one side
to provide expertise and an Expo official on the other, to make sure
everything said on air was positive and to provide the Expo expertise.

The main problem was that the canoe expert and the Expo official hated one another and Tom was almost a one-man show. While Tom was in the midst of this tension, Lloyd Robertson—then with the CBC—was nearby, merrily and smoothly describing the arrival."[58]

Pat Marsden heard on The Fan 590 radio in Toronto was another colourful personality whose departure from CFTO was under circumstances that the most hot tempered Irishman could hardly have anticipated. Marsden arrived in 1966 at CFTO to replace Tim Ryan who had moved to California to be the play-by-play man for the Oakland Seals, a new team in the expanded National Hockey League. Marsden's radio career had taken him to three Ontario communities: Blind River, Niagara Falls and Ottawa. When he arrived in Blind River, Marsden was taken aback. He told sportswriter Earl McRae: "The day I drove into the town the bank manager had been shot in a robbery and there he is lying in the middle of the dirt street, dead as a door nail."[59] At Ottawa radio station CKOY, Marsden became known for his signature sign-off that had a charming ambiguity: "If you win say little, if you lose say less." He took over the television play-by-play from Esaw after the Grey Cup football classic in 1972 and with commentator Mike Wadsworth, a Notre Dame graduate, broadcast football for nine seasons on CTV before the CBC took over the broadcasting rights.[60]

Marsden was dismissed from CFTO after he tried to punch out Ted Stuebing, CFTO's Vice-President of News and Public Affairs. A human error forced Marsden to take an electronic feed from Global television on the hockey highlights of a game involving the Toronto Maple Leafs. After the development, he was beside himself and wrote Stuebing complaining about "incompetents" and saying that he was most grateful for Global's contribution. In response, Stuebing suggested that Marsden go work for Global. The Stuebing remark was the catalyst that ignited Marsden's Irish temper and he exploded. As he explained to McRae: "I chased him [Stuebing] into his office and heaved him over his desk. He landed on his head, and I jumped on top of him, swinging. It was broken up, I didn't hear anything until the next day when the guards at the gate said they couldn't let me in, I'd been fired."[61]

CTV SPORTS AND the vibrant personalities involved had provided viewers with a new style of fare in a manner reminiscent of the other entertainment programming that the network had offered in its schedule.

From *Telepoll* to *Laugh-In* to the *Sports Hot Seat*, the private network offered a popular fare that touched the sensitivities of Canadians throughout the 1960s. From the early 1960s to the beginning of the 1970s, television came of age as a truly visual medium.

During the period, 1962–1972, politicians, advertising agencies, sponsors and the broadcast regulator came to recognize that the television landscape had changed forever from its beginnings in 1952. Politicians had to adjust their political rhetoric to meet the requirements of the medium; advertisers became more willing to adopt television to sell consumer products in a growing economy that would enhance Canadian affluence; and while Canadian programming was mandatory, viewers were unwilling to be denied access to the most popular fare available in North America, especially American programming. Through the 1960s, the noble high culture that the Massey Commission had advocated in 1951 was surpassed largely by a dominant mass culture which television as an entertainment medium nurtured and to which CTV specifically catered as an alternative, general interest service.

With reference to the Massey Commission and its description of American influences as "alien," Professor Frank Underhill wrote in 1951, the year of the report's release and 40-odd years before the Canada-United States Free Trade Agreement: "These so-called 'alien' American influences are not alien at all; they are just the natural forces that operate in the conditions of twentieth century civilization."[62] Spencer Caldwell would have agreed. Clearly the CTV network was at one with mid 20th century Canada when the structure of the broadcasting system had undergone a major transformation. The CBC had suffered a wrenching experience when its public affairs show *This Hour Has Seven Days* was taken off the air. The private television sector was able to fill a television void. The CBC's noble cultural mandate appeared to be compromised by Canadians' predilection for popular fare.

Perhaps nowhere was the difference between CBC and CTV more apparent than in their approach to entertainment programming especially sports broadcasting. CTV's adventuresome style allowed for the introduction of shows, such as *Laugh-In* which CBC acquired later. The private network's sports programming was clearly more opinionated, close up and personal, the way Johnny Esaw had envisaged it. "So with Bobby Orr and Muhammed Ali and the figure skating, the '60s, it was the greatest decade in history," said Esaw, "and I had it all. You know I had it all....I was doing the football, I was doing the skating, well anything else we were doing, I was doing it. I was the front man. I was self-ish I guess, but I felt I could do it and I did. And that then rebounded, because I could walk through any door and come back with sales."[63]

Still some of the best entertainment programming was yet to come. CTV was to enter the 1970s amidst a nationwide hoopla. The network won the broadcast rights to the memorable Canada-Russia hockey series when Paul Henderson's goal with the clock ticking gave Canadians a welcome shot of national adrenaline. Following the FLQ October crisis of 1970 and the election of a minority Trudeau government in 1972, Canadians finally had something they could rally around.

Murray Chercover, President of CTV, 1968–1990.
Photograph courtesy of CTV.

SIX

Canada AM, the Arrival of Lloyd and a Short-lived *CTV Reports*

1972–1979

To REMAIN A SUCCESSFUL Canadian network and operate as a viable business, CTV realized that its news and public affairs division could become a major growth area. The network moved from the infant age to at least adolescence in its coverage and analysis of news developments throughout Canada and the world. During the 1970s, CTV News began to show signs of becoming a profit centre for the network. President Murray Chercover had recognized the need for an expanded news operation. Still the immediate driving force behind the network's accomplishments in the growth period crystallized in two vibrant characters with considerable CBC experience as news correspondents: Tom Gould and Don Cameron.

Gould had joined CTV in the mid 1960s succeeding Ab Douglas as the network's parliamentary bureau chief and subsequently moved to the administrative level when Charles Templeton, the network's Director of News and Public Affairs, left in 1969. An aggressive reporter, Gould later held the position of Vice President of News. Cameron joined CTV in 1972 as a news executive after several years with the CBC and the NBC in New York. Both men were forceful personalities who pushed hard to expand the network news department throughout the 1970s and were prepared to do battle with affiliates to achieve their aims. CTV became more centralized in its news operation and the struggle between the network and its stations as it related to news gathering seemed less of an issue.

Tom Gould presented an interesting "Backgrounder" news analysis on the *CTV National News*. Photograph courtesy of CTV.

Harvey Kirck recalled Gould's style of demanding performance. "Tom was good....He'd go into [Murray] Chercover's office and pound the desk until he got what he wanted." Don Newman, a former *Globe and Mail* correspondent, who became a member of CTV's parliamentary bureau in the early 1970s, recalled Cameron's nickname which was "craze," short for crazy, "and in some ways that was a pretty good description." Newman who went on to CBC Newsworld saw Cameron mainly as a "programmer and a producer" who ended up being "a bit of an administrator which he was wasn't very good at and hated." Perhaps because of his experience in the United States with NBC, Cameron was determined to expand the network's international news coverage and the overall reach of CTV. "I think his attitude to budgets was more or less mine," said Newman, "maybe that's where I acquired it. Push them to the limit and if the shows are really good and the stories are really good, then in the end people will remember them rather than the fact that they went over budget."[1]

At the start of the 1970s, it is fair to say that CTV network news went "uptown" from its earlier lacklustre beginnings. In 1972, three developments took place. The network, which had been confined largely to the three cities of Toronto, Ottawa and Montreal in its news service, opened two news bureaus in Washington and Vancouver. The network also started an early morning news program, *Canada AM*, on 11 September 1972, a program which has had lasting impact. In addition, about the same time, CTV hired Michael Maclear, a familiar face to CBC viewers, to head up the first bureau in London, England. Maclear recalled his contact with Gould: "When I...departed from CBC over differences...I was the CBC London correspondent and I phoned up Tom Gould and I said 'look I am leaving CBC, do you need a London correspondent' and he just laughed and hung up. And a couple of hours later he called me back and said 'you're on'."[2]

As the news department's growth continued, Lloyd Robertson, the long established CBC television news anchor, joined CTV in 1976 in a move that was seen as a major coup for the private network and a sharp setback for the Corporation. Robertson was the quintessential trained announcer who was schooled in the niceties of CBC diction and demeanor. He joined Harvey Kirck whose appeal was more to the "overalls" set of viewers whom CTV had attracted with its more populist style of presentation. By the mid 1970s, CTV boasted the two most recognized network newscasters in Canada. The intent of CTV's marketing strategy in wooing Robertson was seemingly to entice more of the country's opinion leaders and cultural enthusiasts, earlier CBC viewers, to join CTV's "rent a movie crowd." The private network obviously hoped to expand its audience, build ratings and increase revenue.

The 1970s was not free of a notable failure for CTV. *CTV Reports*, a public affairs show perhaps ahead of its time, had a short-lived experience. The show, which included a large cast of noted journalists, lasted a matter of weeks at the start of the 1977–78 season. The network gambled on a new magazine style format and lost. Still the growth of the news service culminated in a major breakthrough in 1979 when CTV became the first broadcaster in North America to establish a bureau in Beijing, China, six years after Prime Minister Pierre Trudeau's historic mission there in the fall of 1973.[3]

CLEARLY THE PROGRAM *Canada AM*, the country's longest-running early morning news and information program, brought a new dimension to CTV News and Public Affairs. It was a daring move in the early 1970s for the network, because such morning shows had virtually no track record on which they could be judged. CTV had originated an early morning program called *Bright and Early* back in the Spence Caldwell era and *Canada AM* was really a relaunch of the earlier program. The first morning program was considered to be premature for the network and its affiliates. The idea to introduce *Canada AM* originated with the network's executive committee. Ray Peters, who represented British Columbia Television Broadcasting System Limited (BCTV), was responsible for raising the prospect of an early morning show. Murray Chercover, the CTV President, told the Canadian Radio-television Commission in November, 1972: "One of the executives of the executive committee, Mr. Peters, said, 'What about reactivating the morning show idea which would be useful to all of us and to the country,' and the rest of the executive committee supported that view, and we were directed to proceed to immediately reactivate the project."[4]

Peters lobbied the network to get the morning news program. Earlier in his career, he had spent time in New York and was an avid watcher of the *Today Show* on NBC when Dave Garroway was the host. "I said to myself one day," Peters recalled, "God damn it, why is all of Canada watching NBC New York in the morning? Why can't we create our own morning show on CTV? Why don't we develop a morning show which can compete with radio and everything else?" Peters remembered that his conversations with Chercover went on for a year or so. John Bassett too had to be brought on side. "I finally convinced John," said Peters, "that it was a good idea only if the production was done in his studio which it still is. It was the only way he liked the idea. And we gradually developed *Canada AM*."[5]

The CRTC was curious about how the lead-up costs to introduce *Canada AM* were financed. "Where did the loot come for this?" asked Commissioner Harry Boyle. The network had proposed a "permanent rotating program development fund" of $50,000 to develop new program ideas. In the case of *Canada AM*, startup costs of $42,000 had come out of the fund prior to the airing of the morning program. The only model available to judge whether such a venture could be successful was the NBC *Today Show* in the United States. From an advertising standpoint, the NBC program was not a financial success for a period of four years, but by 1972 it was one of the network's major profit centres. Still Chercover failed to see how *Canada AM* could ever be a financial bonanza for CTV: "I would think that the program would subsequently generate substantial revenue and be more self-supporting, but unlike the United States…it will be a good advertising vehicle and it will contribute funds toward production, but it will never be a profit centre. We just don't have that kind of a market."[6]

When *Canada AM* went on the air in September, 1972, the first hosts were skilfully chosen and underlined the extent to which CTV has always tried to leverage popular personalities to the fullest. The early morning pair of Carole Taylor and Percy Saltzman could appeal to a wide audience. Taylor, a former Miss Toronto, was an attractive host with a quietly forceful and gracious manner. She was a protégé of the Bassetts. John F. Bassett, son of *The Telegram* publisher, urged Taylor to become involved in both the newspaper and CFTO television when she was in high school. A new newspaper section entitled "After Four" which appealed to a youthful readership was developed; later Taylor joined Bassett on a program with the same name on CFTO. *After Four* was also seen for a brief time on the CTV network. Saltzman was a well recognized personality by the time he was introduced to viewers of the private network. A regular on the early CBC-TV show *Tabloid*, he was probably most memorable for his signature sign off after his "weather-man" reports. Saltzman would take the viewer through the day's weather in a clear, concise manner and at the end of his report pro-nounce, "and that's the weather," as he simultaneously tossed the chalk he had used on the map of Canada into the air, generally managing to catch it. Taylor and Saltsman were able to appeal to a range of viewers from the then young baby boomers to various segments of the middle class.

Taylor remembered Don Cameron's invitation to host the program and how she underwent a kind of baptism of fire at CTV. "It was quite unexpected, I thought I was just going to go in and sit down with Don Cameron and he'd talk to me casually. But he was very organized and there were at least half a dozen people around a table and me sitting at the end of the board room table and they just started saying, 'How many troops...in Vietnam? What's the prime minister's policy on this?' [They] just started throwing all these political questions, I guess to see where my knowledge base was." Obviously those in the CTV board room saw Taylor as something more than just another pretty face. She admitted to being captivated by the rapid fire questioning from the male dominated boardroom: "I thought that was great and so when they asked me to do it I said 'yes' which was a bit nuts, because I had to get up at 3:30 in the morning for *Canada AM*." Then in her first of two marriages, Taylor also had a new baby: "So I was up at two o'clock for the feeding, at 3:30

for the show, and it was pretty hard to do but a...really great show."
Taylor was an avowed fan of Cameron: "He was tough but good to
work with, because he would listen and you could go back and forth
and argue your case and sometimes win and sometimes not. Tom Gould
was tougher and more remote and I don't think I ever won any arguments with Tom Gould."[7]

Female journalists began to make major inroads in network broadcasting during the early 1970s in Canada. Besides Taylor, the names of
Helen Hutchinson, Gayle Scott, Pamela Wallin, Jan Tennant, Barbara
Frum and Adrienne Clarkson became familiar to many Canadians. Still
in her case, Taylor recalled having to struggle to transcend the male view
that female journalists should be confined to stories directly related to
women. To be a woman in media could be a handicap as well as an
advantage. Taylor often struggled to avoid covering stories related to
cooking and fashion: To be a woman "was a positive in that I believe a
lot of networks were beginning to feel that they should have more
women on so that was an advantage that I was coming along. The negative was that they still really believed that women, even...on *Canada
AM*, you would do the soft stuff and the guy would do the political.
There was still an underlying sense that a woman does women's issues."
Taylor got "a lot of support from Don Cameron in fighting that and in
fact I would say I was quite comfortable with what they had me doing
on the show and also at W5. But it was behind the scenes a constant
struggle...."[8]

When it came to salary, it was no contest. Men were undeniably front
and centre. Taylor was flabbergasted when she learned what her cohost
Saltzman made each year, even though they were sharing the host duties.
When she joined *Canada AM*, Cameron offered her a salary of about
$20,000. "I'm not a negotiator," Taylor said, "I knew from nothing and
so I said, 'well as long as you believe that's fair, that's fine with me.'" As
the first season progressed, an incident arose that got Taylor's back up
and galvanized her into action: "One day Percy Saltzman was very angry
at the producers about something, I have no idea what it was. He went
running through the office and...said 'you can take your $40,000 and
stuff it.'"[9]

When she heard Saltzman's loud pronouncement of a salary double
her own, it was too much for the calm co-host who had to rise in the
early hours of morning to feed a baby before she faced the nation. Not
surprisingly, Taylor did some rapid calculation: "I'm sitting there going,

we were co-hosts, equal, right! I'm going $40,000. I'm making 20, you're making 40." Taylor decided it was time to confront Cameron in his office: "I said Don, 'you know, naive me thinking maybe Don didn't know this.' Don, you know you're not going to believe this." In the end, Cameron's responded: "Face it Carole! Life is not fair." On this score, Taylor found that she was up against the media environment of the 1970s: "And that was it. Didn't change my salary, didn't adjust it, nothing. That's just the way it is kid. It would never happen these days. But that's how women got started, you know. That's how it was at the beginning."[10]

Taylor moved to the program *W5* after only a brief stint on *Canada AM*. An interview conducted with Margaret Trudeau, wife of Prime Minister Pierre Trudeau, which aired on *W5* following the 1974 federal election was a memorable event for CTV which attracted much attention. Staged on the lawn in front of 24 Sussex Drive at the prime minister's residence, the interview showed two young women engaged in a thoughtful conversation about the important issue of the personal lives of public figures. The prime minister's wife had been a popular campaigner for the Liberal party in 1974, although after the election she admitted in her book, *Beyond Reason*, "I felt that I had been used."[11]

The circumstances surrounding the celebrity interview caused a backstage rift between Taylor and Cameron over a question of journalistic ethics. Shortly before the interview was to be conducted, Margaret Trudeau had called to cancel for emotional reasons and to inform Taylor that she would be entering a Montreal hospital. "At that point," Taylor recalled, "no one knew that, the press didn't know." Trudeau urged Taylor to maintain silence about her hospital visit and in return she promised her the first interview when she emerged from her stay in hospital. "I felt that this was not only the honorable thing to do," said Taylor, "but in fact from a journalism point of view, if I ended up with this major interview, it would be good for CTV."[12]

Cameron's instincts for pure journalism did not allow him to endorse Margaret Trudeau's notion of a *quid pro quo*. "Well Don Cameron knew that it was going to be done and knew that it had been cancelled," Taylor recalled. "And I wouldn't tell him why and so he was very unhappy, because he felt that my responsibility as a journalist, if I knew something, was to go to air with it. So we came down on different sides but I think in the end it worked out well." CTV viewers of *W5* were able to watch a candid exchange between two young women in different circumstances and accustomed to the public's scrutiny. "I certainly had empathy for her situation and I think it was at that point really a load on her, the responsibilities and the position," said Taylor. "I forgot whether it was Chinese food or pizza, but one of them, that she couldn't even order in…there were so many rules and barriers so it was very hard for her."[13]

There was another assignment in 1974, beyond several foreign stories, given to Taylor, who was emerging as a rising star at CTV, that Cameron later regretted. She was dispatched to Vancouver to interview Art Phillips, the city's mayor, on immigration issues. When his worship caught sight of the luminous former Miss Toronto as journalist-interviewer, for him any notion of western alienation was bid good-bye at least temporarily and, from her central Canada perspective, lotus-land took on new meaning. They married. When Taylor met her future husband, she was separated with a son Christopher. She had also received a phone call from CBS news anchor Walter Cronkite asking if she would be interested in moving to New York. She turned down the offer, but continued to host the 1975–76 season of W5 by commuting after her move to Vancouver.

When she transferred to the west coast, Taylor approached BCTV, the WIC Western International Communications owned network affiliate, hoping possibly to originate a network show from Vancouver. As a Bassett protégé, she maintained her initiative was not well received: "My coming out here I was seen as a Bassett girl. So they weren't very keen really to continue the relationship." She saw her reception as a reflection of CTV's internal struggles: "That was just the WIC versus Baton. And I was clearly with the Bassetts." Taylor later started a public affairs show, *Pacific Report*, for the CBC: "But it…was CBC who was far more interested and so I started working for CBC at that time."[14] Later the first female host of W5 ran as an independent in civic politics and sat on various corporate and community boards. Taylor was appointed chairwoman of the CBC in July 2001.

IT WAS THE ARRIVAL of Lloyd Robertson from the CBC that was undeniably the major development for CTV during the 1970s, especially after the private network's news organization had entered a major growth period that was to see it emerge as a rejuvenated challenger to the CBC. Robertson, a native of Stratford, Ontario, was the well-known news

Lloyd Robertson. Photograph courtesy of CTV.

anchor on *The National*, the flagship newscast seen at eleven o'clock on the CBC's English language television network. CTV lured Robertson in 1976 with a reported million dollar contract over ten years. He was to join Harvey Kirck, the long established CTV news anchor. The rationale behind the move was to gain for CTV the two most watched anchormen on network television in English Canada. The arrival of Robertson again reflected the attitude of Tom Gould that shrewd personnel choices could make up for a shortage of technical and financial resources at the private network. Kirck viewed the hiring of Robertson in positive terms: "If you can't lick'm join'm in reverse sort of thing. I think it was a good move. First of all, it got us a hell of a splash in the paper."[15]

The figure of one million dollars that Robertson was reportedly paid has to be clarified, because news reports at the time focused heavily on his annual salary. The metaphorical portrayal of Robertson's departure for CTV by CBC News Executive Knowlton Nash, as "a million dollar baby in a five and ten cent store," could not help but reinforce the media's preoccupation with a million dollars. Robertson placed Nash's humorous quip in the context of the negotiations at the time: "Well it was a great shot and it was funny, but it wasn't true. Because I had started at $85,000, it went up $5,000 a year until it got to $100,000 in year four. And then there was an option going my way for another five years, but the amount of money during that five-year period was not determined at that time." Robertson concluded that the million dollar figure was assumed: "Now it is obvious that you would probably start at $100,000 and go up from there at the end of five years, but the amount was not laid out. That was not determined. It was just that I think people made assumptions, because figures were being thrown around as a result of negotiations." Looking back on the negotiations, Kirck is inclined to agree with Robertson: "I don't think there was ever any talk about a million dollars....If there was, I never heard it."[16]

For his part, Kirck refused to take a back seat to Robertson when CTV hired the former CBC news anchor. "I know he increased my pay," said Kirck. "That's for sure. It was about 100 thousand dollars that Lloyd got and I got 113 [thousand]." Kirck argued for an increase based on his longevity in the anchor role at the private network from 1963 to 1976: "I said, I want the same thing as Lloyd, but I want a thousand dollars for every year I've been here." Laughingly Kirck remembered, "So I got 113, I had been 13 years there alone. I don't know whether you should print that or not, I don't even know whether Lloyd knows that!

Just a little recognition, that's all!" As for Nash's "million dollar baby" comment, Kirck opined, "I think he was sorry because it wasn't him."[17]

Robertson insisted that he wanted Kirck to have the same amount of money as himself and made his co-anchor's salary a condition of his joining the private network. "What I knew when they talked to me about going over was that this would only work if Harvey were on side," said Robertson, "and if Harvey got the same amount of money that I got. I knew first of all...he had his following, if he were bumped that was not going to look well on me and also I honestly thought that I liked Harvey, I knew him, I didn't want to do it to him and I told them, if this is bumping Harvey Kirck, forget it! I won't be part of it." From what Robertson knew at the time, Kirck's salary was to be similar to his $85,000 starting salary with a $5,000 increase over a five-year period. "As far as I know, Harvey's was exactly the same."[18] Based on Kirck's reading of his negotiations, he could argue that his salary was higher than Robertson's.

While the joining of the two noted anchormen looked smooth and friendly, such was not the case. Certainly not from Kirck's standpoint despite Robertson's consideration of the long established CTV anchor. "I suppose if I am really honest there was some resentment there," said Kirck. "It didn't fit the CTV image, but then the CTV image I think at that time wasn't going anywhere anyway. And so this was complete change....I really couldn't get too upset, because I knew it was happening, knew what was coming on and I knew damn well that I was getting tired. And it gave me a chance to do some other things as well with Lloyd there. There was a continuity that we couldn't maintain otherwise."[19]

An obvious potential for a clash of egos existed when Robertson and Kirck were paired together, but no major upheaval seemed to occur. "We never had an argument," said Kirck. "We got along pretty well, surprisingly well. Once in awhile, we would get into a battle over who was going to do what. There would be something special coming along and who was going to do it? But I figure I wound up the best of it." In the negotiations, Robertson recalled, it was decided, "The only difference was that I was to do more of the specials than he was doing." Indeed Robertson's capacity to improvise during specials and big event programming was his forte. "He was stuck in the studio most of the time," said Kirck, "because he did most of the specials. He was better at the bullshit than I was, he was better at ad libbing, he could sit there and go on for hours. And I couldn't. I did a lot of humming and hawing. But I got a chance to go out and do some reporting on stories. And that got me out of the...studio, out of the country a lot of times. I liked that." The CTV broadcasts sponsored by Texaco that Kirck anchored on the Apollo space program in the United States, and aired through agreement with the NBC, had extended into the 1970s and were, in his words, "the best time in my career I'll tell you."[20]

"We had a lady named Mary Gorman," Kirck remembered. "She worked downtown with [Bob] Conroy. She was the "Gulf watcher." Gorman played an important backstage role in each broadcast. "Because NBC was sponsored by Gulf," said Kirck, "and we were sponsored by Texaco, we took an eight-second delay on everything. So when we were taking NBC, and they went to a commercial, she would yell and we'd switch it over to the eight-second delay and miss the introduction of Gulf and do our own [commercial] for Texaco." Kirck recalled that CTV went "gung ho on all of the Apollo program launches." He would visit the Johnson Space Centre in Houston before some broadcasts to familiarize himself with the latest developments. CTV's broadcast combined material from the National Aeronautics and Space Administration (NASA) and from NBC with in-studio models to explain the space program. "We got to the point where we didn't really use much of NBC anymore, we were originating all of our studio stuff ourselves."[21] This kind of big event news programming coupled with the hiring of Robertson gave CTV a news presence it did not possess earlier.

When Robertson agreed to join CTV, Tom Gould recalled that the news anchor urged the private network to hire Tim Kotcheff, a CBC executive producer, who joined CTV and eventually became Vice-President of News, Features and Information Programming. In an interview with *Broadcaster: Canada's Communications Magazine*, Gould explained: "I guess he (Robertson) felt that it was a bit of culture shock coming from the public to the private sector."[22] Kotcheff remained with CTV until 1992 and then returned to the CBC when the Corporation underwent yet another management realignment.[23] With Gould, Cameron, Robertson and Kotcheff, all former CBC employees and occupying prominent positions at CTV, the private network could not help but come under the influence of broadcasting practices that characterized the behaviour of the public broadcaster, its competitor.

The chief difference in the two networks was that CTV's financial resources for news gathering paled in comparison to the Corporation's funds that could be devoted to news and public affairs. Beyond the question of money, by the mid 1970s CTV still needed to build the kind of solid reputation that the CBC had acquired over the years. CBC news had continued to expand following the sound coverage its correspondents had provided on radio during World War Two. CTV News had begun only in the early 1960s.

Not surprisingly, Robertson's decision to join CTV created a wave of controversy; not only did the newscaster's lucrative contract draw attention but a great deal was made of the opposition Robertson had encountered from the Canadian Wire Service Guild and the question of his freedom to report the news as well as to read it. Television critic, Blaik Kirby, wrote in *The Globe and Mail*: "On several occasions at the CBC, he [Robertson] said yesterday, members of the Canadian Wire Service Guild, who gather the news, had walked out when Robertson, a member of a different union, took over a reporting function. CTV has no union for its news-gathering staff."[24]

Scott Young, a *Globe and Mail* columnist, criticized the CBC's Knowlton Nash for his reaction to Robertson's move: "I thought it uncharacteristically simple-minded of CBC's news chief Knowlton Nash to attribute Lloyd Robertson's move to CTV as being a matter of money....The interference of the Canadian Wire Service Guild with what Lloyd Robertson had a perfect right to think was his natural function—to go out and do some reporting from time to time—was intolerable and nobody with any guts would take it for long." Young noted that at a certain point, "money means little or nothing, but career fulfillment means more and more as a person gets older."[25]

Young drew a comparison between Canada and the United States and underlined the greater potential for Robertson, if the newscaster had been employed with an American network: "If he'd had a parallel career in the U.S. he would have had a choice of places to go; people waiting on his doorstep the instant the word was out that he might be available. In Canada there is only the one place, and CTV was just plain smart enough, and cared enough about his talent, to give him what he wanted." With characteristic humour, Young speculated on the impressionistic nature of television and how Robertson's elegance might complement the dissipated appearance of Harvey Kirck. Robertson could even be made to look like a Hamilton Tiger-Cats football lineman: "I'm pretty sure they'll take him as he is, too, in looks, but if not he can always go to a plastic surgeon and say, 'I want to look like Vince

Mazza.' That way, Harvey Kirck would wind up as just another pretty face...."[26]

Following the announcement of Robertson's intention to move to CTV, perhaps the most significant development in Canadian broadcasting during the 1970s, comics and radio talk-shows found the subject a new source of entertainment. Their attitude underlined the extent to which television news had become personality driven. *As It Happens*, the popular CBC radio network show hosted by Barbara Frum, held a contest to determine Robertson's successor as newscaster for *The National*. Blaik Kirby explained the range of characters who were seen as possibilities: "In a week of auditioning, *As It Happens* had considered everyone from Margaret Trudeau to the Cookie Monster, from Charlie Farquharson to Earl Cameron—who, after all, held the job longer than Robertson, for seven years ending in 1966." The winner of the contest was Robert Stanfield, one-time Conservative leader, who had struggled as a national party leader to survive his media treatment and adapt to the dictates of the televisual age. Stanfield's persona generally was not considered to be telegenic. Tom Gould maintained that he was "terrified" to have CTV face Stanfield on the nightly news. Stanfield reacted with a humourous quip: "So I've become a national personality now, eh?"[27]

Still Robertson's move to CTV, along with Kotcheff, was not greeted with universal applause at the private network. In time Robertson became the country's most trusted newscaster and by 1994 was the winner of two Gemini awards for being judged the best Canadian news anchor/interviewer.[28] Still the clash of cultures between the private and public broadcasters, and the heavy competition between both networks, prevented a totally smooth transition for Robertson and Kotcheff to CTV.

Don Newman, who coincidentally moved to CBC from CTV at the time Robertson and Kotcheff joined the private network, thought that CTV made "a terrible mistake" in its determination to woo Robertson. When Newman, the CTV Washington correspondent, later moved to Newsworld his reputation soared following his thorough reportage during the first ministers' debate over the Meech Lake Constitutional Accord. In retrospect, he maintained that CTV "panicked" after a dubious rating period in the spring of 1976: "In fact, I sort of took the view that I think a lot of people at CTV did [which] was 'wait a minute, we worked like hell for four or five years, we've caught up to these guys, one bad rating period and suddenly you go out and give the two best jobs in the company to two people from the outside...."[29]

The notoriety surrounding the arrival of Robertson and his high salary concealed the fact that CTV at the time lost Newman to CBC news and Eric Malling, a member of the CTV Ottawa bureau, to the *fifth estate*, an established CBC public affairs program. Ultimately Robertson and Kotcheff enhanced the credibility of the *CTV National News*. But in the process the departure of Newman and Malling, two journalists with undoubted capacities for growth in television news, offset to some extent the advantage to be gained by the acquisition of Robertson. The network's reporting capability was weakened. In addition, the hiring of Kotcheff for a senior administrative position had a demoralizing potential at CTV. Newman, who worked for both television networks, argued that in effect what CTV management accomplished in 1976 was to transpose "a lot of CBC ideas into the place without the money to execute them."[30]

INTERNAL TENSIONS THAT could affect programming still existed at the network even during a successful decade. While CTV News and Public Affairs gained new stature during the 1970s, the need for the network to have a proper access to its affiliates was crucial and the matter of pre-emption was often a source of tension. Typical of the tension that could arise between the network and its affiliates over the pre-emption of station time was an incident that occurred at CFTO television when United States President Richard Nixon announced he would resign the presidency on the night of 9 August 1974. A series of events that swirled around the political storm known as "Watergate" had forced the president's resignation. Don Newman, the CTV's Washington correspondent, had flown to Toronto to provide analysis of the much anticipated Nixon speech. Not surprisingly, CTV had decided to broadcast the Nixon address "live" given its international significance.

A CFTO executive entered the CTV newsroom which was located in the station and refused to carry the Nixon broadcast. He asked Newman, "what are you doing?" Newman replied that Nixon was about to resign and "we're carrying him live" on the network. The CFTO representative shot back promptly: "Not on our station, you're not!"

Regularly scheduled programming on CFTO, and on the other network affiliates, would have to be interrupted for the Nixon broadcast. After Newman telephoned Cameron to clarify the matter, CFTO carried the Nixon speech. In their operation of CTV News, both Cameron and Gould had a considerable measure of success in their attempts to stabilize the network's relationship with its affiliated stations. Newman recalled: "Gould and Cameron were network players and knew how to play the network but also they got enough money that the shows were good enough that they didn't look mickey mouse" and could satisfy the affiliates.[31]

During the mid 1970s, a greater level of stability developed between the CTV network and its affiliates. The new climate was prompted by regulatory demands for changes to an earlier affiliation agreement and initiatives undertaken by Gould and Cameron to argue the network's position. Two amendments to the affiliation agreement called for the number of hours of network service to be increased from a minimum of 48 hours to 60 hours. Secondly the network obtained the right "to pre-empt affiliate station sales time for programs of paramount national importance." At a public hearing before the CRTC in November, 1975 when CTV applied for a licence renewal, the latter amendment received considerable discussion. The hearing revealed that the pre-emption amendment "provided only for the right to pre-empt within that part of the overall station broadcast time which is classified as network service, i.e., the station service portion of the network service time." As a result the CRTC was of the view that "this amendment does not go far enough, in that it does not give the network the opportunity [on its affiliated stations] to pre-empt beyond network service time."[32] CTV now had more latitude to air programming, because it could pre-empt programming in the "station sales time" period in addition to "network sales time."

The CRTC was undoubtedly mindful of the potential conflict within CTV over its ownership structure and how network programming at all levels, news, sports and entertainment could be affected by recalcitrant affiliates. If the stations refused to carry network programming and would not allow for pre-emption of their own service, CTV could not function as a licensed network. When the Commission renewed the network's licence for three years until 1979, it put the CTV affiliate owners on notice. The network's interest was to take precedence over any individual affiliated station.

Thus the CRTC concluded: "The Commission recognizes that anomalies and conflicts can result from the fact that the CTV Network is owned by its affiliates. The Commission considers it important that, in instances where the interest of the network might conflict with the interest of an individual affiliate, the network interest should prevail. Because of the significance of the CTV Network as an integral part of the Canadian broadcasting system, the Commission considers it to be extremely important that the member stations fully participate in ensuring the achievement of the network's objectives."[33]

The CRTC believed that CTV had made "a very useful contribution in the field of children's programming with its Saturday morning hour, *Kidstuff*."[34] Still CTV's resources and emphasis remained focused heavily on news and sports programming throughout the 1970s. The wide appeal of sports programming was an effective vehicle to build audience and to enhance revenue.

As a noteworthy contribution to Canadian broadcasting, the Commission singled out the network's public affairs program *Maclear*. Hosted by Michael Maclear, a former CBC correspondent and thoughtful investigative journalist, the regulator characterized the program as "an example of a lean, efficient production, with the major proportion of the budget directed to production with a minimum of administrative and supervisory expense." When the CRTC renewed the network's licence in 1976, it noted critically that *Maclear* was the only "non-entertainment Canadian program which can be seen in the peak viewing hours between 8.00 P.M. and 10.00 P.M. The time block relies on U.S. sources for nearly 90% of its programming. All CTV regularly scheduled non-Canadian series presently listed on the 1976–77 schedule are American originations."[35] Clearly the Commission would be looking to CTV, as a dominant player in the country's broadcasting system, to play a more active role in the Canadian cultural experience. The network was perceived too readily as a carrier of U.S. programming attractive as such fare might be for many Canadians.

The program *Maclear* seen on Thursday nights in the CTV schedule was again an attempt by Gould in 1974 to bring personal journalism to the private network in the hopes of compensating for a lack of financial resources to match the CBC. Maclear's reputation, which was greatly enhanced when he reported from Hanoi at the time of North Vietnam leader Ho Chi Minh's death in September, 1969, was expected to carry the news program. Maclear remembered fondly "the creative freedom they gave us." With producer Don McQueen, the program had considerable scope. Maclear and his team could choose their own stories to be broadcast. "We could see something develop, we'd move almost instantly," said Maclear. "It was probably...the most creative days I had in television. So I have fond memories of CTV for that and especially of Tom Gould who took a flyer on me." The program *Maclear* often drew a million or a million and a half viewers.[36]

CTV REMAINED INTENT on exploiting news personalities to the fullest in the hopes of building audiences through well known journalists, even if the resources were not always available to match ambitious program formats. In the case of *CTV Reports* which lasted a matter of weeks, the program was top heavy with news personalities who seemed to transcend the show's format and its capacity to deliver the style of journalism that Maclear, as Executive Producer, had envisaged. The intent was to assemble a program that was to emphasize "live" programming with a corps of hard nosed commentators offering penetrating insights on the leading issues of the day. The personalities included Bruce Phillips who had served as CTV's Ottawa bureau chief; Peter Trueman, a news anchor familiar to viewers of Global Television in Ontario; writer Barbara Amiel; a respected Quebec journalist, Andre Payette; and author William Stevenson. Trueman who recalled "a horrendous traffic jam at the make-up room" wrote: "CTV, perhaps leery of the fact that my unlovely face was unknown nationally, apparently urged Maclear not to let his own face disappear from view." The net result was that no one commentator was able "to make any kind of an impression on the program or the viewers."[37]

The two senior producers of *CTV Reports* were Don McQueen, formerly with *W5*, and Andrew Cochrane, who had joined the network in its growth years. In about a seven-year period, Cochrane had held various positions with *W5*, *Canada AM*, *CTV Reports* and the *CTV National News* before departing for the CBC in 1979. Cochrane believed that *CTV Reports* failed because it came too early: "It was a fabulous idea that was before its time. I think it was demanding more largely from the technology than the technology of the day could deliver. In a lot of cases, I think some of the things that Michael had in his mind were really things that...[became] commonplace...on *The Journal*...the last half of *The National* on CBC. That sense of mixing some shows that had real in depth reports with the live head, bringing in somebody from another city to talk in the studio, all that kind of stuff."[38]

Controversy seemed to surround *CTV Reports* almost from the beginning even when it came to naming the program. Maclear wanted the title to be *The Reporters*. As he recalled, the network's President Murray Chercover "didn't like that at all." Maclear also envisaged the show's format to be reminiscent of *60 Minutes* seen on CBS in the United States and built around popular journalists who seemed to draw even more attention than the content of the stories they reported. With the noted commentators on *CTV Reports*, Maclear commented that much "audience interest could be built on these journalistic personalities. Never had a chance to prove that one."[39] In the end, the timing of the program in the network's schedule in the 1977 fall season could be seen as a crucial factor in its demise.

The network's plan was to have a half hour of the new public affairs program replace Maclear's earlier 30-minute Thursday night show and also take the place of the hour long *W5* seen on Sunday nights. Companion shows for one hour and a half a week would be grouped under the umbrella *CTV Reports*. Maclear was opposed to the timing: "CTV, I think, is to be commended for having the idea, but it simply didn't have the pockets." He argued strenuously against the timing "because Sunday night the world is shutdown, government doesn't operate, almost by definition there is no news, and if the attempt was to be up to the moment, then Sundays was a bad choice. But I couldn't budge them from that."[40]

While the public affairs program had a strong editorial team on camera, as Maclear remembered it was also "a very costly one." From the technological standpoint, CTV did not seem to be up to the challenge that airing such a program involved especially the concept of going "live" in the broadcasts. "Nobody had done it," said Maclear, "since the early days when you had to do it. And we were to discover...that going live for the sake of it is not necessarily a good idea. We wanted to be up to the moment, but it doesn't necessarily mean you got to be live, just sticking your cameras out on the street and saying here we are...." When the CBC introduced *The Journal* in the 1981–82 season, the network developed what is known as the "double-ender" to facilitate the network in going live. The Corporation explained to the CRTC the process involved in the technological innovation: "The host in Toronto conducts a telephone interview while the guest is shot by our on-site crew. Picture and sound of the guest are transmitted back to *The Journal* where both ends of the interview are edited for broadcast."[41] However *CTV Reports* did not enjoy the technical advantage of the "double-ender" in the late 1970s.

In the end, Maclear was called into Chercover's office when it was evident that *CTV Reports* could not hope to make it in the schedule. The ratings, which are ever important in private broadcasting, simply were not there. "I am not going to get into what he said, nor what I said," explained Maclear, "it was a little heated and I understood I was being removed. The problem was that I had a locked-in five-year contract. Thus the network didn't quite know what to do with me. They wanted me to sort of go on W5 and I declined that. So for a time they put me back in my old Thursday night slot...on a shoestring budget and the audience went back up to a million."[42]

Still Maclear held no animosity towards Chercover: "I don't know that Murray could have found any more money. I don't blame Murray. I think he has served that network tremendously well over the years. At that time it certainly coincided with, I think, the height of his boardroom battles which were pretty never-ending. And there were certainly times when one wanted to get to Murray to talk to him about issues and one couldn't. And I think more so than him, there were others behind the scenes, outside of the network immediately who, when they saw this wasn't getting the ratings, it wasn't an instant hit, must have put tremendous pressure on, because this was really costing money. And it was a much harder type show than they were used to."[43]

By the time *CTV Reports* was taken off the air, Tom Gould had left the network and Maclear followed later. The one-time CBC correspondents who had become familiar to Canadians on the public affairs program, *CBC Newsmagazine*, now had learned the entrails of private network television. "Tom Gould had left earlier," said Maclear, "and there were the two of us who were two of the earliest correspondents ever to go to CTV sitting in the Yorkville coffee shops wondering what to do next for lunch."[44] Andrew Cochrane also departed CTV in 1979. He had difficulty adapting to the fact that the network's news division had become more profit driven and to the more bureaucratic systems approach that Tim Kotcheff had introduced following his arrival with Lloyd Robertson in 1976.

COCHRANE RECALLED THE HUGE growth in expenditures for news throughout the 1970s at CTV: "We were hiring people left and right, starting new shows, doing this, opening bureaus, all kinds of things going on. And so there was financial pressure too...but that to me was the early seeds of really putting the financial reins on things, trying to wring more dollar efficiency out of everything and turning news into a profit centre. All of that...and the more systems approach that Kotcheff brought." Under Kotcheff, Cochrane sensed a new focus on process: "He was sort of the senior news person at CBC, very large system. And there was some of that systems thinking I think that he brought to the news area at CTV where process was as important, if not more important, than outcome. Until that time, everything in the news department had always been very outcome driven. Did we get it on the air? Was it better? Was it faster?" In short, CTV News, though a leaner operation, began to adopt the CBC administrative model. "But at that point with me," said Cochrane, "I felt it was a different style than what I had been used to certainly with Cameron's leadership. Cameron was very much, get the story, bring it back, bring it back better than anybody else. That was the dominant value of the place. That was the value that resonated with me. And it felt that there was just a different kind of emphasis going on in the department, at that point, and that wasn't the one that I was comfortable with."[45]

The CTV network had tried to establish its news division during the 1970s and had achieved notable successes with the establishment of news bureaus and the acquisition of Lloyd Robertson who was to give the network a news credibility in the years ahead. In expanding CTV News, the network was building on strength. When it chose to introduce the short-lived *CTV Reports*, the network could be seen to be guilty of over-extending itself. "Certainly the culture at the time," said Cochrane, "both by Gould and Cameron, and then certainly continued by Cameron was to really encourage innovation, to really push the boundaries, to really try new stuff." CTV executives, formerly employed at the more bureaucratized CBC, had a broad field of action which they were eager to exploit. "It was to go ahead of the CBC," Cochrane remembered, "but it was also kind of, hey we are free of that environment, we can go out and we can do this. We don't have to check with those guys anymore, we can do this."[46]

The problem for CTV was that as the 1970s progressed, the stakes got higher because news and public affairs programming was expected to contribute steadily to the economic well being of the network. If news was to be a profit centre, experimental programs such as *CTV Reports* could not last long, if they were unable to maintain sufficient audience ratings. They had to be thoughtfully conceived from a budgetary stand-point and implemented effectively making proper use of the broadcast technology and available resources. On this score, *CTV Reports* simply did not measure up. In a broader context, news programming on the whole was to face new competition.

During the 1970s, individual CTV affiliated stations also developed their news programming which continued to draw large audiences. The program that drew the most attention for BCTV in British Columbia was *News Hour* with Tony Parsons which attracted more than 500-thousand viewers early in 1978. Ray Peters had hired Parsons away from CTV to anchor the newscast which became enormously popular. BCTV decided to develop a dinner hour news program to compete with noted CBS news anchor Walter Cronkite who dominated the early part of the evening in Canada. After the CTV network refused to introduce an early evening newscast, Peters focused on his own market: "My thesis at the time was that we really should be either creating another one [newscast] at six o'clock or move the eleven o'clock news on CTV to six o'clock in the early evening. So I got so damn mad at the network not accepting what I thought was a good strategic move [that] we developed our own early evening news hour....we finally...beat Walter Cronkite [and] we cracked open the champagne."[47] The popular *News Hour* had a wide reach, because of the rebroadcasters that had been established throughout British Columbia in places such as Kelowna, Kamloops, Prince George, Dawson Creek, and Prince Rupert. "That was the start of our developing our own thing," said Peters, "and that snowballed with other stations starting to do their own thing. When I say 'thing', starting to develop a stronger local program schedule and not leaning on the network to do everything."[48]

Similarly in Ottawa, the CJOH *Newsline* in the evening with Max Keeping was highly successful. In the early 1970s, Keeping left CTV in the Parliamentary Press Gallery to join the Ottawa affiliate. He adopted a news marketing technique of Frank Ryan who had owned radio station CFRA in Ottawa. Keeping explained the Ryan approach to John Ruttle in the *Broadcaster*: "That is to build a loyal following around the rural audience. I looked at our entire viewing area as one big riding and made sure that I was in every part of that riding…whether it was by invitation or just going there to get my own sense and feeling."[49] CBOT, the CBC affiliate in Ottawa, struggled to compete with the popular, private station.

From the beginning, Baton's CFTO, Toronto placed a heavy emphasis on news and deep community involvement. The practice was followed by Baton's other stations across the country. Throughout its history, the company focused on providing a shared experience for viewers with programming on its stations but still underlined the extent to which each station has contributed to its individual community. A company annual report noted: "Each BBS [Baton Broadcasting System] station is unique in its home market, playing a key role in the social fabric. Wherever there are BBS stations, their local news draws the largest ratings, and BBS staff are closely involved in the life of their communities."[50]

Trina McQueen who rose to become head of CTV Inc., remembered her arrival at CFTO in the mid 1960s as a TV journalist when the philosophy of the need for close identification with the city was readily apparent. "I had come from the *Ottawa Journal*," said McQueen, "and even the *Ottawa Journal* didn't seem to be as much into…the city council and the courts a hundred percent and I always admired that." She found a different outlook when she arrived at the CBC: "When I got to the CBC, I noticed how that was kind of missing from their local news in some kind of sense that I can't really define." McQueen said the close identification between CFTO and Toronto has remained a defining characteristic: "There was really a sense that that station belonged to Toronto and Toronto belonged to that station. And I think still you see that they are absolutely 100 percent focused on Toronto. It's like *The Toronto Star* in some ways. Well, what does it mean to Metro? Everything was seen through that filter." She remembered the sharp focus on prominent civic leaders: "You had to know the city councillors, you had to know the judges, you had to know the cops. And it was that kind of very strong local news reporting even in the beginning."[51]

The intense local news orientation of CFTO has remained throughout the station's history. In a background study for the Task Force on Broadcasting Policy undertaken in October, 1985, authors Walter I. Romanow, Stuart H. Surlin and Walter C. Soderlund underlined the differences in news coverage among the three Toronto stations, CFTO,

CBLT and CITY TV: "Newscasts of the privately owned CFTO were seen as having a strong (72%) local resources base and a minimal dependency upon CTV network supports (only 3%, as opposed to 28% from the CBC owned CBLT)." At the same time, "The focus of coverage beyond the City of Toronto and the Province of Ontario was greater than the other two stations: 50% as opposed to 41% from CBLT, and 13% for CITY."[52] With the network and its affiliates boasting impressive news operations, and through a skilfull selection of popular American programming, CTV was able to serve Canadians with program offerings that seemed to satisfy them in both categories. Canadians appeared relatively indifferent to whatever other fare the network was able to offer. Certainly after two decades, there appeared to be no groundswell of public opinion demanding that CTV provide viewers with more Canadian content.

BY THE END OF THE 1970s, the Canadian television industry had undergone a profound change. CTV and CBC confronted a new Ontario network, Global TV, and the growth of cable television in Canada had produced greater audience fragmentation. Another innovation—Pay-TV—was on the horizon with its capacity to provide still greater competition for conventional networks. Private broadcasting generally had seen a shift from small, individually operated entities to large business ventures. Pierre Camu, the President of the Canadian Association of Broadcasters, had underlined this transition and raised the possibility of greater federal intervention in the broadcasting industry. Columnist Sheri Craig explained in *Marketing*: "In line with this, Camu said that the role of the private broadcaster has changed from the original entrepreneur operating his own one-man show in a completely open environment to the businessman running broadcasting as a business. The third generation now coming up will have to be administrators operating in a public responsibility type of environment and dealing with both the public and private types of restrictions."[53]

The behaviour of Global television after its introduction in January, 1974 was a dramatic illustration of the criticism frequently raised by apologists for public broadcasting against private broadcasters; lofty promises made to attain broadcasting licences often go unfulfilled. *Maclean's* columnist Ron Base underlined the network's shortage of cash in November, 1975, some 15 months after Global went on the air: "Although it started out with an innovative lineup of Canadian shows, the network has degenerated into a cheapjack delivery system for American reruns. Indeed Global has become such an embarrassment to the CRTC that it invited the network before it this month to explain why it seems to be as much as six hours a week short on Canadian programming."[54] The Global network had got off to a shaky start on 6 January 1974. Its founder, Al Bruner, soon gave way to Allan Slaight whose company IWC Communications took over the young network which had lost some 16-million dollars in its first year and a half.[55] Brian Nolan, a former CTV producer, who was familiar with the launch of Global described Bruner as "a very charming guy" and also "a visionary" but he was "impractical." In Nolan's words, "Bruner thought like Disney," but he had "a budget like CJOH," the CTV affiliate in Ottawa.[56] Nolan was instrumental in Bruner landing William Cunningham, a veteran CBC correspondent, as Global's Vice-President of News. Nolan recalled that "Bill really liked this flamboyant character and they got along really well; Bruner liked Cunningham because Bill had a lot of style."[57]

After Slaight took over Global, a number of Canadian shows such as *The World of Wicks, The Braden Beat*, and *The Great Debate* were cancelled. The dictates of the marketplace that drive the North American broadcasting environment had a sharp influence on Global. To produce *The Braden Beat*, it cost Global $17,000 for each episode; an American program could be imported for only $3,000. Critic Base focused attention on Slaight's request for a relaxation of the Canadian content quotas as they pertained to Global: "Despite howls of derision from performers and broadcasters, Slaight stoutly maintains that by constantly repeating the few Canadian shows Global has left it is just about meeting the CRTC's Canadian content requirements. But that didn't stop him from desperately seeking a Canadian content dispensation."[58]

Global eventually would become an enormously profitable operation under the ownership of CanWest Global Communications Corp. The head of CanWest, I.H. "Izzy" Asper was determined to establish a third national television network in Canada. By the end of the 1970s, the CTV network had a formidable rival in Global, an Ontario service that was to expand across the country in the coming decades and become the most profitable television broadcasting system in the country. Clearly the Canadian broadcasting environment was about to change from the earlier era dominated by two national networks. CTV remained a major player, but the private network was soon to operate in a multi-channel broadcasting universe where there would be a virtual explosion of viewer choices.

SEVEN

CTV Scores!

1972–1979

Sports programming had become a staple for CTV as the network continued to position itself as a populist service to win viewers and appeal to advertisers. The *Wide World of Sports* and the *Sports Hot Seat* had been innovative program formats for sports fans. Still the Canada-Russia hockey series in 1972 captured the nation. CTV scored a major triumph when the network won the broadcast rights to televise the event that had a profound impact on the favorite pastime of Canadians and was a defining moment in international competition.

Many Canadians, even those with a casual interest in history, have fond memories of where they were on 28 September 1972. Even children born during the early 1960s would have vague memories of the tumult that Paul Henderson's goal at the Lenin Central Stadium in Moscow created throughout the country. Succeeding generations would see incessant replays on television of the historic moment that unleashed a new wave of optimism about Canadian hockey when the sport was in urgent need of it. Foster Hewitt's excited play-by-play account of the goal with its crescendo and climactic pronouncement, "Henderson has scored for Canada!" could not help but touch the sensibilities of all Canadians. Hockey arguments, a common occurrence in Canadians households, can be divisive. But when Henderson fired the puck past Vladislav Tretiak, on a second try after getting his own rebound, Canadians were clearly at one with their sport.

The Canada-Russia hockey series at the start of a new decade was one of those rare occasions when Canadian nationalism came alive and a proud citizenry acted boastfully in a most uncharacteristic manner. Not surprisingly the players on Team Canada who won the much publicized series in 1972 were judged Canada's sports team of the twentieth century in a survey of sports editors and broadcasters by the Canadian Press and Broadcast News.[1] At the time, *The Globe and Mail* offered this assessment of the impact of the Canadian victory in the eighth game of the memorable international series: "Henderson's goal in the game on which international hockey prestige was balanced, completed an incredible comeback by Team Canada, and left the place of sports, Lenin Central Stadium, echoing to 'O Canada.'"[2]

PRIOR TO THE HOCKEY SERIES between Canada and Russia, the Canadian television networks, CTV and CBC, had watched developments closely as controversial hockey promoter Alan Eagleson showed a steely determination to arrange the matchup between the two countries. Such an important international sporting event was bound to draw a sizable audience. The television networks and advertisers could not afford to overlook the exposure that the series would provide. The excitement surrounding the Canada-Russia confrontation inevitably raised the question of which television network would be able to acquire the rights to broadcast the series. At first glance, the publicly-owned CBC would have seemed to be the natural broadcaster for the series given its historic mandate to reflect the social and cultural fabric of the country to Canadians. The sport of hockey was undeniably an integral part of Canadian culture.

Unlike the fledgling CTV, the CBC had history on its side. Early viewers had grown accustomed to *The Hot Stove League* seen on the CBC during the 1950s in the pioneer days of television before watching *Hockey Night in Canada* became a regular Saturday night routine for hockey enthusiasts. However the television rights for the series went to CTV, the private network, in a somewhat curious set of developments backstage. Johnny Esaw, the CFTO Sports Director, who was a central figure in the negotiations to obtain the rights for CTV, wrote that "by the time 1970 had come along...a hockey world hunger was being created for a major confrontation between the hockey superpowers, the Soviet Union and Canada."[3]

The personalities of the characters involved played perhaps as important a role as the circumstances of the day. The name of Alan Eagleson, a lawyer and one-time Ontario politician, is well known to hockey fans in Canada. He was the agent for Bobby Orr, the legendary Boston Bruin defenceman. Before Eagleson's initiatives culminated in the Canada-Russia series, there were other prominent figures who saw possibilities in international hockey events, notably Gerald Regan who was to become Premier of Nova Scotia and a federal cabinet minister. Both Regan and Eagleson would later face unrelated criminal charges in the late 1990s. In 1998 Regan was acquitted of eight sex related offences but the following year was facing eight indecent assault charges dating back more than 30 years.[4] Eagleson was found guilty of fraud in 1998 in a case that involved the theft of hundreds of thousands of dollars from international hockey that was to go to the National Hockey League Players' pension fund.[5]

Regan was active behind the scenes as a hockey promoter in the 1950s. The Montreal Canadians had built a powerful dynasty that was to last through five Stanley Cups. The improvement each year in the CBC television coverage of NHL games after the new medium arrived in 1952 seemed to parallel the growing strength each season of the Canadians. Their daunting power play that entertained countless viewers included Doug Harvey and Bernie "Boom Boom" Geoffrion on the points; the smooth Jean Beliveau at centre ice with Bert Olmstead, a strong corner man, on left wing, and the legendary Maurice "The Rocket" Richard on the right side. While the Canadians were atop the NHL most seasons, the Boston Bruins were annually relegated to the basement. That was before Bobby Orr, Phil Esposito and Derek Sanderson.

In recalling the period of hockey history before the 1972 series, Johnny Esaw underlined Regan's enthusiasm for international competition: "By coincidence, there was a young lawyer in Halifax who knew something about promoting events and, being something of a hockey nut, saw a future in Canada-Soviet hockey relations. Gerald 'Gerry' Regan had put himself through Dalhousie law school as a play-by-play announcer in the long forgotten Nova Scotia South Shore League (senior or intermediate, nobody seemed to know for sure)." Regan also had ties to the Boston Bruins and organized Maritime tours for the Bruins who would play local senior teams. Regan succeeded Danny Gallivan on radio station CJCH, Halifax as hockey play-by-play announcer when Gallivan moved to Montreal to become the voice of the Canadians. He was a provincial premier from 1970 until 1978 and later the Minister of Sport in the government headed by Pierre Trudeau.[6]

Esaw recalled that Regan's determination to arrange a Canada-Soviet Union hockey event was unknown to many Canadians, because his initiatives were carried on beyond the public's view: "This is a part of hockey history few people know, or remember. Anyway, Regan could act on impulse and at one point took off on his own for Moscow. He had a great time there, used his great personality and the gift that had him nicknamed 'Gabby' and got the Russians seriously interested in Canadian tours. Alas, when Regan arrived home, happy with his work, he had an immediate letdown." Officialdom in the hockey world was not impressed. "When he contacted the governing Canadian Amateur Hockey Association (CAHA) he was told that he was unofficial and unauthorized, that any international dealings were federation to federation but, yes, they [would] be delighted to take up where he left off. The CAHA in effect snatched the prize from Regan and, without any initiative of its own, was able to begin tours."[7]

In his recollection of the early Soviet tours, Esaw remembered the players' stoic manner: "The Soviets arrived as mystery men, dour faced, fur-hatted, uncommunicative. They played senior teams in the smaller cities and arenas, drew crowds of curious spectators and made some money for all concerned—nothing compared to what would be involved later but, what the heck! this was the real beginning!" Still knowledgeable hockey observers such as Wren Blair who had scouted Bobby Orr when he was a 12-year old playing in Parry Sound, Ontario watched the Russians closely and contemplated the future. "A standing joke among media and spectator," explained Esaw, "revolved around how copiously the Soviet coaching staffs took notes during games." The Soviets had entered world tournaments in 1954. In that same year, they stunned the hockey world by winning the world championship when they defeated Toronto's East York Lyndhursts 7–2 in Stockholm, Sweden.[8]

Stockholm was also the scene of the World Championships in 1969 when Canada fared poorly. Alan Eagleson, whom Bunny Ahearne, President of the International Ice Hockey Federation, is said to have called an "office boy with no authority anywhere," was galvanized into action following the disappointing Canadian performance. Esaw remembered Eagleson's passionate assertion: "We'll show the Russians where the best hockey in the world is played and it sure as hell isn't in the Soviet Union." Whatever Eagleson's shortcomings, Esaw characterized him as "the one who almost single handedly put the memorable series together. His metamorphosis [sic] from Bunny Ahearne's alleged office boy to international hockey's powerbroker, left Ahearne dizzy and disillusioned." From Gerald Regan's forays to the Soviet Union until the series was held in 1972, Esaw observed that "the road to 1972 was long, eventful and involved more than the obvious upfront people."[9]

THE CANADA-RUSSIA SERIES was an eight-game affair with four games to be played in each country. Eagleson "had to convince the NHL players (and some owners)," Esaw wrote, "that this was a worthwhile series for both image and pocketbook and he finally swung them over. By the time he was finished explaining the benefits to their pension fund, the players couldn't refuse. Patriotism might have been nibbled at but money was the more functional arguement [sic]." Naturally Canadian advertisers and television networks were also interested in the monetary aspects of the series. Esaw was to play a central role in acquiring the broadcasting rights for CTV.

The backstage manoeuvring that enabled CTV to win the rights involved both determination and timing on Esaw's part. The interplay among advertisers, Eagleson and the television networks was conducted in an excited atmosphere with hopeful prospects for a lucrative series. The fact that Art Lennox, the advertising manager of Labatt's Breweries had provided Eagleson with $800,000 was illustrative of how the advertising world envisaged the series potential. "The Eagle was as busy as a proverbial one-armed paperhanger with hives," wrote Esaw. "He 'worked' all his political angles, calling in IOUs, applying pressure where needed and generally bringing heavy hitters onside. At the same time, he was burning the telephone lines to team managers, coaches, players, trainers and executives throughout North America."[10]

The manner in which Eagleson arranged for the network telecasts of the series served to underline the level of control he exercised over the many facets of the hockey encounter between the two countries. When the broadcasting rights were available for negotiation, Eagleson informed Esaw by telephone that the CBC "had made a pretty good pitch." Meanwhile Esaw had received the go-ahead to try to get the broadcasting rights for the series from CTV President Murray Chercover and John Bassett, the Chairman of the network's Board of Directors. Esaw quickly contacted Eagleson and in the process stretched a point or two: "On the pretext of a severe emergency, I managed to convince Eagleson's office that I just HAD to speak to the overworked and almost over-extended Eagle. He was in a closed door meeting with External Affairs Minister Mitchell Sharp in Ottawa but he managed a recess to speak with me and answered my question by telling me that the TV rights were still for sale. With that information, I set up a meeting with Alan for the following morning in Mr. Bassett's CFTO office."[11]

The phone call between Esaw and Eagleson was a hurried exchange. "So I phoned Eagleson and I said 'emergency call!'" Esaw remembered. "'Get him out of that meeting!' So he came out and I said, 'Are the rights sold?' He said, 'No.' I said, 'Can they be sold?' He said, 'Yes.' I said, 'Well I want 'em! When can we meet? How about tomorrow morning?' He said, 'Good.' I said, 'Meet me in John Bassett's office at eleven o'clock.'" Esaw arrived at Bassett's office fifteen minutes early in the hopes of discussing privately what CTV was prepared to pay for the television rights to the series. However Eagleson had also chosen to arrive before eleven A.M. preventing Esaw and Bassett from having a chance to discuss in detail their proposed offer. "Eagleson being a good Tory came early and they're talking politics," Esaw explained. "I don't get a chance to talk to Bassett about how much we are going to charge or pay."[12]

The three participants were in Bassett's office at CFTO only briefly when Bassett said it was time to start the negotiations. The network that means business was up against a shrewd promoter and bargainer in Eagleson. The opening salvo came from Bassett: "We're prepared to pay you $900,000 for the rights." But Eagleson promptly responded with a pronouncement that stunned both Bassett and Esaw. "The rights are not for sale," he said. "I'm here to buy your network." As wily bargainers themselves, Bassett and Esaw soon realized that Eagleson had carried out "a masterful stroke," because he was operating from a position of strength. Esaw remembered a crucial moment in the meeting: "He [Eagleson] already had $800,000 of Labatt's money in the bank and, by making this move, he was looking to make all the profits of commercial time he could sell on the telecasts."[13]

The onus was now on the two CTV representatives to ask a price that would be acceptable to Eagleson. Obviously taken by surprise, Bassett looked straight at Esaw and said, "I suppose we COULD sell." Esaw gulped, flew by the seat of his pants and came up with a figure: "$1.1 million is the least we could accept." Without hesitation, Eagleson responded: "Make it a flat million and it's a deal."[14] The three participants shook hands and the meeting was over. Eagleson had bought the network; CTV had the rights to the Canada-Russia series.

NOT SURPRISINGLY, the CBC was irate when its competitor obtained the television rights. Still CTV, which operated solely in English, had to find a way to serve French language broadcast outlets. Esaw was prepared to take the CBC in as a partner in the deal to solve the problem. But the response he received from the public broadcaster was something less than favorable: "I called Thom Benson, Head of Programming for the CBC English language network to inform him that CTV had been awarded the rights and that we'd like to work with CBC on the coverage. The air turned blue with his response as he gave vent to his feelings. He stated bluntly that the series wouldn't appear on CBC under any circumstances, in view of this development with CTV having the right [sic]. I advised him to call the Eagle, the arbiter of all things, in the hope that Alan would wade through Benson's pique, calm him down and change his mind."[15]

Eventually Esaw dealt with Gordon Craig, Head of Sports at CBC and later Chief Executive Officer of The Sports Network (TSN), on the plans for the broadcasts of the series. The two conditions stipulated by Esaw in the discussions with the CBC involved the on-air talent and the priority list for the network telecast of the games. Foster Hewitt, a familiar hockey voice to Canadians, was to be the play-by-play broadcaster. As well Brian Conacher, a former member of the Toronto Maple Leafs, would be the colour commentator. The choice of Hewitt caused little sensation, although Danny Gallivan who was familiar as the television broadcaster for the Montreal Canadians was also a preference. But the main contention surrounded Conacher who had written a book critical of the NHL and its owners. The teams' owners anticipating the audience the telecasts would draw were not inclined to have Conacher in such a high profile position. John Bassett's intervention settled the question. Esaw recalled a phone call he received in Ottawa where he had gone to broadcast a Canadian Football League game: "Mr. Bassett obviously wasn't amused by the NHL owners trying to exercise talent-control and, when I took the call in the hotel lobby, I'm sure his crackling voice could be heard by everyone. I know I held the receiver away from my ear....Mr. Bassett, I now learned, had made it crystal clear to Eagleson that Conacher was to be on the telecasts or there would be no Canada-Russia series on CFTO [the CTV flagship]. Eagleson told Mr. Bassett not to worry and was as good as his word, as usual. Conacher was the color commentator."[16]

When it came to the second condition, which involved CTV having the choice of games to telecast, Esaw, by his own admission, "out-smarted" himself. However the rationale for his decision seemed accept-able given the conventional wisdom that a Team Canada made up of NHL players would make quick work of the Soviet Union. Without being able to predict what would happen, he handed the CBC a major advantage: "Having the choice after my agreement with Gordon Craig, I decided CTV would cover the first game. I knew the audience for that one would be awesome and, if it meant giving the eighth game to CBC on our rotation, who cared? The series would be decided in six, seven games at the most. Nudge, nudge, wink, wink." Esaw foresaw "a token viewing audience for a token eighth game. Now you have another exam-ple of the 'you can't win them all' rule and, by the eighth game I was try-ing to be as gracious as possible while kicking myself in the butt." The eighth game seen on the CBC turned out to be the deciding thriller. Esaw was "seething inwardly" and had to admit, "If nothing else, we couldn't have written the script any better for the People's Network."[17]

Other backstage issues that proved difficult when the series shifted to Moscow after the fourth game involved the question of commercial breaks which called for a stoppage in play so that advertising messages could be inserted. A television and newspaper correspondent from the Soviet Consulate in the city of New York, Igor Charikov, was sent to Canada to watch the telecasts so that the Soviets could understand the process. Still the Russians seemed unable to understand that the com-mercial messages about consumer goods would not be seen in their coun-try but only in Canada. The Canadian practice is for the referee to be equipped with a beeper that the producer of the broadcasts can trigger when the commercial ends. But the Russians said no to the notion of the referee having any kind of wire. A compromise was worked out aimed at satisfying the Russians. Oliver Babirad, CTV's Business Manager and Assistant Director of Sports, assumed a position in the penalty box and took directions from the producer. Babirad who stood six feet, five inches would stand up for the commercial breaks so the referee could see him.[18]

The arrangement worked well for awhile in the opening game in Moscow. But as Esaw explained, the practice had to be abandoned under the watchful eye of Soviet officialdom: "Then a messenger came rushing past me and went directly to the penalty box to see what the stoppages were all about....Shortly after his penalty box visit, the messenger came to me and said, 'No more stoppages," while pointing to the VIP box. Sitting there was the Soviet Union leadership, [Nikolai] Podgorny and [Leonid] Breshnev, among others. Obviously, they were not too thrilled by this capitalistic practice and the orders came down. Now we were flying in the dark, guessing at our commercial time outs. Fortunately, we didn't miss a goal to the relief of our sponsors and certainly the fans in Canada."[19]

Another problem that would not have been seen by Canadian viewers was the difficulty encountered in allowing the television crews to move throughout the production areas in the arena. Esaw dealt with this predicament by interviewing Anna Silinkina who was in charge of the Soviet Figure Skating Association. She also oversaw the arena management and was delighted to go on Canadian television. After the interview, the Canadian production crew had no problem circulating throughout the arena.[20]

THE SERIES WAS AN EYE-OPENER for Canadian hockey fans. The Russians had obviously learned from the earlier visits to Canada over the years and watching how the game was played. The Russians won the first game 7–3 at the Montreal Forum. Canada came back to capture the second one at Maple Leaf Gardens in Toronto by the score of 4–1. It was on to Winnipeg for the third contest which ended in a 4–4 tie. In the fourth game, the Soviets won 5–3 at the Pacific Coliseum in Vancouver. The results meant that the Soviets headed to Moscow with two victories, one loss and one game tied.

After the Soviet victory in Vancouver, Esaw conducted a memorable on-ice interview with Phil Esposito, a member of Team Canada, who communicated passionately the feelings of the Canadian players who had received a wide-ranging criticism from disappointed Canadian fans and the mass media. "This was raw emotion," Esaw recalled, "and Espo was speaking for all his mates. He's Italian ancestry and the emotion is never far below the surface." The strength of television as a medium is that it has an extraordinary capacity to communicate experiences like no other form of communications. When Esposito, up close and personal and drenched in sweat, kept up the passion in the interview, Esaw waved off the "cut" signals he had received from the floor director, because he realized that "this was what television was all about, that the raw nature of it all was taking our viewers where they had never been before in hockey."[21] The interview was a stirring moment in Canadian television.

Esposito spoke straight from the heart to hockey fans from coast to coast to coast: "For the people across Canada, we tried. We gave it our best. For those people who booed us, gosh, all the guys are disheartened and disillusioned in some of the people." Team Canada could not believe the booing and the bad media coverage. Esposito's hot-blooded Italian ancestry was palpable when he struck a patriotic chord: "Everyone of us 35 guys who came out and played for Team Canada, we did it because we loved our country and not for any other reason. They can throw the money for the pension fund out the window. We came because we love Canada. And even though we play in the United States, Canada is still our home and that's the only reason we came. I don't think it's fair that we should be booed."[22]

In a Canadian Press retrospective look at the series in November 1999, Neil Davidson wrote: "Esposito's impassioned plea seemed to be a turning point in the series and [coach Harry] Sinden said it was a different Canadian team that arrived in Europe."[23] However the Soviets won the fifth game in Moscow 5–4. Clearly Team Canada was up against it. The Canadians came back to win the next two games, 3–2 and 4–3. Paul Henderson scored the winners in both outings. With each team having three wins, three loses and with one game tied, game eight would decide the series.

Even in the crucial, final game, the Canadians did it the hard way. The score was 2–2 at the end of the first period, but in the second the Soviets looked strong and held a 5–2 lead. As he recalled his interview with Esposito, Esaw gave his version of the memorable, final period: "Then everything that Esposito had said in Vancouver about pride and wanting to win kicked into overdrive in one of the most amazing finishes in any sport, ever. Team Canada came at Tretiak in waves and finally Esposito put it within reach at 5–4, only one goal down. Little Yvon Cournoyea, the fabled Roadrunner of the Canadiens, made it 5–5 and that set the stage for bedlam."[24]

With 34 seconds on the clock and world hockey supremacy hanging in the balance, Paul Henderson fired twice from in front of the net; the second shot off his own rebound went past Tretiak, the outstanding Soviet netminder, to give the Canadians a 6–5 win and the series. It was Esposito's tireless effort in forechecking and getting the puck over to Henderson that set up the goal that beat Tretiak. Harry Sinden, the

Team Canada coach, explained to Davidson the irony of the moment: "I was trying very, very hard to get Phil Esposito off the ice and, having coached Phil for a long time in Boston, I knew how difficult that was in any particular game." Not surprisingly, Sinden expressed pleasure that "he didn't hear me."[25]

In retrospect, Esaw described the Henderson goal as "the most single thrilling moment of my 40-year career": "Forgotten were the disputes, on and off the ice, the Eagle defying an arena filled with unfriendly faces and giving them a finger and arm signal....Forgotten were the many incidents. My own problems with commercial time-outs and Esposito's obsession with his hotel room being bugged, became merely amusing anecdotes. I suppose I didn't even really care on whose network the big moment was shown." Jack Ludwig writing in *Maclean's*, observed that the Canadian players broke free from their NHL straight-jackets, made use of their latent talent and beat the Russians at their own game: "I suggest that hidden behind the show biz shoot-it-in-and-chase-it hockey played by the NHL was the natural hockey talent Team Canada players didn't always have to use in the NHL." Following the 7–3 loss in Montreal, "each and every one of the players painfully dredged up his memories of hockey past."[26] Although the CTV network did not get to broadcast the deciding encounter between Canada and Russia, the private TV network had managed to obtain the broadcasting rights to the most memorable international hockey event that had a lasting resonance with Canadians of all generations.

The success of CTV in acquiring the rights to the renown international hockey series was a milestone in the history of the network. CTV would continue to accentuate its sports coverage which was seemingly a program category where boardroom directors and affiliated stations could often find common ground. The universal appeal of sports especially the game of hockey could transcend regional interests and grievances. Based on the U.S. experience, sports telecasts could build audiences. Still the production of other forms of entertainment programming would often produce dissension within the network.

DURING THE 1970s, independent production companies did not have the pride of place that they would later have in Canadian television and in the CTV program schedule. The CTV affiliated stations in the various regions hoped to produce their own in-house programs and sell them to the network for national exposure. "We...had what at that time was a very important production company called Glen Warren Productions," John Bassett recalled, "and I knew that over a period of time there would be a lot of Canadian programs that would have to be promoted, produced and that we'd get the bulk of the business." Bassett wanted to look at "the whole of Canada as our playground, not just Toronto."[27] Inevitably rivalries that reflected regional differences in the country developed over the amount of production that any one affiliate should be allowed to air on the network. The programming issue, which was watched closely by the broadcast regulator, could not help but exacerbate latent, regional tensions between the principal network affiliates in Toronto and Vancouver. Both affiliates, CFTO and BCTV, continued to be intense competitors in the production of network programs.

The question of program origination by affiliates received a full airing at a CRTC hearing in 1972. The Commission's counsel, John Lawrence, inquired from Bassett about the dominant position that CFTO held in program production compared to other affiliates. As it was with the CBC, the Commission was concerned about the question of regional input on the private network. "In looking over the 1972–73 schedule of the network," said Lawrence, "I am struck as anyone would be to the number of programs contributed to the network by CFTO." Bassett was ready for the question: "I thought we might be asked this." The CFTO owner went on to cite extensive figures that played down CFTO's involvement in the network. CFTO's total production business in the year ending 31 August 1972 was $7,171,000. The station's billings to CTV amounted to $2,205,000 or 31 percent. Boasting that he had "the best single production house in North America," Bassett told the Commission that the remainder of the billings were from other sources, "largely American sources which came up here to use our facilities and take advantage of our trained personnel."[28]

Bassett argued that 35 percent of the more than two million dollars was billed directly to the network for use of the facilities at CFTO. He noted that CTV did "W5 out of our facilities, the news out of our facilities...but to us the key figure is the top 31%, because there is the impression, only partially correct...the facilities we have are totally dependent upon network business. Network business is very important to us: 31% is a very significant figure. But 69% of our production came from other sources." Before the Commission and with Murray Chercover, the CTV President, beside him, Bassett left no doubt that he was the dominator of CTV: "So I think, Mr. Lawrence, it is a combination of all of those factors which make CFTO such an important center of production for the network...there is the very psychological strength we have because, as you know, I dominate the network." Later in the exchange with Lawrence, Bassett replied that he made no apology that when it came to "[program] pilots and so on in competition with other affiliates, I want it all." When Bassett expressed the view that it was difficult for anybody "in any field" to live in any place other than Toronto, Lawrence inquired if he were suggesting that the CRTC should move to that city. "No, absolutely," said Bassett, "let them stay far away."[29]

After Bassett's pronouncement at the hearing, WIC's Ray Peters and Allan Waters, head of CHUM Limited, dealt with the issue of regional input on the CTV network. Peters underlined the need for three components before a station could provide major productions to be aired nationally: good technical people, a pool of talent and the necessary technical facilities. "With reference to Mr. Bassett's point," Peters told the Commission, "I guess I must concede that the largest source of good potential talent is in Toronto, if you are speaking about the English sector of the country, but the second is Vancouver." Waters explained that his company, which had developed the Atlantic Television System which gave the east coast access to CTV, was primarily concerned with the question of extension of service. But he hoped eventually to become involved in national productions: "As far as the talent is concerned...and I believe there is good talent in Halifax and in the other areas in the Maritimes— perhaps not as much as in Toronto or in Vancouver or Montreal, but there is talent there and we do hope to develop it along with programs as we are able to increase and improve our facilities."[30]

Bassett's boastful comments before the CRTC seemed to stimulate Peters's determination to get his company's share of the program production on CTV. The rivalry between Baton and WIC showed no sign of dissipating. Moreover a trend in the 1970s began to emerge especially among the major regional players in the CTV network such as Baton, WIC and CHUM Limited. In news and entertainment programming, the strong regional broadcasters began to spend more money and improve their individual program schedules beyond the 65 hours for which they relied on CTV. This development had important implications for the future of the network. By the mid 1990s, Ray Peters assessed the cumulative impact of the growing strength of the regional broadcasters that had begun 20-odd years earlier. He noted that "the individual stations were getting stronger in developing their own program schedules. To the point now where the CTV network is...reduced to some 40 hours of programming."[31] The strong, regional players showed signs of outgrowing the CTV network which was forced to operate in a new context.

Among the WIC produced programs seen on CTV was *Story Theatre*, a production that featured vignettes of satirical, funny and serious material. Peters described it as "the ancient form of *SCTV*," a comic style of programming. *Story Theatre* was sold also in the United States and Europe.[32] Other network programs produced at WIC for CTV included: *Mantrap* hosted by Al Hamel; the *Paul Horn Show*, a musical show "in a Gassy Jack's Gastown setting," as Roy Shields described it; *The Oscar Peterson Show* recorded at CHAN because of its refined sound equipment ideal for piano music; and *Banjo Parlor* featuring Mary Gillan and Kathleen Payne. The latter show first aired on CTV on 15 December 1973 at 7 P.M. and faced the sport of hockey as its competition in the time slot. As Shields noted, "Nevertheless, across the country it should have the instant appeal—and more—that greeted Bassett's...pub show, *Pig n' Whistle*. *Banjo Parlor* featured 'old favorites and contemporary songs in a flashy setting, with classic cars and dancing girls.'"[33]

On the east coast, CHUM Limited was active in the 1970s through its development of the Atlantic Television System (ATV) that consisted of CJCH, Halifax, CJCB, Sydney, CKCW, Moncton and CKLT, Saint John. The stations and rebroadcasters covered nearly the full population of the two million people living in Nova Scotia, New Brunswick and Prince Edward Island.[34] After watching its operation, John Porteous writing in the *Financial Post* highlighted a distinctive aspect of the ATV system's operation: "ATV aggressively 'covers off' incoming CTV logos much of the time with its own emblem and the voice-over, 'This has been an ATV color presentation.' But there's no indication that CTV minds." He noted that as the only representatives of the CTV network in the three Maritime provinces "perhaps the tail has become weightier than the dog." The system's programming was inclined to lean "toward the bland and haphazardly produced."[35]

In 1976, CJON-TV in St. John's, Newfoundland had its licence renewed and Don Jamieson, then the federal Minister of Industry, Trade & Commerce, received CRTC approval to transfer his 49 percent interest in the company to a trust operated by his brother, Colin, and Allan Waters, head of CHUM Limited. Geoff Stirling held the remaining 51 percent in Newfoundland Broadcasting Co., which operated CJON.

According to Michael Harrington, the quality of CJON broadcasts had received regular criticism: "The quality of the private station's transmission and programs has been frequently attacked by local critics and viewers for lacking original and imaginative local programming." With most of the province being able to receive only two channels, the "lack of choice has stimulated demands for cable-TV."[36]

Baton Broadcasting Inc. had continued its expansion across Canada. In addition to owning CFTO, the company acquired CFQC, Saskatoon, another CTV affiliate. Baton also tried unsuccessfully to gain CFCF television in Montreal from Multiple Access Ltd., a division of the Bronfman family holdings. Speculation at the time centred on Bassett's desire to gain control of the CTV network. Typical was the view expressed by Margaret Lewis in the *Financial Post*: "Control of CFCF, CFTO and Bassett's other CTV affiliate, CFCQ [sic] in Saskatoon, would place about 38% of the entire CTV network's revenues in Bassett's hands— three times as much as any other single interest. Moreover, these three stations together account for about 72% of the Canadian programming of the entire CTV network."[37] Clearly the major broadcasting groups in CTV were in an expansive mode as the broadcasting system faced a new era of media concentration. The growing number of acquisitions by the principal broadcast-owners of the network invariably meant that conflicts would arise between their positions as owners of CTV and as powerful regional broadcasters in their respective areas of operation across Canada. The CRTC maintained a watchful eye on the rapidly changing private broadcasting industry, an era when developments had serious implications for the future of the network.

GAME SHOWS HAD dominated CTV's programming during the 1960s. By the 1970s, the network provided a somewhat greater range of programming though the formats were still largely predictable. Musical programs were more in evidence and, for the first time, CTV undertook the production of its own "sitcom" entitled *Excuse My French*. According to Arthur Weinthal, the network's Vice-President of Programming, the sitcom was a "moderately successful" program. Regulatory pressure on CTV to produce suitable dramatic programming would continue to build into the 1980s. Although CTV could claim no notable success in drama production, it had reluctantly tried to respond to regulatory prodding. A production fund that CTV had established early in the decade had helped to improve the network's programming performance. The CRTC had noted "with approval an expenditure of nearly $570,000 on this account during 1973, 1974 and 1975."[38]

The CTV produced musical fare during the 1970s included *Rollin on the River*, a musical series that featured a rising star, singer Kenny Rogers; the *George Kirby Show,* which entertained audiences with Kirby's versatile performances; *Nashville North,* which later became the *Ian Tyson* show; *Shake, Rock and Roll* and *Pig n' Whistle*, a musical program set in an English pub that ran successfully for ten years on CTV. The program *Banjo Parlor* from Vancouver, helped to round out a network schedule that gradually began to have more variety in its programming.[39]

The program *Here Come the Seventies* was a "pop public affairs show" about newsworthy developments in a new decade. CTV also produced a "mind" show featuring *Kreskin* later known as *The Amazing Kreskin*. Still the network was not without game shows such as *Mr. and Mrs.*, the program format that had been a staple of the 1960s. Other fare seen on CTV during the 1970s included *Star Lost*, a science fiction program produced with 20th Century Fox for CTV and the owned and operated stations of the NBC in the United States. *Star Lost* marked the beginning of what became known as a "co-production," a controversial form of programming in which production costs were shared for the programs aired on TV networks in the participating nations. Critics argued that such programming tended to lose its indigenous quality, because it was designed to be sold worldwide rather than solely for the Canadian market. No Canadian movies were seen on CTV and TV drama was virtually nonexistent.[40]

Though often controversial and the brunt of criticism, co-productions were to play an important role in CTV's programming schedule. Murray Chercover told the CRTC in November, 1972 that co-productions were a "field which we have pioneered and persevered with." In his appearance before the Commission's hearing into the network's licence renewal, Chercover responded to the frequent criticism made against co-productions—insufficient Canadian identity and their lack of indigenous quality. In defence, Chercover drew the Commission's attention to the series *Untamed World* and the production *Story Theatre*, which he argued had been critically acclaimed: "Now in spite of critical comments, at worst our co-production activities have resulted in a greater expenditure on Canadian artists, performers, craftsmen and facilities than would have been the case if we were producing wholly within our own resources. At best, they have enabled us to develop such series as *Untamed World*, widely acclaimed critically, wholly written and produced by Canadians shown in over 31 countries; *Story Theatre*, a unique experimental form of drama for families and young people, universally acclaimed critically, well received, exposed in the United States and on the BBC in Great Britain."[41]

Still in its decision to renew CTV's licence from 1 October 1976 to 30 September 1979, the Commission lamented the loss of *Excuse My French* from CTV's schedule after two seasons and the lack of drama on the network. The CRTC had shown that it would concentrate more on the content of the broadcasting system in the years ahead and focus less on such issues as extension of the private network's service. The sitcom produced at station CFCF had employed both English and French Canadian performers. Clearly the Commission saw the loss of the program as a deficiency in the CTV schedule and in a program category the Commission had tried to nurture: "The series, which is not being continued, ran two seasons, achieving the third highest rating among CTV's Canadian programs in the winter of 1975–76. The Commission expects the network, in future schedules, to correct the deficiency of no weekly Canadian drama in the 1976–77 network schedule."[42] The regulatory demand for drama production on the network, regardless of its cost for private broadcasters, would continue to challenge CTV.

By 1979, the CRTC had concluded that the production of dramatic programming had to become a high priority for the network. The Commission had served notice that in the next decade it would place even greater emphasis on the need for such fare in the network's schedule: "The Commission considers that CTV has been very successful in the area of information programs and sports, and should be commended for the high quality of the news and public affairs and sports staff which it has assembled and developed. However in the opinion of the Commission CTV has not yet in the main achieved comparable results with distinctive Canadian entertainment programming, particularly in the field of drama."[43]

In short, as a populist service that provided credible news programming and appealing sports coverage, CTV was entitled to some self-congratulations. But its future as an alternative private network would depend heavily on the extent to which it could respond to the demands for more drama production, an expensive form of programming that faced serious competition from the popular entertaining fare seen on

United States television. American entertainment models had influenced viewer behaviour ever since the pioneer days of television. As the 1980s approached and the growth of cable television and satellite delivery provided expanded viewer choice, nothing appeared ready to alter the established viewing practices of Canadians. Home-grown productions would have to be costly to remain competitive against American programming.

THROUGHOUT THE 1970s, CTV remained preoccupied with its structure which could not help but have impact on its performance as a national network. A major restructuring of CTV had paralleled its expanded programming service in news and sports fare. The realignment was aimed at making the network more economically efficient and causing less division among its owner-affiliates. A more clearly defined network organization, it was argued, would enable CTV to play an enhanced role in the Canadian broadcasting system.

A new affiliation agreement in 1973 was intended to bring order to the private network's operation in specific areas. It called for a realignment of the network, a restructuring that divided the affiliates into three distinct classes: full affiliate, affiliate and supplementary affiliate. A full affiliate was a TV station whose revenue in the preceding fiscal year from all transmitters, and re-broadcasters owned by the station amounted to a minimum of two million dollars. The second category, an affiliate, was a station with revenue less than two million dollars. The third classification, supplementary affiliate, had to meet three criteria. First, such a station had to be located in a market not a priority for national advertisers; second, it was to be incapable of participating in the financial support of network operations; and third, the station had to become what was known as a "twin stick," because the addition of the CTV service could threaten the economic base of the station's position in its market.[44] A "twin stick" television operation such as CKPR, Thunder Bay was a station that had two transmitters, one that broadcast CBC programs and the other was affiliated with CTV.

The new affiliation agreement was a significant document. The arrangement established the basis for the future financing of the network. The cost of the network operations was to be the responsibility of the "full affiliates" and the principle of one station, one vote contained in early agreements still applied. The affiliation agreement in 1973 noted specifically: "It is intended that...the obligations of the Network will be borne on a proportional basis by those stations qualified to do so, i.e. the Full Affiliates, and...for the purpose of operating the Network each shareholder from the Full Affiliates or Affiliate Class will retain only a single vote and voice in Network policy. In those instances where more than one station is effectively owned or controlled by a single company or individual, there shall only be one voting representative on the Board of Directors for all stations so owned and controlled."[45] The notion of CTV as a co-operative was reiterated. Major affiliate-owners of the network such as CFTO, Toronto, British Columbia Television Broadcasting System Ltd., operator of CHAN-TV, Vancouver and Multiple Access Limited, owner of CFCF, TV Montreal would still have only one vote at the directors' table. The new affiliation agreement placed heavy financial responsibilities for the network's operation on the shoulders of the full affiliates.

AT THE END OF THE 1970s, the structure of CTV had expanded greatly. The network consisted of 14 full affiliates, two affiliates, four supplementary affiliates and 216 rebroadcast transmitters. The technological structure of CTV enabled it to cover 95 percent of the English-language population in Canada.[46] CTV still had to reconcile its need to adhere to the dictates of the marketplace with the demands placed upon it by the CRTC and the cultural objectives of the Canadian broadcasting system. The network was about to face the Commission again to seek a licence renewal at a time when the tension between both the network and the broadcaster regulator seemed to intensify.

A letter in September, 1978 from Murray Chercover to J.G. Patenaude, Acting Secretary General of the CRTC, raised several issues that were illustrative of the network's determination to respond to the regulator's concerns. Chercover was forced to deal with several matters that the Commission had raised: a demand for more Canadian drama, a concern about a shortage of independent Canadian television productions on the network and a Commission questioning of the centralization of programming on CTV stemming from the dominance of CFTO.

The CTV President wrote to the Commission: "During the broadcast season just recently concluded [1977–78], CTV produced and scheduled a successful, weekly half-hour adventure drama series entitled *Search and Rescue* and, for the current 1978/79 season planned, invested in, developed and committed to produce and schedule a science fiction-drama half-hour series, *The Shape of Things to Come*. Both projects were the product of international co-production agreements with independent producers." Chercover informed the Commission of the problems that CTV had encountered in its efforts to make greater use of independent producers: "The latter property [*Shape of Things to Come*] has been deferred indefinitely as a consequence of the failure of independent Canadian financial partners, despite the co-producers and ourselves having delivered theatrical distribution with monetary guarantees, U.S. and foreign television distribution with substantial financial guarantees and our own Canadian license contracts—all of which conformed to their expressed needs and requirements."[47]

In his response to the CRTC's lament that independent productions were not listed regularly in CTV schedules, Chercover noted that "CTV and its stations are themselves Canada's largest independent television enterprises which, we would hope, the Commission recognizes."[48] Still Chercover's boast to the Commission about the production capabilities of individual CTV affiliates could not conceal the alienation felt by some independent producers towards the network.

A study of *The Independent Production Industry with respect to English language programs for broadcast in Canada* by the Centre for Communications Studies at the University of Windsor outlined the role of the production houses owned by powerful CTV affiliates. Among them were CFTO's Glen Warren Productions; Carleton Productions Limited and Champlain Productions which belonged respectively to CJOH, Ottawa and CFCF, Montreal. The study in 1976 under principal investigator Professor Hugh H. Edmonds explained the attitude of independent producers towards CTV: "What the independent producers tell us is that by and large they have a very unreceptive audience for their proposals. Again, the explanation may be rather simple: the Network simply cannot afford the direct costs involved unless it is entering into some co-production arrangement in which the co-producer recovers the balance of his costs through international or U.S. distribution." Among the comments from independent producers questioned in the study was the following: "Our major market, CTV Network, has now closed its doors to independent producers and buys only from its stations or their subsidiaries—Glen Warren (CFTO), Champlain (CFCF, CJOH, B.C.-TV.)"[49]

In his letter to the Commission, Chercover had noted a fundamental dichotomy between the role of the independent producer and the network he headed: "While the objective of CTV and its affiliates is to provide programming which will first serve the interests of our Canadian viewers, independent Canadian producers are, of necessity, more likely motivated by the need to extract profit and to meet the demands of other potential markets as well as their investors."[50] In the next decade or so, independent production houses in Canada would grow more profitable and Canadian TV networks would have greater reliance on them when programming their schedules.

The CRTC was always concerned about the question of regional input on CTV and the need to have programming that originated from network affiliates beyond central Canada. In the eyes of the Commission, a heavy Toronto orientation in the CTV schedule was to be avoided. The broadcast regulator had underlined the fact that in the 1976/77 schedule "nearly 50% of CTV's Canadian programs will originate in Toronto." In response, Chercover simply turned the argument back on the regulator: "The same comment, looked at positively, is far more significant in that *more than 50%* of CTV's entertainment programming continues to be produced by other member stations other than Toronto! We feel this de-centralization is a rather remarkable achievement and should be regarded as such by the Commission." On the issue of regional contribution from network affiliates, the CTV President drew a comparison with other broadcast systems throughout the world: "Moreover, such de-centralization does not conform to the professional practices in any other developed nation—the U.K., France, Italy, Germany and even the United States, nor does it maximize our competitive performance potential, which could best be achieved by marshalling maximum creative and technical services."[51]

Whatever defence of its performance that CTV advanced before the Commission, Chercover had no choice but to address the sensitive topic of Canadian content requirements. The CRTC's definition of the peak viewing time between 8:00 P.M. and 10:00 P.M. was when CTV had often presented the popular American programming that drew large audiences for advertisers. The Commission preferred to see Canadian entertainment programming aired in this time period. Chercover challenged the regulatory notion: "For example, the peak viewing hours designation, referred to above, is artificial. If it were sensibly adjusted during the winter period, 7:00–9:00 P.M. would be so classified. In summer, 9:00 to 11:00 P.M. would be more applicable, but only for mass appeal general audience programming. It should be noted that peak viewing for most sports events is weekend afternoon time. Similarly, service shows, soap operas and strip game shows find their particular peak audiences on a daily basis in morning and afternoon periods."[52]

Chercover's observations were in flat contradiction to the Commission's position on the placement of popular Canadian fare. Aware of the time segments when CTV could draw the largest audiences, he saw no advantage to be gained by positioning popular home-grown programs against strong American programming in the prime-time period: "The Commission must recognize that Canadian programming suffers most when facing U.S. network prime time, high cost competition in the 8:00—11:00 P.M. period. Moreover, we have demonstrated that significant Canadian programming such as *Question Period* and *W5*, or entertainment shows such as *Stars on Ice* or drama programming such as *Search and Rescue* perform more competitively when scheduled other than against U.S. network programming in the 8:00–11:00 P.M. time period."[53] Clearly there was a disconnect between CTV and the broadcast regulator. The historic difficulty in reconciling the cultural imperatives of Canadian broadcasting with market forces was readily apparent in the exchange between Chercover and the Commission over CTV's forthcoming licence renewal.

By the late 1970s, network television in Canada had to contend steadily with the growing impact of cable television which had caused extensive audience fragmentation. Chercover told the Commission that the policy of *simultaneous program substitution* was "the only viable regulatory policy" that had contributed to "the repatriation of lost audiences to Canadian stations." Under this regulation, when a Canadian and an American station showed the same program in the same period, cable operators substituted the Canadian signal for the U.S. channel. The initiative gave maximum exposure to Canadian advertising and blocked out American commercial messages. "The purely quantitative Canadian content regulation," argued Chercover, "has produced a predictable 'watering-down' of the competitive quality of Canadian-produced television programs, particularly in the face of escalating foreign program costs, created by the licensing by the Commission of many new Canadian outlets."[54]

LOOKING TO A NEW DECADE, Chercover appeared ambivalent about the future of private broadcasting. Major challenges faced Canadian broadcasters in the 1980s: "The program season just recently begun is our last of the decade of the 70's. The license we seek to renew with this letter of application and subsequent appearance before you, will carry us into the next decade; a decade feared by some as the Orwellian 80's and eagerly anticipated by others as the decade of significant technological advancement."[55]

Despite the tension with the CRTC, the CTV network still had managed to build audience largely at the expense of the CBC English language service. As a mass entertainment programmer, and with no widespread protest among Canadian viewers over the fare that it offered, CTV could take a somewhat supine approach to the question of regulation. The network undoubtedly remained conscious of Canadians' eagerness to watch popular American programs. Having fallen short of expectations in categories such as Canadian drama, the network's populist programming thrust had continued to attract a growing audience of viewers.

The *Report of the Federal Cultural Policy Review Committee* (Applebert) under the co-chairmanship of Louis Applebaum and Jacques Hébert assessed the Canadian broadcasting system in the early 1980s and commented on the loss of audience that the CBC had experienced. By 1980, a fundamental realignment in the broadcasting system was underway amidst a new electronic media environment that showed CTV in the ascendant: "Between 1968 and 1980, according to CRTC and CBC figures, the share of audience watching CBC English-language television fell from 35 percent to 18 percent, while that of its affiliated stations fell from 12 percent to 5 percent. In the same period, CTV audience rose from 25 to 30 percent, and that of the US channels from 24 to 32 percent. (These percentages do not total 100 because independent and other stations are not included.)"[56]

Given its share of Canadian viewers, the CTV network would have to be seen as a success on the eve of a new decade. After starting the 1970s by winning the broadcasting rights to an international hockey event that will be long remembered, the network through both its news and sports coverage had presented a clear alternative to Canadians viewers who seemed attracted to its colloquial style of presentation. After two decades, the programming contrast with the more formal CBC presentation had appealed to a wide audience of viewers. Still the network was not without its critics. CTV would have its licence renewed in 1979 but not before the talent unions, notably the Association of Canadian Television and Radio Artists (ACTRA), would deliver a scathing criticism of the network's operation before it could welcome the 1980s.

EIGHT

The Dominator Retaliates
1979–1985

CHARLES JOSEPH CLARK, the youngest Prime Minister in Canadian history, came to power on 22 May 1979 when the Conservative party ousted Pierre Trudeau and the Liberals. The short lived Tory administration was defeated on a budget in the House of Commons and lost the February election the following year to the Liberals. However the Clark government was in power long enough to make changes to federal agencies such as the CRTC. John Meisel, a Queen's University professor, replaced Pierre Camu in 1979 as Chairman of the CRTC. The appointment of Meisel followed in the year after a major public hearing where the CRTC had denied the application of Baton Broadcasting Inc., and its owner John Bassett, to acquire control of CFCF television in Montreal from Multiple Access Limited, a division of the extensive Bronfman holdings, the licensee of the TV operation.

"Oh yeah, I tried to buy it," said Bassett, "I was defeated by a vote of 5–4 and it's the first time in the history of the CRTC that they presented two reports: they presented a minority report you know....But it shows you that it's a long road that has no ashcans."[1] Bassett believed that other factors were at work that cost him the Montreal licence, beyond the question of ownership concentration. Allan Beattie, Chairman of Baton, remembered the Commission's focus on the question of concentration in the mass media. "There was a lot of concern in the '60s and '70s about control in the media and single ownerships owning too many different vehicles. There was talk that no one broadcasting company should be allowed to own too many licences and so at the end of the 70s Baton was actually turned down in its efforts to try to own Montreal."[2]

In the late 1970s there was regulatory skepticism towards concentration of ownership or what has become known as "convergence." The denial of Baton's application came only eight years after the release of the *Report of the Special Senate Committee on Mass Media* (Davey Report) under the chairmanship of Senator Keith Davey. The committee, which drew a great deal of public attention, recommended the establishment of a Press Ownership Review Board to review mergers in the print industry only. The CRTC would continue to deal with broadcasters: "The Canadian Radio-Television Commission now has authority over broadcasting mergers, and has exercised this power in a series of licensing decisions which add up to an evolving policy on ownership concentration. The intent of this series of decisions, as we define it, is that the C.R.T.C. is already following the same broad guideline that we propose for the Press Ownership Review Board: concentration is bad— unless proved otherwise."[3]

The Senate Committee's report could not help but serve as a recent backdrop to the Commission's decision involving the Baton application to purchase CFCF. The Commission could have taken into account the Senate Committee's finding that most of Canada's television networks and stations have broadcasters eager to produce quality programs. Still the Committee had added a qualifier: "But these organizations also feel a very deep obligation to continue their role as the principal medium for advertising soap, cosmetics, and instant coffee. And the competition between the demands of these differing roles is not being resolved in favour of public service or social responsibility."[4]

An examination of the Commission's decision on the Baton application leaves little doubt that its decision was influenced by its consideration of the important question of ownership concentration and the fear that too much Canadian media would fall into too few hands. The first line of the CRTC's decision on 12 October 1978 underlined its principal concern: "In the Commission's opinion, the most significant issue raised by this application is concentration of ownership and control within the Canadian broadcasting system." At the time, the decision noted, Baton "a public company controlled by the Eaton and Bassett family trusts" owned CFTO-TV, Toronto, CFQC-TV Saskatoon, and four radio stations, CFGO, Ottawa, CKLW and CKLW-FM, Windsor and CFQC, Saskatoon. Baton also owned Glen Warren Productions Limited, described as "the largest and best equipped privately owned television production facility in Canada, and one which enjoys an enviable international reputation."[5]

Specifically, the CRTC focused on Baton's dominant role in CTV: "Within the CTV network, Baton is by far the largest group, receiving more than twice as much air time sales revenue as the second place group, which is in fact Multiple Access. In 1976–77, Baton received 52.3% of all sums paid by the CTV network to member stations for the production of programs. Multiple Access received 20.1%." The Commission's fear was that if the application were approved, "Baton would control CTV licensees reaching 30% of the Canadian population, receiving almost 40% of the total air time sales revenue of all CTV stations, and accounting for over 70%, in dollar terms, of all production for the network."[6] Baton also would obtain two major English language radio stations in the transaction, CFCF and CFQR-FM.

At a public hearing on 13 April 1978, Bassett tried to meet head-on the arguments against media concentration. With greater resources in both facilities and personnel, he maintained that "we can utilize the talents that exist in Montreal and the Province of Quebec and present these talents to the rest of the country in a way that has not been done heretofore, and if approval is granted, I undertake to do so." He argued that "only through such concentrations of broadcasting strength can Canadians hope to develop programming that will woo our audiences away from U.S. programming." However the Commission did not accept Bassett's argument about the advantages to concentration. The CRTC considered that "the improvements to Canadian television programming suggested by Baton were essentially presented in general rather than specific terms and that it was not concretely demonstrated by Baton how combined control of the licensees of CFTO-TV and CFCF-TV would improve the level and quality of Canadian programming."[7]

A dissenting opinion was receptive to Bassett's position. The minority report dealt with the question of diverse points of view in the media and challenged the majority findings by stressing the notions of economies of scale and profitability that gave advantage to multi-media owners: "Diversity in the domestic and international sources of opinion and information available to Canadians from within the program schedules and formats of the private elements of the Canadian broadcasting system is a function both of the extent and nature of the concentration of ownership and of the resources such economic strength or lack of it makes possible for news and informational programming." The commissioners who dissented concluded that concentration had improved rather than weakened the broadcasting system. Concentration had increased, and not lessened, the diversity of views in the media: "It is our opinion that an examination of the private element of the Canadian broadcasting system over the past decade would reveal that as the degree of concentration increased the sources of opinion, news, information and independent commentary within schedules and formats made possible increased as did the job opportunities for reporters, writers, commentators, editors, freelancers and stringers, etc."[8]

The media coverage of the CRTC ruling on the Baton application, "the first split decision in its 10-year history," focused on a central problem facing the broadcasting industry. In the *Financial Post*, Margaret Lewis dealt with the crux of the matter: "The case highlights the dilemma of the Canadian broadcasting industry—namely, can Canada hope to produce high-calibre domestic programming that can compete with U.S. imports without allowing concentration of ownership in the media?" Lewis reported that "industry sources claim the final decision was carried by a narrow vote of five to four, indicating that the issue is probably far from settled. The dissenting minority supported the argument for better Canadian programming through some degree of concentration of ownership."[9]

The issue of ownership concentration appeared to be a major factor in the Commission's decision to deny Baton the control of CFCF. Still Bassett was of the opinion that he had failed to get control of CFCF because of behind-the-scenes circumstances that occurred earlier and went beyond the issue of concentration. In his view, the decision against Baton was the extension of previous developments that involved the Canadian Association of Broadcasters.

The reasons for the denial of Baton, according to Bassett, were rooted in circumstances that had occurred back in April, 1970 when the CRTC under its chairman Pierre Juneau had conducted hearings into the question of Canadian content. The Cancon hearings involved the CAB, the private broadcasters' lobby group, which had an uneasy relationship with Baton. Bassett's interpretation of "the story behind the story" of Baton failing to get CFCF focused around the role played by both the

CAB and Pierre Camu, at one time a CAB President, and later a CRTC Chairman. Camu was Chairman when Baton was denied the licence for CFCF.

AS WAS ITS RELATIONSHIP with the Canadian Press, Baton was a reluctant member of the CAB. "I never wanted to join because of my experience in Canadian Press," Bassett said, "whereby metropolitan dailies had very little in common [with smaller papers]. You know what did *The Toronto Telegram* have in common with the *North Bay Nuggett*? Nothing, and you had all these smaller papers....But the same was true in the CAB." Bassett claimed that he "had been talked into joining the CAB" and "paid our dues," although he took no interest in a controversial CAB brief on the subject of Cancon that was presented to the CRTC hearing.[10]

When Bassett saw the CAB brief that was submitted to the hearing, he became irate and resigned his membership. "In any event at this hearing in Ottawa, the CAB came out with a brief, an absolutely unreasonable, terrible critical brief on the question of Canadian content," Bassett remembered. "But somebody brought me in the thing off the wire and I called Ottawa long distance right away. And I got Stu Griffiths [CJOH, Ottawa] who, although we disagreed from time to time, [we] were very close in our ideas on programming and were strongly in favour of Canadian programming." Bassett dictated a statement to Griffiths who communicated with the Commission: "I dictated a thing which he took down in which I publicly disassociated myself from the CAB brief and resigned my membership. And Griffiths did the same. Well of course Juneau was delighted, just delighted. Anyway the CAB were devastated."[11]

The backstage story continued to unfold. "Well time went on," said Bassett, "and a group of what I would call senior broadcasters decided to reconstitute, renovate the CAB and make it more meaningful. Ray Peters was very active. Philippe [de Gaspé] Beaubien who was a friend of mine was very active and one or two senior, serious people." Still Bassett refused to join the CAB: "They came to see me and I said 'oh, to hell with it.' I said 'tell you what I'll do. If you want to form an association of large broadcasters, I'll be glad to join.' So I refused."[12] The senior broadcasters went ahead with their plans to revitalize the CAB and appointed Dr. Pierre Camu as President. Later he succeeded Harry Boyle as Chairman of the CRTC.

When he was the CAB president, Camu paid a visit to Bassett at Baton's office on Richmond Street in downtown Toronto. The meeting was intended to bring Bassett on side and to get him to rejoin the CAB. "So Dr. Camu came to see me," said Bassett. "I was polite to him. He was a pompous fellow....took himself very seriously and so on, and I treated him in a very cavalier manner, politely, but dismissed him. I certainly was not going to join the CAB." From Camu's standpoint, his objective in arranging the meeting was to bring Bassett back into the CAB, "because he was a very important player." Camu thought the meeting "went well." Moreover he had thought "it was normal for me to increase the membership as much as possible in order to represent the voice of private broadcasting in this country."[13]

Recalling a familiar John Diefenbaker metaphor about "a long road" having "no ashcans," Bassett ultimately characterized the denial of the Baton application as a Camu move to stop him: "He became chairman of the CRTC and he cast the deciding vote against me when I [made] the Montreal application...."[14] The CFTO owner was incensed. Still Bassett, a prominent Tory who seemed to enjoy the role of king-maker, decided to play a final card. The Liberal reign of Pierre Trudeau was about to be interrupted by Joe Clark and the Conservatives. Bassett, a noted Ontario party stalwart among the Tory establishment, supported Clark from High River, Alberta. At the time, tension existed between the Ontario and Alberta wings of the federal party.

Bassett had been especially critical of Jack Horner, an Alberta MP who later joined the Liberals, and had stood for the party leadership in 1976 against Clark. Bassett said several times that Horner was both "a bully [and] a redneck." With a sense of humour, Bassett recalled an interview between Horner and CFTO journalist Fraser Kelly on *Canada AM* following the 1976 Tory leadership convention in Ottawa when Bassett, Eddie Goodman and their wives were in the Chateau Laurier hotel preparing to catch a flight back to Toronto. "Kelly had asked Horner, 'well how do you explain you did so badly?'" said Bassett. "'Oh,' he said 'the media defeated me.' He said 'John Bassett attacked me all the time.' He said 'I know you. The fellas like you. You think John Bassett's a prince. But I spell that prince: prick!'"[15]

Laughingly Bassett remembered: "So I came back to Toronto, poor Kelly damn near died! I roared with laughter. But I...took a very serious view of it. And I called CTV right away...and I said 'you'll be hearing from my lawyer, I want a public apology and so on.' And I had them serve a writ on Horner which I never pursued. But CTV made a public apology and the whole thing. That was a famous *Canada AM*." Bassett had never really intended to pursue the matter: "Oh, I wasn't going to sue CTV, but they publicly apologized and that was the end of it. Ha Ha!" In his eyes, Horner was "a big bully, somebody should have flattened him!"[16]

Clearly Bassett was not one to be found lacking a sense of occasion. With the election of the minority government headed by Clark, Bassett felt a need to retaliate for what he considered to be an improper CRTC decision on his attempt to expand Baton through the acquisition of the Montreal station. Bassett was prepared to exercise his backstage influence: "Joe Clark became Prime Minister. I supported him. He wasn't there very long, but he was there long enough to fire Camu. So I cost him his job...but he cost me the Montreal licence."[17]

Obviously Bassett was bitterly disappointed over his defeat. Bill Neville, Joe Clark's Chief of Staff, had offered Camu the post of Deputy Minister of Transport. But instead Camu resigned as CRTC Chairman for "personal reasons" and returned to the private sector. "I believe that Bassett was very influential in the Conservative party," said Camu. "He succeeded in working his way and saying 'I want his head' and he got it. That's my view." On the question of the level of media concentration at the time, Camu said he "was very concerned with it. Mind you I was not alone."[18]

A prominent member of the CTV network had lost an important CRTC ruling, a decision that seemed to foreshadow a new era when the broadcast regulator would demand a higher level of performance from private television broadcasters. CTV was about to face sharp criticism from talent unions, government inquiries and the CRTC. Beyond the question of CTV's performance, as Canada entered the 1980s the country's broadcasting system was to undergo profound changes that were to have lasting impact on conventional TV broadcasters.

REGULATORY PRESSURES would build on Canadian private broadcasters and networks such as CTV to provide enhanced Canadian programming, especially home-grown dramatic productions. The network maintained an uneasy relationship with talent unions such as the ACTRA.

The tensions between CTV and the broadcast regulator, as well as ACTRA's intervention at a CRTC hearing in February, 1979 were indicators of the need for the private network to reconcile its reliance on mass programming and advertising with the cultural objectives of Canadian broadcasting.

The evidence was clear that conventional Canadian television networks such as CTV faced a new era of competition especially with the sustained growth of cable television. Alphonse Ouimet, a former President of the CBC, underlined the significance of "The Television Revolution and the National Interest." He singled out cable TV as "the most important agent of change": "With 50 percent cable saturation, Canada is the most cabled country of any size in the world. This figure is the general average for all parts of Canada including remote locations which couldn't possibly have cable, even if they wanted to. Considering urban areas alone, the percentage is much higher, with many cities, such as Vancouver and here in London [Ontario], nearing full saturation with over 90 percent."[19]

The growth of cable and its extraordinary capacity to deliver an extensive array of foreign TV channels could not help but have a dramatic impact on Canadian broadcasters. Additional levels of competition for conventional broadcasters included the licensing by the CRTC of six Pay-TV licences in 1982 and of the first satellite-to-cable specialty channels, MuchMusic and The Sports Network in 1984. With the arrival of a new decade, CTV and CBC, the principal players in Canadian television, faced a broadcasting environment that provided viewers with a greatly expanded choice of TV services.

At the February, 1979 hearing into CTV's application for its licence renewal, ACTRA was exceedingly critical of the network. The talent union's brief emphasized its disenchantment with the performance of the private network and showed how uneasy the relationship was between CTV and one of Canada's major artistic groups. ACTRA's negative assessment of CTV, and the network's determined response, illustrated the difficulty the CRTC faced in trying to strike a balance between the economic and cultural aspects of Canadian broadcasting.

ACTRA made three forceful arguments against CTV. First, the talent union accused the network of fighting vigorously against the CRTC's attempt to Canadianize the television broadcasting system in Canada. ACTRA's 13-page brief explained: "The network's schedule currently contains 64.4 percent Canadian programming. But—and it's a significant but—in the Fall and Spring schedule only 7 percent of Canadian programming, three hours a week, is broadcast in prime time. Alternatively, 68 percent, 15 hours a week, of American production is aired during the hours when most Canadians are watching television."[20] ACTRA considered prime time television to be between 7:30 P.M. and 11 P.M. The assessment of the amount of American production did not include Canadian-American mixtures such as *Wide World of Sports* which could include sporting events and athletes from both countries.

Second, ACTRA charged that CTV was a "private club" which existed solely for the "profit of its members." Specifically, the union focused on the profits made by the network's affiliates: "CTV has continuously worn beggar's garments although many of the member stations have enjoyed increasingly higher profits. In 1975, for example, CTV cried to the CRTC that the network had lost $800,000 (out of $35 million). Yet, since 1972, the number of stations which have prospered to the point of becoming full affiliates has increased from eight to fourteen. Last year Baton Broadcasting Inc. showed a profit of over seven and a half million dollars, up 22 per cent from the previous year. Bushnell Communications Ltd., Multiple Access Ltd., CFCN Communications, and others, also report substantial increases."[21]

ACTRA chose to rely on Canadian author Pierre Berton who had received early television exposure on CTV. "In an ACTRA submission to the CRTC in the 1971 Licence Renewal Hearing he [Berton] said, 'It has been to their (the station owners') advantage to finance CTV in such a way as to keep it poor. This has given the private broadcasters a weapon. By crying poormouth, CTV is trying to persuade the CRTC and public opinion that Canadian programming doesn't pay...'" The ACTRA brief noted also the conflicts within the corporate structure of CTV: "The network is suspect since there is a conflict of interest inherent in its basic structure. It is in the financial interests of the private broadcasters to hang on to as much local time as possible, to spend as little as possible on network productions and yet these are the people who are making the decisions at the CTV network."[22]

Significantly, ACTRA drew the CRTC's attention to the "vicious circle" that had resulted from both the network and affiliated stations raising advertising rates and blaming each other for the increases. ACTRA sought to explain how the affiliates had used the network "to their own advantage" in ways that were not always visible to the public: "In September of 1977, the network increased its advertising rates from between 17 to 26 percent. The official excuse given was that the cost of buying American shows has increased from 40 to 50 percent. But those in the advertising industry say there is another important reason. Local stations had or were about to boost their advertising rates by over 30 percent so that it would have been cheaper for an advertiser to buy time on the whole network rather than combinations of two or three stations."[23]

"A vicious circle" had resulted in the marketplace that drove CTV's operation. ACTRA was unequivocal in its avowed, cultural nationalist posture: "The individual stations can justify their price increases because of network increases; the network can justify its increase because of local increases." ACTRA argued that "it has been shown time and again that advertisers faced with high rates will buy nothing but large-audience American programs. They will not risk thousands of dollars per 30 second commercial on unknown Canadian productions. They too have been brainwashed that we as a nation are simply without the creative skills to produce interesting programming."[24]

The third main argument raised by ACTRA against CTV dealt with the extent to which the network had "continuously disregarded CRTC's recommendations." The union underlined the lack of Canadian drama in CTV's schedule: "The CRTC…noted that there was no weekly Canadian drama in the 1976–77 schedule. There is no weekly Canadian drama in the 1978–79 schedule either. *Excuse My French*; *Swiss Family Robinson*; *Police Surgeon*; all were popular shows, all have disappeared. *Search and Rescue*, which was broadcast last season, is gone. The half-hour science fiction series, *The Shape of Things to Come*, scheduled for this year is cancelled, a victim, says CBC [*sic*] President Murray Chercover, of Canadian financiers who pulled out of the production."[25]

ACTRA questioned CTV's reliance on "co-productions," its lack of the use of independent productions and the central Canada domination of local production by stations. The union asked, "Does co-production mean more Americanization of Canadian television since many such programs have no Canadian orientation, and fit just as nicely into the social milieu of Toledo and Pittsburgh as Hamilton or Regina?" Moreover the ACTRA brief argued, "There are no independent productions planned so far this season [1978–79] to be shown by CTV; the majority of programs bought by the network from other member stations are still produced in Toronto."[26] Clearly ACTRA had presented a forceful intervention at the hearing in 1979. CTV had no choice but to respond.

From the network's standpoint, CTV tried to counter the ACTRA brief which had a destructive potential on the outcome of the network's licence renewal hearing. The network challenged ACTRA's argument relating to CTV's scheduling of American programs in prime time and the union's position that the private network had worked against the Canadianization of the television system. According to CTV, it had to function within certain regulatory imperatives designed to bolster the overall broadcasting system: "Canadian broadcasters must take advantage of the audience appeal of those more expensive American television shows and schedule them, wherever possible and practical, simultaneously with their release on the U.S. networks—thus implementing the commission's regulation which provides for simultaneous program substitution. The American networks only program from 8:00 to 11:00 P.M. Therefore, we can only schedule those shows in that time period." CTV argued that ACTRA chose "to disregard this imperative, as do some of the other critics, despite the fact that these procedures minimize the audience loss and provide the funding to produce more and better television programs in Canada."[27] The CTV response underlined a fundamental dichotomy in Canadian broadcasting; revenue from American programming helps to pay for Canadian productions.

CTV maintained that ACTRA was incorrect "when they calculate our Canadian content with their artificial definition of prime time." The network challenged ACTRA's claim that "68%, 15 hours, of the network's schedule, in their arbitrarily re-defined prime time period," was American programming. "In fact," argued CTV, "the network's American content in that artificial, ACTRA-classified, prime time period is 7 hours, out of a total of 13, or 53.8%." ACTRA had failed to understand the differentiation "between network sales time, our reserve time programming and station sales time programming." CTV argued that "the measurement of content insofar as the network is concerned only applies to reserve or network sales time in two defined categories, overall and from 6:00 P.M. to midnight."[28] It will be recalled that network sales time was that portion of the total CTV service where network programming was aired on time that was reserved for the network on the affiliated stations. Station sales time allowed affiliates a greater flexibility in the times they showed programming that had been provided to them by the network.

As for ACTRA's argument that CTV was "a private club" that existed for the profit of its member stations, the network threw the ball back in the union's court: "ACTRA has a substantial investment resource of its own—the ACTRA pension fund—yet hasn't invested a penny of it directly in support of any aspect of the Canadian production industry, particularly in the development of speculative program ventures." Still ACTRA demanded "that CTV do more, much more, so it and its members—the real 'club' in Canadian broadcasting—can be guaranteed to prosper."[29]

Finally CTV charged that ACTRA operated in a time warp when it countered the union's lament that the network had repeatedly disregarded CRTC's recommendations and the concerns expressed about the disappearance of certain shows from the 1972 schedule: "That is a little bit like asking why *Have Gun, Will Travel* is still not on CBS or why *Lucy* is still not on the air. The programs they identify were, over time and in the natural course of the ebb and flow of audience interest, replaced by other shows such as *Swiss Family Robinson* and *Excuse My French* which, in turn, have been replaced in subsequent seasons by some expensive and popular shows such as *Circus, Stars On Ice, Live It Up,* et cetera." As for its relationship with the independent production industry in Canada, CTV argued that "every season for the past six years such independent ventures have been part of our regular schedule."[30]

Still intervenors such as ACTRA that emerged at the public hearing were not the only critics determined to hold CTV accountable. CTV and the private broadcasting industry received a further harsh assessment both from a federal inquiry and a prominent arts organization as the 1970s came to a close and a new decade began. The Consultative Committee on the Implications of Telecommunications for Canadian Sovereignty (Clyne Committee) under the chairmanship of J.V. Clyne singled out the private television sector including CTV as negligent in the production of Canadian programming: "Taking this group as a whole, while recognizing individual differences in markets and programming performance, we do not believe that they are doing all they could and ought to do in the way of Canadian program production."[31]

Relying on a brief submitted by CAB, the Clyne Committee underlined the historical ambivalence in the Canadian broadcasting system that related to the desire of Canadians to watch United States programming: "Canadian broadcasters buy American programs because they attract large audiences; the advertising rates charged are therefore higher, and the resultant revenue helps to pay for Canadian program production. It is estimated that the Canadian broadcasting industry buys distribution rights for U.S. programs to the tune of $50 million a year, a sum that represents about 20 per cent of all U.S. producers' foreign sales."[32] As a Canadian network operated as a business, CTV had no choice but to rely on popular U.S. programming for its survival.

A major recommendation of the Clyne Committee called upon the CRTC to introduce "a points system for measuring Canadian content combining qualitative, quantitative, and prime-time aspects, without relinquishing the present concept of a minimum quantity, but with strong emphasis on quality." This approach to the historic Cancon issue represented a break with established practice and put the private broadcasters on notice that they must produce a greater range of quality Canadian programming. The Canadian content rules governing both the CBC and private broadcasters had been "only quantitative, expressed only in percentages and related to different periods of the broadcasting day and week."[33]

The Canadian Conference of the Arts in a major study entitled *A Strategy for Culture*, urged still greater governmental and regulatory initiatives to force the private broadcasters to play a more meaningful role in the Canadian broadcasting industry. The arts community recommended that "through a combination of regulations and incentives (wherever the latter are justified), the federal government take action to ensure that a significant proportion of the gross revenues of the private television broadcasters, and of their program production budgets, are committed to Canadian program production and the purchase of Canadian programs from independent producers." Specifically in relation to CTV, the report called for the CRTC to review "the financial structure of the CTV network, as proposed in the network's 1979 license renewal decision, with a view to reorganizing CTV financing in a manner which would more reasonably reflect the profitability of its affiliates."[34] The network's reliance for business reasons on American programming was certain to come under close scrutiny in future.

CTV FELT THE HEAVY impact of the CRTC's regulatory might when its licence was renewed for three years on 3 August 1979. The decision appeared to show a more interventionist broadcast regulator of the Canadian broadcasting system. The CRTC seemed prepared to place a greater reliance on "conditions of licence." The CRTC made it a condition "of the renewal of the CTV network licence that 26 hours of original new Canadian drama be presented during the 1980–81 broadcasting year, and 39 hours of original new Canadian drama be presented during the 1981–82 season." Moreover in planning these dramatic programs or series, "a minimum of 50% should be entirely domestic, rather than co-productions with foreign partners." The CRTC insisted that the focus "should be on Canadian themes and the contemplated productions should be intended for telecasting in the peak viewing periods of the evening schedules."[35] CTV's electronic feet had been put to the fire.

The broadcast regulator had offered a stiff challenge to CTV as the network prepared to enter the 1980s. No longer was the CRTC seemingly prepared to accept the conventional private broadcasters' argument that Canadian dramatic productions were too expensive and therefore difficult to produce. The Commission recognized that the condition of licence imposed in 1979 would necessitate "a substantial increase in the funds provided for the development and production of Canadian programs at a time when many other network costs are increasing." But it was satisfied that the resources of the CTV system were sufficient "in terms of financial and production capability" to provide programs that would show Canadians "a significantly greater production effort." The CRTC would look for a clear commitment from the network's member stations "to employ these resources adequately."[36]

By the 1980s, CTV had expanded its reach as a network, developed its news, public affairs and sports offerings and had brought entertaining programming to Canadians, much of it American. What could be described as the low culture offered by the private network had resonated with a sizable audience of Canadian viewers. But following the CRTC decision it became imperative for the network to Canadianize its schedule with a higher quality of Canadian programming and to rely less on co-productions.

CTV appealed the CRTC's decision renewing its licence subject to the condition requiring a specific number of hours of original Canadian drama; the network wanted its licence to be renewed unconditionally. The Federal Court of Appeal set aside the decision and referred it back to the Commission. The CRTC subsequently appealed and CTV cross-appealed to the Supreme Court of Canada. In the end, the Supreme Court allowed the CRTC appeal and dismissed the CTV cross-appeal.[37] CTV had to accept the Commission's decision of August, 1979.

John Travers Coleman, a CTV executive for over two decades, wrote in a private perspective entitled *Canadian Television's 'Game Scenarios' for the Nineties* that the absence "of specified procedure for the attachment of conditions of licence" rather than "the substance of the conditions in question which dealt with Canadian content programming" caused CTV "to pit itself" against the CRTC before the Supreme Court of Canada.[38] Whatever the network's rationale, the combative posture of CTV brought a surprised reaction from the Chairman of the Commission.

The Supreme Court of Canada delivered its judgement to allow the CRTC appeal in the CTV case on 5 April 1982. In his notes for an address to the Broadcast Executives Society in Toronto on 11 May 1982, John Meisel compared the Canadian content quotas in the broadcasting system with the efforts by other countries to nurture their own cultures. Specifically, he found it curious that CTV would go to extreme legal lengths to avoid regulatory measures imposed by the Commission: "Many of the other countries have adopted measures much more stringent than those we know here. I think of Australia, for example, and of France, the Netherlands, Belgium, Italy, and a host of other countries in Africa and Asia. And yet CTV felt compelled to challenge in the highest court of the land the CRTC's requirement that it produce a measly 26 hours of new Canadian drama for 1980–81 and 39 hours the following year."[39]

Indeed the Supreme Court's decision was some solace for the CRTC and its regulatory approach to the question of Canadian programming. Meisel's notes for a speech to the Canadian Film and Television Association on 15 April 1982, shortly after the court's decision and the Commission's licensing of six pay-television services, underlined the significance of the Supreme Court's verdict and the promise it held for independent television producers: "Sometimes it is assumed that pay television is the *only* source of money to support the production industry. But although it is important, particularly at this time, pay television is not a panacea. Fortunately, there are other very promising signs. The recent Supreme Court decision upholding the conditions of licence given to CTV is a most welcome and encouraging sign for the Canadian production industry. Its implications are there to be pondered."[40] Clearly the private broadcasting industry would be expected to make a greater contribution to Canadian programming in the 1980s as Canada entered a new broadcasting era.

Three separate initiatives in the early 1980s, a federal inquiry, new CRTC proposals on Canadian content and a Department of Communications policy statement on broadcasting served to illustrate the extent to which Canadian broadcasters, especially the "privates," faced the challenges of a competitive broadcasting environment. Viewers would be able to enjoy a range of choices with the growth of cable TV, the advent of pay-TV and satellite-to-cable specialty services. Direct-to-home-broadcast satellites or DTH services were on the horizon.

The Applebaum-Hébert *Report of the Federal Cultural Policy Review Committee* (Applebert), a federal inquiry that dealt with the broad field of Canadian cultural institutions, was none too flattering to private broadcasters. The report drew a comparison between the costs that Canadian content regulations and conditions of licence imposed on private stations and the thrust of public policy that allowed these same stations to become profitable. Specifically, the Applebert report cited three measures: Section 19.1 of the *Income Tax Act* that disallowed Canadian companies the right to deduct as a business expense advertising on United States stations whose signals were received in Canada; the CRTC's simultaneous nonduplication rule that allowed Canadian stations to have their advertising substituted for that of American stations when the same program was broadcast on both stations simultaneously; and the 100 percent Capital Cost Allowance provided for investments in Canadian film and video including productions for television. The report had a pointed message for the CRTC and private television: "It is imperative that in setting content requirements and in granting licences, the CRTC consider the costs and benefits of all measures affecting private broadcasters. Private television broadcasting, in our view, does have a cultural responsibility—to provide information and quality entertainment."[41] In other words, CTV was no longer seen to be able to rely mainly on the importation of American programming regardless of how accepting audiences were to such fare. Applebert had seen the need for CTV programming to have a greater cultural dimension.

Canadian private television broadcasters also came in for sharp criticism when the CRTC released its Policy Statement on Canadian Content in Television on 31 January 1983, which seemed to foreshadow a new broadcasting environment. The Commission reiterated a statement contained in its 1979 announcement on Cancon: "With the exception of the Canadian Broadcasting Corporation, Canadian English-language broadcasters offer Canadian audiences virtually no Canadian entertainment programming in peak viewing periods and next to no Canadian drama—light or serious—at any period in their schedules." The Commission proposed a points system to provide for a clearer definition of Canadian content and expressed its intention to place greater reliance in the 1980s on conditions of licence: "Where circumstances warrant, the Commission intends to rely to a significantly greater extent than in the past on the use of conditions of licence to stimulate improvements in Canadian television programming."[42]

However in a dissenting report two commissioners, John Grace and Jean Louis Gagnon, did not share the view of the majority of the Commission, especially the proposal to tighten Canadian content requirements for conventional television broadcasters: "The position now being put forward by the Commission fails, in our view, to recognize sufficiently the new broadcasting reality: the growing, even overwhelming, abundance of viewer choice from both licensed and unlicensed sources. The Commission is proposing regulations for a broadcasting world which no longer exists." Specifically, Grace and Gagnon questioned the Commission's intention to rely more heavily on conditions of licence: "Licensees who might have volunteered to exceed minimum content requirements—and some now do—will hold back in the event of additional demands being placed upon them by a Commission that they will have been given some justification to fear as unrealistic."[43] Whatever their past behaviour, CTV and other private broadcasters appeared to face a harsher climate where the regulator would be concerned over the maintenance of a Canadian presence amidst an explosion of viewer choice.

Following the CRTC's proposed policy on Canadian content, Communications Minister Francis Fox outlined a new broadcasting strategy on 1 March 1983 that placed even more demands on the private industry to enhance its performance and improve Canadian programming. The minister's policy had a specific private sector thrust that was aimed at encouraging private broadcasters "to fulfill an expanded role in increasing both the quantity and quality of Canadian programming." Private TV broadcasters were to receive support from a new Canadian Broadcast Program Development Fund which would support at least half of their Canadian programming. The Liberal government's broadcast strategy placed emphasis on new, specialized, TV programming especially in the areas of children's and cultural programming. Recently licensed pay-television services in Canada as well as private Canadian TV broadcasters were expected to provide this style of programming: "The federal government intends to encourage private Canadian broadcasters to use their present production facilities, their expertise in Canadian programming and their knowledge of the Canadian advertising market to acquire a hold on this important new market."[44]

The regulatory and legislative initiatives pointed to a new broadcasting environment in which all players in the Canadian broadcasting system—both public and private sectors—would be expected to provide the kinds of Canadian programming that had been underrepresented in the broadcasting schedules of earlier years. The private sector was expected to play an increasing role in ensuring a Canadian presence in a crowded broadcasting universe. In the mid 1980s, CTV would be called upon to increase its drama production even though as a business it knew the high costs involved in presenting such programming.

WHEN CTV ENTERED the 1980s, the network's programming focus shifted from the quiz shows of the 1960s and the musicals of the 1970s to a genre described as "unique variety programs." Canadians were able to watch *Stars on Ice*, *Circus*, and *Big City Comedy*. In the case of *Stars on Ice* and *Circus*, the network intended to develop new programs around popular appeal events. The network's sales department had reservations about trying to sell an ice show to advertisers on a weekly basis. Still Arthur Weinthal was insistent that the programming notion was endemic to Canada "where we have a relationship with ice." *Stars on Ice* also represented CTV's first effort at selling a wholly created Canadian show abroad. The network had considerable success with the foreign sales of *Stars on Ice*. The program was sold to about 30 countries including the United States. Curiously Saudi Arabia was among them. Weinthal had "a vision of people, Bedouins sitting in tents watching *Stars on Ice*."[45] Still the programming focus remained a populist one which CTV emphasized to distinguish its programming from the public broadcaster.

The show *Circus* was in the same mode as *Stars on Ice* and was an attempt to develop popular programming that could be related to live events. The style of fare capitalized on television's capacity to communicate experiences and its strength as an intensely visual medium. "I always thought," said Weinthal, "that you see a circus from afar [but] you never see it...close and...television can afford that. You can put a camera inside a lion's cage and you can have a camera inches away from the hands of the flyers as they grab each other" on the trapeze. He noted that CTV "had circus acts from...all over the United States and Canada and some from Europe; we rapidly ran out of circus performers so we changed their names."[46] *Circus* was the second CTV produced program that the network was able to sell to the United States and internationally. The production later was aired on the specialty channel YTV.

Big City Comedy with John Candy, then a rising comedian star, made its appearance in the 1980–81 network schedule. This program along with *Littlest Hobo*, an adventure show involving a German shepherd dog who came to the assistance of distressed people, *Stars on Ice* and *Circus* were aired weekly starting at 7:30 P.M. As Sandy Stewart noted, *Littlest Hobo* was "one of the most successful, middle-market shows. It doesn't try to compete in the prime of prime time but always does well in early evening."[47]

The average program cost per telecast hour for the production of regularly scheduled Canadian programming in prime time had increased dramatically in just a decade. Network documents show that the average cost per telecast hour for the 1970–71 season was $14,087 compared to $41,349 for 1980–81, a difference of $27,262 and a 193.5 percentage increase. For an hour of the program *Circus* in 1980–81, the cost of production was $23,000; *Stars on Ice*, another half-hour show, cost $30,000 per telecast hour. *Littlest Hobo* and *Big City Comedy*, two other half hour productions aired at 7:30 P.M. in the 1980–81 season, were produced for $32,500 and $16,000 respectively. The figures represented a sizeable increase over the cost per telecast hour for the 1970–71 season. For example, an hour of *Nashville North* cost $9,900; *Pig n' Whistle* $6,016; *Here Come the Seventies* $10,300 and the hour-long *Barbara McNair* show was produced for $13,500.[48]

The total cost per telecast hour for the production in 1970–71 of six regularly scheduled Canadian shows in prime time, *Untamed World*, *Nashville North*, *Pig n' Whistle*, *Barbara McNair*, *Here Come the Seventies* and *Sports Beat* was $49,306. In 1980–81, the total cost per telecast hour for seven regularly scheduled Canadian shows in prime time, *Circus*, *Stars on Ice*, *Ronnie Prophet Show*, *Headline Hunters*, *Littlest Hobo*, *Bizarre* and *Big City Comedy* amounted to $144,720.[49]

The fact that CTV functioned as "a handmaiden of the stations" that owned the network had a direct impact on the style of programming and the amount the network could spend to inform and entertain its viewers. In short, the corporate structure of CTV tended to reinforce a populist approach especially when viewers responded to mass entertainment. Other than regulatory prodding, no motive existed to provide a more uplifting form of programming. In the words of Arthur Weinthal, there were a lot of "trade offs, a lot of quid pro quos, a lot of you do this and I'll do that." The affiliated stations "made a lot of money and the network slipped around...doing lofty programming of any kind because that wasn't going to return a profit to the co-operative."[50]

Network records show that the total net payments to the affiliates went from $9,766,100 in the 1979–80 season to $32,417,400 in the 1984–85 season. In 1979–80, the network's total network sales time revenue was $60,373,700. Total programming costs against that revenue were $39,639,900. Other network time costs such as administration, distribution and overhead costs amounted to $10,967,700. The remaining amount—$9,766,100—was passed on to the affiliates. In 1984–85, network sales time revenue was $135,258,500. Total programming costs were $82,304,100; other network time costs amounted to $20,308,000 leaving total net payment to the affiliates of $32,417,400.[51]

Still the network would soon learn that much greater demands would be placed on it for certain kinds of program categories such as drama that were under-represented in its schedule. By the mid 1980s, the CRTC under a new chairman, André Bureau, was adamant that in specific programming areas previously neglected, the CTV network had to be more responsive and move beyond the news and sports genre. As Arthur Weinthal commented, "the crunch hearing was in the '80s [1986] with André Bureau in which he lowered the boom on the network and made demands on us; drama, expenditures, program categories and thou shalt do!"[52]

CTV and private broadcasters generally had continued to receive considerable adverse commentary on their performances. The prevailing view was that private broadcasters too often made high-minded programming promises only later to have the broadcast regulator modify the original promises or expectations. The CRTC also had come in for sharp criticism. Typical was an article entitled "A peculiar people" on 6

January 1981 by Geoffrey Stevens, *The Globe and Mail*'s national affairs columnist. Stevens was critical of what he saw as an unholy relationship between the CRTC and the private broadcasters: "Broadcasters are expected to live up to the performance promises they make when they get their licences—or else! Or else what? Broadcasters can—and do, every day—thumb their noses at the CRTC and ignore their performance promises, secure in the knowledge that their licences will be automatically renewed."[53]

BEFORE THE NETWORK faced a strenuous licence renewal hearing in 1986, CTV had suffered three setbacks in the early part of a new decade. John Travers Coleman, as project manager in each case, undertook three initiatives in the hopes of stabilizing CTV's operations at a crucial time in its history. The first issue related to CTV's growing concern about the impact of cable television in fragmenting the audiences of the affiliates and the network. Coupled to the cable issue was the development of Canadian Satellite Communications Corporation (CANCOM) which was licensed originally to provide Canadian broadcasting services to remote areas of Canada. As the Caplan-Sauvageau *Report of the Task Force on Broadcasting Policy* noted, "Although CANCOM is not a broadcaster, it is licensed as a network. Its service is really analogous to cable, as it is a distributor of other people's broadcasting signals and not directly involved in the content."[54] However in 1983 the CRTC allowed CANCOM to add the three main American networks, NBC, CBS and ABC in addition to PBS. Clearly the development was a rebuff to CTV which had hoped to corral cable and confine CANCOM to providing an indigenous Canadian service to remote areas.

CANCOM originally was owned co-operatively by a number of the largest broadcast entities in Canada. Among them were WIC Western International Communications which owned CHAN in Vancouver, a CTV affiliate; Selkirk Communications Limited through its ownership of CHCH Television, Hamilton; Allarcom Limited, owner of the independent TV station CITV, Edmonton and Télémédia of Montreal. The involvement of WIC in CANCOM could not help but produce tensions within CTV. As John Coleman recalled, "it was a very difficult situation for Ray Peters [WIC] to be in, because as Chairman of the Executive Committee [of CTV] and [as] issues would arise of concern about

CANCOM, he had to exempt himself from the discussion because of the conflict of interest. It was not an untypical conflict of interest."[55]

A second setback for CTV in the early 1980s was the network's abortive attempt to win a pay-TV licence in co-operation with the TVA French language network in Montreal. The CRTC licensed one national and three regional pay-TV services, a performing arts channel and a multi-lingual service. Coleman recalled: "I think the Commission was concerned about putting that large a weight of influence in the hands of the two largest private broadcasters in Canada. And they opted for alternatives."[56] Four of the six services that the CRTC licensed in 1982 failed in the first two years.

The third rebuff to the management of CTV was its failure even to make a presentation to the network's Board of Directors for an all-news network operation, a project which Coleman had led for several months. He remembered this particular disappointment: "The night before we were to present it to the Board, they changed their minds and the next morning we were forbidden even to make a presentation to the Board that we had spent three or four months developing....It put us in CTV's terms, in my opinion, behind the eight ball because of the circumstances that prevented us from achieving any one of the three objectives." Among the three initiatives, the CTV Board's disapproval of an application for an all-news network operation was perhaps the most disconcerting: "An all news service...could have added an impetus to the network's operations, in a morale sense, and would have benefited the bottom line...at a time when it really needed it." CTV still experienced operational difficulties: "We were still going through the struggles of trying to come to grips with an equitable affiliation agreement with the stations."[57] Eventually under President John Cassaday CTV obtained a licence for an all news service CTV News1 which became NewsNet on 8 September 1999.

WHILE THERE HAD been defeats, CTV also had an upside as it entered the 1980s. The network's foundation, its news service, was established as a firm competitor to the CBC. Commentators and the viewing public had become increasingly aware of CTV's news growth throughout the 1970s. In November, 1981, Dennis W. Jeanes wrote in *TV Guide*: "In 1970, nine years after CTV began broadcasting, *CTV National News* had roughly half the viewers of CBC's network news, but today both newscasts split the audience down the middle. It's probably safe to say that CTV leads in urban markets, whereas CBC leads in small-town and rural markets." Jeanes had relied on CTV News Executive Tim Kotcheff to explain the network's integrated approach to news and public affairs: "The newscast is a news bulletin at 11 P.M.; *Canada AM* does a follow-up on world news; *W5* digs more deeply into stories; and *Question Period* deals once a week with key issues and key parliamentarians. So we try to spread our impact." The CTV network budgeted for a great deal more money and resources for the national newscast in the early 1980s compared to a decade earlier. The network figures showing the average program cost on a per hour comparison for regular programming are revealing. They show the average cost per telecast hour for producing the CTV news in 1970–71 was $9,932 compared to $42,999 in 1980–81.[58]

Despite the network's advances in news, CTV suffered an embarrassment in 1984 as did its correspondent Brian Nelson who was fired by the network. Nelson had been assigned to cover Prime Minister Pierre Trudeau's trip to the Commonwealth Conference in New Delhi and to the Persian Gulf. Nelson ended up reading the news on Abu Dhabi state television on 30 November 1984. The newscast contained references to Israel as "the Zionist entity" and to Israeli Prime Minister Yitzhak Shamir as a "terrorist." In the end, CTV fired Nelson because he had "performed the role of a newscaster on the network of a foreign country without prior approval of the management of CTV, which is inconsistent with established journalistic principles in most democratic countries." Journalist David Frum writing in *Saturday Night* magazine concluded that the dismissal of Nelson was justified: "Nelson has since defended himself by maintaining that he was only 'fulfilling a diplomatic courtesy at the request of the prime minister's office.' But is fulfilling diplomatic courtesies at the request of the PMO what reporters abroad—or at home—should be doing?" Frum's assessment was that "Brian Nelson the man deserves the sympathy of his colleagues, but the firing of Brian Nelson the symbol was justified."[59]

Clark Todd, a CTV foreign correspondent in Lebanon, was killed when he was hit by shrapnel while covering fighting between the Druze and Christian Militias in the Shouf mountains at the time of an Israeli troop withdrawal. In recalling the incident, Peter Kent described Todd's death as "the worst bloodying that CTV experienced in terms of a correspondent dying in the field." Harvey Kirck commented that Todd's death was a devastating blow, especially when it had to be reported on camera: "But I have never been so sorely tried in my profession as the night when I had to read Clark's obituary." CBC news executives Tim Kotcheff and Don Cameron went to the Middle East, entered a virtually unknown place called Kfar Mata, from where Todd had reported, and recovered his body found in a room in the mountain village. His body was brought back to London where it was received by his wife and children.[60] Indeed the growth of network television news in Canada with a greater emphasis on international coverage was not without its pitfalls and perils.

In the early 1980s with the arrival of Ted Turner's Cable News Network (CNN) in the United States, television news would serve increasingly as a vehicle to build audience. Indeed the medium in North America would be more than ever personality-driven and become even more profit oriented for networks. In Canada, Lloyd Robertson's controversial move to CTV in the mid 1970s had seemed to both accentuate the network's determination to compete and to build audience ratings around a more personalized form of newscast. In 1984, Harvey Kirck would step down from the anchor desk leaving the job solely to Robertson. Eventually Peter Mansbridge would become a major news personality on the public network replacing Knowlton Nash. Commenting on the state of television and its personality focus in June, 1980, Morris Wolfe had asked, "Finally, if Knowlton Nash remains news reader, would someone please teach him how to say goodnight?"[61] Network news anchors on both CTV and CBC would continue to receive close scrutiny from audiences and critics.

Illustrative of the extent to which private television would stretch to bolster ratings in a competitive marketplace was the gaffe committed by the Global television network when it rolled the dice and gambled on a totally inexperienced junior press aide to Pierre Trudeau in the hopes of turning her overnight into a credible news anchor. Global's behaviour was as desperate as it was remarkable and the closest Canada had come to having glitz and entertainment encroach on news values. Suzanne Perry's face had been seen regularly on the nation's TV screens as she accompanied Trudeau around the corridors of Parliament Hill and when he appeared in media scrums. Global's intention was to match her on the news set with Peter Trueman, an established anchor, in the hopes that some kind of chemistry between them would appeal to viewers. Perry's attractiveness and Trueman's experience were expected to be reinforcing qualities. The problem with the innovation was that television, as well as being impressionistic, can also be brutally honest and revealing.

Perry, the mother of actor Matthew Perry and wife of Keith Morrison, who was fired from CTV news in the early 1990s, lasted a matter of weeks. The experiment was a failure. The incident also had its colorful sidebars. With reference to a *Playboy* interview of Matthew Perry, later a leading actor in the popular sitcom, *Friends*, Gillian Cosgrove recalled the media impact of his mother's short-lived stay on the anchor desk and how Global had tried to hype her appearance: "Then all hell broke loose when a former boyfriend from the supposedly idealistic '60s—the cad!—sold carefully cropped (to make them seem more racy) old photographs of her topless on a beach on the French Riviera to a skin magazine. He had neglected to mention that everyone else was topless on that beach."[62] Clearly the Global innovation had taken the notion of the personalized newscast to extremes.

For better or for worse, with its personalities and crisp style of presentation CTV had impacted on the CBC. The public network showed Canadians a much faster paced newscast, *The National*, at 10 P.M. in January, 1982. The newscast was followed by *The Journal*, a program that was to bring national recognition to interviewer Barbara Frum. CBC's influence on CTV lay in the credibility which the public network had managed to acquire and which the private network knew it must emulate to build audience. Still CTV sought to provide an alternative to the CBC not only in news but in entertainment programming. Thus its accent on becoming increasingly a populist service with its own approach and agenda and its willingness to leave the transmission of high culture to the CBC.

Spencer Caldwell, the founder of CTV, had recognized from the start that the network's future rested on the extent to which it could distinguish itself from the publicly owned Corporation. The private network that the entrepreneurial Caldwell had established in 1961 showed signs of promise at the start of a new decade. Still in the new broadcasting age of the 1980s, far greater regulatory demands would be placed on both television networks. CTV and CBC would continue to go head-to-head in certain program categories with CanWest Global Communications

Corp. in hot pursuit. Canada's television landscape was on the verge of a major transformation with audience fragmentation certain to rise in a highly competitive marketplace. In the midst of it all, the CTV network was about to face the most demanding licence renewal hearing in its 25 year history before the country's broadcasting watchdog. Chairman André Bureau and the CRTC were about to show CTV that the broadcast regulator too "means business!"

NINE

Chairman Bureau Gets Tough
1985–1990

COMMUNICATIONS MINISTER Marcel Masse established the Task Force on Broadcasting Policy in April, 1985 less than a year after the Conservatives led by Brian Mulroney had ousted the Liberals under John Turner, the successor to Pierre Trudeau. The Task Force was to make "recommendations to the Minister of Communications on an industrial and cultural strategy to govern the future evolution of the Canadian broadcasting system through the remainder of the century, recognizing the importance of broadcasting to Canadian life."[1] The co-chairmen of the broadcasting task force had links to both the New Democratic Party and Radio-Canada. Gerald Lewis Caplan was the NDP's national campaign director in the 1984 federal election; Florian Sauvageau, a university professor, had been a radio and television journalist and a host with Radio-Canada.[2]

CTV, the leading English TV network, was singled out along with the Global TV network for relying too heavily on talk, quiz and game shows: "In 1984 CTV filled no less than 324 hours of its schedule with three talk shows and 260 hours with two quiz shows. These five shows, therefore, account for 82 percent of the total broadcast hours of the CTV schedule devoted in 1984 to Canadian performance categories (this, of course, excludes CTV's other Canadian programs in news, sports, etc.)."[3]

Regardless of whether CTV operated as a business, Caplan-Sauvageau expected the network to nurture the goals of the Canadian broadcasting system to a greater extent. Specifically, the Task Force underlined the enormous profits that had accrued to the network's affiliated stations that were owned by several prominent private broadcasters such as Baton, WIC and CHUM Limited. Thus Caplan-Sauvageau concluded: "CTV and its affiliates earned 51.5 percent of all national television advertising revenues in 1984, up from 47.4 percent five years earlier. While the CTV share of all television advertising also increased over this period from 44 percent to 48 percent, the affiliates' profits before interest and taxes of $85.7 million in 1984 represented 25.3 percent of their total revenues of $339 million. The network functions as a co-operative with virtually all of its net income distributed to the affiliate-owners."[4]

In its defence, CTV attempted to provide its own interpretation of the Caplan-Sauvageau findings. Murray Chercover questioned the accuracy of the data developed by the task force in support of its recommendations. He explained to the House of Commons Standing Committee on Communications and Culture: "For example, while the report states that in 1984 only 1% of CTV's programming between 7 P.M. and 11 P.M. was Canadian drama, the full schedule actually included 7% Canadian drama." He stressed that the CTV network was measured by the CRTC only on the network reserved-time portion of its schedule. Specifically, that part of the network schedule that is under the direct control of CTV and which could not be altered by any of the affiliated stations which surrendered their time for specific network programming. "When the network reserved-time portion is examined," said Chercover, "the only element of the schedule controlled by CTV and measured by the CRTC, the percentage of Canadian drama was 12.5%."[5]

A recommendation in the Caplan-Sauvageau report which Chercover supported was that "Canadian specialty services should remain on a discretionary cable tier and the carriage of competitive signals from the United States should be prohibited." At the same time, the CTV President stressed that the network's future growth would come in the development of competitive Canadian programming given that American programming had reached a saturation level in the Canadian television marketplace. He was adamant about the need for improved Canadian programming: "We at CTV regard Canadian programming in our service as our highest priority, as evidenced by the fact that CTV will spend over $400 million on Canadian programming over the next five-year period [1987–1992]. Notwithstanding our desire to do more and better Canadian programming, it is difficult for us to forecast the sources of financing in support of that objective."[6]

THE RELEASE OF THE Caplan-Sauvageau report and the earlier appointment of André Bureau, former President of Canadian Satellite Communications Company, as CRTC Chairman brought a new era for Canadian broadcasting. In the fall of 1986, both CTV and CBC faced crucial licence renewal hearings. The CRTC could be expected to take an aggressive approach towards both networks. The broadcast regulator now under scrutiny and pressure to demand a greater Canadian programming contribution from the private sector let it be known that CTV must perform at a higher level.

Arthur Weinthal commented on the Commission's newly-found vigorous attitude that prevailed in the mid 1980s: "That was the first time the CRTC said, 'you network have been coming in here on a few occasions barefoot and pregnant and penniless. And we've listened to you and we've examined it and we see that you are penniless. However we've examined the system of which CTV is a part and, in our view the system, the system being CTV and its affiliates...are doing very well thank you very much! So CTV this is what we want you to do and get whatever money you have to get out of the stations in order to do it.'" CTV had no choice but to respond, because "the veil was lifted and the shell game came to a stop."[7]

At a public hearing on 17 November 1986, Bureau served notice on opening day that the Commission intended to delve deeply into the structure, promise and performance of CTV as one of the principal players in the Canadian broadcasting system. In his opening remarks, he noted that a half dozen of CTV's affiliates "are among the ten most profitable stations in Canada" and left no doubt that the hearing would carry out a thorough cross examination of CTV's role as the leading private TV network in Canada. In an assertive manner, he declared: "Let us be clear. The Commission expects to be convinced during the hearing of the true desire, clear plan and firm commitment to combine the substantial capacity in resources of the entire network to enhance the quality of the Canadian portion of the network service. This public hearing process should demonstrate the drive towards distinctiveness of the private sector element in the Canadian system."[8]

The commissioners did not take long to focus on their chief concerns about the network's operations: its structure, financing and the level of Canadian programming service. Commissioner Monique Coupal led off the pointed questioning of CTV executives on the opening day of the hearing. She noted that the structure and finances of CTV had impact on the level of Canadian programming that the network provided. In the interplay between the network and its stations, she concluded that generally the network provided "the Canadian content at night and a lot of the Canadian content during the daytime is provided by the station." She characterized the relationship between CTV and its affiliates as a "very complicated balancing act" in order to ensure that the network had sufficient money "to do the programs that will attract audience at night."[9]

In a verbal exchange with Chercover, Commissioner Coupal probed the relevant issue of peak viewing time. With reference to the CRTC's 1979 licence renewal of CTV, she noted that the Commission expected Canadian programs to be shown in the 8 P.M. to 10 P.M. mid-evening hours. Given that programming from the United States seemed to dominate the peak time period stipulated by the CRTC, she asked wryly if a Canadian service could be defined as one "that starts to be Canadian in the morning and then gets to be American." A somewhat indignant Chercover responded: "Commissioner Coupal, if I was just to tell you that the audience available, and this happens to be a given, at 7:00 P.M. on a Monday was 9,260,000 total viewers watching television, whereas at nine o'clock that same night there was only 8,900,000 viewers watching, would that surprise you?" The exchange underlined the extent to which the cultural imperatives of the federal regulator clashed with the dictates of market forces that govern private broadcast schedules. Chercover argued that the interconnection between certain kinds of programming and available audience had to be considered: "Peak viewing time is more specifically related to a program than it is to a clock. The reality is that Superbowl Sunday, four o'clock in the afternoon is absolute peak viewing time. For a program like *Night Heat*, ten o'clock is peak viewing time."[10]

Bureau was not impressed with Chercover's outline of the rationale for the network's programming decisions. The CRTC Chairman jumped into the fray: "Mr. Chercover, we will not play with words. The decision of the Commission in 1979 said explicitly on page 7 that those [Canadian] programs should be scheduled between 8:00 and 10:00. That is on page 7 of the Decision. Whether we call it peak time or whether in fact it was peak time or not is not the subject of the discussion here. Commissioner Coupal is asking you how did you perform, considering what was put in the Decision in 1979." At that point, William McGregor, Chairman of the CTV Board of Directors, defended the network's scheduling of Canadian programs. At the same time he had to concede: "Mr. Chairman, obviously we have not followed the Decision. However, it was our view that the priority here was to establish Canadian drama and that took a higher priority than the establishment of Canadian programming between 8:00 and 10:00." The CRTC had won this specific argument.[11] Clearly the regulatory hearing in 1986 was to be the most challenging that CTV had faced in its 25-year history.

Beyond the question of program scheduling, the Commission also delved deeply into the matter of Canadian content. The crux of the issue at the hearing was whether CTV had lived up to its Canadian content commitments. Commissioner Coupal argued that CTV did not meet the Cancon requirements of 50 percent Canadian programming in prime time when the "full network service" was taken into account. She perceived the full network service to be the more than 60 hours contained in two categories: network reserved sales time and station sales time.

The hearing learned that the prime time period between 7 P.M. and 11 P.M. of some 28 hours each week included about 12 hours of network sales time and 16 hours of station sales time. "If my calculations are correct," Commissioner Coupal said, "you are doing, in prime time, 26 hours and 20 minutes of programming; and to maintain the percentage, you would need to do half of that, which would be 13 hours and 10 minutes, which would mean an additional five hours, almost six hours of Canadian programming." After an examination of the network's programming, the Commissioner concluded that "the network is the arm of the Canadian content, and the stations are the ones distributing the American programs, the U.S. programs."[12]

CTV challenged the commissioner's interpretation of the Cancon regulations as they applied to the network. Network officials maintained that the Cancon regulations should apply only to the network reserved sales time period which in prime time amounted to just

12 hours. Chercover told the hearing that the network's affiliation agreement had been developed in consultation with both the CRTC and its predecessor the BBG. He expected the Commission to adhere to the BBG's interpretation dating back to the mid 1960s: "That understanding and the revision in the affiliation agreement to incorporate it to move to 60 hours was premised on the fact that the network reserved time package, or the network sales time package, was the basis of the measurement of the network's performance. The rest of it [station sales time] was merely a delivery service to the affiliates." Still Bureau drew a comparison with the CBC: "It is not different from CBC; CBC has a network licence that covers its entire schedule, but with its affiliates, they have a separate agreement that says: 'you will take at least "X" number of hours', but they still have a network licence for the entire schedule." When John Hylton, counsel for CTV, joined the exchange, his legal position was that "one would hope that the recognition would be that network reserve sales time has provided and met the Canadian content regulations, because if it has not, then, CTV network has been offside almost every year since its creation."[13]

CTV was prepared to spring surprises at regulatory hearings. Typical of such initiatives that could disarm inquisitive commissioners were two dramatic announcements when the sensitive issue of Canadian content was under discussion. On the first day of the hearing, the network announced a new, dramatic series *Mount Royal*, a Canadian *Dynasty*, dealing with a Quebec-based family and their corporate enterprises to be produced with Alliance Entertainment Corporation and involving an initial commitment of $7.4 million. The following day Chercover announced that "we are going to produce in association with Prime Media and BCTV a major production of Cinderella with Karen Kain and her husband and the cast and crew will be in Vancouver presenting this as a Christmas pantomime." The program was to be ready for the Christmas season of 1987.[14] The timing of the announcements was hardly fortuitous.

As the hearing progressed, no one was more aware of the harsh criticism that CTV would encounter than Ray Peters, Chairman of the Executive Committee of CTV. Peters, President of Western International Communications, had hired Bureau to be the President of the CANCOM in which WIC had a 49 percent interest. Peters recalled that Bureau was adamant: "'Some of the questions you are going to get are going to be pretty tough.' And it was during the years that everybody

Ray Peters, President of Western International Communications Ltd. and then Chairman of the Executive Committee of CTV. Photograph courtesy of Peters Management Ltd.

was, and they still are, carried away with drama." At the same time, Peters knew that the CRTC was singularly accurate: "The stations... were taking far too much money out of the network and putting very little back in."[15]

THE EXTENT TO which the affiliated stations of CTV had profited from their relationship with the network was illustrated graphically in a report by Woods Gordon, management consultants. CTV had commissioned the consulting firm to conduct a study of the network's organizational structure. The consulting assignment was undertaken in December, 1985 and completed for a special shareholders meeting and Board of Directors meeting of the network in Vancouver on 24 June 1986. A document entitled "Alternative Ownership Structures for CTV: A Discussion Paper for the Board of Directors" suggested three options for the future structure of the network: the status quo, a single controlling interest or a public offering.

The Woods Gordon discussion paper presented to the CRTC noted that the time payments made by the network to the affiliates were made "in accordance with the 'corporate formula' which is calculated for each affiliate as the percentage of its net advertising revenue to total net advertising revenue for all affiliates for the preceding year." The time payments to the affiliates totalled $25.8 million in 1982 and rose to $37.4 million in 1985. The charges to the affiliates in the station sales time for programs supplied by the network went from $17.5 million in 1982 to $18.3 million in 1985. The net cash flow to the stations, known as the full affiliate net position, increased from $8.3 million in 1982 to $19.1 million in 1985 with a budgeted $10.5 million as the net cash flow in 1986.[16]

Given the highly favourable position held by the affiliates, not surprisingly CTV found itself on the defensive at the November, 1986 hearing. The root cause of the paralysis that had gripped the privately-owned network by the mid 1980s was its basic structure and formula for time payments to the affiliated stations that had endured since the Spencer Caldwell era. Under the 75–25 formula, the network did not have sufficient funds to operate. When 25 percent of the network sales time revenues was not sufficient and a financial loss ensued, a "special assessment" had to be levied against the affiliates. Regulatory pressure and officialdom's view of CTV as a "do nothing" network would force a change in the operation of CTV.[17]

Peters and some CTV Board members realized that the network had to take the initiative. CTV proposed at the hearing that the network alter the long established formula for time payments to the affiliates as part of a financial restructuring. In effect, the affiliate-owners of CTV gave the network more operating room by paying all network direct costs and overhead before deducting their share of the revenue from network sales time. Ray Peters said the network was in "deep trouble" before the Commission, because the expensive programming genre of Canadian drama could not be produced for "a lousy 25 percent of the dollar coming in at the top."[18]

To allay the regulator's fears, the financial restructuring or "flip flop," as Peters termed it, proposed to deal with the problems of network costs *before* the stations got their money paid to them for use of air time. Instead of the stations getting time payments up front as they had in the past, the new proposal called for the entire cost of operating the network including the development of the program schedule and new drama to be deducted at the outset. The balance, or what was left over, from the network sales time revenue would then be divided among the stations. In essence, reduced payments to the affiliates for their station time could result. Peter O'Neill, a one-time Controller of the network, explained: "What the affiliates were really saying is 'look, we'll only take what is left over. That's our commitment to CTV.'"[19]

Peters argued before the CTV Board of Directors that the status quo was inadequate: "I said 'we have got to try to plough some of this money back into [Canadian programming]. We have got to go in our submission to the Commission with an undertaking that we are going to produce at least two hours of drama.' We were producing a half an hour [weekly] at that time and I said 'our image was of doing nothing.'" In the end, it was left to Peters and McGregor to sell the new arrangement for restructuring the network's finances to the Commission. Peters recalled the atmosphere in the CTV boardroom: "Because we were continually having these battles, the Board of Directors said, 'Okay, you two are going to present this new formula and the new program schedule. You're going to try to convince the Commission that this is the best thing since sliced bread!'"[20] Peters and McGregor faced a major challenge before a skeptical regulator.

Was the new CTV financial proposal a major innovation or was it a cosmetic, accounting change largely similar in the final analysis to earlier network practice? Certainly the CRTC Chairman was skeptical. When Bureau asked for an explanation of the long-term objectives of CTV that would enable the network to contribute to the objectives of the *Broadcasting Act* in a new electronic media age, Peters offered a high-minded response: "We are restructuring the network so that when the dollars come in…all of the costs of operating the network is charged against that total revenue.…We are also very anxious to write off all of our inventory or a lot of our inventory that we had to acquire in order to maintain a high standard of both Canadian and American programming."[21]

However Bureau thought that the difference between the practice at CTV, when special assessments had to be applied, and the new proposal to finance the network was inconsequential: "I still have difficulty understanding what is the big difference between having a special assessment, which is a bill that is sent to the affiliate I suppose, and [secondly] telling them, 'Well, instead of receiving that kind of a percentage of the revenues after deduction of distribution and programs and things like that, you will receive less.'…What is the big difference between the two?" Peters responded that the net effect of the change meant that "the stations will get $7 million less for their station time, in this fiscal year we have entered into, than they got last year; that is in definitive terms."[22]

McGregor did his best to show the new CTV arrangement was a sharp break with established practice. He characterized the financial realignment as "a very significant change in the management of the relationship between the network and the stations": "What we have here is really a single commitment, the original commitment—'Mount Royal' being an example—and in effect a blank cheque to pay for it. The stations are going to absorb that additional cost."[23]

Aside from the question of network finances, Bureau wondered aloud about the ownership conflicts within CTV. Directors of the network were also responsible to shareholders of individual, affiliated stations. In addition, stations belonging to CTV competed with each other in individual markets. Bureau asked: "How the hell can you run that CTV network with those conflicts of interest?"[24]

Peters told the hearing that when a conflict occurred between the shareholders and the directors, "the final decision is made in the direction of what is in the best long-term interest of the network, not the individuals who happen to have a conflict with what we were doing." Still Bureau was not convinced. Specifically he cited the example of CHUM Limited, owner of ATV, a group of four Atlantic stations that operated as full affiliates of CTV in which CHUM had an equity interest; CHUM shared in some CTV revenues and expenses. At the same time, CHUM owned CITY-TV, Toronto which was in direct competition with CFTO, Toronto, the network's flagship station owned by Baton Broadcasting Inc. Peters responded that it was "in the best long-term interest for the ATV operation and for the CHUM operation" to have an affiliation agreement with "the strongest possible network." Peters had never known CHUM executives Alan [sic] Waters or Fred Sherratt to favour CITY-TV deliberately when they sat at the CTV board table: "What they do is make their decisions at that Board table, and recommendations and discussions as to what is the best long-term interest of that network, because if ATV is going to be successful, as they are, and continue to be successful, they must have a very strong network, and they know that."[25]

Bureau took a critical look at the financial figures in his assessment of CTV. He expressed concern over the network's debt to equity ratio. When noting that it had risen from 12.25 in 1981 to 28.15 in 1985 and was projected to go to 35.38 in 1991, he concluded that it was "a pretty difficult ratio to classify and maintain." He wondered how "that under-capitalized type of operation can subsist, and at what cost and to whom." The capitalization of CTV at the time was $1,800,000; the network's total debt was $48 million. At the same time, McGregor assured the Chairman that the network had "no difficulty in arranging our lines of credit with the bank."[26]

CTV WAS ON THE receiving end of a detailed criticism of its licence renewal application from the arts community. The Canadian Film & Television Association questioned the proposed realignment of the network's finances and time payments to affiliates. The association described it merely as "an accounting change." Doug Barrett, counsel for the Association explained to the Commission: "If the CTV makes a major program commitment, they [affiliates] know that the bottom line, which is now a floating figure instead of a fixed figure...will come out of their share, so if they own 3.7 per cent or whatever the corporate formula is, each time they make a programming decision it is their money...so the network management is continually trying to get greater and greater resources, knowing that they are directly coming out of the affiliates' pockets."[27]

Reminiscent of Commissioner Coupal's lament, John Ross, a Director of the Association, criticized the network's structure that did not allow CTV to own "its own prime time." Significantly he noted, "Virtually all...of [the] Canadian programming on the CTV network in prime time appears in the network sales time period [12 hours]." Ross noted that the 1985–86 schedule contained a total of seven hours each week of Canadian content that included hockey. A new schedule that had been filed, he believed, provided for just five Cancon hours: "So the network is programming five out of 12 hours of Canadian programming and therefore had seven hours available at its disposal to earn the margins that it refers to, in the richest motherlode of time—the richest time period of the week—to produce all of the Canadian content which appears on the network." Ross underlined the economic advantage enjoyed by the affiliates which had full control over the station sales time from which they derived all the revenue mainly from American programs: "The remaining time in prime time—16 hours of it, 60 per cent of prime time—the network has absolutely no interest in whatsoever, unless we are sadly mistaken about the information we have been given. The stations own 100 per cent of that time and receive all of the revenue from it." In addition, "Less than 1 per cent of all that time is Canadian."[28]

After assessing CTV's contribution to dramatic programming in prime time throughout the 1980s, the Association concluded: "The sum total of CTV's Canadian serial drama production during the past seven licence years boils down to Littlest Hobo, Snow Job, Night Heat, Check It Out and The Campbells, some 106 newly produced hours, or approximately 17 hours per year. 72 of these hours were produced by production subsidiaries of CTV affiliates [Baton's Glen-Warren Productions and Champlain Productions, a subsidiary of CFCF Inc.]; all the rest were U.S. developed co-productions or co-ventures." At the same time, the association's brief underlined CTV's continued reliance on sports coverage: "It is interesting to note that while the amount of dramatic programming in prime time remained flat, the number of broadcast hours devoted to sports programming rose steadily from 303.02 hours during the 1980–81 season to 620.15 hours during the 1985–86 season, an increase of about 105%." The Association recommended that the CRTC give a short licence renewal "of between one and two years" to

CTV and during this time the Commission could call "a special public hearing to determine the appropriate mandate, structure, objectives and need" for Canada's main private national TV service.[29]

In its decision on 24 March 1987, the CRTC renewed CTV's licence for a five-year period, from 1 October 1987 to 31 August 1992. The decision contained onerous conditions of licence. Not surprisingly, the CRTC focused on the question of Canadian programming, specifically drama, in its renewal of CTV's licence. The Commission noted that, from 1981–82 to 1985–86, "CTV expended approximately $203.2 million on Canadian programs." As a minimum, the conditions of licence applied to the network's licence renewal "would require total expenditures on Canadian programs over the five years 1987–88 to 1991–92 of at least $403.0 million." The latter amount represented "an increase of 75.1% by comparison with the five-year period ending in 1985–86." However the minimum dollar expenditures did not take into account the costs of additional hours of Canadian drama that CTV was required to broadcast as a condition of licence.[30]

As a condition of licence, CTV had to broadcast a prescribed average number of hours weekly of regularly-scheduled Canadian drama during network sales time beginning with 2.5 hours in 1987/88 and rising to 4.5 hours in 1991/92. The Commission also narrowed the time frame for the broadcasting of Canadian programming. Clearly it had not been persuaded by Murray Chercover's assertion that peak viewing time had to be more specifically related "to a program than...to a clock." No more than one hour of the specified additional hours of Canadian drama each week could be broadcast before 8:00 P.M.[31] The Commission's decision had raised the level of expectations for the CTV network as a leading player in the Canadian broadcasting system. Moreover the demands of the broadcast regulator had come at a time that was hardly favorable to the private network. The state of the Canadian economy began to sour forcing the private network to trim its operation. Economic conditions produced a turbulent period for CTV in the latter years of the 1980s.

THE CRTC HAD COME down hard on the network. The network was short of revenue and seemed to be in a perilous state. Only days before the CRTC's licence renewal on 24 March 1987, *The Toronto Star* reported that major layoffs were imminent at the network. The round of cuts eventually took a hefty toll on the CTV News and Public Affairs

W5 promotional photograph for 1986–1987 season, just before the well-publicized firings. Hosts: Jim Reed, Bill Cunningham, Helen Hutchinson, commentator Harvey Kirck and Dennis McIntosh (left to right). Photograph courtesy of CTV.

departments. Among the personalities fired were long-time news anchor Harvey Kirck, most recently with *W5*; Helen Hutchinson also of *W5*; *Canada AM's* Wally Macht and Ottawa news correspondent Bob Evans. But the buildup to their dismissal in March and the controversy were something of a public relations disaster for CTV.

Peter Rehak who became Executive Producer of *W5 with Eric Malling*, recalled how Duncan Morrison, an accountant with no experience in broadcasting, was brought in to deal with an adverse economic situation: "The affiliation agreement had no provision for what happens when the network loses money. They had provisions for dividing the profits when there were profits but now all of a sudden it was losing and there was nothing legal as to who was responsible." The network's Board of Directors decided to hire a chief financial officer to balance the books: "So the Board reacted by bringing in a guy from Pittsburgh. His name was Morrison, came from a steel company in Pittsburgh....and he was hired by the Board, he reported to a committee of the Board and that was the first round of cutbacks at CTV."[32]

Kirck, the well recognized front-man for the network, was on a promotional tour for a book he had written with Wade Rowland about his broadcasting career entitled *Nobody Calls Me Mr. Kirck*. During an interview at radio station CKO, Toronto, a station that belonged to a short lived all news Canadian network, Kirck was presented with a copy of *The Star* in which correspondent Sid Adelman reported that major personnel cuts were on the way at CTV including himself and Hutchinson. Not surprisingly, Kirck was stunned. He had no inkling whatsoever that his days with the network were numbered. "Somebody brought *The Star* into me and there was a picture of Helen Hutchinson and I on the front page saying that we were axed," explained Kirck. After making inquiries at CTV, Kirck learned from the office of President Murray Chercover that "it's all speculation, it's not true and so on and so forth."[33]

Kirck went through an emotional roller-coaster for about a week following the newspaper report over his firing. "My departure was a mess," said Kirck. "I got hung out to dry real good." At the same time, the network was on the defensive under intense media scrutiny that followed after *The Star* broke the story of the network firings and the general economic state of CTV. Chercover was forced to issue a press release later reported in *Broadcaster* in reaction to the newspaper report: "The [*Star*] article was speculative in some respects, misleading and, perhaps most important, factually inaccurate," the press release explained. "The speculation about the specific personnel changes (relieving Harvey Kirck and Helen Hutchinson of their duties on the network newsflagship *W5*) and/or budget adjustments are not matters for discussion publicly…"[34]

The extent of the rumours, and the negative publicity to CTV, also prompted Chercover to send an internal memo to the network's staff. Clearly the network's finances were a cause for concern: "CTV is short some $10 million in its revenue forecast for the current operating year and from the preceding year, due largely to shifts and reductions in national advertising expenditures in television. All television broadcasting in Canada and the United States is experiencing the same downturn in advertising revenue, including our affiliated stations which represent the ownership of the Network." According to Chercover, there were to be "no wholesale firings"; nor was the Network "going to be gutted as has been reported."[35]

Kirck was besieged with reporters for about a week following the publication of the story, but he was unaware and uncertain of what the future held for him. "Everytime I went out the door, there was somebody there," he recalled. "I didn't know what was going on." He remembered some curious developments including the lack of viewer response to his dismissal: "I was arrested…for drunk driving. And I got mail by the bucket. When I got fired, I didn't get one piece of mail." Kirck was highly critical of both news executive Tim Kotcheff who had departed for Europe at the height of the network's crisis, and Chercover. He explained: "I don't know who to hate most which is a sad situation. Kotcheff was away on vacation when all this happened and I'm convinced he knew what was happening before he went and he just avoided the whole issue by being away. Murray was the one who just left me hanging. It's an awful feeling to be at a place for almost 25 years and to read about your being axed at work…on the front page of the paper."[36]

Kirck had made no secret of his problems with alcohol in *Nobody Calls Me Mr. Kirck*. While he was "in the throes of divorce" with his second wife, he had been charged for driving with an amount of alcohol beyond the legal limit, his second offence. However he believed that the earlier incidents involving alcohol had no bearing on his eventual dismissal from the network in 1987: "It was long before….If I drink, I drink at home now. Even then, it had nothing to do with [the firing], not that I know of."[37]

THE CRTC'S EXPECTATIONS of CTV, a decrease in the network's revenue and the dismissal of several noted on-air personalities created an unsettling atmosphere at the network. Then the historic divisions within the corporate structure of CTV that had pitted the west against the east, specifically British Columbia versus Ontario, blew wide open for the public to see. Nation's Capital Television Incorporated, a wholly-owned subsidiary of Baton Broadcasting Inc. applied to the CRTC to purchase CJOH-TV, Ottawa from Bushnell Communications Limited. Bushnell was a wholly-owned subsidiary of Standard Broadcasting Corporation Limited, a company ultimately controlled by Slaight Communications Incorporated. Following a public hearing on 26 January 1988, the Commission approved the sale of CJOH to Nation's Capital.

At the hearing WIC's Ray Peters and William McGregor of CAP Communications Limited of Kitchener intervened and took different sides. BCTV, represented by Peters, the Chairman of the Board, strongly opposed the sale of CJOH to Nation's Capital; McGregor, President of CAP, licensee of the CTV affiliate CKCO-TV, was in favour of the sale. The pair had been front and centre together in 1986 at CTV's licence hearing before the CRTC.

Peters who appeared along with Don Smith, President and Chief Executive Officer of British Columbia Television, told the hearing that BCTV was intervening "with great reluctance." It was not the company's practice "to intervene in applications involving ownership transfers that we are not involved with." Peters explained that the sale of CJOH to Nation's Capital would have a damaging effect on the CTV network. In his view, Baton, the parent company of Nation's Capital, "had dominated the CTV network far too long. In our view, the network and its Canadian programming would be much stronger without that domination."[38]

In 1988 it was John Bassett's son, Douglas, who had appeared at the hearing into the sale of CJOH as President and Chief Executive Officer of Nation's Capital and of Baton Broadcasting Incorporated. He listened as Peters advanced a decentralized view of the CTV operation that would take into account the country's diversity as opposed to Baton's more centralized position. Again the regional tensions within CTV were apparent.

Peters argued his company's position forcefully and was hardly restrained in his comment: "The CTV network was established as a programming co-operative in which the shareholders would have an equal opportunity to contribute programming and to influence the decisions of the board and of its individual committees. Today, that opportunity has been severely diminished because of Baton's ability, through its size and its location in Toronto, to force its objectives on the network programming decisions." Peters said that his company had decided not to submit pilots and scripts to CTV for consideration any more: "It is a waste of our time and money. Each time we do, we get skated offside by the Baton machine, and our shows are not properly considered, in our view."[39]

Peters buttressed his position with material filed at the time of the most recent CTV network licence renewal hearing. He noted that CTV had paid Baton about $12 million for programming services, $3 million to CFTO, Toronto and $1.3 million to its Saskatchewan television operation for station time payments. In all $16.3 million from the CTV network to Baton. According to Peters, this amount was "five times more than any other affiliate received last year. No wonder they want to dominate or control the network." Peters concluded that Baton wanted to take over the network: "Baton's stated intent, therefore, commensurate with this application, is to achieve clear cut control of CTV."[40]

Douglas Bassett had specifically questioned the notion of gaining majority control of CTV earlier at the hearing under questioning from Commissioner Louis Sherman: "There was a time, Mr. Sherman, this summer—it was published in the *Globe and Mail.* They ran a picture of the former chairman of Baton and his son, meaning myself, that we are out to control 51 per cent....That is completely false. My father has said publicly for many, many years how he would like to be more involved with CTV, and he is entitled to his opinion." Still as Bassett explained, "the fact of the matter is Baton's position now is a position of not having 51 per cent." Baton wanted a revised ownership structure where voting strength on CTV would be more directly related to the number of stations under the control of individual owners instead of the historic practice of each owner have only one vote regardless of the number stations owned. Bassett told the hearing that "our principal of shareholdings should be commensurate with the responsibility." He believed that the more stations a company owned the greater should be its voting strength. Because if a shareholder "is on the hook for more money, he should have more votes."[41]

Peters countered Baton's argument that, given the proportion of the costs that the company had to bear, it must have board representation commensurate with the level of responsibility: "That argument...totally ignores the effect of the corporate formula. Baton's share of revenues is substantially greater than that of any of the other affiliates." Baton had also argued, said Peters, "in our meetings that someone has to be accountable for the efforts and the responsibilities of the network. I get a little fumy on that because that presupposes that no one else in the country can be responsible, Mr. Chairman, and we of course disagree with that point." Peters said that a Baton takeover of CTV would "undermine still further the national strength and representative character of the network." He stressed the need for regional productions: "Already too much production is concentrated in the City of Toronto. Producers in other regions will have even less opportunity to place their programs in the CTV schedule, and consequently, even less incentive to produce programs with the high production values needed for national exposure. Regional artists, writers and performers will in turn have even fewer opportunities for network exposure."[42]

Baton steadfastly challenged Peter's contention. "There is a fallacy," said Bassett, that a program produced at Glen Warren Productions [a Baton subsidiary], is seen as a Glen Warren show for CTV. "CTV, Mr. Chercover and Mr. Weinthal may do a deal with a producer," he said, "then they will come up and just rent our facilities. We have no money in it....Just like CTV paid for the *Alan Thicke Show*, which came out of British Columbia." Similarly Ted Delaney, Vice-President and Secretary of Nation's Capital, told the hearing that there were "numerous programs, including *Mount Royal*, that are led to believe that they are Glen Warren Productions. The most involvement we have from time to time, if any at all, is that we are involved in some of the editing of it."[43]

The divisions within CTV were obvious when McGregor endorsed the Baton application to buy CJOH. Peters had wanted the CRTC to either deny the application or deliver a strong message in its decision to show that "Baton cannot own more than 25 per cent of the network." McGregor believed that "the granting of the licence under discussion can be beneficial to the network." Though in the years ahead with CTV hoping to devise a new shareholders agreement, he said that "the future ownership of CTV must be representative of the diverse interests of our coverage, with no single entity being in a position to dictate to the other shareholders who...must represent Canada and Canadians as a whole."[44]

When the CRTC approved the sale of CJOH to Baton, the regulator noted that the decision reduced the number of owners of CTV by only one, from eleven to ten. "In other words, approval of this transaction will not alter the existing ownership structure of the CTV Network nor will it increase BATON's voting strength relative to that of the other owners." The Commission also believed that "issues relating to the ownership of the CTV network and regional balance in program sources which were raised at the...public hearing should in the first instance be resolved by CTV itself."[45] Baton appeared to be well on its way to gaining control of the country's only privately owned national TV network, a broadcasting vehicle that industry observers perceived the company to have coveted.

THE NETWORK STILL managed to record some notable programming accomplishments despite the uncertainty surrounding CTV in the late 1980s. As host and domestic broadcaster, CTV's coverage of the 1988 winter Olympics in Calgary was a forerunner of the great emphasis that the network was to place on "Big Events" broadcasting. John Howse wrote in *Maclean's* magazine: "For the 16 days of the XV Winter Olympics, a global audience estimated at 2.2 billion is sharing the Games via satellite signals from the official CTV Host Broadcaster (CTV HB) command post in the International Broadcast Centre." Ralph Mellanby, Executive Producer of CTV HB, explained that the crowd at an Olympic event is really "just ambience." In his opinion, "The real audience is at home watching on TV." Phyllis Switzer, a key organizer of the network's coverage, explained, "We are the eyes and ears of the world."[46]

Canadians seldom get to see the behind-the-scenes activity that often preceded the awarding of broadcasting rights for Olympics coverage. CTV's winning of the rights to the winter Olympics in Calgary was the culmination of a series of backstage events that involved skilfull lobbying and a near endless tenacity. Johnny Esaw, Vice-President of CTV Sports, recorded the developments that led to CTV winning the broadcasting rights and how a consortium of broadcasters was established to ensure the provision of broadcasting services by a host broadcaster at the world Olympics for foreign broadcasting outlets. "The idea of sharing with other networks was primarily initiated to bring Olympic coverage to all of Canada as well as to help one another in being able to afford Olympic rights. Rights were skyrocketing because they were becoming the hottest television properties around."[47]

A sharing arrangement emerged after Esaw had suggested to the CBC that a consortium of broadcasters—the European Broadcast Union, TVA [Quebec private network], the CBC and CTV—be formed to provide host broadcast services for the Olympics. He took the initiative after learning at the Innsbruck Games in 1976 that ABC had bought the North American rights for Lake Placid in 1980 without any obligation to provide services as host broadcaster to other countries. The role of the host broadcaster in Olympics coverage was to ensure that the holders of the broadcast rights in other countries had adequate facilities and technical backup to provide visual feeds for their audiences. While picture material was to be provided, no sound or voice transmission was required from the host broadcaster. "Without such a setup," wrote Esaw, "other rights holders were faced with the prospect, and expense, of shipping in complete production facilities and—even worse—there simply wouldn't be enough camera positions at any site."[48]

With the formation of the consortium to handle the Olympics, Marcel Deschamps, Vice-President Network Operations at the CBC in Ottawa, became Chairman of the summer games negotiations on behalf of the Corporation and Esaw, CTV's representative, assumed a similar capacity in charge of the winter games negotiations. CBC and CTV would split the Olympics coverage; CBC took the summer games and CTV was to broadcast the winter Olympics. "So this was getting ready for '84 in Los Angeles," Esaw recalled, "which we knew there was going to be a big price tag if we were both bidding for it. And then Sarajevo which was the winter games in '84....He [Deschamps] and I would go in and we'd both negotiate and we knew how we were going to share it when we got it."[49] Esaw had approached the CBC with a view to controlling the cost of the coverage, because both the private and public networks were bidding against each other. As he recalled, "I got to the CBC and I said, you know we're crazy, the two of us! We're bidding, there's summer, there's winter games. You take the summer, I'll take the winter, we'll both go in and bid and they agreed that that was right."[50]

The CBC put an end to the sharing agreement prior to the negotiations over who would win the rights to broadcast the Olympics in Calgary, a much heralded event. As Esaw noted, "Prior to negotiations for the rights to Calgary, I asked the latest Head of Sports at CBC, Denis Harvey and his assistant Bill Sheehan, to meet with Ollie Babirad and myself. We wanted to keep the consortium in place for Calgary but, because Harvey felt that CBC would automatically be awarded the rights, his network wouldn't need CTV's help or involvement and to hell with the future." Still Esaw had been lobbying to capture the world event in Calgary since 1981 when he had travelled to Baden-Baden, Germany where the host cities were announced for 1988: "We covered ourselves by wining and dining all groups so that we would have a foundation of contacts in place with whomever we would have to negotiate. But Calgary did get the major share of our attention."[51]

A westerner, Esaw appeared to have an advantage in attempting to win the broadcasting rights in Calgary for CTV. He was on a first name basis with influential figures such as Bill Pratt and Bill Wardle, the President and Vice-President of the Calgary OCO (Organizing Committee Olympique). "I used to do the Calgary stampede as part of my *Wide World of Sports*," Esaw remembered, "I did it every year. And Bill Pratt was the General Manager of the Calgary Stampede. Bill Pratt was the President of the Calgary Olympic committee. So you know the door is wide open." Esaw walked in and reminded Pratt that in its coverage of the 1976 summer Olympics "the CBC spent all this money, government money, bought all this equipment, when the games were over, they took it all home and the Olympic committee paid for it."[52]

Esaw proposed that CTV cover the Calgary event mainly on a rental basis. He told Pratt: "We will do the host broadcasting of the 88 games and we'll do it on a rental basis. We'll keep one set of books and you'll have an accountant and we'll have an accountant and we won't spend a nickel over our bid without your authority." To draw the sharpest contrast he could with the CBC's coverage in Montreal more than a decade earlier, Esaw said that "any equipment that we use will be...on a rental basis the day we start using it and we stop paying the day the games are over. That will keep the price a way down."[53] Esaw had adopted a similar practice in CTV's coverage of the Calgary Stampede.

CTV entered its bid for the broadcasting rights to the Olympics in Calgary in late November, 1983. The network offered to be the host broadcaster for a production cost of $39,072,000. To gain the rights as domestic broadcaster, CTV presented a fee of $4.5 million. CTV and CBC had bid for the rights against each other. CTV emerged the winner. Esaw's sensitivity to western Canada and the entrepreneurial outlook of Calgarians who could be skeptical of central Canadian institutions was of some benefit: "Calgary even today is probably the most commercially minded city in Canada, they loved that. That was the perfect presentation to give them."[54]

Like all such events, the winter Olympics in Calgary had enormous cultural impact on Canada. Esaw recorded the momentous occasion: "We were in John Hudson's Labatt's office in early December, signing our Blue Jays contract. CTV's senior Vice-President at the time, Jack Ruttle and Marketing V-P Peter Sisam were in on the signing. We were interrupted by an urgent telephone call for me. It was OCO President Bill Pratt and Vice-President Bill Wardle. 'You've got it. The vote was eight to none with one abstention.' (The abstention was to satisfy the Federal Government that CTV would supply French-language coverage to Western Canada, which we did). It was a most personally satisfying moment for me."[55]

Still the CBC held the rights to the summer Olympics the same year in Seoul, Korea. CTV approached the International Olympic Committee (IOC) to see if the network could negotiate to broadcast its morning program *Canada AM* from Seoul and offered $250-thousand dollars to gain access to the event. The IOC had to advise the CBC. The Corporation raised the price to $500-thousand dollars which CTV met as its final offer. Esaw remembered that the price kept going up "until they paid a million dollars to keep us out. Now compare that to 1972 when I had the Canada-Russia series and invited them in. Those are the two extremes of the operation of the private sector and the public."[56]

THE OVERALL INTERNATIONAL reach of CTV became more visible to viewers in the late 1980s. In 1989, CTV News expanded further internationally when the network opened a bureau in Moscow and covered extensively the visit by Prime Minister Brian Mulroney to the Soviet Union. In an age of broadcast satellites, the *CTV National News* and *Canada AM* went to air "live" from Moscow during the prime ministerial visit. Eric Morrison, Executive Producer of the National News and Specials, was involved in setting up the Moscow bureau in the late 1980s. At CTV where he later became Vice-President News, Information and Current Affairs, Morrison fashioned a populist newscast which showed a distinctive style especially after the national newscast at 11 P.M. expanded to a half hour towards the end of the 1980s.

Morrison's view of populism was based on the need not to simply explain issues but to show how news stories and the principal developments each day impacted on people. While he rejected a trivial, tabloid approach to the news, Morrison attempted to make the evening newscast with Lloyd Robertson "not just more interesting but more important to people in some way and try to look at how some of these areas affected them." He chose to emphasize the impact of issues rather than adhere to a conventional, standard coverage of institutional news: "My philosophy was…that the audience was not stupid and shouldn't be talked down to but they'd have a lot of things that they'd care about and be interested in. That those are the legitimate topics of what you should be doing.…So there might be somewhat less concentration on the standard leadership elites or the way the country works and more sense about what impact does this have outside of Ottawa or what impact does this have outside the political sphere."[57] CTV had tried to differentiate its news presentation as much as possible from the CBC's.

In the 1970s and the early 1980s, the CTV network news generally carried American material scattered throughout. Morrison attempted to use reports from the United States "much more selectively" and began to refrain from comparing CTV news coverage to the CBC. About the Corporation, he noted: "You always felt that they had very good standards and what you were trying to do was have the same kind of standards but not do necessarily the same sort of stuff."[58]

CTV attempted to play to regional sensibilities as opposed to opting for a central Canada orientation. Morrison saw CTV with an advantage in having a newscast that resonated with the regions: "I think that editorially one of the strengths that we had was to be very well connected to the regions in some sense and to not necessarily be completely driven by the central institutions as much. I do think we listened and took seriously concerns that were coming out of other areas that would reflect in the coverage somewhat maybe more so than our competitor because you would have less weight upon you in some way."[59]

In a speech to the "Round Table" at the Rideau Club in Ottawa on 1 May 1996, Morrison challenged the CBC's Peter Mansbridge for statements in *The Globe and Mail* lauding the public broadcaster: "That's why private broadcasters—including me—responded so decisively to the recent letter from Peter Mansbridge…in which he blindly asserted that only the CBC can and does tell Canadians about their country." On the contrary, Morrison came to his network's defence: "In fact, when one adds up the national audiences for *Canada AM* and the *CTV News*, and adds in the viewership of the local CTV affiliate newscasts at noon, suppertime and late night, it is clear that more Canadians choose to get their information about Canada from the CTV family of broadcasts than any single source."[60]

Despite his bias towards the CBC, Mansbridge acknowledged that CTV is "a competitor and there are a lot of things they do well." But he sees the public broadcaster with a loftier purpose: "They take a different approach on the news...I think they really do. You know they make no secret of it. They will quite often focus on stories people are talking about around the water cooler as they say. So you know it's the old argument. Is news what people are talking about or is news what people should know about?" Mansbridge perceived the CBC's *The National* to be more concerned with the latter and CTV's populist presentation in its national newscast designed to appeal more to the former.[61]

CTV had some notable successes with its entertainment fare at the end of the decade. In 1988, the network joined with France, Italy, Germany and Great Britain in the co-production of *The French Revolution*, a $50 million dollar, eight-hour mini series.[62] Still judging from audience appeal, the network's major achievement came when CTV introduced a new program in its Canadian schedule that soon developed a huge following. The network launched the critically acclaimed *E.N.G,* a one-hour drama set in the frenetic, pressure filled atmosphere of a television newsroom starring Sara Botsford, Art Hindle and Mark Humphrey. The program which ran for five years captured ten Gemini awards including the best dramatic programming series in 1990, 1992, 1993 and 1994. However the popular *E.N.G.* was hardly a smashing, financial success for the network.

Arthur Weinthal observed that the program with wide appeal lost money every time it was aired, an illustration of how expensive the genre of Canadian dramatic programming was to produce in an increasingly fragmented television market: "I told Telefilm and I told anybody else who would listen. *E.N.G.* fully sold out to the best of our ability, everytime we broadcast a show we lost $38,000, every time. And you can look at it up, down and sideways."[63] As with other programs, CTV's success with *E.N.G.* was highly dependent on what advertisers were willing to pay.

Weinthal underlined the profound influence of advertising agencies in determining what will be paid for programs and the importance that must be placed on the interplay between sponsors and audience numbers: "What a program is worth is not determined by a producer, by the

broadcaster or by the critic or by the people who write magazine articles. It is people who sit in front of computers [at] advertising agencies
and say 'that is worth $6,500 for a thirty second spot. A spot in your
morning show is worth $700; a spot in the World Series is worth
$35,000.' That is who determines what programs are worth. And that
determination is made by the number of bums in the number of seats
watching their commercial. And everything else is 'gee whizz'
and...good thoughts."[64]

For much of the 1980s, the broadcast regulator had stressed the
importance of producing more Canadian drama and had become more
intolerant of broadcasters who in the past had made programming
promises that were not kept. With a retrospective look, Weinthal
explained: "Those excuses were generally, if not accepted, they were
certainly not frowned on in such a way as to jeopardize us. And this continued during the growth years, where these [broadcasters] were able, as
many of them would, to take their companies public and become more
significant as businesses." To Weinthal, a network pioneer, the 1986
licence renewal hearing was a major turning point for CTV amidst an
increasingly fragmented broadcast marketplace: "And in fact the irony
of it is that 86 was not only a time when we were called collectively to
account for our profitability, but it was also the time when the
fragmentation really started. It really started to roll and the economy
started to roll back and we were now saddled with the kind of [regula-
tory] demands that would drive us in 90, 91, 92 to the door of extinc-
tion."[65]

Whatever the impact of the CRTC crackdown on the private network, CTV entered a new era in 1990. John M. Cassaday, a 37-year-old
former Campbell Soup executive, succeeded Chercover as President in
early 1990. In the transition to a new Canadian broadcasting environment, CTV shifted to an intensely market-driven operation in all aspects
of its news and entertainment programming. Cassaday had his work cut
out. He was soon to comment: "Actually, I'm getting my share of gray
hair. I walked into a network early in 1990 which, for the first time in
its history, had lost money in 1989, and didn't have a plan to deal with
a $3 million deficit, simply because they'd never had one before." In
addition, "We had a lineup of shows that was dated and aging, a news
and current affairs department that had lost its touch, and an audience
share that was heading south, fast."[66] Then the recession hit big-time at

the beginning of the second quarter of 1990. Clearly Cassaday had to make some major adjustments if CTV Television Network Limited were to survive as a private broadcaster that could serve advertisers, operate as a successful business in future and reach Canadians with attractive programming.

John M. Cassaday, President of CTV, 1990–1997, currently
President and Chief Executive Officer, Corus Entertainment,
2001. Photo courtesy of Corus Entertainment Inc.

TEN

The Soup Salesman Cometh
1990–1993

JOHN CASSADAY'S ARRIVAL as President of CTV ushered in a new era for Canada's national private television network. As successor to Murray Chercover, Cassaday's appointment brought a shift in priorities. A much greater emphasis was placed on the marketing of CTV as a major player in the expanding broadcasting universe. Chercover's forte was programming. In a way, Cassaday's arrival was a throwback to the Spencer Caldwell years. Like Caldwell, Cassaday's strength was promotion, marketing and selling. Cassaday, who had received a B.A. from the University of Western Ontario and an M.B.A. from the University of Toronto, was a skilled marketer but without any broadcasting experience. He had worked for RJR MacDonald and General Foods before joining Campbell Soup where he had served as President (Canada), President and CEO (U.K.) and Vice-President (U.S.). As a soup salesman, he knew virtually nothing about broadcasting.

Why would a 20-odd year old private Canadian TV network turn to a manager such as Cassaday who was without broadcasting experience? Two principal factors that promoted the naming of the former Campbell Soup executive to the top post at CTV were at work. First of all, the appointment was expected to be made from either a pool of current broadcasting executives, a group of former broadcasters, or if necessary a coterie of business managers without broadcasting experience but who could be expected to adapt quickly to the business of network

broadcasting. Cassaday was in the latter category. A CTV selection committee of broadcasters had to agree on a suitable candidate. Initially
there was no interest in Cassaday. He was aware of a struggle that had
ensued within the search committee before he was chosen: "They were
all broadcasters and the likelihood of finding a broadcaster who hadn't
burned a bridge with at least one of them was virtually nil. So by the
time they had gone through the list of all the likely candidates and come
up with nothing they then switched gears and started looking for somebody that had been in the broadcasting business but was no longer in it
and that was a pretty short list."[1] Eventually the search committee was
forced to move to the third category of possible candidates, experienced
business executives with little or no broadcasting experience.

The second factor at work that prompted the appointment of Cassaday was the sense of desperation within CTV at the time. The network
was in a perilous state and on the verge of disappearing. CTV had gone
from a point where it had made time payments to its affiliates in 1984
of some 33 million dollars to where it was operating with a deficit in
1990. As for the shareholders, as Cassaday explained, there was "no
upside either."[2]

Cassaday knew that he faced a formidable task as the new CTV President given the network's past struggles: "You think about the evolution
of CTV; it went from basically being boutique to a fairly large company
but it still had basically a boutique mentality. There was no structure,...no process, and as a result the controls that you would expect to
be in place just simply didn't exist. So...I was brought in to...bring some
management discipline to the organization. That's what I was able to do.
I knew nothing about broadcasting at the time I came in."[3]

BY THE TIME Cassaday assumed the top position, major changes had
occurred on the boards of directors of both Baton Broadcasting Inc.,
and CTV Television Network Ltd. Allan Beattie, chairman of Baton,
recalled the realignment that occurred between the Bassett and Eaton
families and Baton. Beattie observed the changed circumstances by the
mid 1980s: "At the end of '86, I left the law firm [Olser, Hoskin and
Harcourt] and went to work for the family. One hundred percent of my
time with the Eatons. By then I had succeeded John Bassett as chairman
of Baton but my fundamental role I guess was...representing the family
in the inter-relationship between the business itself [Baton], the Bassetts

and the Eaton family." Beattie said that "by the time I became chairman, the Bassett family had really sold their share position in the broadcasting to the Eatons for which they received cash which they were able to go and do other things with." When Beattie became Chairman of the Baton Board, "the Bassetts really didn't own any shares in Baton. But they were still managing and Douglas [Bassett] was managing, succeeded his father."[4]

On the CTV Board of Directors, a new group of younger broadcasters had arrived around the time of Cassaday's appointment, individuals who eventually helped him to restructure the network. Among them was Douglas Holtby, a new representative of WIC Western International Communications Ltd. But as Holtby noted, there were others: "You got to remember I wasn't the only new guy on the block. Ron Osborne was quite new on the block and Maclean Hunter [CFCN] and you know he recognized that this thing [CTV] can't continue the way it is. It has got to be properly capitalized, it's got to be properly operated as a business and not just an adjunct to the affiliates." Holtby recalled the presence of another member of the Pouliot family: "His father was on the board but Adrian [Pouliot] was a new member of the Board....Randy [Moffat] had been there for a long time but what we were trying to deal with was who is going to pick up the deficits...."[5]

Cassaday saw that the embattled network was relying on the momentum it had built up years before and continued to function with "a will to survive as opposed to a will to win." Now the network's corporate board room, renown for its tensions, questionable language and histrionics was faced with a soup salesman who knew little about the regulatory or cultural aspects of Canadian broadcasting such as licence obligations and the cost in meeting Canadian content quotas. What Cassaday possessed was considerable managerial skill honed since he had left honours journalism at the University of Western Ontario in his second year to work for RJR Macdonald Inc. "My memories of the Faculty," Cassaday recalled in a speech at Western, "revolve around...waiting to find out why my latest story was not Pulitzer Prize material—even more to the point, why it wasn't good enough to get me out of first year of Journalism School."[6]

The first meeting of the network's Board of Directors was an eye-opener for the young President. He recognized a managerial flaw that had to be dealt with promptly. "The problem was that management had abdicated its responsibility for running the company to the Board and, in this case, it was a Board of wealthy broadcasters who were also our competitors. And [after] the Board meeting began, it had no beginning, no middle, no end; there was no real agenda. People just came in and talked about the business."[7] CTV appeared to be drifting aimlessly without direction.

Cassaday intervened when he saw that the directors' meeting was without coherence and objectives. "About three o'clock one of the directors got up to leave," said Cassaday, "and then another guy said 'I got to go.'" Cassaday moved to halt the state of drift that had swept the board room: "I just said, 'hold on a second here! You know I've been listening all day and here is what I think the key issues are that we have to deal with. And by the time we get together next time, I'll have developed a point of view for you on these four or five areas.'" The CTV management seemed receptive: "This was not rocket science," said Cassaday. "But…we were beginning to take control of the process again on my first day and that was really key to the turnaround. We had to get the directors back into the role of directors and advisers to management as opposed to managing."[8]

THE BROADCASTING BUSINESS in Canada had undergone a major transformation when Cassaday arrived as the new CTV President. The private TV broadcasting industry had been founded typically by media entrepreneurs in the late 1950s and early 1960s. Many of the first holders of the private television licences had been radio station owners in an earlier era. There had not been in Cassaday's view "a lot of external force brought to bear on the business.…No matter what kind of programming you put on, it sold out." Until approximately the mid 1980s, advertising markets had continued to power ahead. John Bassett, a network pioneer, believed that broadcasters "were not known as financial geniuses anyway."[9] At the start of the 1990s, the impact of audience fragmentation, economic recession and dramatic changes in advertising practices introduced a range of new elements to the private television industry that could not help but affect the day-to-day operations of CTV.

Perhaps the greatest change in the Canadian broadcasting environment that affected the private broadcasters especially CTV was the different approach to advertising adopted by the companies that dealt in packaged goods. These companies had been a driving advertising force in the 1960s and 1970s during the birth and early growth of the private network. By the early 1990s, a major realignment had occurred that saw the emergence of a newly empowered retailer. The retailer began to exercise a great deal more clout with the manufacturer producing a fundamental shift in the marketing mix. The change meant that monies which had previously gone towards the building of consumer franchises through advertising were now diverted to the retailer for price promotion and the funding of retailer programs. Cassaday described the change in the advertising market as "a shift away from advertising to promotion principally trade-oriented promotion": "So a company like General Foods would have seen...a shift of say 70 per cent consumer directed spending, 30 per cent trade to 70 per cent trade, 30 per cent consumer." For CTV such a realignment in the advertising market towards the retailer could not help but have major implications. The packaged goods companies had embraced television in its early years and had been a mainstay of the CTV network. By the early 1990s, only a few of the core group who would have been among the top ten for CTV in 1988 remained on the network's list of prominent advertisers. As he explained, "they've been replaced entirely by advertisers who weren't there at that time."[10]

Cassaday told the CRTC 1993 that "the people to whom we sell, the national advertisers, are responding, particularly in the packaged goods area, to other pressures, notably the concentration of trade." He referred specifically to two national advertisers that had been with CTV almost from the birth of the private network in 1961: "The major players, like Procter & Gamble and Kraft General Foods, are dealing with a food trade that is putting increased pressure on them to reduce the price of their products. That pressure is coming from cross-border shopping to some degree but more importantly from the emergence of these 'category killer' retailers, the Price Clubs and the Costcos of the world." He noted the impact of the new pressure in the food trade: "The result of that is that the moneys they have available for advertising or brand-building is being severely diminished as they are forced to put their money into the cost of their product and provide Loblaws and A&P with a price that is competitive to Costcos and Price Club, who do not advertise at all."[11]

Changes in the world of advertising were paralleled by an increasingly competitive broadcasting environment. With a general economic downturn in the early 1990s, the private network faced a difficult future. The CRTC in 1984 and 1987 had licensed new specialty services which had produced greater audience fragmentation by the 1990s. The success of TSN and MuchMusic had removed considerable advertising revenue from the marketplace for conventional, general-interest services such as CTV. Between 1988 and 1992, CTV had a compound annual growth rate of two percent. The financial return meant that the network had experienced real rates of decline when an inflation factor of 2.5 percent was taken into account.[12]

The continuing objective of CTV in the 1990s was to present Canadians with a television network that was more populist than the publicly-owned CBC. Cassaday planned to achieve this aim by making CTV appear to Canadians as more "main street" Canada through the marketing technique of "branding." When asked by CRTC chairman Keith Spicer in 1993 to articulate the differences between CBC and CTV "in bringing Canadians together," Cassaday noted the principal difference of style: "We really feel that we have much more of a populist approach, that we are much more 'main street' Canada, as opposed to the university halls of Canada." The CTV President explained: "We like to think that we can touch people with our story-telling. We are not trying to educate them. We are trying to inform them—and it is more than a subtle difference to us." According to Cassaday, the notion of "branding" was to make CTV distinguishable to viewers in the multi-channel universe: "We believe that as the marketplace becomes more fragmented and the converter comes to represent more of a buffet table than anything else, with a myriad of choices, viewers are going to opt for something that they are comfortable with." The aim of "branding" was "to make people aware that they have been watching CTV, that they have achieved some enjoyment from it, and perhaps the next time they turn the television on, they will come to us first, or second. If we continue to have good programming, we can hold them."[13]

Given Cassaday's marketing approach that focused on the CTV "brand," his intention was to debunk what he saw as a myth, namely, that Canadians watch programs, they do not watch networks. CTV embarked on a new course aimed at ensuring that viewers would continue to enjoy the security of familiarity offered by the fare on the private network. A fresh set of colorful graphics, and a new positioning for CTV embodied in the call-sign, "CTV, Tuned In To You," set the network on a recovery course for the 1990s. The CTV brand was everywhere. *W5* became *CTV's W5, Canada AM* was identified as *CTV's*

Canada AM and the *CTV National News* began to look like a newscast about to break the 2000 year barrier. In Cassaday's view, Lloyd Robertson, the CTV news anchor was "a 20 game winner" who had been forced to perform "in bush league surroundings."[14]

MARKETING AND JOURNALISM are not always compatible. Cassaday decided to revamp the network news, even if he had to become the antagonist in a clash of network cultures. Skeptical CTV journalists seeking the pure truth generally have no time for marketing wizards, gimmickry and instruments of advocacy designed to build audience. Over time, Cassaday succeeded but not without experiencing opposition. The challenge that the President faced within CTV was accompanied by a high level of outside competition that confronted the network.

Cassaday drew comparisons between CTV and three prominent private broadcasters: CanWest Global Communications Corp., WIC Western International Communications Ltd. and Baton Broadcasting Inc. He argued before the CRTC that CTV was "in a different ballpark" from Global in the programming areas of drama and news. Historically the differences revolved around "the increased commitment on CTV's part to drama," especially since the network's licence renewal in 1986 and, unlike Global, CTV's "national mandate for news." The greatest competition between CTV and Global was in the area of popular American sitcoms and drama: "If you were to ask the person in the street what they would think would come to mind about Global, I would say it would be Thursday night, where Global has done an extraordinarily good job in owning that night, with a bank of popular American shows. We all envy that. It would be nice to have that little cash drawer." As for WIC and Baton, Cassaday explained that from CTV's perspective, "their mandates have tended to be more local....Baton has, through their acquisition process, strung together a number of local stations that will allow them to bring some regional focus together as well. But, the objectives of those two companies are principally to meet the needs of their local audience, which I think is significantly different than the role of CTV."[15]

The President's determination to put his own stamp on CTV could not help but have considerable influence on news and entertainment programming. Perhaps nowhere was the President's style of operating more apparent than in the changes brought to *Canada AM*, and the *CTV National News*, traditional areas of CTV strength. "I infuriated the staff very early on," said Cassaday, "by saying 'you know *Canada AM* needs a wakeup call.' It had become dull and uninteresting [and] far too focused on political and Ottawa's agenda."[16] Indeed Cassaday introduced a market survey approach to all aspects of CTV programming. He saw the need to repatriate CTV's viewers.

In his first year, the network invested some six million dollars in state-of-the-art news and public affairs production facilities. The aim was to get Lloyd Robertson out of his "bush league" surroundings. To revamp the CTV newsroom, Cassaday turned to designer Don Watt, Chairman of Watt International, a strategic branding and design consultancy, whose clients included Grand & Toy, IBM Canada and Labatt. The company had reformatted the Loblaw grocery stores. Cassaday remembered, "You can imagine the eyes rolling back in the news department."[17]

When Cassaday looked at the initial drawings for a restyled newsroom, he was dissatisfied because it resembled every newsroom seen on American networks such as ABC, CBS and NBC. He had turned to Watt to bring a new perspective to CTV. In the end, Cassaday was satisfied and Lloyd Robertson in 1992 went on to be named the country's most trusted news anchor by *TV Guide* for the sixth time. "You know," Cassaday recalled, "we created a logo for CTV and an integration between CTV's major news programs and a look for our newsroom that distinguished us from everybody else. We brought some warmth to the set of *Canada AM* and some authority to the set of the *CTV National News.*" When viewers stopped to ask him about the changes, Cassaday was impressed: "I'd be stopped at a golf tournament, sports fans would say to me 'gee you guys are doing a lot more sports.' Well we weren't doing any more sports than we ever did. But we were 'branding' our sports, 'CTV Sports Presents.'"[18]

The hand of Cassaday influenced not only the form of the CTV news programs but also the structure of the news. The CTV President conducted a systematic analysis of the audience makeup for individual programs such as *Canada AM*. The findings showed that the audience profile changed dramatically between 6:30 A.M. and 9 A.M. when *Canada AM* was on air. To respond to some of the different groups of viewers, the program was sectionalized: a strong business orientation from 6:30 A.M. to 7 A.M.; political and general news from 7 A.M. to 8 A.M.; between 8:30 A.M. and 9 A.M., a more human interest, lifestyle orientation with items such as recipes and entertainment news.

A new conformity was also introduced to the morning program. CTV viewers would know exactly when a specific format would be on air. Again Cassaday drew on his marketing background to realign the network's morning news program. In short, selling a program on *Canada AM* was like selling soap or toothpaste. "I knew from selling breakfast serials and orange breakfast drinks," said Cassaday, "that people's routines in the morning...never change. You shave before you blow dry your hair, you do that every morning." The notion of conformity was transposed to *Canada AM*: "So what we brought into place in *Canada AM* was an absolute certainty that at 6:50 you are going to get this kind of business report, at 7:10 you are going to hear from this, at 7:50 you are going to see the political panel on Thursday come hell or high water." The central aim of having the programming format of *Canada AM* conform to the morning routines of CTV's viewers eventually was achieved. "That show" said Cassaday in 1995 after introducing the programming changes, "after years of clawing has been consistently growing...despite new competition from the CBC and from breakfast programs from independents."[19]

The *CTV National News* also changed. Cassaday's influence went well beyond the staging apparatus that showed viewers Lloyd Robertson with all of the accoutrements befitting a leading network news anchor. The numerous innovations to the network newscast included the introduction of more feature reports that highlighted society trends in health and the new information age. Personal biographies and profiles gave the news a more human dimension. To develop its own news agenda, CTV made a controversial move with the introduction of Dale Goldhawk as a news ombudsman who would "fight back" for viewers with particular grievances. The network seemed determined to become more proactive in its journalism as it was on the verge of seeming to generate the news and not just report the principal developments.

Clearly the network's Board of Directors had reservations; the role of the ombudsman as journalist was a subject that received heated debate in the CTV boardroom. "I think the Board was very concerned about that," said Cassaday. "But we were committed, convinced it was the right thing to do and it has been." His assessment of the ombudsman as a proper innovation was based largely on the high response rate to Goldhawk's reporting: "I mean Dale Goldhawk gets hundreds and hundreds of calls. We are going beyond reporting a story to bringing it to a conclusion." In the process, CTV realized that with Goldhawk helping

Canadians to "fight back," its audience could also be increased. Still Cassaday continued to struggle with the Board of Directors, because he wanted the ombudsman introduced even earlier in the newscast preceding some of the hard news of the day: "I guess the only debate we have right now is that I keep arguing that it should be earlier in the newscast....You know I believe that we should be...with Goldhawk at 11:12 instead of 11:22. And...I've lost that one, because basically we start off with a headline format and then we slide into the features as the show progresses."[20]

The thrust of the changes brought to CTV News was to enable the network to develop its own news agenda and to allow it to become more populist in its news gathering. Under Cassaday's leadership, there was a more aggressive marketing of the network's news personalities. "I use the expression," said Cassaday, "if you put a gun to peoples' heads they probably couldn't name more than three people who work for CBC; but I'd like to think that a lot of people could bring to mind Valerie Pringle...and Eric Malling and Lloyd Robertson and Craig Oliver, Sandie Rinaldo...because we've added a human dimension to these people and...you know you want to go to bed at night and wake up in the morning with the comfort that you know things are right with the world."[21] Reports by Mark Schneider on societal trends and Avis Favaro's medical stories brought a new range of feature material to the newscast that supplemented the harder news items of the day. In the early 1990s, CTV moved into a dominant leadership position in news.

SOME CTV ON AIR PERSONALITIES arrived at the private network after establishing themselves at the CBC. Typical was Valerie Pringle who joined CTV in 1993 after an eight-year stay with the public broadcaster to become a co-host of *Canada AM* with Keith Morrison, a one-time CBC correspondent who had returned to Canada after several years in the United States as a news anchor. Pringle's father-in-law, Donald Pringle, a lawyer, had been on the first CTV Board of Directors in the early 1960s during the Spencer Caldwell era. When she decided to join CTV, CBC colleagues questioned her rationale. "Friends would say to me," Pringle recalled, "'you know they don't have resources, they can't do things properly, they can't research things properly, they can't cover things the same way we do.' And Peter Mansbridge before I left made me feel so guilty." Pringle remembered Mansbridge's lament: "'When CBC is under

Valerie Pringle.
Photograph courtesy of CTV.

siege and under fire we need people like you, you shouldn't be going, and what kind of journalistic assurances do you have they do a good job.'" She credited CTV News Executive Henry Kowalski with support that reassured her: "Oh Henry's lovely. They were smart actually to bring Henry out to meet me, because a lot of other people might have turned me off, but Henry was just the right person to sort of calm me down."[22]

Mention the word "perky" to Valerie Pringle and watch the clouds roll in. Her vibrant personality in the morning when Canadians are forced to galvanize themselves into action fitted the *Canada AM* format. Still her view of the description of her performance as "perky" is that it takes away from any substantive contribution that she makes as a broadcaster: "I find it a dismissive word and in fact my friends, the people who know me, will call me 'perky' to annoy me....However I think people use it always about morning show hosts and female broadcasters...and it does connote that they're kind of blindly enthusiastic and you know often there is a dumbness to it. Like everything is just great, isn't it. I don't feel that way at all. In fact I think most things are not great." In June, 2001 it was announced that Pringle had decided to leave *Canada AM* as co-host.[23]

Sandie Rinaldo.
Photograph courtesy of CTV.

The female personality on CTV who clearly broke new ground was Sandie Rinaldo, the familiar face on weekend newscasts, whose amicable style of delivery has won a steady audience. In 1980, Rinaldo was promoted to co-anchor on *Canada AM*, the first woman to read a daily newscast on CTV. She and Wally Macht shared the newscast responsibilities. As she recalled, someone remarked to her that "there was a buzz all through the studio because a woman was going to read the news."[24] In February, 1985 Rinaldo became the full-time weekend anchor of CTV news.

Rinaldo's reputation as a pleasant personality and newscaster has had both advantages and drawbacks. Graduating from York University in 1973, she tried for a position as a researcher at the CBC. Unsuccessful with the Corporation, she contacted CTV and became a junior secretary to News Executive Don Cameron. Cameron inquired, "Why should I give you this job?" With the brashness and naiveté of youth, Rinaldo answered: "Because I'll be hosting *Canada AM* one day." Rinaldo saw Cameron as a mentor who "changed my life." She recalled he was very "pro active in terms of moving women forward. If you take a look at the women he moved into the network, it's really remarkable. Carole Taylor, Helen Hutchinson, Pamela [Wallin]."[25] Viewers have enjoyed Rinaldo's calm demeanour and intimate delivery. Still she has felt the barbs from print media critics: "The viewers I know like watching me because they like the fact that I'm 'nice.' As far as I am concerned that's been very positive with the viewers and the audience. I have been able to build a strong following as a result of that. Where it has hurt is with the print media, because they often dismiss me having no regard or no understanding of how I've come to this job. In a sense, it is an unfortunate scenario, because many of them have not taken the time to check."[26]

Rinaldo was incensed when *Globe and Mail* columnist John Allemang wrote a story entitled "Who is Lloyd's heir apparent?" in which he rated her and other possible successors to the 65-year-old Robertson. Allemang had described Rinaldo as having an "emotive style" and wrote: "Much better with warm and cuddly stories than weekday's hard news. Journalistic background is spotty."[27] Rinaldo earlier in her career had worked for *World Beat News* at CFTO as a co-anchor and senior editor. While at *World Beat*, she had travelled to Washington to cover the inauguration of U.S. President George H.W. Bush and reported from Moscow on how Canadian businesses performed in the Soviet Union.

After the *Globe and Mail* story appeared, Rinaldo responded to Allemang in a letter and took him to task for the manner in which he had characterized her journalistic background: "I said to him, 'Look! You have every right to say I'm a long shot in the race to replace Lloyd, because that's your opinion. You have every right to say you think I am 'emotive' and nice, because that's your opinion. But you have no right to say…'spotty journalistic background.' Because you have no idea of what I've done.' And when I outlined for him what I had done, he said 'you're right. I had no idea what you had done.'"[28]

CRAIG OLIVER, THE FIRST PRODUCER of *Canada AM* and the network's Ottawa bureau chief, credited Cassaday with rescuing the network. He argued that Cassaday was a saviour for CTV: "John saved us for awhile. He really did. We were going under." To meet the financial commitments to CTV's affiliated stations, Oliver maintained that Cassaday "got blood from a stone." Cassaday managed to get the network to produce more money and essentially turned the Ottawa bureau into a production house. Oliver was able to get a financial return for the network: "Take this operation here….In one month I billed one company 40 grand. We are a production house as much as we are a separate bureau. This is all John's vision. Getting this place generating some amount of money on

Bill Cunningham, *W5*
promotional photograph.
Photograph courtesy of CTV.

its own." Oliver described Cassaday as "a tremendous manager" who
had "really straightened this place out" at least in the short term.[29]

Lloyd Robertson saw Cassaday's arrival as a period when the marketing of the network was placed front and centre. Robertson considered Cassaday's initiatives as a way to differentiate CTV from the public broadcaster and appeal to main street Canadians: "He wanted to
carve a CTV brand into the newscast so that things would be distinctly
identifiable to us like Goldhawk [ombudsman], like Avis Favaro [med-
ical reports]...the Friday file, the funny little end...those kinds of things.
People would say they watched CTV because they liked that. And I
think it was a matter of drawing those identification markers." Under
Cassaday's watch, said Robertson, "we began to carve out a territory for
ourselves."[30]

Though he was without broadcasting experience, Cassaday could be
perceptive in assessing the impact of changes that CTV decided to make.
A case in point was the revamping of *W5*. Peter Rehak, Executive Producer of the program, had joined CTV in 1981. Bill Cunningham, a vet-

eran journalist with wide experience at CBC and Global television, had hired him as a senior producer. CTV had expected the public affairs show to capture audiences of about one million. But in the late 1980s, the program managed some 600,000 viewers. With a view to raising the profile of the show, Rehak decided to hire Eric Malling, a journalist whose provocative style garnered seven ACTRA and Gemini awards. Malling, formerly an investigative journalist on CBC's *the fifth estate*, was a controversial figure perceived to be anti-establishment and a contrarian. The CTV public affairs show was to become *W5 with Eric Malling*.

When Cassaday learned of Rehak's intention to headline Malling, he was curious. Rehak recalled Cassaday's inquiry: "One of the questions that John asked which was very perceptive for somebody coming out of a soup company, he said, 'what are the other hosts going to say about this?' I said, 'Oh, I wouldn't worry about that'....Never have I been more wrong....I totally discounted ego."[31] As a host of the program, Cunningham, who reported foreign stories, was furious about turning W5 over to Malling with his name attached. Rehak recalled: "Cunningham, I had him out of the country, and he was on the phone and he was drafting letters and characteristically I don't think he ever sent them off." Faced with financial cutbacks at CTV and the need for retrenchment, Rehak was forced to fire Cunningham. Cunningham was irate and felt betrayed: "I had hired him and I fought for him, I got him the job. I fought for him with [Don] Cameron...then he stiffed me. Needless to say, he is not one of my best friends."[32]

The backstage dispute between Rehak and Cunningham revolved around their different perceptions of the style of program that W5 should become. Rehak had hired Malling to usher in a hard hitting, provocative format that was modelled on a program called *Edges*. Malling had tried unsuccessfully to sell *Edges* to the CBC. His vision of the program was that it would be public-issue oriented and steadfastly contrarian. "Early on," Rehak recalled, "[we] did a story on the problems with English as a second language. Not an anti-immigrant piece by any means but just pointing out that some districts in Toronto 80 per cent of the students could not speak English. The thrust taken on the story was the federal government makes the immigration rules but the local schools are expected to take up the costs and it does not have happy results."[33]

Perhaps the most controversial story that Malling reported on was in February, 1993. He showed how New Zealand had to take stringent measures to deal with its debt and deficit crises. More than 1.7 million viewers watched the program which caused a major, national stir in the corridors of power. "It came kind of in harmony with the rise of Reform [political party]." Rehak said. "Eric had no ties with Reform and neither do I...but this was something that struck a chord. And I think had real impact. He did an equally good program about deficit fighting in Saskatchewan."[34] However Malling's efforts did not get universal applause especially from leftist leaning commentators.

Two years later, author Linda McQuaig wrote a national bestseller entitled *Shooting the Hippo: Death by Deficit and Other Canadian Myths*. The title made reference to Malling's special report that a baby hippo had to be shot at the Auckland Zoo, because there was insufficient funds to allow the hippo pen to be expanded. By focusing on the budget-slashing undertaken by the New Zealand government, McQuaig argued that Malling had distorted what actually happened: "The real story is about how New Zealand's politicians embarked on a huge experiment in which they transformed their country from an advanced social democracy into a free-market jungle with massive unemployment, growing inequality and a damaged manufacturing base."[35] *W5* was steeped in controversy.

From his standpoint, Cunningham considered Rehak's concept of a *W5* centred around Malling as a fatal error in judgement. No stranger to public affairs shows, Cunningham had been a major contributor to the CBC's *Newsmagazine* in the early years of television. He drew a comparison between *W5* and the popular *60 Minutes* on CBS: "Magazine shows are magazines. You may not like Mike Wallace's piece [*60 Minutes*] that week but Morley's [Safer] coming along and it is a totally different show....And I told him [Rehak] this, I said 'Listen. You turn that show over to Malling, you're going to go right down the toilet! He's a Johnny one note and it will not play. He's a sniper. He's not Peter Jennings. You know, he's not a guy who can carry that.'"[36]

With reference to *60 Minutes*, Cunningham emphasized that the show's producer Don Hewitt "watches...very carefully. He's got 40 items up there that he can pull." But Hewitt "structures those shows....There's a sense of play about them." Cunningham was not opposed to hiring Malling on *W5*: "Hire Malling by all means. I mean he's a really good sniper. And he's a real asset. But don't turn the show over to him, because it'll go down the tubes. People don't like him on a long show. He doesn't play well enough."[37]

Malling eventually departed *W5* and the program was integrated with the news department in a more user-friendly format. Rehak remembered the ratings were in decline by 1996: "His name was on the program and he had his direction, he's a very stubborn guy. It was very hard to get him off the line of 'deficit and anti-government' so you need to change and we didn't change fast enough. By 1996 the ratings were coming down again." Rehak had to contend with "accountants [who] were raising the flag" about the cost of *W5* and said "let's cancel it. John Cassaday understood that this was an important show and he kept it on."[38] At the age of 52, Malling died in 1998 after falling down the steps in his Toronto home. *Maclean's* noted, "In recent years, Malling struggled with alcohol abuse."[39]

THE PRIVATE NETWORK had undertaken some major initiatives after Cassaday's arrival. Still it was helped by an internal reorganization at the CBC which provided an opening for a news competitor like CTV. On 2 November 1992, the CBC moved its network flagship newscast from the 10 P.M. time slot to 9 P.M. as part of a new "Repositioning" strategy. By early 1993, CTV had moved ahead of the Corporation and gained viewers who previously watched the CBC news at 10 P.M. A Canadian Press report noted, "Ratings for *CTV News*, as measured by A.C. Neilsen, have increased considerably since CBC restructured its prime time schedule."[40] The report drew attention to an Environics Research Poll commissioned by CTV which found that the respondents who watched *CTV News* between mid-October and early December, 1992 had risen to 59 percent from 45 percent. The period that was surveyed corresponded to the shift in the CBC's news programming when *Prime Time News* had replaced *The National*, the CBC's flagship, at 10 P.M. and *The Journal*, the magazine style show, that had followed the newscast.[41]

Other observers of the broadcasting industry drew attention to the fact that *CTV News* had expanded its audience. Near the end of 1992, Jim McElgunn writing in *Marketing*, explained, "Figures from Nielsen Marketing Research, Markham, Ont., show that the CTV newscast, which airs from 11 P.M. to 11:30 P.M., drew 1,367,000 viewers (aged 18 and over) in the average minute from Nov. 2 to 15. This was 37% higher than CTV's estimate to advertisers in June."[42]

The unsuccessful "repositioning" concept involved a number of CBC executives who were trying to find a new place for the Corporation in the multi-channel universe. Two of them, Ivan Fecan and Trina McQueen, would later end up in top positions at CTV. The redesigned news format had Pamela Wallin, formerly with CTV, teamed up with Peter Mansbridge as co-anchors. Mansbridge's interpretation of what happened to *Prime Time News* focused on the fact that the CBC had essentially downgraded its flagship newscast. Canadian viewers would have been startled, if they could have been in the studio on opening night. "I can remember Wallin and I sitting there on the first night of this program with the carpenters hammering away trying to make the set," Mansbridge remembered. "There were no dry runs. I think on Sunday night, the night before, we did something just to see what things looked like. But there was no dry run, you know, what was the flagship of this network!"[43]

The program also suffered from a clash of cultures. Wallin's experience at CTV was seen almost as a liability when she arrived at the public broadcaster. "It was a sense...I had that somehow my experience didn't really count for anything," she said. "I had people who came in and you know explained to me how to do an interview and told me the questions to ask and I said, 'well actually I've done this for a couple of years, I actually know that.'"[44] Tony Burman, head of *CBC Newsworld* had attempted to rescue *Prime Time News* in January, 1993. He maintained that Wallin underwent a frustrating time when the focus of the program shifted away from her specific talents as an interviewer. He wondered aloud why CBC management adopted the concept of moving the news to nine o'clock with seemingly no research to assess the impact on audience: "I think for a network as important and large as the CBC to embark on such a dramatic change in programming without that kind of empirical support is mystifying and lamentable."[45] Wallin later was fired from the program.

Tim Kotcheff whom CBC President Gerard Veilleux had appointed Vice-President of News, Current Affairs and Newsworld after he departed CTV insisted there was research that showed a drop in audience if the newscast moved to nine o'clock. Not surprisingly, he questioned the findings: "The answer I got back was 'that's what they said when we did the research to move the news from eleven to ten. And the empirical evidence of that experiment was that we increased our viewership substantially.'" But the move to nine o'clock, according to Kotcheff, "wasn't as cavalier as it looked." When he was at CTV, Kotcheff claimed "their [CBC] ratings fell and they didn't go to ten o'clock because they wanted to, they went to ten because they were losing their numbers." He saw the decision to move the news to nine o'clock in a similar vein: "I can tell you...the decision to move to nine wasn't because it was a great success at ten. They were losing ten per cent a year in viewership....So the repositioning was partly a recognition that the news wasn't doing well at ten."[46]

In 1992, CTV's news programming continued to focus on leading national issues with the production *Canada in Question* which included up to the minute results of the constitutional referendum on the Charlottetown Accord along with reaction from political leaders and guest commentators. The network's news reach continued to expand. CTV Radio News was introduced on numerous Canadian stations to provide greater breadth for the network and to allow Canadians ready access to the CTV news service.[47]

BY 1993, CTV had become the most watched television network in Canada, a fact acknowledged by Friends of Canadian Broadcasting (FCB), a public broadcasting lobby group. At the time of CTV's licence renewal hearing in September, 1993, the supporters of the CBC, whose steering committee included such prominent Canadians as Pierre Berton, Peter C. Newman, Frank Peers and Ian Morrison, filed a detailed intervention before the CRTC aimed at ensuring that CTV enhanced its service to the Canadian public. The intervention began with the observation, "The CTV Television Network is one of the most important sources of shared experience and belonging in Canada today, deserving CRTC defence and protection as a vital cultural instrument under the *Broadcasting Act*." A five-page submission by FCB agreed with CTV that the private network had surpassed CBC as the country's most watched network: "As the applicant points out, as of November 1992, its audience share exceeded that of CBC television by 68%. CTV's share was 23.5% while CBC Television's share was 14.0%."[48]

Beyond the realm of news, CTV showed a renewed interest in "Big Event" programming in the early 1990s to maintain its populist appeal as a national network and to garner advertising revenue. Big Event programming such as the winter Olympics coverage in Calgary, 1988 and in Lillehammer, 1994 enabled the network to create impact and to win large audiences in excess of two million viewers. Big Events were linked to the network's corporate initiative called TOPS (Total Optimization of

Premiums and Specials) which was designed to underline major programming undertakings. Such programs that only a national network could provide for advertisers and particular constituencies were sometimes distinctly Canadian. Traditionally on CTV, big event programming had included such fare as the *Wide World of Sports*. But the style of programming was extended to include the *Canadian Country Music Awards*, the *Academy Awards* and mini series such as *The French Revolution*.[49] CTV remained a mass market, general interest network service though it faced steady competition as the multi-channel broadcasting universe continued to evolve.

THE CRTC CONDUCTED a thorough examination in 1993 of new shareholders and affiliation agreements that the CTV network had arranged with its members stations. The new shareholders agreement had come into effect on 27 January 1993. Long-term affiliation agreements with the network's stations came into force on 1 September 1993. The aim of both initiatives was to put the network on a firmer financial footing and to establish a more satisfactory relationship between CTV and its affiliates.

John Cassaday was determined to change the network's method of operation. The "co-operative" nature of CTV most recently had seen eight shareholders—Baton Broadcasting Ltd., CHUM Ltd., Maclean Hunter Ltd., WIC Western International Communications Ltd., Electrohome Ltd., Moffat Communications Ltd., CFCF Inc., and Newfoundland Broadcasting Co. Ltd.—each hold 100 common voting shares or a 12.5 percent interest in the network. Each owner continued to have an equal voice in network business affairs and an equal vote regardless of the number of stations he owned.[50] Such a shareholders' co-operative arrangement could cause a paralysis in the operation of the network.

Cassaday had succeeded in getting the directors of CTV to devise a new shareholders agreement which changed fundamentally the network's structure. The network was allowed to operate along the lines similar to a conventional company with a Board of Directors that would have greater latitude than in the past. In future, the composition of the network's Board would be determined by the common shares held in CTV. Significantly, the veto power awarded to each director under the previous co-operative arrangement was removed. All resolutions now were to be passed by a majority of votes cast at meetings. Two other aspects of the new shareholders agreement were also relevant. First, the ownership of shares in CTV was not a pre-condition for network affiliation and shares could be sold or assigned. Second, the seven owners who eventually signed the new shareholders' agreement—Westcom TV Group Ltd. [WIC], CFCN Communications Limited [Maclean Hunter], CFTO-TV Limited [Baton], CFCF Inc., Electrohome Limited, Moffat Communications Limited and CHUM Limited—had each agreed to purchase a two million dollar debenture to recapitalize the network. Each debenture was to be convertible to two million common voting shares. When it renewed CTV's licence in 1994 for a five-year period, the CRTC concluded that "the Commission considers that the new agreement holds the potential to put an end to the impasse of recent years and enable the network to respond more quickly to a changing environment."[51] Newfoundland Broadcasting Co. Ltd., "NTV" was not a signatory to the new shareholders' agreement but it remained a CTV affiliate.

Similarly the new affiliation agreement that the CTV's owners had worked out was designed to provide a smoother relationship between the network and its affiliates. The CRTC noted that in the past "co-operative arrangements [between CTV and its affiliates] proved workable only so long as the network continued to operate at a profit and was able to compensate affiliates for use of their facilities at a level they deemed acceptable." A major problem arose in the late 1980s when CTV's profits declined and "the affiliate/shareholders found themselves unable to agree on the means to cover those losses."[52]

Under the new affiliation agreement reached in 1993, "network sales time," when CTV rented time on the stations for its programming, was to total 40 hours weekly including 12 hours between 7 P.M. and 11 P.M. However "affiliate sales time" or "station sales time," which the stations paid CTV to provide, was all but eliminated leaving only 2.5 hours per week. The affiliates, many of them now in large ownership groups, such as Baton and WIC, preferred to purchase their own programming. This arrangement for just over 2 hours covered the first half hour of the program *Canada AM* each week Monday to Friday from 6:30 A.M. to 7:00 A.M.[53]

Clearly the greatest distinction between the old and new affiliation agreements was the provision that guaranteed the time payments the network's affiliates would receive for CTV's rental of their air time. The original affiliation agreements were no longer appropriate when the network began to experience deficits. Before 1993, as Cassaday explained, "All of the affiliates would submit their revenue for the year to an independent audit and if your combined revenue was 35 percent of the total pot then your distribution from CTV was 35 per cent." But there had been no provision made for a time when the network began losing money such as the late 1980s. He said that "at the time they made the agreement, no one contemplated deficits. So they never discussed how they would split up deficits."[54]

Under the new affiliation agreement, the CTV affiliates were guaranteed cash payments for their air time. The payments to the affiliated stations were to rise from $14.8 million in 1994–95 to $21.8 million in 1998–99. By the end of seven years, the payments were to increase to $25.2 million. According to Cassaday, such payments would amount to a return of about 14% on CTV's projected revenue, an amount the affiliates had been accustomed to in the past. The CRTC noted the advantageous position that the affiliates continued to enjoy: "The Commission considers that CTV's compensation to its affiliates for use of their airtime is, at the very least, generous. Because the compensation is fixed in each year, and is thus independent of the network's profitability, these arrangements could affect CTV's ability to meet its responsibilities should revenues fall short of projections in any given year." The Commission discounted such an eventuality but expected "the licensee's shareholders and affiliates to act responsibly should such an event occur, and ensure that the network has adequate resources to fulfil its obligations."[55]

The new agreements had been hammered out between 1991 and 1993 in a series of ongoing meetings among the participants. Cassaday had come to believe that dispute resolution was all about process. That is one reason why Roger Fisher, a Harvard university professor and a specialist in conflict resolution, was brought in to help put an end to the struggle that had dominated the CTV board room. Fisher had been involved in some major international disputes. In the case of CTV, Fisher and Cassaday sought to get closure on the various elements that would create a shareholders' agreement separate and apart from the affiliation agreements with the members stations. "What we did in the affiliation agreements was to identify what the network's responsibility would be to the affiliates," said Cassaday, "identify the schedule of payments that would be made to compensate them for their air time. On the shareholders' side, we drafted a document that talked about representation on the Board, votes and responsibilities."[56]

Two meetings in particular, at The Briars resort north of Toronto and a following session at the Sutton Place Hotel in Toronto, were central to Cassaday's success in creating a new structure for CTV and to recapitalize the network. He recalled how a crisis financial situation had forced the network to go to the barricades: "In 1991 the bank [CIBC] came in and said, 'you know it's all over! We're not prepared to finance you anymore'....And you know they said that 'we have just realized that we own this place and we're not having any fun!'" Cassaday found himself facing an unfamiliar situation: "You know I came from rich organizations like Campbell Soup and General Foods. Quite frankly even though you had cash flow statements you never looked at them, because there was always cash. I mean the bank was Campbell Soup Company. So here we are for the first time...faced with a situation where we have no cash." He received help when "CRTC gave us approval to delay our payments to them of our licence fees, our program suppliers supported us in extending our terms of payment to them."[57] With a dismal financial backdrop and regulatory pressure coming from the CRTC, Cassaday gathered the network's directors together for what appeared to be a moment of truth for CTV.

The Briars located on the south short of Lake Simcoe is a resort with 17 cottages, a golf course and boasts attractive, rich landscaping.[58] The peaceful surroundings of the resort seemed an ideal setting to solve a lingering dispute over the financing of the network. But Fisher arrived in a somewhat ruffled condition when the car bringing him, his assistant and Gary Maavara hit a deer that went through the windshield on Highway 404 going to Lake Simcoe.

WIC's Doug Holtby who was at the Briars meeting crystallized the central dilemma that CTV faced: "The reason that John Cassaday put this thing together was the network had always been stripped of its retained earnings. Basically the affiliates took all of the...net revenue and the network had no retained earnings....So when things got a little tough for the network, there were no resources within the network to resolve things and John needed to have some injections of capital." From an accounting standpoint, Holtby was mystified when he learned how CTV had operated and he could not believe it: "I mean you can't strip a company like that."[59]

Holtby went into The Briars meeting with four hats for all the participants to wear. He sought to demonstrate the various positions each held as a CTV ownership-director, affiliate owner and competitor. The

284 CTV—THE NETWORK THAT MEANS BUSINESS

fourth, a network management hat, underlined the extent to which the meeting was involved with the management of network affairs. "To me it was an issue of recognizing them," he said, "and when you...walked through that door as a board member, you had to take those hats off. And you had to sit down as a director of a company and make decisions that were in the best interests of the company. Not your own. When I say 'the company' I mean CTV."[60]

The two dominant players in the network remained WIC and Baton Broadcasting. Baton's Douglas Bassett led off with a proposal. Holtby was not impressed with Bassett's offer to purchase CTV: "So it was an interesting meeting....And you know Doug started the meeting off with an offer to purchase and it was so inadequate that you know...everybody said 'you can forget it.'" Holtby maintained that Bassett "didn't want to pay anything for it....So, of course, Roger Fisher had been through these things. He told us he had been involved with the Baltic states and...South Africa. But he had his hands full there." A number of the participants would have "a long litany of issues" and Fisher would attempt to identify the most salient aspects.[61]

Bassett remembered that Fisher pursued the issues doggedly at The Briars meeting: "Well he just kept at it and kept at it. Different scenarios. All these pieces of paper on billboards going. I mean he wore us all down and we all decided what is best for the network. We had to take off our own hats as CEOs of our own companies and try to say what's best for the network and what's best for the Canadian broadcasting system. There's going to be a change. What is the best change in the structure?" Bassett and other directors felt the intense pressure of the broadcast regulator demanding a realignment of the network's operation: "And knowing full well that the CRTC wanted, in fact almost commanded all of us, to straighten this thing out. And in fact it was very hard, because...they didn't own anything, the network." At The Briars meeting, Bassett recalled that the notion of Baton or any one owner getting control of CTV was a subject far removed from the proceedings: "I could see [one owner] as everybody else could eventually one day if somebody bought out shareholders, but nobody was figuring at that time that Maclean-Hunter was going to sell their Calgary [TV station] or that Pouliot was going to sell CFCF...or that Electrohome was going to do a deal with us."[62]

At The Briars, the directors resolved how to deal with the ownership question and a plan was formulated to recapitalize and restructure the network. "I guess the main resolution at that time," said Holtby, "was that it [the network] has got to be set up as a business. It's got to have its own capital, it's got to have its agreements with the affiliates and...it has to have the ability to operate as a business and have the commensurate resources."[63] At The Briars, a framework had been developed; the next step—the implementation—was more difficult.

The stage was set for a crucial meeting at the Sutton Place Hotel in Toronto at the end of January, 1992 where the recapitalization of the network was to happen. In other words, how much capital were the affiliate owners prepared to inject into the network's operations. "That's when we were actually doing our proposals" Holtby recalled, "I went to my Board and said 'I think we should take as much as we can and, of course, we didn't know what the others would be doing." The meeting at the Sutton Place had a surprise in store. As Holtby remembered, "So when we went there, went around the table and said 'we're in'...Doug [Bassett] said he was out. Actually we left the Sutton Place and he [Bassett] was not involved in the network."[64]

Three affiliate owners, WIC Western International Communications Ltd., Maclean Hunter Ltd., CFCF Inc., each were to have a 30 percent interest in the network with two owners, Electrohome Ltd. and Moffat Communications, each having a five percent stake. The network was to receive a capital injection of 20 million dollars. John Partridge underlined the significance of the meeting in *The Globe and Mail*: "It was to auction off shares of that $20 million—the first equity infusion in CTV's 31-year history—and, in the process, come up with a new ownership structure."[65] Baton had decided to be an affiliate only of CTV.

In the end, the arrangement with Baton having only affiliate status proved unworkable. Douglas Bassett found himself isolated: "It wasn't the most pleasurable of times in all our lives...There were tensions. My colleagues, my confrères, some of them not all of them certainly, were somewhat antagonistic. They wanted to freeze out Baton notwithstanding the fact that we owned more television stations that were affiliates than anybody else." Bassett knew the steep costs involved with Baton serving as an affiliate only: "So some said I called their bluff. I just finally said, having checked with my Board of Directors of course, look we'll just be affiliates. You can have the responsibility and you come and make a deal...and you are going to pay us fair market value. Because it is not a co-op anymore. And Baton being a public company had a responsibility to the shareholders." Bassett remembered that "when they looked and saw what the time was going to cost, when we had the time valued by...reputable advertising agencies and they looked at that, well it wouldn't work."[66]

Still Baton eventually became a signatory to the final shareholders agreement involving seven owners that was worked out in 1993, the same year new affiliation agreements came into effect. Two major factors had served as an impetus to bring the various factions in the network together. CTV had no formula to deal with operating deficits and the network owed the bank heavily. The recession of the early 1990s exacerbated the problem.

THE CRTC SEEMED to show a cautious approval of the new agreements when CTV applied for its licence renewal in September, 1993. Obviously concerned about the network's capacity to finance its Canadian programming obligations, Keith Spicer, the Commission Chairman, asked Cassaday if it wasn't true that "the affiliates, under the new arrangements, have more financial power over you than they did before?" Cassaday responded that it was "quite the opposite. Under the new Agreement, the [seven] shareholders have offered to put forward $14 million in equity. So in fact they have for the first time provided an equity base in the Network. This Network was completely financed on the basis of debt prior to this historic accord."[67]

Cassaday explained to the Commission that there were two distinct interests that had to be considered. An affiliate of CTV wanted the best programming that the network could provide in the 40 hours of network sales time. A shareholder, on the other hand, wanted a return on investment in CTV: "Importantly, and again one of the breakthroughs in this new Agreement, we have separated the interests of the affiliate from the interests of the Shareholder. Quite frankly, in most cases, we are talking to two different people."[68]

Commissioner Ed Ross questioned the new corporate arrangement of the network in comparison to the earlier co-operative where each owner had an equal voice: "Under this new Shareholders' Agreement, don't you feel that perhaps the Company has lost some stability and is now subject to more changes than existed under the old Agreement, and could that be detrimental to the Network?" Cassaday challenged the notion by explaining that "the old structure was in effect paralysis of the Network. As a co-op, if one individual member of the Group felt that it was not in the interest of the Network to go forward on a particular proposition, then the Network would have been precluded." The CTV President underlined how the need for unanimity tended to hamper the network: "Getting unanimity on anything is darn near impossible, and now all we are going to be simply asking for is the same conditions as any other company trying to do business in a tough environment such as we are in today, which is that the majority of the Board approve it."[69]

Perhaps the most significant aspect of the new shareholders' agreement was that it contained provisions for the transfer of shares and stations in CTV and allowed for one owner to eventually control the network. Under the old co-operative arrangement, one owner could own as much as 90 percent of the stations belonging to the network and still would be allowed to appoint only one director to the Board. Gary Maavara, CTV's Vice President of Sports and Public Affairs, told the Commission: "That was clearly a big deficiency under the old scheme. The new scheme allows a shareholder inside the Company either to transfer their shares to the others or to a third party—and there is a scheme for that. Or if you want to sell your station or buy one of the other Shareholder stations, you have the ability to get their shares as well." Maavara envisaged the possibility of one owner getting control of the network, a long sought objective of Baton Broadcasting: "What that would do then...is that someone could buy stations and, as a result of that, could logically also acquire control of the Network, and I think there would be an element of the symbiotic relationship in doing that."[70] By November, 1997, Baton would have control of CTV.

AS WELL AS HAVING to decide on the appropriateness of the new CTV structure, the CRTC carefully assessed the promise and performance of the network as it sought a seven-year licence renewal that would take it into the 21st century. Perhaps the most controversial aspect of CTV's application in 1993 was again the question of Canadian programming expenditures. Specifically the CRTC questioned the network on its decision to reduce its spending on Canadian programming after it had lost access to revenue from broadcasts of the Toronto Blue Jays baseball games and the Canadian Football League.

In 1987, the CRTC had renewed the network's licence for a five-year period. It was set to expire on 31 August 1992. The Commission issued a short-term licence for a nine-month period from 1 September 1992 to

31 May 1993. This licence was subject to the same terms and conditions as the last year of the licence granted in 1987. As a condition of licence (COL), CTV was to spend 93.3 million dollars "in respect of Canadian programs in Network Sales Time" in 1992–93.[71]

The network's behaviour in choosing to adjust the COL to new market conditions underlined the tensions that had arisen periodically between CTV and the broadcast regulator. At issue again was the question of the private network's contribution to Canadian content and its adherence to the objectives of the broadcasting system. Clearly CTV had appeared to shape the conditions of licence to the marketplace.

Commissioner Adrian Burns charged that the network had not met the Canadian programming spending requirements in 1992–93 when it chose to spend $67 million rather than the $93.3 million stipulated in the earlier conditions of licence. Cassaday disagreed and explained the rationale for the roughly $26 million reduction. "One of the opportunities we had" said Cassaday, "as per the CRTC guidelines, is to average over-expenditures from the previous year. In fact, in 1991–92 we had expenditures of $103 million-plus. So approximately a $10 million over-expenditure in year five of the licence period." CTV then proceeded to make a major adjustment relating to its licence. "The first thing we did in 1992–93 was to apply that over-expenditure against our commitment for 1992–93. The second thing we did was to back out approximately $17 million, the combination of Blue Jay baseball and CFL football." Cassaday argued that "those two factors were involved or were included in the Base Year spending on which the expenditures were arrived at for the licence period. So certainly it is our interpretation, our belief, our conviction, that we did in fact meet the condition and the expectation and certainly the spirit of the expenditure requirement for 1992–93."[72]

Commissioner Burns persisted with the utmost candor: "Do you not believe, Mr. Cassaday, that the intention of the COL (conditions of licence) on Canadian programming expenditures would require that those budgeted amounts which you have backed out after 1991–92 on those lost programming rights should have been directed towards other programming?" Cassaday's response underlined the historical challenge that has faced the Canadian broadcasting system: the attempt to reconcile public policy objectives through legislation and regulation with the demands of the marketplace to which private broadcasters must respond. The CTV President was hardly restrained in his answer: "No, we do not. We believe that there was not an independent producer that lost an order because of this, that there was no injury to the system whatsoever. The only thing that happened was that the Toronto Blue Jays baseball team got a cheque from Baton Broadcasting instead of CTV, and Larry Smith at the CFL got a cheque from TSN instead of CTV."[73] Cassaday said CTV saw no extra programming obligation arising from the loss of the Blue Jays games and CFL football: "On the subject of additional programming, we felt no inclination to go out and acquire programming to simply spend an additional $15.6 million, because it was not felt that we could add significant value to the program service that we already had in place."[74]

Finally Commissioner Burns asked, "Are you aware of any precedents whereby the Commission has accepted lower expenditures on Canadian programming because programming was not available to a licensee as it had planned?" Cassaday responded: "I am probably the wrong person to ask because I do not have a lot of history here, but what I can tell you is that the cumulative condition for the five years of the licence [1987–1992] was $402,961,700 and we in fact spent $416,601,900. So we exceeded the condition by a substantial amount of money—$13,640,000 to be precise."[75] Clearly the CRTC had reservations about the private network's behaviour especially the practice of reducing Canadian programming expenditures, when the programs that CTV had anticipated at the time of its licence renewal in 1987 were not available.

After its review of the network's performance, the Commission concluded that CTV had fallen short of the conditions of licence that had stipulated the amount of Canadian drama the network was to provide. As a result, CTV's licence was renewed for five years instead of seven.[76] The CRTC imposed stringent conditions of licence that called for CTV to spend $18 million on Canadian entertainment programming in the year ended 31 August 1995, an amount $3 million more than the network had projected for 1994–95. The network had to broadcast a minimum of three hours each week of regularly-scheduled Canadian drama for the first three years of its new licence term and 3.5 hours weekly in the last two years. The Commission also stipulated that the drama programming had to be aired in peak viewing hours. In addition, CTV was to air a minimum of 48 hours of Canadian dramatic features and mini series which could be averaged over the licence term. Chairman Keith

Spicer said the public review had discovered "significant non-compliance in terms of the network broadcasting less regularly-scheduled Canadian drama than it was required to offer viewers."[77]

WHATEVER THE PROGRAMMING demands of the CRTC, CTV management continued to envisage the network as a vehicle to serve mainstream Canada. Arthur Weinthal borrowed a quotation from Les Brown, a leading observer and commentator on the role of television, and cited Brown's notion that "television used to be a cultural campfire and sitting before the set one felt something vaguely important about the shared national experience." Weinthal told the Commission: "Our vision, our point of view, is that we want to be the national campfire, and we want to have our programs of such a quality and importance that there is a gathering of Canadians, whether they are watching programs to be informed, or entertained, or enlightened."[78]

CTV with a new, young President had come to realize that the broadcasting universe of the 1990s, with numerous specialty channels and a steady audience fragmentation, presented a formidable challenge. John Cassaday perceived the television market of the future as an extension of other consumer markets where a polarization of interests had occurred: "If you were to look at the ice cream market, you would find that the growth is in the super high indulgent, high-fat Häagen Dazs kind of products and, at the other end, the low-fat, low-calorie ice creams. The stuff in the middle, the conventional fare, has basically been eroded." In other words, Canadian television was expected to polarize between the high quality, generalist services such as CTV and CBC at one end with a range of services provided by specialty channels, "the niche players" at the other end.[79] Whether CTV could become the "Häagen Dazs" of Canadian broadcasters remained unpredictable as the private broadcasting business confronted a tortuous decade.

ELEVEN

Gordian Knot Before the Triumph of Baton

1993–1997

JOHN CASSADAY had achieved a major objective by arranging for a new shareholders agreement allowing for a transfer of shares within the companies that owned the network. As he explained to the CRTC in July 1997 when Baton applied to take over the network, "The shareholders' agreement provided the mechanism for a controlling shareholder to emerge. The only question at that time was what shareholder would emerge to control CTV, and when."[1]

A controversial Cassaday initiative in the mid 1990s that became known as "Gordian Knot" was both novel and nearly successful. After he departed CTV, Baton Broadcasting Inc. became the sole owner of the network. Cassaday joined Shaw Communications Inc. and became Chief Executive Officer of Corus Entertainment Inc., a company specializing in radio and specialty television. Ivan Fecan, a much travelled broadcasting executive, was to become head of Baton Broadcasting, which eventually managed to obtain control of CTV.

To hear Cassaday describe "Gordian Knot," which was an attempt to devise a strategy to break out of the ownership knot that had limited network operations, his initiative was well intentioned. The conventional wisdom had been that one day CTV probably would have a single owner who would emerge from the powerful CTV affiliates, perhaps Baton or WIC. Cassaday had envisioned another scenario: the possibility of CTV supporting itself in the future as a separate entity without ownership by its affiliates. He thought it possible to have an arrangement whereby CTV basically bought the broadcasting assets of the owners and contracted with them to provide a television network service.

Still what he and the CTV management proposed could also be seen as a "power grab," a view of which Cassaday was well aware. He recalled the risks involved: "We are explaining to the directors what we think is in the best interests of everyone. However the management of the various operations may well have been threatened by it, by the fact that it looked to some like a power grab. But quite frankly, we did not envision life after this."[2]

"Gordian Knot" had a somewhat unusual genesis. Cassaday adopted the strategy following negotiations between himself and David Stern, President of the National Basketball Association (NBA), over the television rights to the broadcasts of the Canadian entrants in the NBA. "We had just negotiated a contract for CTV to be the national broadcaster of the NBA on the occasion of the NBA coming to Canada, the Toronto Raptors and the Vancouver Grizzlies," Cassaday recalled. "And after a series of lengthy negotiations, David and I were together and just talking casually and I said, 'how did you get this turned around' because remember in the '80s, the NBA was in tatters, they had drug problems, they had ownership issues, big financial problems.'" Stern's response struck a chord with Cassaday: "He said, 'well I convinced the owners that it was better to have a small piece of a big pie than a big piece of a small pie.'" Cassaday was impressed. "So the penny dropped for me," he said, "and our entire focus up to that point had been to have one shareholder emerge and take control of the network. So I said, 'what if we did it the other way and the network took control of the affiliates?'"[3]

Without the approval of the CTV Board, Cassaday and his management team including Tom Peddie and Gary Maavara worked closely with Doug Cunningham of the investment banking firm, Wood Gundy, hired for the project. Cassaday foresaw a situation whereby the network could become a strong entity by taking over the affiliates: "What we conceived was a scenario where everyone would roll in their affiliates...without incurring any debt and what we would end up with was a company with great assets, no debt and a company that we would take public and I think at the time we sort of used Baton as the linchpin."[4]

Cassaday saw clear advantage for the affiliates and the network itself,

because at the time "Baton was trading at about eight dollars and we
thought that the stock would trade at at least 12 dollars." The CTV
President underlined the consolidation that would take place in the
operation of the network that would appeal to the owners: "We identified 35 to 50 million dollars in synergies by taking out redundancies in
the system and we felt that it would have been a good way for the
Pouliots to retain their interest in CFCF, for the Griffiths to retain their
interest in WIC, for the Eatons to retain their interest in CTV and Baton,
all of which are gone now, by virtue of the fact that we would have created an outstanding broadcasting company with no debt."[5] Maavara
who became later Senior Vice President, CanWest Interactive, remembered that the proposed structure would remove the problem of the network not owning its affiliates: "You would have had this big company,
CTV Inc., that owned its affiliates, that was owned by a bunch of people, but it would have been a different kind of thing, because the affiliation agreement wouldn't have been an issue anymore because the network would have owned the stations."[6]

Cassaday refuted any notion that the initiative was a power grab on
his part or the CTV management and explained how the proposal was
presented to the CTV Board of Directors: "The way we ultimately presented it to the Board was 'we have taken this initiative on our own and
you can be critical of that. However the fact of the matter is that each
of you has a veto, so no one is required to do what they don't want to
do, no one is going to be bullied into what they don't feel is right for
their company, so criticize if you wish, however we've done what we
think is best for the system.'" From a personal standpoint, Cassaday saw
the CTV Board fully in charge of the decision making process. He
informed the Board: "In terms of our own personal stake in this you
decide how you want to run it when we're done. But there is no quid pro
quo that if you agree to this, you agree to us as the management of this
new organization. So we're clean. This is what we think is the right thing
to do. If at the end of it, you do it and there's not a role for us here, we're
gone."[7]

Cassady's initiative required the unanimous consent of the shareholders. "I think that Douglas [Baton's Bassett] was supportive," said
Cassaday.[8] In the end, Cassaday succeeded in winning over every CTV
shareholder to his adventuresome proposition but one. The lone hold-
out was WIC. "It never happened, but it came very close," said

Mavaara. "We were at the St. Charles Club in Winnipeg. The Board voted and Doug Holtby voted against it. To this day I don't know why he did it....WIC voted against it and it is interesting, because it really would have established kind of a Bell Globemedia ahead of the game, two years or three years before it happening." Maavara envisaged that with "Gordian Knot" CTV would have become "an American type of company...where the network owned the affiliates which was what Bell Globemedia is now or what CanWest is now."[9]

Cassaday insisted he was comfortable with the approach taken, because of the "change of control" clause in the contract he had signed when he joined CTV in 1990: "The expectation always was that there would be a change of control. And my job was to try to get the network back on a footing where it was self supporting, where its debt had been brought back under control and where it was possible for someone to take it over. And at that time I had the right to trigger a change of control clause in my contract and leave. So from the financial point of view, it was almost impossible for me to justify staying."[10]

Cassaday maintained he was indifferent to whatever happened after "Gordian Knot" was presented to the CTV Board: "So I was quite comfortable saying that 'this is what I think is the right thing to do, if you wish me to stay, great, but...my personal stake in the network was going to be realized regardless of what happened. I was indifferent to the outcome. The important thing was my job as an executive was to find a solution for CTV. And how that ended up for me was not of any concern to me." Still the perception of a "power grab" rested with some network shareholders who wondered why Cassaday had undertaken his plan without Board approval. Cassaday drew an analogy with Air Canada: "It's like Bob Milton and Air Canada....the guy's in the job for a week and all of a sudden somebody wants to take his airline over. Might be the right thing to do, but not on my watch. So there was undoubtedly anxiety created by this amongst the larger affiliates as to what in fact our agenda was."[11]

ONCE THE "GORDIAN KNOT" STRATEGY was unsuccessful, it became apparent that the future of CTV would eventually involve a single owner who could bring stability to its operations. Baton with the Eaton family as the controlling shareholder was perceived to be the likely company that would emerge as owner of the network. Cassaday recalled how Baton's eventual control of CTV originated: "Once we did not receive unanimous support of the shareholders, it was like shooting a bear and not bringing him down. Because now we had identified significant savings that were possible and we were very conservative. So how can you as a business executive sit there and know that within your system there is 35 to 50 million, possibly 100 million dollars of cost savings....So that led to the next best solution which is for an affiliate to begin to buy up the other affiliates."[12]

Before the shareholders agreement that had governed the network's ownership was modified, no one affiliate could increase its shareholdings in the network by purchasing another affiliate. Baton now had the latitude to purchase other stations and gain control of CTV. "So the first step then was to go out and purchase Electrohome," Cassaday recalled. "We had identified as part of 'Gordian Knot' that option. The next piece of the puzzle was to buy CFCN in Calgary." During the negotiations over buying CFCN, Cassaday met J.R. Shaw, founder of Shaw Communications Inc., a company he would join in 1997 after leaving CTV. "The Shaws had the opportunity to buy that station [CFCN] as part of the swap with Rogers," Cassaday remembered. "They approached me and said 'what do you think?' I said, 'well I think if you want to control the network this is a good, first step. However if you simply want to own an affiliate, then I think you should pass, because I think it is more important that the network ownership be consolidated.'"[13]

J.R. Shaw agreed with Cassaday's advice. "We then talked to Ted [Rogers]," said Cassaday, "and I told George Eaton that I thought he should approach Ted about purchasing CFCN. And that's how that piece came together." Baton needed only one more transaction to go over the top and gain control of CTV. "That was to swap the Ottawa [sic] and London stations for the interest in ATV [Atlantic Television System]. And now they had effective control of the network."[14]

John Cassaday announced his resignation as President of CTV network on 27 June 1997. His departure from the network, which actually took place before Baton had control of CTV, was negotiated between February and April, 1997. Ivan Fecan had been hired in January 1994 as Senior Group Vice President of Baton. He became President and Chief Executive Officer of the company in December, 1996. Baton Broadcasting was to become CTV Inc. in 1998.

Cassaday's departure drew considerable media attention given the fact that Baton seemed on the verge of getting control of CTV and had a young executive in Fecan who would assume the top post at CTV. Cassaday's leaving created interest as to what extent a power struggle had taken place. Still Cassaday maintained his departure was smooth and amicable. "It was very clear to me," said Cassaday, "that the way it worked out that George Eaton owned the network. George Eaton was going to be able to select his person to run [the network]....I'm a corporate warrior. I understand that. They got control of the network. How many times does somebody buy somebody else and the guy that gets bought ends up staying? Never!"[15]

When it became apparent to Cassaday in February, 1997 that Baton would acquire ownership of the network, he proposed to Eaton that he trigger a change of control clause that was included in his contract when he had joined the network seven years earlier. "Ivan and I never had one discussion, ever," Cassaday recalled. "The original discussion I had was with George Eaton, Fred Eaton and Allan Beattie and then all my discussions were with Fred Sherratt [CHUM] resolving the terms of my departure. It was all worked out amicably and quickly between February and April, 1997."[16]

When Cassaday was hired to become President of CTV, it was a widely held company with several shareholders. "In the event there was single owner," he said, "my job would have changed to the point that...it would have been quite different circumstances under which I was hired. So on that basis, I suggested...we would simply have an arrangement laid out in the contract which would dictate the terms under which I could trigger my leaving." Cassaday refuted any notion of having had a dispute with Fecan: "So this whole thing about Ivan and I having had battles, we...had none, zero! And the thing that's complicated is that since I have come to Corus [Entertainment Inc.]...as I said to the reporter the other day, we're already in partners with CTV. We own the Comedy channel together, I am on the Board, we attend board meetings together, we attend corporate functions together."[17]

The curiosity surrounding Cassaday's departure from CTV was in direct response to the "Gordian Knot" initiative that he had undertaken. He had been hired at CTV to stabilize the network and modernize the company. He maintained his plan was to leave eventually after that was accomplished: "I mean the thing that people forget is that I was brought in to consolidate CTV and then at that time...I would leave. Because it was always the thought that one of them [affiliates] would buy us."[18]

Cassaday's attempt to reverse the process and take over the affiliates was an unexpected development: "The only thing that confused the issue was that just prior to that we tried to buy them. Without 'Gordian Knot,' the whole evolution would have been as natural as can be, because then no one would have assumed for a moment that the company that gets bought ends up running the company that bought them, it never ever happens. If Chrysler buys Mercedes Benz, the President of Chrysler is in charge." Cassaday said "The Eatons knew that Douglas [Bassett] and Joe [Garwood] were...not going to be there forever. They brought in Ivan as the successor to Douglas and Joe. He obviously performed up to their expectations...."[19]

DURING CASSADAY'S SEVEN years at CTV, the network had some impressive successes in its programming initiatives. Whatever shortcomings CTV might have had in drama, one notable success was the popular entertainment program *Due South*, the winner of numerous Gemini awards. When CTV applied for its licence renewal in 1993, the program then in development was described for the CRTC as an exciting new series: "A lightning-paced hour action/comedy in which a polite, by-the-book Canadian Mountie from the frozen North is teamed up with a wise-cracking Armani-clad Chicago cop with a flexible sense of morality. *Due South* stars Paul Gross as R.C.M.P. Constable Frobisher [*sic*] and David Marciano as his unwilling partner, Ray Vecchio."[20]

The program produced by Alliance Communications Corp. was a major success and drew favorable response from television critics. In April, 1995, Christopher Harris wrote in *The Globe and Mail* about the show's international acclaim: "The Canadian action-comedy series *Due South*...is popular with TV critics in Australia, where the two-hour pilot premiered Easter Sunday. The series, broadcast on CTV in Canada, was praised in several Brisbane papers and chosen as the top holiday pick by the Sydney *Morning Herald*'s Robin Oliver. 'Slick, deliberately unbelievable police action, brilliant dialogue and particularly engaging humour' was how Oliver described this 'first-rate Canadian production.'"[21]

CTV's Arthur Weinthal recalled the length of time it took to get *Due South* on the air. The program was carried by CBS in the United States in the fall of 1994 after considerable effort on Weinthal's behalf: "Sixteen years ago I made my first foray into CBS not to buy their Jackie Gleason show or the Andy Williams show or Ed Sullivan show, but [he inquired] 'how about if we produce some shows in Canada you'll buy and we can both run them on our networks.'" Weinthal remembered the astonished reaction from CBS executives: "They looked at me like a side order of asparagus that they hadn't ordered and patted me on the head and said, 'gee nice to see you. And next time you're in Los Angeles come and visit us again, OK. What's your name again?'" Weinthal attributed the success of productions such as *Due South* to economics, more skilled Canadian talent and the role of Telefilm Canada, which has helped to finance Canadian television programming: "It's economics that made it happen and it's the skill of our people that have got a lot better, better and better over the years. A lot of that has been due to initiatives like Telefilm and by regulations pouring down on our head and other heads and the fact that sometimes you get so hard up for material you wind up scraping the top of the barrel!"[22]

BEYOND THE GENRE OF DRAMA, a controversy arose in the mid 1990s over the question of sports programming that served to underline the different attitudes toward the role of network broadcasting between CTV and CBC. CTV objected strongly to the extent of such fare on the public broadcaster and argued that the costs of programs devoted to sports actually drained resources away from the CBC. As CTV President, Cassaday objected when the Corporation outbid the private network for the Canadian broadcast rights to the 1996 Summer Olympic games in Atlanta, Georgia. The private network responded by commissioning a report entitled "A Perspective in the CBC" which was released in July, 1994. The report maintained that each year sports broadcasting was costing the CBC between 60 and 70 million dollars a year and predicted that the Corporation would not make a profit on the Summer Olympics in Atlanta.[23]

In an appearance before the House of Commons Committee on Canadian Heritage, Cassaday raised two salient questions: "Should CBC divert scarce public funds from programming which makes it a distinctive world class public broadcaster, programs such as *The Nature of Things*, news, public affairs and Canadian dramatic programming, to programming which other television services can and do provide?" Cassaday also questioned whether the public broadcaster should take initiatives that go beyond its mandate: "Finally, if CBC is under-funded, should it move into new ventures that do not relate to its mandate, such as Specialty Services and international ventures."[24] CTV argued that both questions should be answered in the negative.

For its part, the CBC countered CTV's claim by releasing an unaudited financial statement that the Auditor-General had assessed. The evidence showed that in its professional sports programming the revenues the Corporation gained were $1.9 million beyond its expenses for 1993–94. The clash between both networks took on a slightly new tone when the Corporation's employees in English broadcasting argued that the broadcasting of professional sports produced a profit closer to $20 million before adjustments for a range of expenses associated with the broadcasts. The Standing Committee on Canadian Heritage seemed stumped in its effort to reconcile the dispute between the two networks: "We think the Corporation should try to end this interminable debate by thoroughly examining the costs question. Specifically, it should evaluate the costs and the benefits of its professional sports programming over an appropriate period to assess the net effect on its other programming and report its findings to the Minister and this Standing Committee."[25]

The debate over sports programming was fuelled still further when Anthony S. Manera, President of the CBC, wrote a commentary in *The Globe and Mail* and argued that profit was not the main reason for sports programming on the public broadcaster. While he argued that "the profits [sports programming] earned by the CBC...help to pay for the coverage of other non-profitable programs," there was another argument to be made for broadcasting Canadian football or the Olympics: "Sports is an important part of our culture and provides many opportunities for shared national experiences that focus on what unites rather than what divides us."[26]

The same day that Manera's commentary appeared in *The Globe and Mail*, the newspaper itself jumped into the fray and awarded a "technical knockout" to CTV: "Is broadcasting Blue Jays games, or even *Hockey Night in Canada*, part of the CBC's role of reflecting Canadians to ourselves? Would our national identity suffer if the CTV logo appeared on the screen instead of CBC's exploding pizza?" The newspaper's editorial concluded that the CBC should rid itself of covering professional sports such as *HNIC:* "With the 500-channel universe nearly upon us, CBC needs to focus on the things that make it distinctive, the things that others fail to do. Sports is not one of them. The CBC should hang up its sports blazers and let private broadcasters take the mike."[27]

By January, 1996 when the Juneau report of the Mandate Review Committee on the CBC, National Film Board and Telefilm was tabled, the "commercial ethos" at the CBC was seemingly full-blown. The Juneau report reflected the findings of the CTV network in its study of the CBC's sports coverage when it concluded that "the CBC English network now devotes 25% of its prime time schedule (based on its 1993–94 season) to sports, and attracts about 37% of its prime time audience from sports. And CBC television now schedules almost as much sports in prime time as its drama, variety, arts and science programming combined." With such evidence, the CBC could not help but be seen as having "lost its sense of proportion."[28]

UNDER CASSADAY'S LEADERSHIP, the CTV network scored a major success in September, 1996 when the CRTC awarded it four specialty television services including a licence for a headline news channel. The CRTC's decision was some solace for Cassaday after the broadcast regulator had denied the network at an earlier stage. "It was very clear to me" said Cassaday, "that CTV could not succeed and would not be able to deliver value to the shareholders or the viewers if it was ghettoized in a 40 hour service." In the past CTV management had to struggle with its Board of Directors to make such applications. Cassaday said that opportunities were denied by Board members who would argue that "the bulk of my assets are tied up in my own company." Board members were inclined to ask, "why would I encourage or invest in an enterprise that I have only 12 percent?"[29]

After winning the headline news channel, CTV News1 which later became NewsNet, the network was able to move beyond its conventional service. The CBC had been awarded its Newsworld specialty channel in 1989. CTV's growth in the mid 1990s created an intensely competitive news environment. In the midst of the heated competition, major controversies involving two noted news personalities arose at both television networks. The notoriety in April 1995 served to high-light specific cultural differences between both the public and private broadcasting sectors.

THE DISMISSAL OF Pamela Wallin, a one-time CTV broadcaster, from *Prime Time News* on CBC television and Cassaday's firing of Keith Morrison from the popular CTV morning show *Canada A.M.* served to reveal an underlying level of turmoil at both networks. Instead of sim-ply moving the earlier programs, *The National* and *The Journal,* to 9 P.M., CBC news executive Tim Kotcheff felt that a more positive and identifiable approach was necessary and decided to integrate the two programs into one hour—*Prime Time News*—with Mansbridge and Wallin as co-anchors. "My feeling was that we just can't move to nine, we have to come up with a revitalized program and we have two anchors so let's build it, give...a reason not only for watching at nine because it is a changed time, but a reason to watch because it is an improved program. I think it was too much for people to absorb at once."[30] Kotcheff wanted to re-launch CBC news and public affairs: "We've got two of the three best journalists in the country on air together. Why the hell can't we make it work? We have an hour. Why do we have to divide it into two? Let's keep the news at the top and then we'll try to get back to a lively, dramatic back end and kind of restore the vigour and vitality of CBC news and magazine."[31]

Unfortunately Wallin whom Kotcheff had hired was accustomed to the private sector and had difficulty adjusting to the public broadcasting culture at the CBC. She joined the network the day after the national ref-erendum on the Charlottetown Accord held 26 October 1992. The working environment at the CBC was more formal and bureaucratic: "Maybe what I was a little naive about was that everything that had been done at CTV the way my working relationships were both with my colleagues and with managers...was essentially done on a handshake. You know that was goodwill. We'd like you to go to the Ottawa bureau and become the bureau chief....I learned here at the CBC if this isn't written in triplicate, with a pretty strong contract, it isn't worth much." Wallin underlined the fact that unlike the CBC, the private network never received federal funding: "The organizations are just fundamen-tally different. And it is a different culture....The sizes are different, the

Pamela Wallin and J.D. Roberts on the set of *Canada AM* in the early 1990s. Photograph courtesy of Watt International Inc., the firm that designed the *Canada AM* set, the *CTV National News* set and logo.

decision-making process is different and because CTV doesn't have federal funding they are not as obliged to respond to all the politically correct...motivations that are also part of the journalistic world."[32]

Wallin had her eyes opened early to the public broadcasting culture at the CBC when she tried to book a plane ticket: "One of my first weeks here, I had to go to Ottawa for something and so I picked up the phone and said 'book me an airline seat, I'll pick it up at the airport.' I was kind of politely told that that is not how it worked. People would book the airline ticket and after eight signatures later an airplane ticket arrived on my desk. Well I have a short attention span, let me put it that way." After her dismissal from *Prime Time News,* a *Maclean's* magazine story by Scott Steele drew attention to what was described as Wallin's disputatious attitude towards CBC staffers and how she amusingly became known as "the Pamatollah." She agreed that there were differences in opinion and struggles with fellow workers: "Oh absolutely, I mean I was very aggressive and I saw that as my job. I worked in a format where we had [*Canada*] *AM*...four minutes to get a politician to answer a question. You don't have a lot of time for niceties and formalities at that point. And I think there was a sense at the CBC that somehow it was not appropriate...although Barbara [Frum] could be a very aggressive interviewer."[33]

Still the culture clash showed in other ways. Kotcheff argued that the reception he received at CTV in 1976 was more positive than when he returned to the Corporation in 1992: "When we went over to CTV, there was less animosity but more a kind of 'glad you're here to help' and they saw it as a benefit rather than somebody muscling in from across the street. When I went back to CBC, it was 'what can people from private television tell us here in public television?' And I felt the animosity something awful."[34]

Kotcheff concluded that Wallin simply did not fit into the public broadcasting culture, especially when she had been accustomed to researching her own stories and "doing her own footwork" in the smaller and leaner operation at CTV: "They felt she wasn't playing the game and everyone had their rice bowl and they should be doing their job and she should be doing hers. There are divisions and territorial imperatives and on and on and on it goes. So naturally some of the staff in that environment didn't take to it. They didn't take to her there. The fact that she is probably one of the best journalists in the country had nothing to do with it. Secondly, she came from the private sector."[35]

Kotcheff was in a position to see the extent of any tension between Wallin and Peter Mansbridge who shared the news anchor role with Wallin. Certainly in the beginning the two anchors appeared to have a harmonious relationship. "Peter agreed to have her," said Kotcheff, "we discussed this, it wasn't just out of the blue." Indeed Mansbridge's accepting attitude towards Wallin at the start simplified the process for Kotcheff when he decided to hire Wallin: "In fact, I made it very plain that there were other candidates that I pursued internally, they didn't want the job, and that because of Pamela's position and her status as a journalist, that I wasn't going to subject her to any harassment or subject Peter to any harassment, if he didn't agree to it ahead of time." Subsequently Mansbridge and Wallin had lunch; Mansbridge telephoned Kotcheff and exclaimed: "we have to have Pamela."[36] Wallin remembered that she talked with Mansbridge "to see if he was up for all of this and he was at the time."[37]

Still the two anchors would have to learn to work together; one schooled in private broadcasting and the other in the public sector. Kotcheff believed that Mansbridge might have been able to create a more collegial atmosphere between the pair on the news program: "So having decided to take the plunge, I think that he could have worked a lot harder to create the environment of...co-operation. And I think he found it difficult as any anchor does and I would be lying to you if I said that Harvey [Kirck] wasn't uncomfortable with the two. Why would he be? Why would Lloyd [Robertson] be comfortable with having to defer and hand over?"[38]

Mansbridge insisted he was supportive of Wallin: "I mean I was supportive for the whole time she was here. She was an extremely strong person in that program and an extremely good interviewer." When the concept of a one-hour integrated program did not work for the CBC which lost viewers, Mansbridge was determined to get the newscast back to its original time slot in the familiar format of separate news and current affairs segments: "And I went to Pam and said 'look I am going to argue that we go back to the original format. And I know she was never particularly comfortable with that....but I said 'look you know this is the argument I am going to make, make whatever argument you want to make, but I am going to make that argument.'" Eventually the CBC returned to the old format. "The choice was made," said Mansbridge, "that I would stay with news and Pam would have current affairs. What happened after that is between the people responsible for the program. A year after that, Pam and the CBC parted company."[39]

Wallin's career did not seem to lose immediate momentum. Although let go from *Prime Time News*, she emerged with her own production company and as the popular host of *Pamela Wallin Live* on CBC *Newsworld*. Later Wallin returned to CTV and hosted the popular program, *Who Wants to be a Millionaire: Canadian Edition*.

STILL THE RATINGS battle between the national news on CTV and CBC has continued. A major development occurred in the spring of 1997 when the CBC decided to introduce advertising on its flagship newscast. According to *Maclean's* magazine, the legacy of *Prime Time News* had continued to haunt Mansbridge. As Marci McDonald explained, "Ever since the network's disastrous 1993 experiment with moving its news hour to 9 P.M.—when its market share plunged to second place and stayed—Mansbridge has anguished over every fluctuation in its numbers. According to insiders, that anxiety turned into an obsession this spring when the CBC introduced commercials into its once—sacred newscast and its average audience of one million viewers promptly plummeted to 844,000." At the same time, Nielsen Media Research showed the *CTV News* with "an average audience of 1.4 million."[40] The CBC later removed commercials from the newscast portion of a restructured news hour.

The other controversy, Cassaday's firing of Morrison who had been seen as a successor to Lloyd Robertson, took place at nearly the same time as Wallin's leaving *Prime Time News*. The CTV Board of Directors knew it was coming, but the move was a surprise especially to Valerie Pringle, Morrison's partner on *Canada AM*. "We knew he was going into see John," said Pringle. "When I got the phone call that he had actually been fired, I was stunned! And I had the hideous job of having to go on the air the next day and say, 'Hi, you know Keith's not here.' And it was sort of just the news. And Pam had been fired the day before." As Pringle noted, "No one gets fired in Canadian broadcasting really much, not from those kinds of jobs. So to have Pam and Keith gone in a day was stunning, stunning."[41]

The national media paid close attention to the rare happenings in Canadian broadcasting. *The Globe and Mail*'s front page on 4 April 1995 reported: "Wallin, Morrison depart networks, claim firing." *Maclean's* featured both journalists on the front page and tried to explain "How CTV pulled the plug on Keith Morrison" and "Why *Prime Time News* fired Pamela Wallin."[42] Morrison had been seen as taking over from Lloyd Robertson as news anchor. With that end in mind, CTV had renewed his contract in 1994 with a view to Robertson stepping down in 1996.[43] However it became apparent with Robertson's capacity and energy for the job that the two-year time frame originally contemplated was going to be elongated. Pringle described Morrison as "a nice man, a really nice man": "I was very fond of him. Working with him at *Canada AM* became harder I thought than it had been at *Mid-Day* [CBC]. He was doing a lot of freelance work for NBC. So he would often go down after doing *Canada AM*...and work there for the day and then fly back and then come in the next morning. You do that enough mornings and you are a basket case! So he was struggling with that."[44]

Cassaday told *The Globe and Mail's* Liam Lacy that the decision to let Morrison go was "personal and organizational, and it's as simple and as complicated as that" while denying any connection between Morrison's leaving CTV and Wallin's departure from *Prime Time News.* Morrison said he "was terminated" and that there was "no reason given," but he was not departing the network voluntarily.[45]

BY THE TIME OF THE BROUHAHA at both networks in the mid 1990s, the Canadian broadcasting environment had undergone a major change. The Juneau report had underscored the realignment that had taken place especially with the steady growth of specialty channels and the decline in audience share for the English language networks: "In the latter half of the 1980s, both CBC and CTV lost between one-quarter and one-fifth of their overall viewing share. Since 1989–90, however, CTV has levelled off at around 22% of the full-day audience, while CBC has slipped from 16.1% to 12.9% on a full-day basis." However the CBC also measured its audience "reach"—which is "the number of viewers who tune in at least once a week." The measurement of audience "reach" told a more positive picture of the CBC as a public broadcaster serving Canadians. The number of viewers who watched the CBC for at least a 30-minute period weekly were surveyed: "The latest available data for the 30-minute threshold, from the 1993–94 season, show that 63% of English speaking Canadians watched the CBC in an average week. This compares to a weekly 30-minute reach of 72% for CTV."[46]

Whatever the extent of competition between the private and public networks, CTV could rightfully continue to argue that it was the most watched network in Canada. In June, 1996, an economic analysis of Canadian television broadcasting by Nesbitt Burns Inc., entitled *The Outlook for Television Broadcasters: Regionalization, Rationalization and Ratings,* by analyst Tim Casey concluded: "The CTV Network is the most watched television service across Canada based on an overall market share of 18%." The report argued that a rationalization of the CTV network's ownership structure would usher in a profound change in the Canadian broadcasting market: "As the operator of the single largest CTV affiliate, CFTO-TV, Toronto, Baton is the logical owner of the network. However, we believe WIC's British Columbia franchise provides it with sufficient critical mass to legitimize a control position at CTV."[47] By the end of 1997, Baton had achieved effective control of

CTV, the culmination of a process that the company had begun in the mid 1980s. Baton's takeover of the network involved numerous transactions over a number of years.

Since 1986, Baton had undertaken a series of moves that positioned the company to apply to the CRTC to become the majority shareholder of CTV. From the mid 1980s to the mid 1990s, Baton had built its broadcasting infrastructure through several major purchases: the acquisition of TV stations in the province of Saskatchewan, CJOH-TV, Ottawa, Mid Canada stations in Northern Ontario, CFPL-TV London and CFCN-TV Calgary. Baton had also formed a strategic alliance with Electrohome Limited, another transaction designed to enable the Toronto based company to get control of CTV. Bruce Cowie, Executive Vice-President and Chief Executive Officer of Baton, told the CRTC on 15 July 1997: "These applications have entailed expenditures of more than $446 million, including tangible benefits of more than $125 million. This is the context in which we are now applying to become the controlling shareholder of the network."[48]

It should be recalled that the CTV network too had undergone a fundamental change in its capital structure on 29 September 1994. That was when seven shareholders exchanged a total of $14,000,000 in convertible debentures for 14,000,000 common shares in the network. BBS Ontario Incorporated, CFCF Inc., CFCN Communications Inc., CHUM Limited, Electrohome Limited, Moffat Communications Limited and Westcom TV Group Ltd. each acquired 2,000,100 common shares, 50,000 preferred shares and a 14.24% voting interest. Newfoundland Broadcasting Company Limited, the eighth owner of the network, made no investment in the debentures. Prior to this arrangement, each of eight owners had held a 12.5% interest in the network.[49] During the next three years, several major developments would lead to Baton's majority control as of 28 August 1997.

A CRTC decision on 21 June 1996 was an important turning point for Baton in its quest for CTV. The Commission approved Baton's application "for authority to transfer effective control of CFCN, licensee of CFCN-TV Calgary and CFCN-TV-5 Lethbridge, through the transfer of all of the issued and outstanding shares in the capital of CFCN from RCI [Rogers Communications Inc.] to BBS Western [BBS Western Acquisition Corporation]." This decision related directly to Baton and CTV; the voting interest in the network outlined by the CRTC at the time as 14.28% held by RCI, through CFCN, would pass to Baton and be held by BBS Western through CFCN. The CRTC decision also related to a series of transactions between Baton Broadcasting Incorporated [BBI] and Electrohome Limited that involved a Strategic Alliance Agreement between the two companies. The Commission approved "the application by BBI for authority to implement a voting agreement which results in Electrohome delegating control of its 14.28% voting interest in CTV to BBI." Significantly, the CRTC concluded that "following this series of transactions, BBI will have control of 42.9% of the total voting interest in CTV and will nominate three of the seven shareholder-nominated CTV board members. The Commission notes that BBI will consequently have a significantly stronger voice in CTV matters."[50]

Still another step on the way to Baton's control of CTV occurred on 14 January 1997, when the company filed an application with the CRTC for a strategic "merger" with Electrohome, as opposed to an "alliance," and for the "acquisition" of Electrohome's 14.3% interest in CTV. Baton's supplementary brief to the Commission noted at the time: "The effect of this strategic merger is to convert the nature of Baton's control of Electrohome's CTV shares from a delegated power pursuant to the voting agreement to an ownership interest." Clearly the Canadian TV broadcasting environment was in the midst of a profound change that would involve many of the noted regional players. Following the Commission's approval of the strategic alliance between Baton and Electrohome, the two companies began to discuss the possibility of an even closer affiliation: "Both realized that although our strategic alliances brought a higher degree of co-operation and co-ordination..., the inefficiencies and duplication involved in two sets of management and two different operating companies were unsustainable in the evolving environment. As well, the strategic alliances did not include CFRN-TV Edmonton and Baton's principal Ontario stations."[51]

The realigned economic framework of the broadcasting system in Canada was of concern to both Baton and Electrohome as they faced strong competition from other powerful regional broadcasters who acquired a near national scope. In August, 1996 the CRTC had approved licences for Toronto based CHUM Limited and Western International Communications Ltd. to add re-transmitters in Ottawa. WIC, the owner of CHCH-TV Hamilton, was actually able to cover several major markets in Ontario. Another chief competitor, Global, operated its Ontario service from a single location allowing it to be more cost efficient. Baton's brief to the Commission underscored the changing nature of the broadcasting landscape: "All of Baton's principal competitors—WIC, CHUM, and Global—now have access to markets throughout Ontario without local programming obligations outside their main markets. In contrast, Baton, which serves all of these same markets, has significant local news programming obligations throughout the province. Meanwhile, these competitors enjoy cost efficiencies because they generate virtually all of their Ontario programming from one central facility in Toronto [Global] or Hamilton [WIC] for province-wide broadcast, providing them with efficiencies in both programming and infrastructure."[52]

Baton argued that the more competitive broadcasting environment had created "downward pressure" on regional advertising rates and had reduced its "selective advertising" revenue stream. "Selective buys" by advertisers represent the additional purchase of advertising beyond their national and regional buys to help them reach their target audiences. Baton maintained that these revenues were critical especially in small and medium-sized markets to help to cover the full cost of local programming and the infrastructure of local stations: "Over the last few months, national selective advertising in Ontario has been drastically curtailed, because advertisers obtain access to our selective markets at no extra cost when they buy cost-efficient regional advertising on WIC, CITY, CFMT, WUTV or Global. These broadcasters are able to sell the time at highly competitive rates because they have no local obligations outside their main markets."[53]

In May, 1997 Ivan Fecan, head of Baton, could see the pieces coming together to take over CTV assuming the company was able to manage CRTC approval. He summarized the extent of Baton's activity in its quest for the network: "We are shareholders of CTV," he said. "We own 28 percent currently of the shares and we have a voting trust with Electrohome for another 14 percent. We applied to buy Electrohome's stations and therefore their CTV shares, so at that point our economic interest would be approximately 43 percent." The other arrangement involved CHUM Ltd.: "And we are through a swap of assets looking to buy for no money but swap the ATV (Atlantic Television System) stations and for some cash its CTV shares which would give us an economic interest in the range of 57 percent."[54]

The CRTC approved Baton's acquisition of all of Electrohome's television holdings including its 14.3% share in CTV on 28 August 1997. Electrohome was to hold 23% voting interest in Baton. At the same time, the Commission approved a major swap of assets: the transfer of ATV and its 14.3% share of CTV and the Atlantic Satellite Network (ASN) from CHUM to Baton. CHUM in turn received from Baton CHRO-TV Pembroke, CFPL-TV London, CKNX-TV Wingham and CHWI-TV Wheatley. The Commission's decision thereby transferred effective control of CTV to Baton giving the company a 57.1% majority interest.[55] Baton had achieved its long sought objective.

In its decision on 28 August 1997, the CRTC underlined how the Canadian broadcasting system would be changed with the approval given to the applications by Baton and certain of its subsidiaries, CHUM and CTV relating to the transfer of assets or to the effective control of CTV: "Their approval will reshape and consolidate, on a local, regional and national basis, the broadcasting operations of two key industry participants, namely Baton Broadcasting Incorporated (Baton) and CHUM Limited (CHUM). Approval will also result in the transfer of effective control of CTV Television Network Ltd. (CTV) to Baton, and the withdrawal of Electrohome Limited (Electrohome) as a television licensee."[56]

The developments that occurred between the unsuccessful "Gordian Knot" initiative and the triumph of Baton in gaining control of CTV had a lasting impact on the private network and the Canadian broadcasting system. Gary Maavara saw Ivan Fecan as a major player dependent on events evolving a certain way: "Because I mean if CTV [Gordian Knot] had succeeded,...it would have come down to who is the boss? Ivan or John [Cassaday]? It was pretty clear to everybody that each guy had his own ideas as to what should transpire from that and Ivan's only real hope, I think, was that the deal didn't happen which it didn't."[57]

Fecan had more latitude when he became President of Baton at the end of 1996. "Well I mean in a strict corporate sense Joe Garwood and Douglas [Bassett] were running the show" said Maavara. "It was pretty clear" that Fecan "was working the Eatons to get control of the company." When Garwood and Bassett left Baton, "Ivan took over the company." In time, said Maavara, Fecan "did the deal with CHUM and the Electrohome deal. He effectively became the irresistible force to take over the network. The irony is that we set it up, did all the leg work to get it in place where he could do this."[58]

With the synergies and savings that "Gordian Knot" had identified for the network's owners, it appeared to pave the way for an eventual takeover by a large broadcaster-owner of CTV such as Baton. With "Gordian Knot," said Maavara, "one of the problems we had, John had in particular was…that…our corporate obligation was to treat everybody fairly. So we couldn't go and work on convincing Fred Eaton or George Eaton to do a particular thing. It was both unethical and also I felt that it was contrary to our corporate obligations to do that. And that's the problem that we had being 'inside' the game." In the final analysis, Maavara maintained that the network's structure evolved as it should have: "It was a confluence of a whole bunch of environmental and corporate factors which caused the end result. And at the end of the day, I think the end result whether John Cassaday or Ivan…is really irrelevant. It's 'did we get to the right place?' And I think the answer is 'yes.' It's where the company [CTV] had to evolve. All the rest of it is just personalities."[59]

Significantly Baton managed to obtain control of CTV the year that its founder John Bassett retired from the Board of Directors. The company's annual report in 1997 paid tribute to Bassett who had applied successfully 37 years earlier for a Toronto private television licence when Baton was known as Baton Aldred Rogers Broadcasting Ltd. On behalf of the Board, Fredrik S. Eaton wrote: "It's hard to believe that most of the members of the present board were in university or school on Wednesday, March 16, 1960 [sic], when John Bassett and his associates presented the original application to the Board of Broadcast Governors in the Oak Room of Union Station in Toronto."[60] Clearly Baton's acquisition of CTV had ushered in a new age of Canadian private broadcasting.

Looking back to the early years of CTV, John Bassett speculated on his prospects if he had attempted to buy the network from Spencer Caldwell: "I'd have bought it obviously subject to Board of Broadcast Governors approval and it's questionable whether they would have approved it, I don't know. Questionable, I don't think they would have. But if I had bought it and been approved, I would have then set up an affiliation agreement. We were well financed, we were doing well, in which I would have guaranteed the payment of the time I got from them as the CBC did with its affiliates."[61]

Subsequent to the CRTC decision giving Baton majority control of the network, Baton acquired the 14.24% voting interest in CTV held by each of three principal players: WIC Television Ltd., CF-12 Inc. and Moffat Communications Limited. Baton's interim report to shareholders for the three months ended 30 November 1997 noted, "The Company completed the purchase of the remaining blocks of shares of CTV on November 12, 1997, at a total cost of $42 million."[62]

CTV FACED A MAJOR CHALLENGE as it looked to the 21st century. The network under new management had to continue to duplicate in the entertainment programming category the success it had experienced historically in the programming of news and sports. Indeed that was essentially the vision that Baton put forth to the CRTC in its attempt to get control of CTV in July 1997.

The company emphasized "building critical mass and mobilizing resources to concentrate on creating high quality, popular Canadian programming." Baton had made a commitment to great Canadian programming that would be national in scope: "Despite the difficulties in creating and bringing it to the screen, Baton firmly believes Canadian programming with cultural resonance is crucial to the long-term viability of Canadian broadcasters." Mindful of the 23 new specialty channels that the CRTC had licensed in 1996, Baton was still optimistic: "In a world of almost limitless choice, Canadians will choose Canadian broadcasters only if they can provide something unique and relevant to them. For Baton, that uniqueness and relevance will come from our focus on Canadian stories and Canadian experiences—and from opening a Canadian window on the world."[63]

Baton proposed a Canadian literature initiative, a one million dollar "top-up" fund over the remaining CTV licence term "to help independent producers bring Canadian literature to the screen by providing funding over and above the usual licence fees." A Halifax development office, estimated to cost $2,275,000 over seven years was to provide "a solid on-ramp to link the creators and independent producers of the Atlantic provinces into Baton's pool of national licence fees and platforms." Baton also proposed six new episodes each year of *The Storytellers,* which was a special series devoted to "half-hour dramas designed to offer new and emerging independent producers a first opportunity to begin telling their own stories in their own voices."[64]

From the early 1960s to the late 1990s, CTV network as a business had evolved from a network of outside private investors and broadcasters, to a co-operative of station owners, to a streamlined company and ultimately to a single owner. As the new millennium beckoned, and if CTV were to continue to take on CBC, its historic competitor, and CanWest Global, a more recent threat, the challenge for Baton was to ensure that CTV would continue to be the most watched network in Canada with a new range of attractive and compelling Canadian programming. Whatever its past evolution, the CTV network was about to undergo still another ownership change that would see it become part of a major communications convergence.

Ivan Fecan, President of CTV, 1997–2001.
Photograph courtesy of CTV.

TWELVE

The New CTV

1997–2001

THERE IS NO QUESTION that the Eaton family as the controlling shareholder of Baton Broadcasting Inc. saw Ivan Fecan as the broadcasting executive who would take the company into a new century. Fredrik Eaton, a long-time board member, described him as a broadcaster who combined imagination with an entrepreneurial outlook: "I think he's extraordinarily imaginative and he brings an entrepreneurship to the company. I mean he's a little guy from nowhere, worked his way through the business, understands the business and so I have the greatest respect for his judgement."[1] Fecan became President of Baton Broadcasting Incorporated in December, 1996 as the company prepared to enter a new era that would see it gain control of the CTV network, a long sought objective of the Bassett family.

Douglas Bassett, a one-time President and Chief Executive Officer of Baton, explained the rationale for Baton's initiative in gaining control of the network: "We always believed, and I personally always believed, that the network could be operated more efficiently and get better programming with having a majority owner who owned affiliates. Because…a CTV trademark is one of the great trademarks in Canada. But it didn't own anything. It was a forty-hour service. No stations." The earlier co-operative structure of CTV meant that "if Murray Chercover when we was President or John Cassaday…wanted to go out and buy the rights to the Olympic games, they had to go to the affiliates and say can 'we get time from you?' And sometimes they would say 'yes,' sometimes they would say 'no.'" In contrast to CTV, the immensely profitable CanWest Global Communications Corp., a major CTV rival, owned its own stations. As Bassett noted, "Having your own O and Os (owned and operated stations), that is the whole key. Mr. Asper (Izzy Asper) owns all his own stations. How do you think he does so well?...They own the programming undertaking vehicle. CTV didn't."[2] As owner of CTV and through its ownership of affiliates in British Columbia, Alberta, Saskatchewan, Manitoba, Ontario and the Maritimes, CTV Inc. by 2001 was in a position to clear the broadcast time for national distribution of network programming.[3]

As head of CTV Inc., the new name given to Baton in 1998, Fecan had the potential to exercise considerable influence over the Canadian broadcasting system and its programming content. Not surprisingly his rising stature caught the attention of the Canadian media. The Report on Business in *The Globe and Mail* described him as "The new king of Canadian broadcasting."[4]

Fecan had a lightning-like ascendancy in the broadcasting industry. He held positions in news, current affairs and entertainment programming in both public and private broadcasting before becoming President and Chief Executive Officer of CTV Inc. His near meteoric rise had some notable sidebars. Born and bred in Toronto to a Russian mother and Ukrainian father, Fecan attended York University and enrolled in its four-year honours program in fine arts. He never graduated.

York University would not adjust its undergraduate requirements to meet Fecan's preference for advanced courses. Even in his university days, he was a young man in a hurry. "I was a victim of my own fast talking," Fecan remembered. "I was bored by the first year courses....Basically I ended up in second year courses. So I just finagled my way in. And so it was a four year program....and I did my second year and my third year and my fourth year." When he was ready to graduate, York University blew the whistle. At the time, Fecan was restless and eager to enter broadcasting: "I am sure they would have been happy if I had taken some other fourth-year courses, some other third-year courses, and at that point I was ready to go out in the world and I just couldn't wait to start working."[5]

The radio revolution arrived in the 1970s when the medium revived itself in the face of television which had emerged as the communications' vehicle of national attention. CBC radio was in the forefront of the new wave. Fecan produced the first year of the show *Quirks and Quarks* on the public broadcaster. He was also a producer on the program *Sunday Morning* for a few years. For Fecan, his early CBC experience "was my graduate education."[6] He recalled the fascinating people at CBC radio, personalities who were to gain prominence in the years ahead: Margaret Lyons, Mark Starowicz, Peter Gzowski. "Barbara Frum was there," Fecan remembered. "I shared an office with Barbara Frum for couple of years, it was a very amazing time....I learned how to write, I learned about stories and I learned about the country in a lot of ways. I was ready. I just couldn't see going back [to university]."[7]

Next came television. From the time Fecan was a child, the medium held an extraordinary fascination: "I am fascinated by what's on the screen."[8] Fecan moved quickly through the television industry during the 1970s and the 1980s. He was a co-developer of CITY PULSE NEWS at CITY-TV in Toronto, held executive positions with the CBC and with NBC in Los Angeles before returning to Canada in August, 1987 as Director of Programming for the CBC network. Prior to joining Baton in 1996, he was Vice President Arts and Entertainment at the CBC network and later head of the CBC's English television networks. Fecan has been a man in motion whose fast paced career largely paralleled the evolution of the North American television industry.[9]

A calm and engaging individual, Fecan clearly impressed the Bassett and Eaton families when a choice had to be made between him and John Cassaday. "There were two people who could have run CTV as it subsequently turned out....and we knew both of them," Fredrik Eaton remembered. "And it was a question of whether we would go with a guy who is already working with us or we would throw him out, because he wouldn't work for Cassaday and Cassaday wouldn't work with him. So they were both chief executives and they couldn't have worked together. Ideally, of course, if they could have that might have been good. But they couldn't. And so we simply had to make a choice and we bet on the horse we already were riding."[10]

Clearly in the decision to choose Fecan, Baton's focus was on production and programming: "He was a production guy whereas Cassaday was a marketer. Now nothing against marketers, but we have always believed that the product is so important to a television station and so we went with a guy who was with the product and not with the guy who was the marketer." Eaton recalled that the transition to Fecan from Cassaday went smoothly and without rancour: "We just said to John, 'you know we are going to stick with the guy we have.' And he said, 'fine, that's ok.' I mean he understood the game. He came and saw us, he knew we had to make a choice between him or Ivan and we did. I mean we all parted friends. I sit on a board with John....I have the highest regard for him."[11]

In 1999, Allan Beattie, Chairman of CTV Inc., saw Fecan as a young executive with the capacity to leave a major legacy: "To begin with, Ivan Fecan had established a unique reputation himself and he was ready to make a move. So he in effect was successfully recruited to come first of all to Baton and with the concept that he would succeed ultimately to the top job at Baton, now CTV." The company gave Fecan several incentives to perform: "He has an attractive salary. He has an attractive number of stock options....You know he looks out at 45 years of age as to what he might be able to accomplish by the time he is 65. He has the potential to leave a very attractive legacy of something or other behind him. All the while doing well for himself financially and personally. Look what all of this did for John Bassett senior and for Douglas too for that matter! And it's all there, so he has lots of motivation to want to make a first class job."[12]

The *National Post* reported in December, 1999 that Fecan in the last year was paid $1.11 million, a 20 percent increase from the previous year. Basing the figures on a company information circular, Garry Marr wrote in the *Financial Post*, the newspaper's business section: "Mr. Fecan earned $650,000 in base salary and $460,000 in bonus last year, compared with $550,000 and $369,000, respectively, in 1998."[13] Whatever the future of Canadian television, CTV Inc. had decided to place their trust in Fecan to build the enterprise.

Trina McQueen, hired by Fecan to become Executive Vice-President of CTV Inc., saw him possessing two strong qualities: "First of all, he has the quickest ability to learn or the ability to learn more quickly than any human being I have ever met. I once said that he doesn't have a learning curve, he has a learning dot. It's just, you know, he's there." McQueen noted his ability to deal with many aspects of the business: "He can go into the news department and argue about a set design for the election and then come right out of that and then go into a merger discussion of buying a sports team and go from that to whether we should float a stock and go from there" into a question about the company's Christmas party. His second strength, according to McQueen, is his capacity for marketing: "He can seize on the central point of something and convey that message very dramatically, quickly and easily."[14]

Fecan admits to being a sensitive individual, one of the reasons why he never considered a role as a performer on television when his interest in the medium began at an early stage. "I don't know whether my interest at that time was that well defined," he recalled. "I don't think I have the thick skin necessary to be a performer in any country, particularly ours. You know the plight of the Canadian star has been much talked about. So I think my interests probably were more in the news, journalism side....and as many people in content at a certain point you decide whether you want to stay in content or whether you want to move to management." Eventually Fecan went to the management side: "And for whatever reason, I grew interested in this other thing after many years of content. And so that was a transition and I guess the benefit was that it allowed me to manage something I knew a little bit about."[15] In a relatively short career span, the "little guy from nowhere" had found himself.

Fecan drew praise for the manner in which he handled the transition from CTV Television Network Ltd. to Baton after the company took over CTV in 1997 and management personnel were replaced. Peter O'Neill had joined the network to work in the mail room in 1968 just seven years after CTV had been launched. He had held several management positions that included Vice President of Finance, Vice President Administration and Vice President Public Affairs. "We all knew that something was up," said O'Neill, "and we didn't know exactly where our futures lay. We all had separate interviews with Ivan. So Ivan interviewed all the management group. He asked where I saw myself fitting into the new group, what I could add in terms of value to the new CTV." O'Neill was impressed with Fecan's approach: "I have to tell you that Ivan was really quite a gentleman. You know he met with all of us. I can just tell you of my experience. He met with me, spent three quarters of an hour talking about his challenges, reminiscing about some of the meetings we'd been together, he was quite gracious. He allowed us to come back the next day and we cleaned out our office....The next day we came back to our offices...and we just said good-byes to people and it was quite professional."[16]

Similarly Ray Hazzan, a former CBC journalist, documentary producer and President of the Toronto Television Producers Association, remembered Fecan's gracious manner at meetings when he represented CBC management in discussions over network issues. Fecan, recently returned from NBC in Los Angeles, had become Vice President of CBC

Arts and Entertainment. "My impression of him was, and is, of a very polite, very engaging young man, softly spoken, quiet, not pushy or that kind of thing. So you know it was pleasant dealing with him." Hazzan had a second impression totally subjective and based on conversations between himself, as a producer in news and current affairs, and other drama producers. Hazzan had learned from those in drama production that Fecan was a broadcasting executive "who was very, very, very hands on, who knew what he wanted and was determined to get it." Fecan was "somebody who wanted to keep his hands on everything that was happening in the drama department" even last minute script changes. From the producers' point of view, "it had to be passed by Ivan before anything was done."[17]

Fecan's presentations before the broadcast regulator have seemed to combine a somewhat charming salesmanship with a self-congratulatory undertone that can hardly fail to impress a nationalistic-minded listener. In October, 1998 he told the CRTC at the hearings on a review of Canadian television policy: "Programming is my passion, and I'm proud of the fact that I have spent 24 of my 26 years in broadcasting doing everything I could to enable Canadian programs to thrive, both creatively and financially. And the passion remains undiminished." By drawing on his public broadcasting experience, he presented the Commission with a list of his "proudest achievements" in the genre known as long-form drama: "*Love and Hate, Conspiracy of Silence, The Donald Marshall Story*, and *Boys of St. Vincent*; dramatic series such as *Road to Avonlea, Street Legal*, the Montreal-based *Urban Angel* and *Degrassi Junior High*; and comedies such as *Codco, Air Farce, This Hour Has 22 Minutes* and *The Kids in the Hall*."[18]

Fecan is inclined to debunk the idea of moving from the general to the specific when it comes to dealing with the subject of television programming and how it can be sold abroad. His belief is in flat contradiction to the notion: "I believe in the adage that in the specific, you will find the universal. It is no fluke that some of the most Canadian of our programs have been the most successful abroad. Think of Anne of Avonlea's PEI; the vulnerable Newfoundland orphans and their complex tormentor in *The Boys of St. Vincent*; or Paul Gross's brilliant and funny evocation of the differences between Canadians and Americans in *Due South*. Vibrant characters, rooted in a strong sense of place, speak to viewers everywhere. And these are precisely the kinds of programs in which we take pride...because they speak *to* us, and *about* us."[19]

Fecan's sensitivity was apparent when he responded to media criticism on the fact that he was a party to the "repositioning" strategy at the CBC, a major debacle in the early 1990s when the CBC flagship newscast was moved to 9 P.M. Afterwards Fecan left the Corporation to go to Baton. Obviously a media watcher, Fecan responded to *Maclean's* magazine after a story appeared in March, 1999 on "The perils of CBC." Anthony Wilson-Smith wrote that news anchor Peter Mansbridge had recalled the dubious undertaking to move the CBC flagship newscast to 9 P.M: "Mansbridge cites the ill-fated 1991 move of the nightly news to 9 P.M.—a decision made, ironically, by Ivan Fecan, now the Chief Executive Officer at CTV, when he was at CBC—as 'a disaster in every way that took us years to recover from.'"[20]

Fecan did not let the report that had interpreted his managerial behaviour pass without a clarification. In the *Maclean's* issue of 29 March 1999, the magazine informed its readers: "In the issue of March 15, *Maclean's* may have inadvertently left the impression that Ivan Fecan, now CEO of CTV, was responsible for the decision to move the CBC national TV news to 9 P.M. when he served as a CBC Vice-President. In fact, the decision in 1992 to move the news was made by a team of CBC executives, journalists and producers, approved by the CBC board and announced by then CBC president Gerard Veilleux."[21] As he had explained in 1993, Fecan with others had been involved in the "structural concept" which called for the development of three new time zones as part of repositioning the Corporation.[22] In retrospect, Trina McQueen who was also a party to the repositioning decision at the CBC, remembered the division between her interests on the news side and Fecan's concern about entertainment programming: "I can't say that he and I were a team on this. I was fighting for my resources in news. And he was fighting for his resources and the opportunities that he would have out of this, because he believed very strongly that the CBC was doing just fine in news."[23] In time both Fecan and McQueen would gain the top positions at CTV. A great deal of their experience as broadcasting executives has been built with the public broadcaster.

THE PRIVATE TELEVISION INDUSTRY continued to evolve throughout the 1990s. CTV's principal competitor had become CanWest Global. Perhaps the most salient aspect of the evolution was the emergence of a handful of major broadcasting groups. By the middle of the decade CTV and CBC were by no means the only major players on the national level. Five other private TV broadcasting groups had become significant forces in the industry which continued to undergo consolidation: CanWest Global Communications Corp.; WIC Western International Communications Ltd.; CHUM Ltd.; Baton Broadcasting Inc.; and Craig Broadcasting Ltd. Until 1997, WIC and CHUM along with Baton were also shareholders of CTV.

Fecan explained the dynamics of the private TV industry as it related to CTV up to 1997 when Baton assumed control of the network: "In the end what you.... [had was] four or five groups that have very much the same infrastructure tools and resources that CTV does. And...three of those groups [WIC, CHUM and Baton]...[were] shareholders of CTV. And so you...[sat] around the table and you [asked] where [was] the value?" A central problem with the duplicate infrastructure within CTV was that it "drained resources away from being competitive on the screen. And that's where the slide begins." As did other CTV watchers, Fecan argued that network's structure after 30-plus years stymied network growth: "As long as you're trapped in a 40-hour network system, with no hard assets beyond the rental agreement of...airtime...the shareholders' agreement, the affiliate agreement gives you plenty of independence and protection. But in a competitive environment, it prevents your ability from growing or changing as well. So what protects you also suffocates you."[24]

In a nutshell, that was the dilemma that CTV faced as it looked to the new millennium. The answer lay in a complete and fundamental restructuring of the network under a majority owner and in consolidating the network's infrastructure costs for such items as microwave, master control rooms, marketing teams and administration groups with one of its shareholder groups. Baton eventually had emerged as the group that obtained control of the network.

Fecan recalled the curious relationship between CTV and its shareholders as the broadcasting universe in Canada changed and as the major broadcasting groups grew by acquiring more stations along with the addition of new specialty services: "When you looked around the table at the CTV Board, you had WIC which was a CTV shareholder and competed against CTV in Alberta and Ontario; you had CITY-TV which was a CTV shareholder [through CHUM] and competed with CTV in Ontario and with the Atlantic satellite network throughout all of the Atlantic provinces; you had Rogers which at the time had a seat

for CFCN and it competed with CTV in Ontario through their multi-
lingual station; you had Baton which, at the time,...had one independent
group of stations in southwestern Ontario which competed with CTV."
There was also "Randy Moffat who in terms of conventional broadcasting had a CTV affiliate in Manitoba but competed against CTV with
the Women's Television Network. And...you had Electrohome which
[was]...the only pure CTV...broadcast owner [CKCO-TV Kitchener,
CFRN-TV Edmonton]." Electrohome owned no competing conventional or specialty television operations. The conundrum at CTV directors' meetings was that "everyone around the table both were part of
CTV and competed with CTV."[25]

The ownership structure of CTV held numerous implications relating
to the potential success of the network. For example in a broadcast week
of some 130 hours, from 6 A.M. to midnight, a local station might have
between 20 and 30 hours for its own programming leaving roughly 100
extra hours. CTV provided its affiliated stations including those owned
by Baton with a 40-hour network service. The cumulative impact of the
consolidation that groups such as Baton enacted within their own organizations was that the remaining 60 hours were largely common among
the various stations the companies owned. In short, on its CTV affiliated
stations, Baton could operate a network in hours larger than that of
CTV. According to Fecan, "40 hours a week doesn't make it."[26] A similar viewpoint came from Ray Peters, a former WIC executive, who had
been with the network almost from the beginning: "40 hours a week is
nothing."[27]

Baton's interest in getting hold of CTV was in direct response to the
evolving structure of the company and its bottom line. By the end of
1997, Baton's conventional broadcasting stations included 17 CTV affiliates, six CBC affiliated stations, one independent station, CIVT-TV
Vancouver and ASN (Atlantic Satellite Network), an independent satellite television service. The CRTC had awarded the Vancouver licence to
Baton on 31 January 1997, the first new TV station in Vancouver since
1974. Given Baton's heavy reliance on the success of its CTV affiliates,
control of the network seemed a logical extension of its continued
growth that had seen it acquire a number of network affiliates. Indeed
that was the essential argument Baton advanced when it received the
licence for the independent station in Vancouver.

Fecan explained that Baton naturally was inclined to focus its money
and energy in what was in its best interest: "We argued in Vancouver

that the person who has the most interest in success of CTV ought to be given control of CTV or certainly ought to be entrusted with CTV because when you have conflicting interests, even with full disclosure, even with the best of all possible intentions, when you stretch you are going to stretch in the direction that is in your best interests at that particular moment." Clearly the majority of Baton's revenues came from its CTV affiliated stations. Baton's CBC affiliates in northern Ontario and Saskatchewan were really "just extensions of service for CBC" and not really "material to the company." Fecan said that in the long term it was better for Baton to concentrate on CTV: "And so strategically you know once we got Vancouver...we could have begun to contemplate going independent at the end of the affiliation agreement. But we felt that our long-term interest in CTV, the glory of Canada's premier private television network, the fact that most of our economic interest now currently resides with CTV affiliated stations, we thought that that would be our preference." Such a move, the CTV President explained, would allow Baton to have "a larger position in CTV to have the financial wherewith all so that we could take the risks to grow CTV in future, because it will require a fair amount of stretching to catch up with Global. We felt that for all those kinds of reasons that we had more at stake in terms of CTV than anyone else around the table even though we also had conflicts."[28]

Baton faced a potential conflict in British Columbia where it was a CTV shareholder and at the same time owned the newly licensed independent television station CIVT, Vancouver. BCTV, Vancouver was a CTV affiliate. Baton had to address the situation when it applied to the CRTC to gain control of CTV recognizing that it would own both CIVT and hold a majority ownership of a CTV service which programmed 40 hours a week on BCTV. The Toronto company addressed the problem through three arguments. In its application to the CRTC, Baton explained: "These 40 hours, which constitute the CTV schedule, have a national mandate. In direct contrast to the intensely local nature of CIVT, CTV programming cannot be skewed for one market without jeopardizing its appeal in the remainder of the country. This reality provides a practical and powerful limit on any programming decisions Baton might influence or make." In addition, Baton was prepared "to make a commitment that in any case of conflict between the Baton schedule and the CTV network schedule, the interests of CTV will prevail, within the parameters of governance provided by the Shareholders' Agreement and the Affiliation Agreements." As well, "CTV's Program

Committee, made up of affiliates and CTV management, continues to provide a forum for input by all affiliates into CTV's programming. All shareholders of CTV continue to have additional input at the board level."[29]

Prior to getting control of CTV, Baton as owner of the network's flagship station CFTO-TV, Toronto, had three formal relationships with CTV unlike most of the other affiliates. The company had a distinctive connection with CTV in that it was a shareholder, affiliate and landlord. Baton was a shareholder in the network and had an affiliation agreement as did other affiliates. But in addition, Baton was a landlord for the network. CTV had a head office and some studio and technical facilities in downtown Toronto. The network's entire news division was located at CFTO; the network rented floor offices, studios and camera crews from Baton.[30] Among the network's stations, Baton appeared as the leading affiliate to take over CTV. After getting the Vancouver licence, majority control in CTV and launching specialty channels, The Comedy Network and The Outdoor Life Network, in which it was a managing partner, Baton could rightfully claim that by the end of 1997 the company had been transformed "from an important regional player into a national broadcaster."[31]

THE FUTURE OF CTV again became a matter of the utmost significance in January, 1998 when Eaton's of Canada Ltd. decided to sell its 40.65 percent ownership interest in Baton held through Telegram Corporation Limited in a public offering. In effect, this development meant that the CTV network was without a controlling shareholder. Robert Brehl explained in *The Globe and Mail*: "There had been an agreement between the Eatons and Electrohome to control Baton." In approving the modification to Baton's ownership, the CRTC explained to the Toronto broadcaster: "The Commission notes that as a result of these transactions, the effective control of Baton controlled licensees will change from a position where the Eaton family was in a position of control to a situation of no clear-cut control."[32]

With Newcrest Capital Inc. as their agent, the Eatons had begun to explore options as to what they would receive if they sold their shareholdings in Baton. A decision was made that the best value could be obtained by selling the shares to the public markets, a move that would affect the ownership of CTV controlled by Baton which would become

Fredrik S. Eaton. Photograph
courtesy of White Raven
Capital Corporation.

a widely held common share company. In the process of the Eatons
wishing to sell their shares, Baton also wanted a capital infusion. Newcrest advised both the Eaton family and Baton that both deals should be
done together at the same time and at the same price. The public offering amounted to some 462 million dollars. It had two essential components: a sale by the Eatons of their shares in Baton and a "newly mint-
ing" of shares by the company. The Eaton family honoured a prior
obligation to Ivan Fecan to enable him to make a profit on his share
position when they sold. Fecan's profit amounted to about eleven million dollars.[33]

The T. Eaton Co. Ltd., a retailing giant for some 130 years, hit hard
times in the late 1990s. The insolvent company was eventually taken
over by its rival Sears Canada Inc. The setback for the family's retail
business was far more devastating than the decision to sell the Baton
[CTV Inc.] shares. Fredrik Eaton agreed it was a wrenching experience:
"I was very emotional about the Eaton side. I didn't feel quite the same

about CTV. Baton and CTV were companies that I had seen growing and I had been on the Board and everything, but I never really felt the same connection, didn't have the same emotional connection to CTV....I felt extraordinarily sad about it and wished it didn't happen. I knew many, many people who worked in the company for years."[34]

"It was really a function of estate planning," said Eaton, "and the fact that we felt as a family that we had gone about as far as we could go with this company [Baton]. We couldn't make it bigger by buying things, and it would require a huge bankroll to continue in this business and, as it subsequently turned out, BCE provides that, that tremendous financing so they can go ahead." Eaton had never seen a permanent relationship with Baton: "We had always envisioned that we would get out of it and it just seemed a good time to do it and we did it....Well I knew what was available on the table and I didn't know what was going to happen in the future. There are all kinds of things that can happen in the future. So a bird in the hand is worth two in the bush. That's really what it was. We decided ok we can see what we can do, we've done very well off this, let's go."[35]

Clearly the Eatons had recognized that a new age of convergence had arrived, an era that was unpredictable: "We are entering another age almost. We started out with television, just television in Toronto, but now what's going to happen to TV companies is beyond my comprehension. I just don't know what's going to happen. But something is going to happen, something big...both Global and CTV are making alliances with newspapers and...it's a completely different game. And it requires a huge amount of money." CTV "was a great business, but there is only one Eaton in CTV now, in fact, he is the only one who ever worked there. That's Henry [Vice-President Strategic Planning and Business Development], my brother John Craig's son."[36]

Allan Beattie maintained that the timing was right for the sale of the Eaton's shares in 1998: "Well it's pretty obvious that starting whenever, certainly the whole world knew about it two or three years ago, things weren't going well in the retail business. And Eaton's [was] obviously as an investment...vulnerable there. It just happened that coincidental with that the television business had been doing very well....The realistic potential of solving the CTV problem was now apparent. The stock had moved from six or seven dollars a share up to something close to 20 and they [Eatons] thought that maybe to protect their own financial circumstances it would be good to diversify the family holdings." With all their family holdings in essentially just two baskets, broadcasting and retail, "just as they said publicly, for family investment purposes, [they] thought this was an appropriate time to convert to cash their interest."[37]

Not long after the Eatons sold their interest in Baton, John Bassett, the company's founder, died after a lengthy illness on 27 April 1998. The sale of Eaton family shares and John Bassett's death seemed to reflect a momentary throwback to CTV Inc. as a prominent family owned regional player in Canadian broadcasting. Bassett's son Matthew recalled his father's resilience following a major heart attack in 1994: "He had a massive heart attack which he almost didn't live through that night. And I was at Western and I got a call from my Mom. And then he had bypass surgery which once again he almost died on the table there....he went right to the brink and he'd come back. Tremendously resilient." Bassett's individualistic spirit showed to the end: "The most difficult thing was that after his bypass surgery he didn't exercise. You know you are not going to tell John Bassett what to do. We got him a physical therapist and I think he fired her the second day. When you have bypass surgery, you have to exercise to build up the muscle...so he did his own thing." Bassett was alert up to the time of his death. "We had some great moments," said Matthew, "we were able to say good-bye to each other. You know he had a lot of dignity. He would have loved his funeral."[38]

Not surprisingly, Bassett's funeral was attended by prominent personalities in politics and business. Ethel Kennedy, wife of Bobby Kennedy, attended the funeral. Bassett had been a pall bearer at her husband's funeral when he was assassinated in 1968 while campaigning for the Democratic presidential nomination. The connection with Bassett had lasted ever since he had invited Kennedy to a Toronto Maple Leafs hockey game after the U.S. politician had delivered a speech in Toronto. Bassett was then Chairman of the Board of Maple Leaf Gardens. Bassett's wife, Isabel, recalled his ties to the Kennedy family: "[W]hen we were married we went down to Hyannis Port and they came up. In fact the first night in our house on Binscarth [Rd.] we were there, they came up for a dinner dance we gave. They slept on the third floor." Ethel Kennedy's attendance Isabel Bassett described as "very like her," because she is "loyal and an amazing person."[39]

WITH ITS OWNERSHIP of the CTV network, Baton by the end of the 1990s became truly national with the leading general interest network broadcaster that offered Canadians the most popular mainstream service. Towards the end of the decade, the arrival of new management for CTV Inc., the purchase of specialty channels, an area of growth in Canadian broadcasting, and the eventual acquisition of the company's licensed broadcasting undertakings by BCE Inc., a global communications services company, signalled a profound change and new era for the CTV network.

Trina McQueen arrived at CTV Inc. in August, 1999 only a few months before the company made application to become the controlling shareholder in NetStar Communications Inc., a company that included among its holdings the popular specialty channel, The Sports Network. For McQueen who was born Catherine Janitch, it was a return to the station that provided her first television experience which was not all that pleasant. Trina later married Don McQueen, a television producer. In the mid 1960s and before women had made major inroads in the television industry, she was hired by Peter Reilly who had been chosen to head up the public affairs program W5.

Her hiring underlined the precarious state of CTV finances at the time and the delicate relationship that existed between the network and its affiliates such as CFTO. "They didn't have enough money to pay all the full time hosts," McQueen recalled. "So the deal was that I was to work a few days for W5, but my actual employment was with CFTO and I was loaned to W5 parttime." She has a vivid recollection of joining CTV: "I was hired by Peter Reilly. The interview was done in his sauna as I remember it. He and I were both in the sauna in his house on Belmont Avenue. Now mind you his wife was in the laundry room just across from the sauna."[40]

Still McQueen had an uneasy relationship with CFTO management. Her arrival at the station was somewhat unorthodox in that the network had hired her and afterwards a deal was made with CFTO: "So I was not somebody that CFTO had personally gone out and recruited. I was kind of landed on them. I was the first woman reporter that they had ever hired." A young, blonde woman at the time, McQueen took her case to John Bassett when she was told by CFTO News Director Doug Johnson that she would either have to join W5 full time or she would have to be let go. Word had come down that she had been perceived as lacking authority on air. "So I went to big John Bassett," McQueen

Trina McQueen, President of
CTV, 2001–   Photograph
courtesy of CTV.

remembered. "I burst into tears in his office and he phoned Ted Delaney
[CFTO executive] and said 'let's make sure that we give this woman a
chance.'" Eventually McQueen began to look elsewhere for employment
and eventually joined the CBC. At the 1967 Progressive Conservative
leadership convention in Toronto, she was a member of the CBC news
team and was seen doing floor reports on the style of dress worn by
Olive Diefenbaker, the wife of former Prime Minister John Diefenbaker.
"It is kind of like the good news, the bad news," said McQueen. "The
bad news is that you are doing the woman stuff, but the good news is
that you were one of the team."[41]

   McQueen held top positions at the CBC and at the Discovery Channel before joining CTV Inc. in 1999. In the company's 1999 annual
report, Fecan described McQueen as giving the company "strong and
deeper management bench strength." He portrayed her as "one of

North America's most highly respected television executives." As Executive Vice-President, McQueen, was given a wide mandate "responsible for the programming, sales and administration of CTV's network, stations and specialty channels." Indeed former CBC personnel were much in evidence in the executive team that Fecan had assembled around him. McQueen joined two other female executives previously employed at the Corporation: Susanne Boyce, Senior Vice-President, Programming and Suzanne Steeves, Senior Vice-President, Sports and Specialty Development.[42] McQueen later became President and COO of CTV Inc.

McQueen appeared with Fecan before the CRTC when the company made application to gain majority control of NetStar Communications Inc. CTV's Inc.'s detailed application in December, 1999 provided insight into the future direction that Fecan's team intended to take the network, stations and specialty channels in a new era of Canadian broadcasting. The CBC had struggled with finances and tried to redefine itself in a new age of broadcasting. On the eve of a new millennium, CTV's principal competitor remained CanWest Global Communications. Indeed Izzy Asper, head of CanWest, had chided Fecan in 1998 when Global had led private broadcasters by winning eleven Gemini awards. Asper challenged Fecan: "Step up to the plate and join us in producing quality Canadian programming."[43]

HOWEVER CTV INC. was to score big time early in the year 2000. The company applied to get control of NetStar after CanWest had tried unsuccessfully to acquire the equity of Canadian shareholders. A supplementary brief filed by CTV Inc. with the CRTC in its application to acquire majority interest in NetStar noted the earlier involvement of CanWest. On 20 January 1999, CanWest had announced an agreement with the Canadian shareholders of the company previously known as Labatt Communications Inc. (LCI). The Canadian shares amounted to about 68 percent "of the company's issued and outstanding voting shares." The remainder of the shares were held by ESPN Sub, a wholly owned subsidiary of ESPN, a U.S. company that operated four sports programming services. ABC Inc., which was an indirect subsidiary of The Walt Disney Company, had an 80 percent ownership interest in ESPN.[44]

A NetStar shareholder agreement allowed ESPN Sub the right "to seek an alternative buyer on terms and conditions at least as favourable as those of the CanWest offer." When ESPN Sub exercised that right, CTV then offered $409 million for the NetStar shares held by Canadians. On 10 February 1999 the offer was accepted and the shares subsequently held in trust pending a CRTC hearing in December. CTV had seen NetStar's three specialty services as important to its future strategy. Besides its ownership of TSN and Le Réseau des Sports (RDS), NetStar owned 80 percent of The Discovery Channel in addition to a controlling interest of nearly 25 percent in Viewer's Choice Canada Inc. In its brief to the Commission, CTV Inc. underlined how the specialty services were a suitable fit with its conventional TV network service: "NetStar's licensed specialty services complement CTV's existing conventional and specialty services. TSN, RDS and Discovery are all widely recognized for their excellence, innovation, world-class programming and devotion to their viewers."[45]

The CRTC approved CTV's application to gain control of NetStar on 24 March 2000 subject to several conditions, among them a requirement that CTV "file with the Commission for approval an application to divest of its interest in the SportsNet regional specialty service." Reflecting views that had been expressed by both the CBC and the Global Television Network, the divestiture of SportsNet was intended to satisfy the "Commission's concerns related to CTV's potential ability to dominate in the field of sports programming and its potential unfavourable consequences for other broadcasters."[46]

The NetStar acquisition was one of Fecan's bolder moves as President of CTV Inc. Market analysts looked at Fecan with some curiosity when he was appointed head of CTV, because he had never managed a company. Tim Casey, a Managing Director at BMO Nesbitt Burns, explained that Fecan deserved a great deal of credit: "They essentially got TSN when CanWest thought they had it....the swing vote in that was ESPN, U.S. super programmer. What ESPN did is essentially play two Canadians off each other brilliantly and just extracted better terms and a better price. But they also played on the very litigious reputation that CanWest has. And once again Fecan was able to strike a deal by purporting himself to be a more benevolent partner. And by getting TSN, that radically changed their position in that they now have a very compelling portfolio of specialty channels." Casey noted that "beer companies and car companies love sports channels and it's one way to attract a very desirable demographic to get at which is young men."[47]

STILL NOT ALL WENT well for CTV in the early part of the New Year. A major furor involving a young, female CTV NewsNet broadcaster on probation arose after controversial remarks she made inadvertently went to air. Avery Haines had been with the headline news service only a couple of months. On 15 January 2000 after she flubbed an introduction to a news report that was pre-recorded, she made a joking comment about equal opportunity that resulted in her dismissal. In her words, "I kind of like the little stuttering thing. It's like equal opportunity, right? We've got the black, we've got the Asian, we've got the woman. I could be a lesbian folk-dancing black woman stutterer...in a wheelchair...with gimping, rubber legs. Yeah, really, I'd have a successful career, let me tell you."[48]

Haines apologized and wrote a front page defence of her miscue in the *National Post*: "I messed up a line, then tried to limit the embarrassment with a quip about employment equity. I'm a woman, for crying out loud. I've benefited from equal opportunity policies. I'm the first to admit that I've probably landed jobs because of my ability, and the fact that I bring (what the bigwigs in media like to call) a female presence on the air."[49] In an editorial entitled "Lesbian folk-dancing," *The Globe and Mail* offered this comment about Ms. Haines's predicament: "Oh dear. Of all the causes it is dangerous to mock these days, identity politics ranks at the top. The status of the victim has never been higher, and membership in victimhood is now due to everyone except younger white males (who are now getting even their sympathies)."[50]

As did many journalists, The *National Post* came to Haines's defence: "Risqué comments to be sure. But should they have cost Ms. Haines her job? It is interesting to note that nothing Ms. Haines said was actually racist; or sexist; or even anti-Lesbian. Satirizing affirmative action is not in itself objectionable—unless one takes the logically absurd step of characterizing this kind of joke as a species of hateful expression."[51] CTV was conspicuously silent throughout the affair which became a much talked about subject on shows hosted by noted media personalities such as Barbara Walters and Howard Stern.

The decision to fire Haines was a collective one. "The recommendation would come from the news director to me," said McQueen. "Henry Kowalski to me and because it was a sensitive thing, I would have checked with Ivan. But all three of us had no doubts and still don't." Why was Haines fired as opposed to suspended? McQueen underlined two important elements in the decision: "One her remarks were offensive and they were offensive to people inside the organization as well as to people outside. The second thing is that she was on proba- tion." Moreover said McQueen, "She knew she was in a studio. She knew there were microphones and cameras....So what you have is a pro- bationary employee who exhibits highly unprofessional behaviour and in a way which violates our policy [respect for everybody]. So because she was on probation she had to go." McQueen maintained that had Haines been a five- or ten-year employee, the result would have been dif- ferent: "Probably a suspension. But she wouldn't have been let go. The probationary thing was a huge issue."[52] Two employees associated with the incident, which allowed the wrong tape that contained the miscue by Haines on air, were suspended.[53]

In retrospect, McQueen considered CTV's passive role throughout the controversy to be possibly a public relations mistake. "We didn't say anything," said McQueen. "And you know Avery certainly behaved absolutely honourable and professionally afterwards, although she was under great pressure to...scream and yell and stuff like that....God bless her. She's a good announcer and I am sure she will do very well." Haines later joined the CHUM owned CITY-TV in Toronto. But CTV's silence could have given the wrong impression: "We had no idea it would hit the fan the way it did," McQueen recalled, "and that's partly because every journalist is outraged when another journalist is fired....You know I wish we had done panels on *Canada AM* with pros and cons of this. I wish we had done an item on the news. I think we were too silent about the issue on our own network and it looked as if we were hiding...."[54]

WHATEVER SETBACKS that occurred for CTV Inc. early in 2000 were overshadowed later by one of the largest transactions that the CRTC would consider in its history: Bell Canada Enterprises' (BCE Inc.) offer to purchase all of the outstanding common shares of CTV Inc. and thereby take over the CTV network. Ever since the Eatons had divested their holdings in CTV Inc., there had been considerable speculation about what company would eventually get control of the broadcaster. The news media raised several possibilities including BCE, CanWest Global Communications Corp., Power Corp., Quebecor Inc., and Corus Entertainment Corp. Speculation about Corus's intention had height- ened in December, 1999 when the company announced that it owned nearly 10 percent of CTV Inc.[55] The fact that John Cassaday, head of

Corus, was a former President of CTV added to the Bay Street rumour mill.

However Cassaday discounted any notion of Corus wanting to get control of the CTV Network: "I don't think so. I think that there's value in CTV. I know because there's no controlling shareholder, somebody is going to take a run at it some day and when that day comes, you know, we want to be there." Cassaday described the Corus move as an investment: "So I think from our point of view, we just said 'look without a controlling shareholder what's the likelihood that this is going to go into play at some time in the future? A hundred percent.' So whether we would get a reward in terms of the appreciation on the value of our shares, whether we would get a piece of CTV if it gets broken up...it's an investment. Am I going to take a run at CTV? No."[56]

Fredrik Eaton had let it be known that he considered BCE to be "the logical company" to take over CTV Inc. "Jean Monty [BCE Chairman] went to see Ivan or phoned him," he recalled. Eaton encouraged Fecan to strike a deal with BCE. "I phoned Ivan...[and said] you should talk to these people, because these are probably the best partners you're going to get. He already knew that or at least he said, 'I know. I have phoned them'...mind you he had to keep all the others into play too. He was trying to get naturally the best deal for the shareholders. It turned out to be BCE." Eaton recalled the extent of Fecan's role in the negotiations: "We as a board never dealt with him [Monty]. Ivan dealt, he would come back to the committee and discuss what had been going on, but all I know is that he [Monty] has a good reputation. BCE has a good reputation and he is a good manager....I think it's a great company and I could see that they would have the deep pockets to look after CTV."[57]

BCE announced a cash bid on 25 February 2000 to acquire the outstanding shares of CTV Inc. at a price of $38.00 a share, later revised to $38.50. The amount BCE paid for the CTV Inc. shares was about 2.3 billion dollars. On 15 March, BCE announced that it had signed support agreements with both CTV and Electrohome Broadcasting Inc. (EBI), the single largest shareholder in CTV Inc. At the same time, the CTV Board of Directors, the EBI Board and EBI's majority shareholders had endorsed the BCE offer.

At a CRTC hearing on 18 September 2000, Canadians got their first look at the new BCE/CTV. BCE offered a glitzy presentation in its application "for authority to effect a change in ownership of the licensed broadcasting undertakings held by CTV Inc." Jean Monty, Chairman of the Board and Chief Executive Officer of BCE, portrayed CTV as "the cornerstone" of a new media company [Bell Globemedia Inc.] that would serve as a dramatic illustration of convergence. The new conglomerate officially launched on 9 January 2001 would include *The Globe and Mail* newspaper, CTV and the Sympatico-Lycos Internet portal. Monty presented a lofty vision to the Commission in his opening remarks: "BCE wishes to contribute to the continuing excellence of CTV as a broadcaster of high quality, compelling Canadian content. We are determined to create a future where English-language Canadian programming is as commercially successful as U.S. programming."[58] BCE offered the largest ever benefits package: $230 million, 92 percent of it to be applied "on screen."[59]

Françoise Bertrand, the CRTC chair, questioned Monty forcefully on the opening day of the hearing about the reasons why BCE, a telecommunications company, was determined to take over the leading private television network in the country. She described BCE's initiative as a "drastic change": "You are pointing out, a telecom company acquiring a broadcasting company, there has to be reasons for it. It is not out of interest strictly of content per se. It is definitely because it fits in the strategy of the future."[60] When Monty was asked to explain "the elements for you that helped you sell it to your board and the shareholders," he cited four criteria that CTV had to meet: build customer satisfaction, remain a growth enterprise, increase profitability and participate successfully in a new media enterprise that included *The Globe and Mail* and the Sympatico/Lycos Internet portal. "We all know that CTV is a fine enterprise today," explained Monty, "but on a profitability basis there is one system in Canada [CanWest] that is much more profitable than CTV, and through...the relationship with its stakeholders, journalists, creators, the customer; and with growth can CTV become a more profitable enterprise in order to deliver on its promise, on its dream?"[61]

Monty foresaw improvement in services if the notion of convergence could bring a leading national newspaper, broadcasting network and internet service together successfully. "I guess the Globe and Mail capability of how we can work the system together and providing even better products and services to enhance the broadcasting capability and services I think will be an interesting set. But I would use that as a subset of the growth of the system." Bertrand wondered aloud if BCE's strategy seemed to somehow be "speeding up the breakdown of what is mass media to get into more narrowcasting and eventually almost bringing back the individuality of a telephone conversation?" Monty replied that Ivan Fecan "has convinced me that the conventional broadcasting system is far from death. The numbers prove it." But looking at the unpredictable environment of convergence, Monty explained that "as we grow the conventional broadcasting system," there was at the same time "something else brewing out there."[62]

The CRTC approved the BCE application on 7 December 2000. The Commission was "convinced that approval will ensure the ongoing growth in improvement of the services offered by the national television network, the local television stations operated by CTV Inc., as well as by the various pay and specialty services in which CTV Inc. has an ownership interest."[63] Clearly the Canadian network television broadcasting landscape had undergone profound change. Two major alliances had emerged in the year 2000.

CanWest Global had reached agreement with Hollinger Inc. to purchase several of the company's newspapers and had received CRTC approval in July, 2000 to acquire a number of TV stations from WIC Western International Communications Ltd. In effect, CanWest had become a third network force in Canada, a long sought objective of Izzy Asper, its founder. The Commission noted in its July decision: "It gives CanWest Global ownership of television stations that provide service over the air to viewers in every province except Newfoundland."[64] The new media alliances between TV broadcasters and newspapers, and in CTV's case a merger that involved BCE, the country's major communications company, were illustrative of the extent to which the notion of convergence, for better or for worse, had come to dominate the corporate strategies of the principal players in Canadian broadcasting.

WHEN CTV APPLIED for a licence renewal before the CRTC in April 2001, CTV Inc. had been a division of the new Bell Globemedia for just over three months. The hearing was significant for two reasons. First, CTV as a division of a new BCE enterprise, was linked directly to the growing concentration of ownership that had accompanied convergence. Second, the hearing into the renewal of CTV's and Global licences was the first to be conducted under the Commission's new framework for Canadian television, *Building on Success: A policy framework for Canadian television,* announced on 11 June 1999.[65]

Under the new policy, multi-station broadcasting groups were generally to have the Commission consider all of the conventional TV licences that they held or controlled at the same time.[66]

The policy was designed to give the private sector broadcasters a new flexibility in a competitive environment. The CRTC policy noted the healthy state of the Canadian television industry: "The TV industry is successful in terms of viewer satisfaction and quality product. It is also a financial success. The profits for both conventional television and specialty services have risen significantly since 1993." The Commission drew particular attention to conventional television: "Notably, conventional TV remained profitable in spite of the introduction of new conventional, pay and specialty services in 1995, 1996 and 1998, with a PBIT [profit before interest and taxes] margin of 11.1% in 1998."[67]

As President of CTV Inc., Trina McQueen told the hearing that "this episode of our great Canadian story has a starring role for a new player: the CRTC's Television Program Policy. That policy sets the stage for the next seven years and gives us all a part to play." McQueen put forth a practical, business oriented vision for CTV: "We want more people to watch our Canadian programs. We want to erase the difference between good business and good popular culture. We want to produce and present high quality, high audience mainstream news and entertainment." The new CTV intended to focus on four program genres: "news, both local and national; drama, especially movies; documentaries; and variety and comedy."[68]

In her presentation, McQueen sought to counter the criticism that had been periodically made against private broadcasters who were seen as trying to shape the regulations to their advantage in the marketplace. "CTV is not here to ask for changes or relaxations, or tweaking, or a little bit different here or maybe a little less there. We are simply here to tell you how we will meet the objectives of the policy." McQueen boasted aloud when she told the hearing that "CTV is pleased to announce that in this fall we have achieved the number one position in average audiences for Canadian drama and comedy, ahead of Global and ahead of CBC." CTV's role in the broadcasting system was significant, because the network accounted "for 40 percent of the viewing to English Canadian television programs and more than 50 percent in peak periods."[69]

Susanne Boyce, President of CTV programming, stressed that the network was not just "a buyer of priority programming" but attempted to bring "tough stories to our audience," often "through supporting emerging producers." She saw the "the diverse, multicultural fabric of Canada" as a main source "for our past, present and future stories." Specifically she drew attention to the story, *Island of Shadows*, a documentary on racism. With fresh optimism, Ivan Fecan, President of Bell Globemedia, told the CRTC that the network was "on the cusp" of a major breakthrough where the production of Canadian programs will make "enormous audience and business sense."[70]

Still one major issue seemed to override the hearing. Beyond the genre of entertainment programming, the Commission was especially concerned about a loss of diversity of views in news reporting given the concentration involved in bringing a national newspaper and a major private network together under one corporate umbrella. This aspect of convergence was given high priority. When the CRTC approved the transfer of the effective control of television network Groupe TVA Inc. (TVA) to Quebecor Média Inc. (QMI), a large media group with newspaper and broadcast holdings, in July 2001, it required QMI to ensure the independence and separation of the different media newsrooms.[71] Bell Globemedia faced the possibility of having to operate separate newsrooms in print and broadcasting similar to Quebecor including separation in newsgathering practices.

CTV was steadfastly opposed to the notion of not being able to share newsgathering resources. At the CRTC hearing, Kirk LaPointe, CTV's Senior Vice-President of News, argued that a code which the network had proposed would ensure "separate news presentation structures, as well as separate management structures and separate budgets." He reminded the commissioners on 25 April that during the intervention process at the hearing they had heard "from eminent academics across the country that, while the diversity of voices is an important concern, the imposition of the Quebecor code was not necessary in English Canada, and indeed might have negative consequences."[72]

CTV did not accept the notion of the need to maintain separation in newsgathering among its reporters in print and broadcast. LaPointe argued that "there is now a very wide range of differing voices in the Canadian broadcast system.": "We do not believe that our affiliation with the Globe and Mail diminishes those voices. On the contrary, we believe that there are opportunities to collaborate and to share resources that will provide a very real improvement in news quality—and in diversity."[73]

Specifically, LaPointe questioned the emphasis placed on newsgathering in the debate over editorial diversity: "The notion that it is in the newsgathering process and only in the newsgathering process that diversity occurs is wrong." He maintained that "sharing resources increases the number of newsgatherers, particularly on the stories that matter most." But equally important, in his eyes, was the selection of interviewees and quotations from the extensive array of information that was gathered on major stories. "The real diversity," he said, "comes in the power to choose the person and to choose the quotes that will be used." He saw the journalistic capacity for influence beyond that of the newsgatherer: "That is the essence of the journalistic power to create diversity, and that is not the task of the newsgatherer. It is the presenters and the managers who make those choices. Our code clearly separates the broadcast division from the print division in these areas."[74]

In its written "deficiency responses" to the CRTC, CTV tied the question of editorial diversity to the notion of good business practices and the different media "brands" involved in Bell Globemedia. The network that had meant business throughout its history saw the matter of editorial independence as an outgrowth of continuing the strong, separate identities of CTV and *The Globe and Mail*: "Both Bell Globemedia and CTV are committed to maintaining strong, diverse editorial voices. The editorial independence of each of our media enterprises is a priority to us. Each of these enterprises has a well-known brand, which is of great value to the overall enterprise; and there is no intention of diluting those brands." CTV argued that diversity formed "the foundation of journalistic excellence" and at the same time contributed "to the core value of these undertakings." As a result, "editorial diversity is not only good for the communities, the viewers and the readers that we serve: it is also good business."[75]

The CRTC renewed the licences of all TV stations owned and controlled by CTV Inc. for the full term of seven years on 2 August 2001. A similar renewal was given to the stations owned by CanWest Global Communications. The decision was some solace for both broadcasters. The Commission acknowledged that "some degree of co-operation and sharing between commonly-owned newspapers and TV newsrooms could increase the amount of original journalism available to Canadians and enhance the quality of news coverage." In other words, there could be some convergence in print and broadcast newsrooms in newsgathering. Still the Commission imposed *A Statement of Principles and Prac-*

tices to deal with the concerns expressed by intervenors at the hearing over the question of potential loss of diversity of voices in the broadcasting system.[76]

The Commission saw the need for separate management and presentation structures: "In essence, the *Statement of Principles and Practices* requires the licensee to maintain separate and independent management and presentation structures for CTV television operations that are distinct from those of any CTV affiliated newspapers. It thus requires separation of news management functions, but not newsgathering activities. Therefore, cross promotion and some cooperation between CTV's television stations and Bell Globemedia's newspapers in newsgathering would be permissible."[77] Following its licence renewal, the CTV network could look to the 21st century with a fair measure of optimism even though the broadcasting environment remained competitive and unpredictable.

IN RETROSPECT, analyst Tim Casey credited Ivan Fecan for the recent upturn in CTV fortunes after an uneven 40-year history: "It was fascinating. When he came aboard in the mid 1990s, he was an unknown quantity on the street and we knew his reputation as an interesting programmer...with some experience in LA [Los Angeles] which presumably would give him contacts, but he had never run a company and so we were interested to see how he would perform in that role. As it turned out looking back, he turned out to be a so-so programmer at CTV but a very efficient, very successful strategic manager...brilliant in fact." He noted that Fecan "consolidated the network...brought it down to one owner, then pulled off the NetStar deal which gave them the specialty channels and disabled his primary competitor CanWest and then sold it into BCE, packaged it up and got a great price for shareholders."[78]

The new CTV was a fundamentally different service from the loose alignment of eight stations that formed the network in Canada 40 years ago by coming together almost accidentally.

As a division of Bell Globemedia, CTV Inc. was a much consolidated television network service. By August 2001, Bell Globemedia owned 18 CTV affiliated stations across the country. VTV (Vancouver) was to become a network affiliate in September and renamed CTV British Columbia. Regulatory approval had been received to purchase CKY, Winnipeg and the transaction was expected to close shortly. CTV Inc.'s purchase of CFCF, Montreal was awaiting regulatory approval. At the same time, the network maintained affiliation agreements with four independently-owned, CTV affiliates: NTV, St. John's (CJON); CJBN, Keewatin; CITL, Lloydminster; and CHFD, Thunder Bay.

With strong economic support and a strategy designed "to erase the difference between good business and good popular culture," CTV's capacity for growth was apparent. Whatever CTV's past failings or the future of Canadian broadcasting, the playing field in Canadian private network television had been levelled by 2001. CTV and CanWest were the principal private players. CTV was a stable network for the first time in its history. On 21 August 2001, the network announced the establishment of five new international news bureaus. The populist service was prepared to offer Canadians a new level of quality programming as the leading, general interest television network in the country.

EPILOGUE

CTV, 2001

AT THE START OF the new millennium, the CTV network had positioned itself for a new broadcasting age that would see a major media convergence in North America. Stand-alone television stations and networks belonged to an earlier era when family-owned companies such as the Bassett-Eaton group entered the electronic media business anticipating that the new medium of television would bring healthy profits. In time, they were proven correct, though CTV experienced a history of struggle before eventually becoming part of Bell Globemedia Inc. Canada's major telecommunications company, BCE Inc., was able to provide a sound, economic foundation for the private network.

CTV's arrival altered the structure of the Canadian broadcasting system. The notion of a network of privately-owned television stations operating as a parallel system to the publicly-owned CBC was hardly anticipated in early Canadian broadcasting legislation. For a long time, Canada had a single broadcasting system of public and private elements with the CBC, established in 1936, holding the regulatory power. The establishment of the BBG as a separate, independent broadcast regulator in 1958, and its subsequent licensing of CTV in 1961, had a lasting impact on the broadcasting system. Private broadcasters gained a new influence and were no longer seen as strictly secondary.

CTV's attempt to give viewers an alternative form of programming to the CBC at the start of the turbulent 1960s was an arduous undertaking. The reasons for the early perception of the private network as a kind of electronic misfit extended well beyond the reported, periodic boardroom tensions that drew regular media attention. As a public broadcaster, the CBC had a high-minded mandate and was designed to explain Canada to Canadians. The Corporation could not help but touch the nationalist sensibilities of many Canadians.

CTV from the beginning was aimed at filling a populist void in a country accustomed to American television but the Massey Commission, in its sweeping examination of the arts, letters and sciences in 1951, had clearly shown a preference for high culture. In many ways, the birth of CTV was a reflection of the embodiment of a fundamental dichotomy in Canadian broadcasting: Canadians will watch home grown programming but will never be denied access to popular fare produced in the United States.

The style of programming that CTV intended to provide was a counterpoint to the CBC's mandate and Massey's definition of culture. CTV challenged the historic notion dating from the Aird Commission in 1929, the first federal inquiry into Canadian radio, that broadcasting had to be essentially a cultural vehicle and instrument of nationhood to uplift a mass population. Indeed Spencer Caldwell, the network's founder, was not that interested in broadcasting as simply a cultural vehicle. His view of television was that it was a medium to provide entertaining programming acceptable to the widest possible audience that, in the end, would appeal to advertisers.

Throughout its 40-year history, CTV's programming has served as a populist voice for Canadians by presenting a distinctive range of fare in news, sports and entertainment. The network's market-oriented approach was driven by both economic imperatives and the meagre resources it had to work with especially in its first decade. Whether it was *Telepoll*, *Laugh In*, the *Sports Hot Seat*, or its outstanding coverage of the 1967 Progressive Conservative leadership convention from Maple Leaf Gardens, CTV enabled Canadians to enjoy a vibrant, energetic and at times "in your face" style of programming.

The 1970s saw a major expansion of the network's news service and its scope in coverage as the country's only national private TV network. In the 1980s, new challenges arose as the broadcast regulator demanded a greater emphasis on Canadian dramatic programming by the network which had spent 25 years building and refining its news and sports programming service to Canadians. By the early 1990s, the wide success of

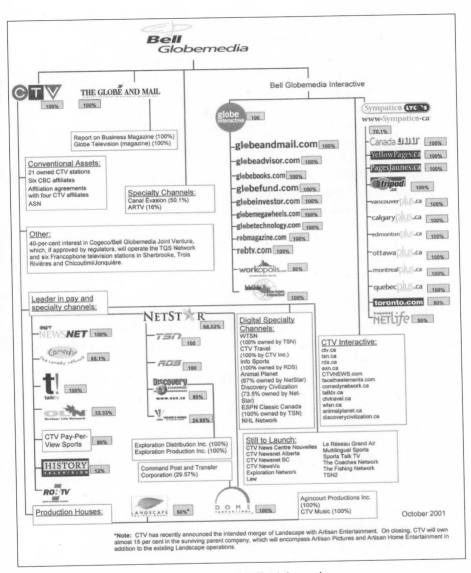

Bell Globemedia Holdings. Courtesy of Bell Globemedia.

the popular program, *Due South*, was evidence of CTV's growth as a network broadcaster able to provide competitive programming in drama, a genre that historically was expensive and required taxpayers' subsidies to produce. The deep pockets of BCE Inc. freed the private network from its earlier reliance on subsidy to produce the kind of fare that could take it to a new level of high quality Canadian programming.

Two main national competitors on the private television broadcasting landscape in Canada have emerged, one in the east and the other in the west: the new CTV and CanWest. Both have adopted different strategies in the evolving broadcast universe. CanWest has chosen to diversify through international investments; CTV's "theatre is national." CTV has chosen to base its growth "on activities within Canada, rather than on international expansion or regional concentration." The network's focus has been described in nationalistic terms as "Canadian television for Canadian viewers."[1]

Given the extent of Bell Globemedia's holdings, in print, broadcasting and new information technology the new CTV appeared prepared to find a populist niche in the unpredictable environment of convergence in the 21st century. "Canadians have always had great writers, great artists," said Trina McQueen. "What they haven't had is what every other...high achieving country has which is a popular culture. Songs that everybody knows, jokes that everybody relates to, TV shows that we all love."[2]

Similarly Ivan Fecan looked to the future of CTV as building on its past by providing appealing, popular fare: "You know my view is that even in an age of infinite choice, people still want to talk about common experiences. And there's always a top ten list. Even the Internet has top ten lists. And so our purpose in the future is to have a lot of items on that top ten list wherever they may be. And I just believe that some of them have to be local in terms of national reflection. I don't mean local as a Toronto; I mean Canada versus Sweden or Canada versus American or Canada versus Britain. Otherwise, why not just get it off the [satellite] dish?"[3]

Whatever the future of Canadian television broadcasting, by 2001 the CTV network had built up a sizeable following of devoted viewers. As a vehicle for popular culture the network, with new ownership, seemed ready to serve Canadian viewers in the 21st century with the highest quality of programming in its four decades of operation. Though envisioned somewhat simplistically in the early 1960s as an "advertisers' network", CTV from *Canada AM* to *Who Wants To Be A Millionaire, Canadian Edition?* to *The Sopranos* to the *CTV National News* had become an integral part of the daily lives of Canadians. From Spencer Caldwell and Gordon Keeble to Murray Chercover, John Cassaday, Ivan Fecan and Trina McQueen, CTV on its 40th anniversary continues to play a leading role in Canadian television as a popular general interest service.

APPENDIX

The Evolution of a Network

—1960s—

1 October 1961[1]   The birth of the CTV Network.

Spencer Caldwell and Gordon Keeble bring together eight stations—seven 'second' private stations in major markets plus CFRN, previously a CBC affiliate and nonbroadcasting owners—to form CTV Television Network Ltd. The original stations were:
CHAN, Vancouver;
CFCN, Calgary;
CFRN, Edmonton;
CJAY, Winnipeg;
CFTO, Toronto;
CJOH, Ottawa;
CFCF, Montreal;
CJCH, Halifax.

23 February 1966[2]   Eleven private stations, the founding group plus three others, apply to the BBG and gain permission to take over CTV from Caldwell's group. The stations and owners (in brackets) were:
CHAN (British Columbia Broadcasting System Ltd.);
CFCN (CFCN Television Limited);
CFRN (Sunwapta Broadcasting Co. Limited);
CJAY (Channel Seven Television Ltd.);

CFTO (Baton Broadcasting Limited);

CJOH (Bushnell TV Co. Limited);

CFCF (Broadcasting Division of Canadian Marconi Company);

CJCH (CJCH Limited).

The three additional stations were:

CHRE/CHAB, Regina-Moose Jaw (CHAB Ltd.);

CKCO, Kitchener (Central Ontario Television Limited);

CJON, St. John's (Newfoundland Broadcasting Company).

Fall, 1969[3]

CKCK, Regina (Armadale Communications Limited) replaces CHRE/CHAB which the CBC purchased.

CKCW, Moncton (Moncton Broadcasting Limited) joins the CTV network as a new affiliate.

CTV has 12 affiliated stations.

—1970s—

Early 1970s[4]

The 1970s saw the CTV network have 14 individual owner-affiliates, a period John Travers Coleman described as the network's "corporate zenith."

The two additional affiliates beyond the 12 outlined above were:

CFQC, Saskatoon (CFQC Broadcasting Limited which previously was known as A.A. Murphy & Sons Ltd.);

CKSO, Sudbury (Cambrian Broadcasting Ltd.).

Consolidation of station ownership intensifies in 1972.

1972[5]

CHUM Limited starts The Atlantic Television System (ATV) that includes:

CJCH, Halifax;

CJCB, Sydney;

CKCW, Moncton;

CKLT, Saint John.

12 October 1978[6]

Canada, *Decision CRTC 78–669.*

The CRTC denies application by Baton Broadcasting Incorporated to purchase CFCF-TV from its owner Multiple Access Limited. At the time, Baton owns stations CFQC, Saskatoon and CFTO, Toronto.

Late 1970s[7]   Over time several internal ownership changes within affili-
                      ates:
                      >   Harvard Communications Limited succeeds Arma-
                      >   dale Communications Limited (CKCK);
                      >   Moffat Communications Limited succeeds MTV Lim-
                      >   ited, formerly Channel Seven Television Limited
                      >   (CJAY);
                      >   Mid Canada Communications (Canada) replaces
                      >   Cambrian Broadcasting Ltd. (CKSO);
                      >   C.A.P. Communications Limited is successor to Cen-
                      >   tral Ontario Television Limited (CKCO);
                      >   CFCF Inc. succeeds Multiple Access Limited (CFCF,
                      >   Montreal).

—1980s—

Early 1980s[8]   WIC Western International Communications Ltd. owns
                      CHAN, Vancouver and CHEK, Victoria, both CTV affili-
                      ates.

                      Still greater consolidation in Canadian broadcasting. A
                      report on *The Economic Status of Canadian Television*
                      notes, "More than 25 television stations have changed
                      hands since 1986."

circa 1986–1988[9]   Baton grows by acquisition on its way to gaining control
                      of CTV.

                      In 1986, Baton purchases
                      >   CKCK, Regina;
                      >   CKOS/CICC, Yorkton;
                      >   CKBK, Melfort.

                      In 1988, Baton purchases
                      >   CJOH, Ottawa.

April, 1989[10]   The CTV network includes 18 affiliated stations and six
                      supplementary affiliates.
                      Affiliates:
                      >   CJON, St. John's;
                      >   CJCB, Sydney;
                      >   CJCH, Halifax;
                      >   CKCW, Moncton;
                      >   CFCF, Montreal;
                      >   CJOH, Ottawa;
                      >   CFTO, Toronto;
                      >   CKCO, Kitchener;

CICI, Sudbury;
CITO, Timmins;
CKNY, North Bay;
CKY, Winnipeg;
CKCK, Regina;
CFQC, Saskatoon;
CFCN, Calgary;
CFRN, Edmonton;
CHAN, Vancouver;
CHEK, Victoria.
Supplementary Affiliates:
CHFD, Thunder Bay;
CITL, Lloydminster;
CHBX, Sault Ste. Marie;
CJBN, Kenora;
CICC, Yorkton;
CIPA, Prince Albert.

—1990s—

1990[11]   In 1990, Baton buys several stations from Mid-Canada Communications (Canada) Corp. consolidating its position still further. The stations are:
CHRO, Pembroke;
CICI/CKNG, Sudbury;
CITO/CFCL, Timmins;
CHNB/CKNY, North Bay.

27 January 1993[12]   New shareholders agreement. CTV no longer functions as a co-operative but is realigned as a conventional company. A previous agreement whereby eight shareholders each held 100 common voting shares (12.5 percent) is replaced by a new arrangement. Seven shareholders (14.24 voting interest each) agree to recapitalize CTV. Newfoundland Broadcasting Company Ltd. is not a signatory to the agreement but remains an affiliate. Provision is made for the transfer of shares and stations in CTV to allow for one owner of the network to emerge.

29 September 1994[13]   Seven shareholders—
BBS Ontario Incorporated (Baton),
CFCF Inc., CFCN Communications Inc. (Maclean Hunter Ltd.),
CHUM Limited,
Electrohome Limited,

Moffat Communications Limited and
Westcom TV Group Ltd. (WIC)—
exchange $14,000,000 in convertible debentures for
14,000,000 common shares in the corporation to recapitalize CTV.

mid to late 1990s[14]   From the mid to late 1990s, Baton moves to gain control
of CTV after a number of transactions involving major
media owners and their stations.

21 June 1996[15]   Canada, *Decision CRTC 96–251* saw the CRTC approve
Baton's application to transfer "effective control of CFCN
Communications Inc. (CFCN), licensee of CFCN-TV Cal-
gary and CFCN-TV-5 Lethbridge, and holder of 14.28
percent voting interest in the CTV Television Network
Ltd. (CTV) from Rogers Communications Inc. (RCI)" to
Baton.

4 September 1996[16]   The CRTC licenses 23 specialty services that include CTV
Television Network Ltd. and its owners CHUM Limited,
Baton, and WIC.

CHUM is awarded six specialty licences in addition to the
earlier obtained MuchMusic (1984) and Bravo! (1994).
New licences (1996):
   Canadian Learning Television;
   MuchMoreMusic;
   Pulse 24 (with Toronto Sun Publishing Corp.), a
      regional news channel;
   Space—The Imagination Station;
   Star-TV;
   Musimax.

Baton wins three licences (1996):
   Talk TV (wholly owned);
   Outdoor Life (Rogers Communications Inc., The
      Outdoor Channel USA and Ellis Enterprises as
      partners);
   The Comedy Network (partners Astral Communica-
      tions Inc., Shaw Communications Inc., and Just
      For Laughs festival, Montreal).

WIC obtains two licences (1996):
   Report on Business Television (ROBTv) (partners
      Canadian Satellite Communications Inc., a WIC
      subsidiary, and *The Globe and Mail*);
   Family Channel whose owners are WIC and Astral

gets licence for Teletoon, an animation channel (partners Nelvana Ltd. and Cinar Films Inc.).

CTV Television Network Ltd. wins four specialty licences (1996):

History and Entertainment Network (minority interest);

Headline News Channel named CTV News1 and later NewsNet;

a regional sports service;

Sports/ Specials pay-per-view service (partner Molson Cos. Ltd. in both sports services).

circa 1997[17]

The transactions prior to 1997 include CHUM Limited and its ATV stations, CTV affiliates, on the east coast:

CJCH, Halifax;

CJCB, Sydney;

CKLT, Saint John;

CKCW, Moncton.

A second owner involved was Electrohome Limited which saw its stations, CKCO, Kitchener and CFRN, Edmonton pass to Baton. Electrohome withdrew as a television licensee.

28 August 1997[18]

Canada, *Decision CRTC 97–527* noted: "Approval of applications by Baton Broadcasting Incorporated and certain of its subsidiaries, CHUM Limited, and CTV Television Network Ltd. for authority to transfer either the assets, or share equity representing effective control, of the CTV Television Network, and of various English-language television and other programming undertakings across Canada."

28 August 1997[19]

Baton obtains majority control of CTV.

1998[20]

Baton's name is changed to CTV Inc.

—2000—

24 March 2000[21]

Canada, *Decision CRTC 2002–86* saw approval of an application resulting "in CTV Inc. (CTV) obtaining an 80% controlling interest in NetStar Communications Inc. (NetStar)." CTV had "to divest of its interests in the SportsNet regional sports specialty service."

6 July 2000[22]

Canada, *Decision CRTC 2000–221* approved the acquisition "by CanWest Global Communications Corp., through its wholly-owned subsidiary CW Shareholdings Inc., of the ownership interests held previously by WIC Western International Communications Ltd. in various conventional television stations and in certain broadcasting undertakings." The acquisitions by CanWest of CHAN, Vancouver and CHEK, Victoria, means that the former CTV affiliates were to change their network affiliation in September, 2001.

7 December 2000[23]

Canada, *Decision CRTC 2000–747.* The decision allows, "Transfer of effective control of CTV Inc. to BCE Inc."

January 2001[24]

CTV Inc. becomes part of Bell Globemedia owned by BCE Inc. and minority partners The Thomson Corporation. and the Thomson family's The Woodbridge Co. Ltd. Bell Globemedia, which brings together CTV, *The Globe and Mail* and Sympatico/Lycos, owns 18 CTV affiliates:
> CJCH, Halifax;
> CJCB, Sydney/Cape Breton;
> CKCW, Moncton;
> CKLT, Saint John;
> CJOH, Ottawa;
> CFTO, Toronto;
> CKCO, Kitchener/London;
> CICI, Sudbury;
> CITO, Timmins;
> CKNY, North Bay;
> CHBX, Sault Ste, Marie;
> CFQC, Saskatoon;
> CKCK, Regina;
> CIPA, Prince Albert;
> CICC, Yorkton;
> CFCN, Calgary;
> CFCN, Lethbridge;
> CFRN, Edmonton.

6 July 2001[25]

Rogers Communications Inc. gets control of SportsNet by acquiring CTV's 40 percent interest subject to regulatory approval.

2 August 2001[26]

Canada, *Decision CRTC 2001–457 and Decision 2001–458.* CRTC renews the licences "of all the television stations owned and controlled by CTV Inc. (CTV) and Can West Global Communications (Global) for a full seven year term." Both CTV and Global "to adhere to a *Statement of Principles and Practices* regarding cross ownership of television stations and newspapers."

2 August 2001[27]   CTV receives regulatory approval to acquire CKY, Winnipeg.

Purchases of CFCF, Montreal and ROBTv are pending regulatory approval.

CTV maintains affiliation agreements with four conventional stations:
NTV, St. John's (CJON);
CJBN, Keewatin;
CITL, Lloydminster;
CHFD, Thunder Bay.

September, 2001[28]   VTV, Vancouver becomes a CTV affiliate and was renamed BC CTV.

Purchase of CFCF received regulatory approval.

NOTES

Introduction

1. For a discussion of the Massey Report, see Frank W. Peers, *The Politics of Canadian Broadcasting 1920–1951* (Toronto: University of Toronto Press, 1969), 413–23 and Frank W. Peers, *The Public Eye: Television and the Politics of Canadian Broadcasting 1952–1968* (Toronto: University of Toronto Press, 1979), 23–28.

2. For details of the 1958 legislation, see Peers, *The Public Eye*, 152–75. See also T.J. Allard, *Straight Up, Private Broadcasting in Canada* (Ottawa: The Canadian Communications Foundation, 1979), 237–55.

3. Michael Hind-Smith papers (privately held), unpublished manuscript, "High Wire: A Life in the Electric Circus (without a net)," Ottawa, 1990, 8. At CBLT, as Hind-Smith has noted, McLean had given him the slogan, "The Network Station with the Local Look." Hind-Smith turned to McLean again for "The Network That Means Business."

4. Andrew Stewart and W.H.N. Hull, *Canadian Television Policy and the Board of Broadcast Governors, 1958–1968* (Edmonton: The University of Alberta Press, 1994), 281.

5. Allard, *Straight Up*, 65.

6. Canada, *Report of the Special Senate Committee on Mass Media (Davey Committee), The Uncertain Mirror*, Volume 1 (Ottawa: Queen's Printer, 1970), 194.

7. *The Globe and Mail*, 31 May 1991.

8. Allard, *Straight Up*, 211.

9. Frank H. Underhill, "Notes on the Massey Report," in J.L. Granatstein and Peter Stevens, eds., *Forum: Canadian Life and Letters 1920–70, Selections*

from The Canadian Forum (Toronto: University of Toronto Press, 1972), 273, 272.

10. Susan Sontag, *Against Interpretation, and Other Essays* (New York: Farrer, Straus and Giroux, 1966), 302, 304.

11. Stewart and Hull, *Canadian Television Policy,* 282.

12. Bell Globemedia (Scarborough), BCE News Release, "Bell Globemedia Launched," Toronto, 9 January 2001. The owners of Bell Globemedia included BCE Inc. (70.1 percent), The Thomson Corporation (20 percent) and The Woodbridge Company Limited (9.9 percent).

13. John R. Bittner, *Broadcasting and Telecommunication: An Introduction,* Second Edition (Englewood Cliffs: Prentice-Hall, Inc., 1985), 85.

14. Interview, John Bassett, 24 March 1993.

15. John Coleman papers (privately held), *JTC*, CTV Corps. Docs., *Television Affiliation Agreement,* 29 May 1962 (Re-typed to incorporate Amendments dated 12 September 1961), 8–9.

16. Canada, *Report of the Committee on Broadcasting,* 1965, Fowler Committee (Ottawa: Queen's Printer, 1965), 375.

17. Ibid., 234–35, 233.

18. National Archives of Canada [hereafter NAC], RG 100, B49, Microfilm (Mf) M-3087, Board of Broadcast Governors Hearing, 23 February 1966, *Transcript of Evidence,* 70.

19. Peter Dempson, "A new era in television service opens as more private stations enter the field," *Canadian Business* (December, 1960): 90, 93.

20. Canada, *Report of the Special Senate Committee,* 7.

21. Peter Rehak papers (privately held), "Notes about W5," given to the author during interview, 12 March 1998.

22. CTV Television Network Ltd. (Toronto), CRTC Public Hearing, Application by CTV Television Network Ltd. for licence renewal, 27 September 1993, Volume 1, *Transcript of Proceedings,* 35–36.

23. Ibid., 37.

24. Interview, Peter Mansbridge, 13 March 1998.

25. Interview, Kevin Newman, 6 October 1999.

26. Interview, Trina McQueen, 1 November 2000.

27. Rae Corelli, "Spencer Caldwell: The Man Who Challenges CBC's TV Supremacy," *The Star Weekly Magazine,* 13 January 1962, 7.

1 The CTV Founder: 1909–1961

1. Hind-Smith papers, "High Wire," 7.

2. Canada, Canadian Radio-television and Telecommunications Commission (CRTC), Public Examination Room, Hearings of the Board of Broadcast Governors, file H–31–6, BBG Public Hearing, "Application by S.W. Caldwell on behalf of a company to be incorporated as Canadian Television Network Limited, for permission to operate a television network in Canada," *Transcript of Evidence,* Ottawa, 13 April 1961, 231, 356. The files from the early 1960s on CTV examined by the author and now in his possession are no longer in the

public examination room. Transcripts of the BBG hearings can be viewed on microfilm at the National Archives of Canada.

3. Nancy Caldwell papers (privately held); Ross McLean, "CTV at silver milestone is going for gold," *Broadcast Week Magazine,* 27 September-3 October 1986, 11.

4. CTV Television Network Ltd. Archives, Toronto, "CTV: Hoopla Network," *The Canadian* (preview issue), (1961): 27.

5. *Financial Post,* 30 November 1963.

6. *The Globe and Mail,* 2 October 1961.

7. Ibid.

8. NAC, MG 31, A17–86–548, Spencer Caldwell papers, Volume 3 of 3, File Caldwell Spencer—1934–1936, *Spencer Wood Caldwell,* 2. The description of Caldwell is from a 1957 article in the Caldwell papers believed to have been written by Kay Kritzwiser but never submitted for publication. Much of the material on Caldwell's life is drawn from this article. For a discussion of Kritzwiser, see David Hayes, *Power and Influence* (Toronto: Key Porter Books, 1992), 93–99.

9. Interview, Gordon Keeble, 7 November 1998.

10. Interview, Finlay MacDonald, 22 April 1993.

11. Interview, Nancy Caldwell, 28 May 2000.

12. Interview, Gordon Keeble, 17 August 1993.

13. Keeble interview, 17 August 1993.

14. Canada, *Report of the Special Senate Committee,* 47.

15. Caldwell papers, *Spencer Wood Caldwell,* 9–10.

16. Ibid. See also Corelli, "Spencer Caldwell," 20.

17. Corelli, "Spencer Caldwell," 7.

18. Allard, *Straight Up,* 22.

19. Caldwell papers, *Spencer Wood Caldwell,* 3.

20. Ibid.

21. Interview, Ray Peters, 23 January 1996.

22. Nancy Caldwell interview.

23. Caldwell papers, *Spencer Wood Caldwell,* 3.

24. Nancy Caldwell interview.

25. Caldwell papers, *Spencer Wood Caldwell,* 4.

26. "CTV: Hoopla Network," 26.

27. Keeble interview, 7 November 1998.

28. Canada, *Report of the Federal Cultural Policy Review Committee,* Applebert Report (Ottawa: Information Services, Department of Communications, 1982), 286.

29. "CTV: Hoopla Network," 26.

30. Keeble interview, 17 August 1993

31. Caldwell papers, *Spencer Wood Caldwell,* 5, 7, and Keeble interview, 7 November 1998.

32. Keeble interview, 17 August 1993.

33. Ibid.

34. Caldwell papers, *Spencer Wood Caldwell,* 5–6.

35. Ibid., 5.
36. Ibid.
37. Keeble interview, 17 August 1993.
38. Caldwell papers, *Spencer Wood Caldwell*, 6.
39. Peters interview.
40. Keeble interview, 17 August 1993.
41. Ibid.
42. Caldwell papers, *Spencer Wood Caldwell*, 1.
43. Interview, Murray Brown, 3 May 1996.
44. Caldwell papers, *Spencer Wood Caldwell*, 6.
45. Ibid., 4.
46. Keeble interview, 17 August 1993.
47. Caldwell papers, *Spencer Wood Caldwell*, 8.
48. Corelli, "Spencer Caldwell," 20.
49. Nancy Caldwell interview.
50. Ibid. Caldwell's life came to an end on 10 December 1983 when the car he was driving collided with a transport truck near his home in Caledon. "He was on highway 50," his colleague Gordon Keeble recalled, "he had gone down to Bolton to pick up a friend who was coming for the weekend. As I understand it, he was driving north on highway 50 and a tractor-trailer backed out in front of him without adequate signals or lights....But anyway he hit it and that was it." Caldwell's guest in the car survived but she was badly hurt. "The lady was Kay Kritzwiser," said Keeble, "That time as I remember she was arts critic at *The Globe*." Keeble interview, 7 November 1998.
51. Caldwell papers, *Spencer Wood Caldwell*, 7.
52. Ibid., 8–9.
53. Interview, Murray Chercover, 3 March 1992.
54. John Bassett interview.
55. *The Globe and Mail*, 19 March 1958, as quoted in Robert J.F. Albota, *The Lobbying Background of the Broadcasting Act, 1958: T.J. Allard versus Graham Spry*, B.A. Honours Research Essay, Carleton University, Ottawa, 1 April 1985, 66. For a discussion of the role of the lobbying surrounding the demand by private broadcasters for a separate, broadcast regulator, see Allard, *Straight Up*.
56. John Bassett interview.
57. Eugene Forsey, *A Life on the Fringe: The Memoirs of Eugene Forsey* (Toronto: Oxford University Press, 1990), 138–39.
58. Keeble interview, 7 November 1998.
59. Stewart and Hull, *Canadian Television Policy*, 66, 325–26.
60. John Bassett interview.
61. For a discussion of the shares transfer, see Frank Foster, *Broadcasting Policy Development* (Ottawa: Franfost Communications Ltd., 1983), 193–96. Foster's study of the evolution of broadcasting policy was undertaken for the Canadian Radio-television and Telecommunications Commission. See also Stewart and Hull, *Canadian Television Policy*, 67–74.
62. Stewart and Hull, *Canadian Television Policy*, 203.

63. John Bassett interview.

64. David Olive, "The High-Wire Act of Ted Rogers," *Report on Business Magazine* 2 (July/August 1985): 28.

65. Interview, Allan Beattie, 28 October 1999.

66. Ibid., and MacFarlane interview.

67. Beattie interview.

68. John Bassett interview.

69. Ibid., and *The Globe and Mail,* 18 March 1960.

70. Beattie interview and Stewart and Hull, *Canadian Television Policy*, 55.

71. Interview, Eddie Goodman, 31 July 1996.

72. Keeble interview, 7 November 1998.

73. Edwin A. Goodman, *Life of the Party: The Memoirs of Eddie Goodman* (Toronto: Key Porter Books, 1988), 168.

74. John Bassett interview.

75. Goodman interview.

76. NAC, BBG and CRTC Hearings, 1959–1973, Microfilm, M-3075, B10, BBG hearing, Toronto, 17 March 1960, *Transcript of Evidence,* 425.

77. John Bassett interview.

78. Ibid.

79. Ibid.

80. Forsey, *A Life*, 143.

81. Keeble interview, 7 November 1998.

82. Johnny Esaw manuscript (privately held), Draft #2, Chapter 4, "CFTO/ CTV: The Beginning," 7. The manuscript written by Johnny Esaw contains 14 chapters detailing his career as a sports broadcaster and as a negotiator for broadcasting rights to memorable sporting events. The author wishes to thank him for allowing access to the manuscript which is in large part a history of memorable sports events and media coverage by a national private broadcasting figure.

83. John Bassett interview.

84. Goodman interview.

85. Stewart and Hull, *Canadian Television Policy,* 76.

86. Ibid., 82–83.

87. Keeble interview, 7 November 1998.

88. Keeble interview, 17 August 1993.

89. John Bassett interview.

90. CRTC Public Examination Room, Public Hearing of the Board of Broadcast Governors, *Transcript of Evidence*, 13 April 1961, 312.

91. Ibid., 242.

92. Keeble interview, 7 November 1998 and CRTC Public Examination Room, CTV Television Network Limited, Toronto, licence application, Vol. 1, File 6–113–340, dated from 14/11/60 to 9/8/63, "*Microwave Rates,*" n.d. The microwave facilities that could link the eastern and western coasts of Canada, and which broadcasters leased, were in the hands of both the Trans-Canada Telephone System and Canadian National and Canadian Pacific Telecommunications.

93. CRTC, Public Examination Room, CTV licence application," *Microwave Rates.*" See also Peers, *The Public Eye*, 239–40.

94. CRTC Public Examination Room, CTV Television Network Limited, Toronto, Licence Application, Vol. 1, File 6–113–340, dated from 14/11/60 to 9/8/63, *News Release*, from *Spencer Caldwell*, Re: *Private Television Network in Canada*, 10 December 1960, 2, and Chercover interview, 3 March 1992. As Chairman of ITO, Chercover recalled that "the stations were prepared to co-operate through ITO in carriage of CFL football. We didn't have microwave capability to interconnect."

95. Chercover interview, 3 March 1992.

96. Keeble interview, 7 November 1998.

97. Ibid.

98. Ibid.

99. CRTC Public Examination Room, CTV Television Network Limited, Toronto, licence application, Volume 1, file 6–113–340, dated from 14/11/60 to 9/8/63, S.W. Caldwell *To Members of the Board of Broadcast Governors*, April 8, 1961.

100. "CTV: Hoopla Network," 27.

101. Stewart and Hull, *Canadian Television Policy*, 95.

102. CRTC, BBG Hearing, 13 April 1961, 280 and Public Examination Room, CTV Television Network Limited, Toronto, Ontario, BBG Hearing on CTV Television Network Ownership Transfer, Volume 2, Application File 6–113–340 from 14/10/60 to 23/2/66, "My name is Ernest Bushnell," 5. Bushnell explained the apportionment of shares at a 23 February 1966 day-long hearing when the stations sought to assume control of CTV as a co-operative.

103. Peters interview.

104. Goodman and Chercover interviews, 3 March 1992 and 31 July 1996.

105. Robert Fulford, "Promises, Promises," *Saturday Night* (July 1987): 6.

106. McLean, "CTV at Silver," 11.

2 The Dominator: 1961—1966

1. Interview, Isabel Bassett, 16 March 2000. John Bassett's first wife was Moira Bradley whom he married in 1938, the mother of Bassett's sons John, Douglas and David. See *The Globe and Mail*, 28 April 1998.

2. Andrew MacFarlane, the 2000 Edward Clissold Lecture, delivered at the University of Western Ontario, 4 November 2000, 4. Andrew MacFarlane, a former Managing Editor of *The Toronto Telegram*, was the founding dean of the Graduate School of Journalism at Western. His speech was delivered to mark the 25th anniversary of the first graduating class. Edward Clissold was a journalist who worked in the 1860s on the *New York Herald* under Horace Greeley and retired in 1910 as editor of the London (Ontario) *Advertiser*. A bequest from the estate of Clissold's relatives enabled the Graduate School to establish an annual series of lectures.

3. *The London Free Press*, and *The Globe and Mail*, 28 April 1998.

4. MacDonald interview and John Bassett interview.

5. Interview, John Coleman, 3 March 1992.
6. Isabel Bassett interview.
7. Interview, Matthew Bassett, 28 October 1999.
8. Interview, Andrew MacFarlane, 8 June 1999.
9. MacFarlane, 2000 Edward Clissold Lecture, 21–22.
10. Beattie interview.
11. Ibid., and Esaw manuscript, Draft #2, Chapter 4, "CFTO/CTV: The Beginning," 7. See also Goodman, *Life of the Party*, 170.
12. Stewart and Hull, *Canadian Television Policy*, 68.
13. Ibid., 71.
14. Beattie interview.
15. Foster, *Broadcasting Policy Development*, 195–96. Foster, a long-time observer of Canadian broadcasting, wrote a study on broadcast policy which was supported by the CRTC.
16. John Bassett interview. For a discussion of CTV's early structure see Michael Nolan, "Case Study in Regulation: CTV and Canadian Broadcast Policy" in Martin W. Westmacott and Hugh P. Mellon, *Public Administration and Policy: Governing in Challenging Times* (Scarborough: Prentice Hall Allyn and Bacon Canada, 1999), 126–35.
17. Hind-Smith papers, *Draft: Re: CTV: A New Concept in Canadian Programming*, Michael Hind-Smith to CTV Board of Directors, 6 May 1965, 1.
18. Gordon Keeble papers (privately held), "GENERAL IMPRESSIONS and NOTES to supplement official 'Minutes' of the affiliates Meeting of October 22, 23, and 24, 1962," 1.
19. Ibid.
20. Ibid., 2.
21. Ibid.
22. Ibid., 3.
23. John Bassett interview.
24. *The Globe and Mail*, 31 August 1961.
25. John Bassett interview.
26. MacDonald interview.
27. John Bassett interview.
28. Ibid.
29. Ibid.
30. Keeble papers, CTV Television Network Ltd., "Proposal—(Confidential)," from CTV to The Affiliates, 4 October 1962, 9.
31. John Bassett interview.
32. Hind-Smith papers, *Draft: Re: CTV*, Hind-Smith to CTV Board of Directors, 6 May 1965, 1–3.
33. CTV Television Network Ltd. Archives (Toronto), internal memo, Vin Dittmer to S.W. Caldwell, 17 June 1964.
34. Interview, W.D. McGregor, 1 September 1992.
35. Keeble interview, 17 August 1993.
36. MacDonald interview.
37. Interview, Arthur Weinthal, 15 November 1994.

38. Ibid.

39. Ibid.

40. *Financial Post*, 1 February 1964.

41. Keeble papers, "Proposal—(Confidential)," 4 October 1962, 10.

42. Ibid.

43. Keeble interview, 17 August 1993.

44. NAC, RG 100, B49, microfilm, M-3087, CTV Television Network Ltd. Ownership Transfer, Board of Broadcast Governors, Public Hearing, Ottawa, 23 February 1966, *Transcript of Evidence*, 25.

45. Public Archives of Nova Scotia, Halifax, *The Mail-Star*, 10 August 1964.

46. Ibid., *The Chronicle-Herald*, Special Section, 14 September 1963.

47. Keeble papers, CTV Television Network Ltd., *Internal Memo, Confidential*, Gordon Keeble to S.W. Caldwell, 15 February 1965, 2.

48. Ibid.

49. Hind-Smith interview, 7 November 1998.

50. Hind-Smith papers, "High Wire," 9 and ibid.

51. Hind-Smith interview.

52. Ibid.

53. Hind-Smith papers, *The Globe and Mail,* 10 December 1966.

54. Hind-Smith interview.

55. Ibid.

56. Ibid.

57. Ibid.

58. Harvey Kirck with Wade Rowland, *Nobody Calls Me Mr. Kirck* (Toronto: Collins Publishers, 1985), 130–31.

59. Chercover interview, 3 March 1992.

60. Hind-Smith interview.

61. Ibid.

62. Interview, Bill Brady, 22 August 1996.

63. Ibid.

64. Ibid.

65. Shirley Mair, "Showdown in CBC's corral: how fast will CTV draw," *Maclean's*, 4 November 1961, 80.

66. For a discussion of the fracas that occurred over the televising of the Grey Cup, see Stewart and Hull, *Canadian Television Policy*, 101–19.

67. Interview, Johnny Esaw, 30 July 1996.

68. Ibid.

69 CTV Television Network Ltd., Archives, "*Wide World of Sports*: CTV" promotional material for 1964–65 season, 4. The document is not numbered. A number was assigned for each page.

70. Esaw interview, 30 July 1996.

71. *Report of the Committee on Broadcasting*, 1965, 236.

72. Ibid., 29.

73. Ibid., 236.

74. NAC, RG 100, B49, Mf. M-3087, BBG Public Hearing, Ottawa, 23 February 1966, *Transcript of Evidence*, 77.

75. Peters interview.

76. *Report of the Committee on Broadcasting, 1965*, 239.

77. NAC, Spencer Caldwell papers, MG 31, A17 86/548, Volume 3 of 3, File Caldwell Spencer, 1934–1936, CTV Press Release, "Gordon Keeble Elected President of CTV Television Network," 1 October 1965.

3 Power Struggles Within the Co-operative: 1966–1970

1. Keeble papers, *Internal Memo, Confidential*, Gordon Keeble to S.W. Caldwell, 15 February 1965.

2. *Report of the Committee on Broadcasting, 1965*, 239.

3. John Bassett interview.

4. *Report of the Committee on Broadcasting, 1965*, 375.

5. Interview, E.A. Goodman, 31 July 1996 and John Bassett interview.

6. Goodman interview and Goodman, *Life of the Party*, 171.

7. Hind-Smith papers, Gordon Keeble to S.W. Caldwell, 6 May 1965.

8. Ibid.

9. Ibid.

10. Goodman interview.

11. NAC, RG 100, B49, Microfilm (Mf), M-3087, Board of Broadcast Governors hearing, CTV Television Network Ownership Transfer, Ottawa, 23 February 1966, *Transcript of Evidence*, 11.

12. BCTV Archives (Vancouver). The archival material on CHAN prepared by Mark Leiren-Young was sent to the author.

13. Ibid., Peters quote is contained in a supplement that appeared in *TV Week Magazine*, October 1990, entitled "A Salute to a Pioneer in Broadcasting: 30 Years of BCTV."

14. Ibid.

15. Peters interview.

16. NAC, RG 100, B49, BBG Hearing, *Transcript of Evidence*, 23 February 1966, 11.

17. Barbara A. Moes, "History and modernism merge at CFRN in Edmonton," *Broadcaster* 40 (October 1981): 26, 24.

18. Ibid., 24.

19. Ibid., Radio station CJCA, Edmonton originally owned by the *Edmonton Journal* went off the air on 1 December 1993. See *The Globe and Mail*, 2 December 1993. For details of the Baton merger, see Canada, Canadian Radio-television and Telecommunications Commission, Decision CRTC 97-527, Ottawa, 28 August 1997, 1, 10.

20. Broadcast House, CFRN archives, Edmonton, company booklet entitled "SUNWAPTA Welcomes You: Know the Company You Are Working With, 1974," 5. See also Moes, "History and modernism merge at CFRN," 24–25.

21. CFCN Television Archives, Broadcast House, Calgary, "Radio Station CFCN: Early History," 1. Gordon Enno, Supervising Producer at CFCN-TV, forwarded this material to the author.

22. Ibid., unauthored article, "Radio Station CFCN: Early History," 3 and

promotional material, message from Terry L. Coles, President & General Manager, CFCN Television, "25 years...and on your side!" The material was sent to the author.

23. Canada, *Report of the Special Senate Committee on Mass Media*, Volume 11, *Words, Music, and Dollars: A Study of the economics of publishing and broadcasting, for the Special Senate Committee on Mass Media* (Ottawa: Queen's Printer, 1970), 91, 93.

24. Gary Bobrovitz, "CFCN-TV stampedes toward 25," *Broadcaster* 44 (June 1985): 11.

25. Moffat Communications Limited Archives, Winnipeg, Corporate History marking the company's growth: 1949–1982, 1. The 20-page history is divided chronologically in decades. The material was sent to the author. (The author assigned page numbers to the document for reference.)

26. "With Moffat in Winnipeg: Decentralized management is the key," *Broadcaster* 40 (April 1981): 27–28.

27. CKCO-TV Archives, Kitchener, "A Brief History of Cap Communications Limited," 1 and "Presenting the Facts: CKCO-TV—Southern Ontario's Leading Station," 1. The material was sent to the author.

28. Ibid., "Presenting the Facts," 1.

29. McGregor interview. For a discussion of the history of CKCO-TV, see Norah McClintock, "McGregor 'CAPS' the Kitchener market," *Broadcaster* 43 (October 1984): 18, 20–21.

30. John Bassett interview.

31. For an account of Marconi's experiments at Signal Hill, see Christine Curlook, "Marconi from Signal Hill...a Canadian retrospective," *Broadcaster* 40 (October 1981): 60, 62–63. See also Allard, *Straight Up*, 4–5.

32. CJOH-TV Archives, Ottawa, "An Application for a private television broadcasting station in Ottawa" by E.L. Bushnell Television Company Limited to the Board of Broadcast Governors, Question 28, *Schedule 16*, 21 March 1960, 1–3. The application material was sent to the author. See also *The Citizen*, Ottawa, 11 March 1986. An advertising feature in the newspaper commemorated the 25th anniversary of the founding of CJOH.

33. NAC, CTV Television Network Ownership Transfer, BBG Public Hearing, Ottawa, *Transcript of Evidence*, 23 February 1966, 17–18.

34. Bill McNeil and Morris Wolfe, *Signing On: The Birth of Radio in Canada* (Toronto: Doubleday Canada Limited, 1982), 186–87, and CFCF Inc. Archives, Montreal, "CFCF, Canada's First Station," 1. The eight-page history on CFCF becoming the first station, which was sent to the author, was prepared in 1969 and revised in 1982.

35. CFCF 12 Archives, Montreal, CFCF Inc., *Annual Information Form*, 15 January 1993, 4.

36. Public Archives of Nova Scotia, Halifax *Chronicle Herald*, 21 June 1960.

37. MacDonald interview.

38. Ibid.

39. Ibid.

40. Carmelita McGrath, ed., *No Place for Fools: The Political Memoirs of*

Don Jamieson, Volume 1 (St. John's: Breakwater, 1989), 153, 181–82.

41. E. Austin Weir, *The Struggle for National Broadcasting in Canada* (Toronto: McClelland & Stewart, 1965), 363.

42. Ibid., 364.

43. Centre for Newfoundland Studies, Memorial University, St. John's, *The Evening Telegram*, 20 November 1986.

44. Interview, Ted Gardner, 30 December 1993.

45. *The Evening Telegram*, 20 November 1986.

46. Centre for Newfoundland Studies, Memorial University, St. John's, Amy Zierler, "Geoff Stirling, Captain Newfoundland," *Atlantic Insight* (October 1980): 45.

47. Ibid., Alexander Ross, "Geoff Stirling's Trip." This five-page article by Ross is in a Biography File at the Centre for Newfoundland Studies. The name file is entitled "Stirling, Geoff" and is dated 26 July 1995. The place of publication and date of the article are not listed. On the back of the first page of the article are the written words: "Stirling-born 1921, article—circa 1969." The last page of the article is numbered 17.

48. Ibid.

49. Ibid.

50. Centre for Newfoundland Studies, *The Newfoundland Herald* TV Week, 8 August 1979.

51. Coleman interview.

52. NAC, BBG Hearing, 23 February 1966, *Transcript of Evidence*, 166–67.

53. Ibid., 52, 64.

54. Ibid., 52–53.

55. Ibid., 59, 53.

56. John Bassett interview.

57. Keeble interviews, 17 August 1993 and 7 November 1998.

58. NAC, BBG Hearing, 23 February 1966, *Transcript of Evidence*, 64.

59. Ibid., 65.

60. Ibid., 66.

61. Ibid., 67, 58.

62. Ibid., 70.

63. Ibid.

64. Chercover interview, 3 March 1992 and BBG Hearing, 23 February 1966, 71–72.

65. NAC, BBG Hearing, 23 February 1966, *Transcript of Evidence*, 72–73.

66. Wallace Clement, *The Canadian Corporate Elite: An Analysis of Economic Power* (Toronto: McClelland & Stewart, 1975), 263.

67. NAC, BBG hearing, 23 February 1966, *Transcript of Evidence*, 212, 217, 230, and *The Globe and Mail*, 24 February 1966.

68. NAC, BBG hearing, 23 February 1966, 227–29.

69. Ibid., 124–25.

70. Keeble papers, *Toronto Daily Star*, 5 March 1966.

71. Keeble and Hind-Smith interviews, 7 November 1998.

72. Esaw manuscript, Draft #2, Chapter 12, "The Boom Years," 20.

73. Hind-Smith papers, G.F. Keeble to Michael Hind-Smith, 2 December 1966.

74. Hind-Smith interview, 7 November 1998 and Chercover interview, 31 July 1996.

75. Hind-Smith papers, Murray Chercover to Michael Hind-Smith, 29 November 1966 and Hind-Smith interview.

76. Hind-Smith interview and Hind-Smith papers, "Statement—Michael Hind-Smith," 5 December 1966 and "High Wire," 10.

77. Keeble interview, 7 November 1998.

78. Hind-Smith papers, "Statement—Michael Hind-Smith," 5 December 1966, 2.

79. Chercover interview, 31 July 1996.

80. Hind-Smith papers, *Toronto Telegram,* 6 December 1966 and *Toronto Star,* 7 December 1966.

81. Vancouver Public Library, *Vancouver Province,* 4 June 1985.

82. Chercover interview, 31 July 1996.

83. John Bassett interview.

84. Chercover interview, 31 July 1996.

85. Ibid.

86. MacDonald interview.

87. Interview, Bruce Phillips, 21 April 1993.

88. Ibid.

89. Ron Base, "Television: How are things going at CTV? OI! Don't Ask!" *Maclean's,* 3 November, 1975, 74.

90. Chercover interview, 31 July 1996. See also *Variety* newspaper, 1 October 1986, 87, 104. The edition of *Variety,* a show business newspaper, contains a special section on the 25th anniversary of the CTV network.

91. CTV Television Network Limited, Toronto, Canadian Radio-television and Telecommunications Commission Hearing into CTV Licence Renewal, Hull, 18 November 1986, *Transcript of Evidence,* Volume 2, 192–93.

92. John Bassett interview.

93. Peters interview.

94. Ibid.

95. Chercover interview, 31 July 1996.

96. John Bassett interview.

97. Chercover interview, 31 July 1996.

98. Esaw interview, 30 July 1996.

99. Chercover interview, 31 July 1996.

100. Ibid.

101. Keeble interview, 7 November 1998 and Keeble papers, J.R. Peters to Murray Chercover, 25 September 1967.

102. Keeble papers, Gordon Keeble to J.R. Peters, 29 September 1967.

103. Peters interview.

104. Keeble papers, Keeble to Peters, 29 September 1967.

105. Ibid.

106. Keeble interview, 7 November 1998.

107. MacDonald interview.

108. Keeble interview, 7 November 1998.

109. Interview, Murray Chercover, 31 July 1996.

110. Keeble papers, *Toronto Daily Star,* 5 March 1966.

111. See Kirck with Rowland, *Nobody Calls Me,* 135, 1 and Barbara A. Moes, "Harvey Kirck, the newsman's newsman," *Broadcaster* 42 (December 1983): 9–10.

112. MacDonald interview.

113. Ibid.

114. Stewart and Hull, *Canadian Television Policy,* 159.

4 "In Colour, the *CTV National News*": 1962–1972

1. Chercover interview, 3 March 1992.

2. Phillips interview.

3. *The London Free Press,* 19 September 1991, C7 and CTV application to the Canadian Radio-television and Telecommunications Commission, *CTV 24 Hour News: Executive Summary and Supplementary Brief,* 1993, 7.

4. Canada, *Report of the Special Senate Committee on Mass Media, The Uncertain Mirror,* 211.

5. Kirck with Rowland, *Nobody Calls Me,* 127.

6. CTV Television Network Ltd. Archives (Toronto), CTV Television Network, Program Schedule, Draft No. 9, 28 August 1962. The 15-minute newscast at 10:30 p.m. was followed by ten minutes of local news on affiliated stations. The entertainment program *Network* followed from 10:55 p.m. to 11:20 p.m., and interview, Larry Henderson, 16 January 1990.

7. Canada, *Good, Bad, or Simply Inevitable? Research Studies for the Special Senate Committee on Mass Media* (Davey Committee), Volume III (Ottawa: Queen's Printer, 1970), 6.

8. Brown interview and Bill McNeil and Wolfe, *Signing On,* 225. For a discussion of the early days of Canadian private radio and Charles Jennings's role as a broadcaster, see Michael Nolan, "An Infant Industry: Canadian Private Radio, 1919–36," *Canadian Historical Review* LXX (December 1989): 496–518.

9. Brown interview.

10. "BROADCASTING: Two at Eleven," *Time: The Weekly Newsmagazine,* vol. 82, 19 July 1963, 12. See also, *The Ottawa Sun,* 12 March 1991, 30.

11. *Time,* 19 July 1963, 12.

12. Ibid.

13. CTV Television Network Ltd., Archives (Toronto), four-page brochure, "Memo to: All ACA Members and Delegates," Toronto, 1962.

14. Pierre Maple, "Canadian Report," *TV Guide,* vol. 12, 25 January 1964, 22–2.

15. CTV Television Network Ltd., Archives, one-page promotional material for the 1964–65 season, "*CTV National News.*" This material features pictures of the four network anchormen.

16. Interview, Brian Nolan, 2 June 1994.

17. Ibid.

18. *The Ottawa Sun*, 12 March 1991, "30 Great Years," Special Thirtieth Anniversary Pullout, 31.

19. *The Globe and Mail*, 22 November 1986.

20. Nolan interview.

21. Robert Black papers (privately held), News Release from CJOH, "A New Type of Political Show Begins," 11 January 1963.

22. Ibid.

23. Ibid.

24. Ibid., CTV Television Network Ltd. (Toronto), Release, "Spontaneous Political Debate New CTV Weekly Program," 30 January 1963.

25. Ibid., CTV Television Network Ltd. (Toronto), "Platform Moves to Prime Time: Replaces Telepoll on Network," 5 April 1963.

26. Ibid., CJOH television script of 1 July 1963 program on Canada's Centennial.

27. Ibid.

28. Nolan interview.

29. For a discussion of the circumstances surrounding the move of the news to Toronto, see Kirck and Rowland, *Nobody Calls Me,* 145–53.

30. Knowlton Nash, *Prime Time at Ten: Behind-the-Camera Battles of Canadian TV Journalism* (Toronto: McClelland and Stewart, 1987), 23.

31. Interview, Harvey Kirck, 13 August 1996.

32. Kirck with Rowland, *Nobody Calls Me,* 148.

33. Nolan interview.

34. CTV Television Network Limited (Toronto), CTV Research and Archives section, Description of the first CTV colour broadcast, 8/31/66; title: CTV colour preview (1966); item number: 0045429.

35. Rehak papers, "Notes about W_5," 6 November 1996, 2 and interview, 12 March 1998.

36. Isabel LeBourdais, *The Trial of Steven Truscott* (Toronto: McClelland and Stewart, 1966).

37. John Saywell, ed., *Canadian Annual Review for 1966* (Toronto: University of Toronto Press, 1966), 423–24. The Mass Media section of the *Review* was written by Wilfred Kesterton.

38. Interview, Ken Cavanagh, 29 October 1999.

39. Hind-Smith interview.

40. Maclean's, *Canada's Century: An Illustrated History of the People and Events That Shaped Our Identity* (Toronto: Key Porter Books, 1999), 304. *Seven Days* was on CBC television from 4 October 1964 to 8 May 1966.

41. Cavanagh interview.

42. Vancouver Public Library, *The Globe and Mail*, 25 June 1966.

43. Interview, Bill Cunningham, 28 October 1999.

44. Cavanagh interview.

45. Jon Ruddy, "The Canadian Report," *TV Guide*, vol. 15 (11 February 1967): 18–1.

46. John Bassett interview.

47. Ibid.

48. *The Globe and Mail,* 16 March 1977.

49. Interview, Hazel Desbarats, 2 May 2001.

50. Robert Fulford, "Reilly was always worth the trouble," *Saturday Night* (May 1977): 10.

51. *The Globe and Mail,* 7 December 1966 and interview, Charles Templeton, 14 August 1996.

52. Templeton interview.

53. Ibid.

54. Ibid.

55. Kirck with Rowland, *Nobody Calls Me,* 152.

56. Kirck interview.

57. Interview, Peter Kent, 29 August 1997.

58. Templeton interview.

59. *The Globe and Mail,* 2 September 1967.

60. Templeton interview.

61. Ibid.

62. *The Globe and Mail,* 11 September 1967.

63. Kirck with Rowland, *Nobody Calls Me,* 155–56.

64. Templeton interview.

65. Kirck interview.

66. For details of CTV's coverage of the King assassination and the Liberal convention, see Kirck and Rowland, *Nobody Calls Me,* 160–61, and Charles Templeton, *Charles Templeton: An Anecdotal Memoir* (Toronto: McClelland and Stewart, 1983), 142–46.

67. Kirck interview.

68. *The Toronto Star,* 6 June 2001

69. Kirck and Rowland, *Nobody Calls Me,* 168–71.

70. *The Financial Post,* 14 and 7 December 1968.

71. Phillips interview.

72. Ibid.

73. Kent interview.

74. NAC, Canadian Broadcasting Corporation Records, RG 41, Volume 831, file 192 (pt. 1), "National News," Knowlton Nash to M. Munro, 16 February 1970.

75. Ibid., CBC records, Volume 831, file 192 (pt. 2), "National News," Knowlton Nash to John Kerr, 7 October 1970.

76. Ibid., CBC Records, Volume 831, file, 192 (pt. 3), "National News," Knowlton Nash to Mr. P. Trueman, Head Daily News & Information—TV, 26 March 1971.

77. Ibid., Peter Trueman to Knowlton Nash, Director Information Programs, 21 May 1971.

78. Ibid.

79. Ibid., CBC Records, Volume 832, file 200 News—News, Knowlton Nash to Denis Harvey, 22 February 1973.

5 *Telepoll, Laugh-In* and *Wide World of Sports:* 1962–1972

1. Canada, CRTC Public Announcement, *Decision CRTC 73–44,* Ottawa, 22 January 1973.

2. Ibid., 1, 4.

3. Broadcast House, CFRN-TV, Edmonton, historical files, CTV Press Release, "CTV Television Network Ltd. Linked from Coast to Coast," 9 January 1974.

4. CTV Television Network Ltd., Archives, Toronto, CTV Colour Preview (1966), item number 0045429, 31 August 1966 and Weinthal interview.

5. CTV Archives, CTV Colour Preview, 31 August 1966.

6. *Report of the Committee on Broadcasting,* 1965, 236.

7. Weinthal interview.

8. Gordon Keeble papers (privately held), "*Proposal—(Confidential),* To: The Affiliates," 4 October 1962, 20.

9. The BBG's "Regulations Governing Television" are cited in Stewart and Hull, *Canadian Television Policy,* 29.

10. Weinthal interview.

11. CTV Television Network Ltd., Archives (Toronto), "Memo to: All ACA Members and Delegates," Toronto, 1962.

12. Ibid.

13. Weinthal interview.

14. Ibid.

15. Canada, House of Commons, Standing Committee on Communications and Culture, *Minutes of Proceedings and Evidence* (Toronto, 1987), No. 65, 4 November 1987, 65:58.

16. Weinthal interview.

17. In November, 1999, John Carpenter, a 31-year-old Internal Revenue Service employee, won a million dollars on the ABC television program, *Who Wants to Be a Millionaire?* hosted by Regis Philbin when he named Nixon as the president who had appeared on *Laugh-In.*

18. Interview, Philip Wedge, 13 April 1994.

19. Alex Barris, *The Pierce-Arrow Showroom Is Leaking: An Insider's View of the CBC* (Toronto: Ryerson Press, 1969), 195–96.

20. Wedge interview.

21. CBC English Networks/Communications, Toronto, "CBC-TV Weekly Program Schedule, 1972–73." The author wishes to thank Sandy Homewood for providing CBC program schedules; and Sandy Stewart, *Here's Looking at Us: A Personal History of Television in Canada* (Toronto: CBC Enterprises, 1986), 72.

22. Weinthal interview.

23. Esaw manuscript, Draft #2, Chapter 1A, "Syrian or Assyrian?" 1–2.

24. Ibid., 5, 12.

25. Ibid., Chapter 3, "Portage and Main," 1.

26. Ibid., Chapter 2, "Regina and On," 3 and interview, Johnny Esaw, 25 May 1999.

27. Ibid., Chapter 4, "CFTO/CTV: The Beginning," 1–2.

28. Ibid., 2–3.

29. Ibid., Chapter 4, 18.

30. Ibid., 19.

31. Ibid., Chapter 5, "Figure Skating or Fancy Skating," 2, 4.

32. Ibid., 6.

33. Ibid.

34. Ibid., 7.

35. Ibid., 8.

36. Ibid., 9.

37. Curtis Stock, "Ice man: Sports visionary Johnny Esaw put figure skating on national television 35 years ago—and watched the ratings soar," *TV Times/The London Free Press*, 16 March to 22 March 1996, 3.

38. CTV Television Network Ltd., Archives (Toronto), network promotional material, *Wide World of Sports* brief, 2. The brief was not numbered; the author assigned a number to each page.

39. Ibid., network records of participation rate schedules, *CTV's Wide World of Sports*, Participation Rate Schedule for 1965–66, effective 18 September 1965.

40. Ibid., CTV *Wide World of Sports* brief, 4.

41. Ibid.

42. Ibid., 5.

43. Ibid., 5–6.

44. Ibid., 6 and 8–10.

45. Esaw interview, 30 July 1996.

46. Ibid.

47. Esaw manuscript, Chapter 7, "*Sports Hot Seat* Which Ali Helped Make Great," 1, 7.

48. Ibid., 3.

49. Ibid., and Esaw interview, 30 July 1996.

50. Esaw interview, 30 July 1996.

51. Ibid.

52. Ibid.

53. Ibid.

54. Esaw manuscript, Chapter 10, "Canada-Russia Hockey, 1972," 1.

55. Ibid., Chapter 6, "Female Athletes," 2–3, and *The London Free Press*, 23 November 1999.

56. Esaw manuscript, Chapter 4, 14.

57. Ibid.

58. Ibid.

59. *The Ottawa Sunday Sun*, 11 December 1994.

60. Ibid., and Esaw manuscript, Chapter 4, 16.

61. *The Ottawa Sunday Sun*, 11 December 1994.

62. Underhill, "Notes on the Massey Report," 273.

63. Esaw interview, 30 July 1996.

6   *Canada AM*, the Arrival of Lloyd and a Short-lived *CTV Reports*:
1972–1979

1. Kirck interview and interview, Don Newman, 28 April 1995.

2. Interview, Michael Maclear, 16 December 1999.

3. *The London Free Press*, 19 September 1991 and CTV Television Network Ltd. (Toronto), Application to the Canadian Radio-television and Telecommunications Commission, *CTV 24 Hour News: Executive Summary and Supplementary Brief*, 7, accompanying letter from Eric Morrison, Vice-President, News, 8 December 1993.

4. NAC, RG100, C44, microfilm M-3103, CRTC Hearing, Application by CTV Network for Renewal of broadcasting licence, Toronto, *Transcript of Proceedings*, 7 November 1972, 53.

5. Peters interview.

6. NAC, RG100, C44, CTV Licence Renewal, Toronto, *Transcript of Proceedings*, 63.

7. Interview, Carole Taylor, 21 April 1999.

8. Ibid.

9. Ibid.

10. Ibid.

11. Margaret Trudeau, *Beyond Reason* (New York and London: Paddington Press, 1979), 175.

12. Taylor interview.

13. Ibid.

14. Ibid.

15. Kirck interview.

16. Ibid., and interview, Lloyd Robertson, 13 March 1998.

17. Kirck interview.

18. Robertson interview.

19. Kirck interview.

20. Ibid., and Robertson interview.

21. Kirck interview.

22. "CTV News, Taking on the Mother Corp," *Broadcaster* 50 (October 1991): 12.

23. *The Financial Post*, 25 June 1992.

24. *The Globe and Mail*, 16 September 1976.

25. Ibid., 17 September 1976.

26. Ibid.

27. Ibid., 24 September 1976.

28. Barbara Righton, "It takes two: Canada's top news anchor, Lloyd Robertson, passes the mantle to Keith Morrison. But he isn't ready to throw in the towel—just yet," *TV times*, 30 July–5 August 1994, 10.

29. Don Newman interview.

30. Ibid.

31. Ibid.

32. Canada, Canadian Radio-television and Telecommunications Commis-

sion, *Decision CRTC 76–395*, Ottawa, 5 July 1976, 5–6.

33. Ibid., 6.

34. Ibid., 4.

35. Ibid.

36. Maclear interview.

37. Peter Trueman, *Smoke & Mirrors: The Inside Story of Television News in Canada* (Toronto: McClelland and Stewart, 1980), 91.

38. Interview, Andrew Cochrane, 29 August 1996.

39. Maclear interview.

40. Ibid.

41. Ibid., and CRTC Public Hearing, CBC English television licence renewal, "Canadian Broadcasting Corporation English Television Network Presentation to CRTC," Denis Harvey Vice-President, 15 October 1986, 3. The author wishes to thank Denis Harvey for providing the CBC material relating to the 1986 hearing.

42. Maclear interview.

43. Ibid.

44. Ibid.

45. Cochrane interview.

46. Ibid.

47. Peters interview.

48. Ibid.

49. John Ruttle, "News Wars in the Nation's Capital: CBOT takes aim at the audience of top station CJOH," *Broadcaster* 49 (February 1990): 25.

50. Baton Broadcasting Incorporated (Toronto), Annual Report 1995, 9.

51. McQueen interview.

52. Walter I. Romanow, Stuart H. Surlin and Walter C. Soderlund, "Analysis of local TV News Broadcasts," Report to the Task Force on Broadcasting Policy, University of Windsor, January 1986, 84.

53. Sheri Craig, "Industry is changing, Camu warns broadcasters," *Marketing* (11 October 1976): 4.

54. Ron Base, "Television: The compounding of the Global disaster," *Maclean's* (17 November 1975): 80.

55. Ibid.

56. Nolan interview.

57. Ibid.

58. Base, "Television: The compounding," 80.

7   CTV Scores! 1972–1979

1. *The London Free Press*, 16 November 1999.

2. *The Globe and Mail*, 29 September 1972.

3. Esaw manuscript, Draft #2, Chapter 10, "Canada-Russia Hockey 1972," 1.

4. *The London Free Press*, 3 December 1999.

5. For details of the charges against Eagleson, see Jane O'Hara, "In the Name of Greed," *Maclean's*, 19 January 1998, 22–26.

6. Esaw manuscript, Chapter 10, 2.

7. Ibid.

8. Ibid., and Chapter 8, "Hockey Memories," 5.

9. Esaw manuscript, Chapter 10, 3, 5 and Chapter 9, "Bunny Ahearne, International Hockey," 7.

10. Esaw manuscript, Chapter 10, 6.

11. Ibid., 7.

12. Esaw interview, 30 July 1996.

13. Esaw manuscript, Chapter 10, 7.

14. Ibid.

15. Ibid.

16. Ibid., 9.

17. Ibid., and 15.

18. Ibid., 13.

19. Ibid., 14.

20. Ibid., 15.

21. Ibid., 12.

22. Ibid.

23. *The London Free Press*, 16 November 1999.

24. Esaw manuscript, Chapter 10, 19.

25. *The London Free Press*, 16 November 1999.

26. Esaw manuscript, Chapter 10, 19 and Jack Ludwig, "1972 Team Canada in War and Peace," Maclean's, *Canada's Century: An Illustrated History of the People and Events That Shaped Our Identity*, selected and introduced by Carl Mollins (Toronto: Key Porter Books, 1999), 90.

27. John Bassett interview.

28. NAC, RG100, C44, microfilm M–3103, CRTC Hearing into Application by CTV for Renewal of Broadcasting Licence Expiring September 30, 1973, *Transcript of Proceedings*, 7 November 1972, 64–66.

29. Ibid., 66–69.

30. Ibid., 90–92.

31. Peters interview.

32. BCTV archives, Vancouver, interviews of personalities dealing with the history of BCTV, material written by Mark Leiren-Young. The material was sent to the author.

33. *Vancouver Province*, 22 September 1973.

34. "ATV: From an alternative to number 1," *Marketing*, 21 November 1977, 47–48.

35. *Financial Post*, 1 May 1976.

36. Ibid.

37. Ibid., 6 May 1978.

38. Weinthal interview and Canada, CRTC, *Decision CRTC 76–395*, Ottawa, 5 July 1976, 2.

39 Weinthal interview.

40. Ibid.

41. NAC, RG 100, C44, M–3103, CRTC hearing into CTV licence renewal, *Transcript of Proceedings*, 7 November 1972, 21–22.

42. Canada, CRTC, *Decision 76–395*, 5 July 1976, 2.

43. Canada, CRTC, Ottawa, *Decision CRTC 79–453*, 3 August 1979, 4.

44. Coleman papers, "*JTC*, CTV Corp Docs.," 3–4. The records were given to the author by Coleman following an interview.

45. Ibid., 5.

46. CRTC Public Examination Room, C.T.V. Television Network Limited, Box-1411 in Records, Volume 13, Examination file, "Re: *Application for Renewal of License—CTV Television Network Ltd. (751072000)*, Murray H. Chercover to Mr. J.G. Patenaude, 25 September 1978, 1. The network was granted a new licence—781895800—on 3 August 1979 until 30 September 1982.

47. Ibid., Chercover to Patenaude, 2.

48. Ibid., 3.

49. University of Windsor, The Centre for Canadian Communications Studies, *A study of* The Independent Production Industry *with respect to English Language Programs for Broadcast in Canada with recommendations for policy action*, Volume 1 (April 1976), 17, 100–101.

50. CRTC Public Examination Room, CTV *Application for Renewal of Licence*, Chercover to Patenaude, 25 September 1978, 4.

51. Ibid., 3.

52. Ibid., 4.

53. Ibid.

54. Ibid., 5.

55. Ibid., 7.

56. Canada, *Report of the Federal Cultural Policy Review Committee*, Applebert Report (Ottawa: Information Services, Department of Communications, Government of Canada, 1982), 280.

8 The Dominator Retaliates: 1979–1985

1. John Bassett interview.

2. Beattie interview.

3. Canada, *Report of the Special Senate Committee on Mass Media*, 71.

4. Ibid., 93.

5. Canada, Canadian Radio-television and Telecommunications Commission, *Decision CRTC 78–669*, Ottawa, 12 October 1978, 3.

6. Ibid., 3.

7. Ibid., 7–8.

8. Ibid., 14.

9. *Financial Post,* 21 October 1978.

10. John Bassett interview.

11. Ibid.

12. Ibid.

13. Ibid., and interview, Pierre Camu, 15 September 2000

14. John Bassett interview.

15. Ibid.

16. Ibid.

17. Ibid.

18. Camu interview.

19. "The Television Revolution and the National Interest," Walter Gordon lecture delivered by Alphonse Ouimet, University of Western Ontario, 25 March 1979, 3–4.

20. CRTC Public Examination Room, C.T.V. Television Network Limited, licence renewal (application number 781895800), Volume 14, IT–2139–2043, Examination file, 1978–1979, "Association of Canadian Television and Radio Artists: A Submission to the Canadian Radio-Television and Telecommunications Commission," Ottawa, 28 November 1978, 3.

21. Ibid., 6.

22. Ibid., 7.

23. Ibid., 8.

24. Ibid., 8.

25. Ibid., 9.

26. Ibid., 10.

27. CRTC Public Examination Room, C.T.V. Television Network Limited, Volume 14, IT–2139–2043, Examination File, 1978–1979, "*The Association of Canadian Television and Radio Artists*," 3.

28. Ibid., 7.

29. Ibid., 2.

30. Ibid., 5–6, 12.

31. Canada, *Telecommunications and Canada: Consultative Committee on the Implications of Telecommunications for Canadian Sovereignty*, Clyne Committee Report (Hull: Minister of Supply and Services Canada, 1979), 33.

32. Ibid., 43–44.

33. Ibid., 38–39.

34. Canadian Conference of the Arts, *A Strategy for Culture* (Ottawa: Canadian Conference of the Arts, 1980), 140–41.

35. Canada, Canadian Radio-television and Telecommunications Commission, *Decision CRTC 79–453* (Ottawa, 3 August 1979), 4.

36. Ibid.

37. [1982] 1. S.C.R. 531, 134 D.L. R. (3d) 193.

38. "*Canadian Television's 'Game Scenarios' for the Nineties*," A Private Perspective developed by John Travers Coleman, 4. The author wishes to thank John Coleman for allowing me the use of his paper.

39. Canadian Radio-television and Telecommunications Commission, Information, "Just and Old Sweet Song: Canadian Content on my Mind": Notes for an address by John Meisel, Chairman, Canadian Radio-television and Telecommunications Commission at the Broadcast Executives Society, Toronto, 11 May 1982, 3.

40. CRTC, Information, Notes for an address by John Meisel, Chairman, Canadian Radio-television and Telecommunications Commission at the Canadian Film and Television Association (an edited transcript of remarks), Toronto, 15 April 1982, 7.

41. Canada, *Report of the Federal Cultural Policy Review Committee,* Applebert Report (Information Services, Department of Communications, Government of Canada, January 1982), 282–83.

42. Canada, CRTC, Notice CRTC 83–18, "Policy Statement on Canadian Content in Television," Ottawa, 31 January 1983, 6, 18.

43. Ibid., 20, 26.

44. Canada, Department of Communications, "Towards a New National Broadcasting Policy," Policy proposals for consultation, Private Sector Thrust (Ottawa: Government of Canada, Department of Communications, 1 March 1983).

45. Weinthal interview.

46. Ibid.

47. Stewart, *Here's Looking at Us,* 187.

48. John Coleman papers, network material was provided to the author. The author wishes to thank Mr. Coleman for the material.

49. Ibid.

50. Weinthal interview.

51. Coleman papers, network material provided to the author, "CTV Television Network Comparisons: 1979/1980–1986/87 Period To 1987/88–1991/1992."

52. Weinthal interview.

53. *The Globe and Mail,* 6 January 1981.

54. Canada, *Report of the Task Force on Broadcasting Policy,* Caplan-Sauvageau Report (Ottawa: Minister of Supply and Services Canada, 1986), 607.

55. Coleman interview.

56. Ibid.

57. Ibid.

58. Dennis W. Jeanes, "The Changing Face of TV News: Canadians will have to decide whether they want to be entertained or informed," *TV Guide* (14 November 1981): 13 and Coleman papers provided to the author, "CTV Television Network Ltd. 1970/71 vs. 1980/81 Average Program Cost Per Hour Comparison For Regular Programming."

59. David Frum, "MEDIA: The Nelson Affair," *Saturday Night* (April 1984) 17, 20.

60. Kent interview and Kirck with Rowland, *Nobody Calls Me,* 218–19.

61. Morris Wolfe, "Television: Good news, bad news, slick news," *Saturday Night* (June 1980): 51.

62. *National Post,* 9 October 1999.

9   Chairman Bureau Gets Tough: 1985–1990

1. Canada, *Report of the Task Force on Broadcasting Policy* (Ottawa: Minister of Supply and Services Canada, 1986), 703.

2. Ibid., 729.

3. Ibid., 117.

4. Ibid., 454.

5. Canada, House of Commons, Standing Committee on Communications and Culture, *Minutes of Proceedings and Evidence*, No. 64, 3 November 1987, 64:131.

6. Ibid.

7. Weinthal interview.

8. CTV Television Network Limited, Toronto, CRTC Public Hearing into Application by CTV for licence renewal, Hull, Quebec, *Transcript of Evidence,* Volume 1, 17 November 1986, 4, 7.

9. Ibid., 60.

10. Ibid., 69, 64–65.

11. Ibid., 73–74.

12. Ibid., 84, 87.

13. Ibid., 89, 95, 93, 92.

14. Ibid., 133 and Volume 2, 18 November 1986, 463, 466.

15. Peters interview.

16. CRTC, Public Examination Room, CTV Television Network Limited, licence renewal (number 861468700), 17 November 1986, Volume 17, file 00TN09, section 2, "Alternative Ownership Structures for CTV: A Discussion Paper for the Board of Directors," April, 1986, 3.

17. Peters interview.

18. Ibid.

19. Interview, Peter O'Neill, 13 April 1994.

20. Peters interview.

21. CRTC Public Hearing into Application by CTV for licence renewal, *Transcript of Evidence*, Volume 1, 161–62, 164.

22. Ibid., 166–68.

23. Ibid., 169–70.

24. Ibid., Volume 2, 211.

25. Ibid., 212.

26. Ibid., 213–14.

27. Ibid., Volume 3, 19 November 1986, 785.

28. Ibid., 766–68.

29. CRTC Public Examination Room, CTV Television Network Licence Renewal Hearing, Volume 14, File 00TN09, 17 November 1986, Canadian Film & Television Association/Association Canadienne De Cinema-Television, Intervention relating to the application of CTV Television Network Ltd., 28 October 1986, 13–14, 22, 27.

30. Canada, Canadian Radio-television and Telecommunications Commission, Ottawa, 24 March 1987, *Decision CRTC 87–200*, 13, 12.

31. Ibid., 18.

32. Rehak interview.

33. Kirck interview.

34. "CTV in the spotlight," *Broadcaster* 46 (May 1987): 8.

35. Ibid.

36. Kirck interview.

37. Ibid.

38. Baton Broadcasting Incorporated, CRTC Public Hearing into an application by Nation's Capital Incorporated to acquire the licence of CJOH-TV, Ottawa, Hull, Quebec, *Transcript of Evidence*, Volume 2, 27 January 1988, 356–57.

39. Ibid., 360.

40. Ibid., 361.

41. Ibid., Volume 1, 26 January 1988, 141–42.

42. Ibid., Volume 2, 362–63.

43. Ibid., Volume 1, 143–44.

44. Ibid., Volume 2, 378, 428–29.

45. Canada, CRTC, *Decision CRTC 88–275*, Ottawa, 8 April 1988, 27–29.

46. John Howse, "A Beaming Effort," *Maclean's* (29 February 1988): 27.

47. Esaw manuscript, Chapter 13, "Olympic Dollars and Sense," 9.

48. Ibid., 5.

49. Ibid., and Esaw interview, 30 July 1996.

50. Esaw interview, 30 July 1996.

51. Esaw manuscript, Chapter 13, 9–10.

52. Ibid., 12 and Esaw interview, 30 July 1996.

53. Esaw interview, 30 July 1996.

54. Esaw manuscript, Chapter 13, 12 and Esaw interview, 30 July 1996.

55. Esaw manuscript, Chapter 13, 12.

56. Ibid., 14 and Esaw interview, 30 July 1996.

57. Interview, Eric Morrison, 16 December 1999.

58. Ibid.

59. Ibid.

60. Transcript of Eric Morrison's address to the "Round Table" Rideau Club, Ottawa, 1 May 1996, 8. The transcript was sent to the author.

61. Mansbridge interview.

62. CRTC, Public Examination Room, CTV Television Network Licence Renewal (Number 93068200), Volume 4, File number 7240–00TN09–X, dated from 27–09–93 to—, CTV Licence Renewal Application, "1987–1993—The Past Licence Term," 7.

63. Weinthal interview.

64. Ibid.

65. Ibid.

66. John M. Cassaday, "Surviving in Tough Times," *The 1992 Toronto Star Lecture on Media Management*, delivered at the Graduate School of Journalism, The University of Western Ontario, London, Ontario, 23 October 1992, 6.

10 The Soup Salesman Cometh: 1990–1993

1. Interview, John Cassaday, 7 March 1995.

2. Ibid.

3. Ibid.

4. Beattie interview.

5. Interview, Doug Holtby, 22 April 1999.

6. Interview, John Cassaday, 23 March 1995 and Cassaday, "Surviving in Tough Times," 5 and *The Globe and Mail*, 12 February 1990.

7. Cassaday interview, 23 March 1995.

8. Ibid.

9. Ibid., and John Bassett interview.

10. Cassaday interview, 23 March 1995.

11. CTV Television Network Ltd., Canadian Radio-television and Telecommunications Commission, Public Hearing, CTV licence renewal, Application number 930682000, Hull, Quebec, *Transcript of Evidence,* Volume 1, 27 September 1993, 147–48.

12. Ibid., 150.

13. Ibid., 35–36, 23–24.

14. Cassaday interview, 23 March 1995.

15. CTV Television Network Ltd., CRTC Public Hearing, CTV Licence renewal, *Transcript of Evidence*, Volume 1, 27 September 1993, 43–44.

16. Cassaday interview, 23 March 1995.

17. Ibid.

18. Ibid.

19. Ibid.

20. Ibid.

21. Ibid.

22. Interview, Valerie Pringle, 25 May 1999.

23. Ibid., and see *The Globe and Mail*, 28 June 2001.

24. Interview, Sandie Rinaldo, 28 October 1999.

25. Ibid.

26. Ibid.

27. *The Globe and Mail*, 28 April 1999.

28. Rinaldo interview.

29. Interview, Craig Oliver, 27 April 1995.

30. Robertson interview.

31. Rehak interview.

32. Ibid., and Cunningham interview.

33. Rehak interview.

34. Ibid.

35. Linda McQuaig, *Shooting the Hippo: Death by Deficit and Other Canadian Myths* (Toronto: Penguin Books, 1995), 4–5.

36. Cunningham interview.

37. Ibid.

38. Rehak interview.

39. "Passages," *Maclean's*, 12 October 1998, 11. For a look at Malling's career, see John Beresford, "The Last Days of Eric Malling: The spectacular rise and drunken fall of a great contrarian," *Ryerson Review of Journalism* (Summer 2000): 42–47.

40. *The London Free Press*, 3 February 1993.

41. Ibid.

42. Jim McElgunn, "Ratings Rising at CTV News," *Marketing*, 21/28 December 1992, 2.

43. Mansbridge interview.

44. Interview, Pamela Wallin, 13 August 1996.

45. Interview, Tony Burman, 12 March 1998.

46. Interview, Tim Kotcheff, 28 August 1997.

47. CRTC Public Examination Room, CTV licence renewal, application number 930682000, Volume 4, file 7240–00TN09–X, dated from 27–09–93 to—, Executive Summary, "Table of Contents," 9–10.

48. CRTC, Public Examination Room, CTV licence renewal, Intervention submitted by the Friends of Canadian Broadcasting, "CTV Television Network Licence Renewal: Public Hearing 1993–7" 27 September 1993, 1.

49. CRTC, Public Hearing, CTV licence renewal, *Transcript of Proceedings*, Volume 1, 27 September 1993, 73, 155.

50. Canada, CRTC, Decision 94–33, Ottawa, 9 February 1994, 3.

51. Ibid., 4.

52. Ibid., 5.

53. CTV Television Network Ltd. (Toronto), Affiliation Agreement between CTV Television Network Ltd. and CFTO-TV Limited, Nation's Capital Television Incorporated, Mid-Canada Communications (Canada) Corp., and STN Television Network Incorporated, Dated as of the 1st of September, 1993, 11.

54. Cassaday interview, 23 March 1995.

55. CRTC, Decision 94–33, 5–6.

56. Cassaday interview, 23 March 1995. See also *The Financial Post*, 17 February 1992 and *The Globe and Mail*, 7 February 1992.

57. Interview, John Cassaday, 16 December 1999.

58. *The Globe and Mail*, 28 August 1999.

59. Holtby interview.

60. Ibid.

61. Ibid.

62. Douglas Bassett, 24 March 1997.

63. Holtby interview.

64. Ibid.

65. *The Globe and Mail*, 7 February 1992.

66. Douglas Bassett interview.

67. CRTC, Public Hearing, CTV licence renewal, *Transcript of Evidence*, Volume 1, 27 September 1993, 54.

68. Ibid., 56.

69. Ibid., 92–93.

70. Ibid., 82–83.

71. Canada, CRTC, *Decision CRTC 92–442*, 3 July 1992, 1 and *Decision CRTC 87–200*, 24 March 1987, 12.

72. CRTC Public Hearing, CTV licence renewal, *Transcript of Evidence*, Volume 1, 27 September 1993, 179.

73. Ibid., 186.

74. Ibid., 187–89.

75. Ibid., 192.

76. Canada, Canadian Radio-Television and Telecommunications Commission, *CTV Television Network Ltd.*, Decision CRTC 94–33, Ottawa, 9 February 1994, 1.

77. CRTC, news release, "More Canadian Entertainment Programming, Especially Drama, Key Conditions of CRTC's 5-Year Renewal of CTV's Licence," 9 February 1994, 2, 1.

78. CRTC Hearing, CTV licence renewal, *Transcript of Proceedings*, Volume 1, 27 September 1993, 33.

79. Ibid., 25–27.

11 Gordian Knot Before the Triumph of Baton: 1993–1997

1. Baton Broadcasting Inc. (Toronto), Transcript of "*Opening Remarks*: In Support of Baton Broadcasting Incorporated's Majority Control of CTV Television Network," CRTC Public Hearing, Hull, 15 July 1997, 3.

2. Cassaday interview, 16 December 1999.

3. Ibid.

4. Ibid.

5. Ibid.

6. Interview, Gary Maavara, 25 April 2001.

7. Cassaday interview, 16 December 1999.

8. Ibid.

9. Maavara interview.

10. Cassaday interview, 16 December 1999.

11. Ibid.

12. Ibid.

13. Ibid.

14. Ibid.

15. Ibid.

16. Ibid.

17. Ibid.

18. Ibid.

19. Ibid.

20. CRTC, Public Examination Room, CTV Television Network Ltd. Licence Renewal, application number 930682000, Volume 4, file number 7240–00TN09–X, dated from 27–09–93 to—, "Table of Contents," Executive Summary, "Series in Development," 47.

21. *The Globe and Mail,* 19 April 1995.

22. Weinthal interview.

23. Canada, House of Commons, Report of the Standing Committee on Canadian Heritage, *Minutes of Proceedings and Evidence*, "The Future of the Canadian Broadcasting Corporation in the Multi-Channel Universe," (June, 1995), 37–38.

24. Presentation to the House of Commons Standing Committee on Canadian Heritage by CTV Television Network Ltd., 25 October 1994, Speaking Notes for John Cassaday, 5.

25. Report of the Standing Committee on Canadian Heritage, 38.

26. *The Globe and Mail*, 27 October 1994.

27. Ibid.

28. Canada, *Making Our Voices Heard: Canadian Broadcasting and Film for the 21st Century*, Mandate Review Committee, CBC, NFB, Telefilm (Department of Canadian Heritage, Hull), 80, 79.

29. Cassaday interview, 16 December 1999 and *The Globe and Mail*, 5 September 1996.

30. Kotcheff interview.

31. Ibid.

32. Wallin interview.

33. Scott Steele, "The Perils of Pamela," *Maclean's* (17 April 1995): 28 and Wallin interview.

34. Kotcheff interview.

35. Ibid.

36. Ibid.

37. Wallin interview.

38. Kotcheff interview.

39. Mansbridge interview.

40. Marci McDonald, "Knights of the News," *Maclean's* (26 May 1997): 30–38.

41. Pringle interview.

42. *The Globe and Mail*, 4 April 1995 and *Maclean's*, "Inside Stories," (17 April 1995): 20–24, 26–28.

43. *The Globe and Mail*, 18 June 1994.

44. Pringle interview.

45. *The Globe and Mail*, 4 April 1995.

46. *Making Our Voices Heard*, 62–63.

47. Nesbitt Burns Inc. (Toronto), Tim Casey, *The Outlook for Television Broadcasters: Regionalization, Rationalization and Ratings* (12 June 1996), 4, 23.

48. Baton Broadcasting Inc. (Toronto), *"Opening Remarks:* In Support of Baton Broadcasting Incorporated's Majority Control," 7.

49. Canada, CRTC Public Examination Room, CTV Television Network Ltd. Licence Renewal, Volume 10, file 7240–00TN09, 27/09/93 to 06/10/94, Peter O'Neill to Mr. Allan Darling, 6 October 1994. The network's new voting share structure is attached as an appendix to the O'Neill letter. See also *The Globe and Mail*, 28 January 1993.

50. Canada, Canadian Radio-television and Telecommunications Commission, Decision CRTC 96–251, Ottawa, 21 June 1996, 3, 21.

51. CRTC Public Examination Room, South West Ontario Television Inc/Vancouver Television Inc/Baton Broadcasting Incorporated/ TV West Inc/BBS Ontario Incorporated, Toronto Hearing, 15 July 1997, Volume 4, File CFPL TV, IA, Re: *Baton Broadcasting Incorporated Merger with Electrohome Limited*, R.A. Fillingham to Mr. Allan J. Darling, 14 January 1997, 2, 7. The CRTC hearing into Baton's attempt to gain control of CTV was held in Hull on 15 July 1997.

52. Ibid., 7.

53. Ibid., 8.

54. Interview, Ivan Fecan, 1 May 1997.

55. Baton Broadcasting Incorporated, 1997 Annual Report, "Building for the Future," 12–15. See also Canada, CRTC, Decision CRTC 97–527, Ottawa, 28 August 1997, 10–11.

56. CRTC, Decision 97–527, 1.

57. Maavara interview.

58. Ibid.

59. Ibid.

60. Baton Broadcasting Incorporated, 1997 Annual Report, 5.

61. John Bassett interview.

62. Baton/CTV, Baton Broadcasting Incorporated Interim Report, For the three months ended 30 November 1997, *Report to the Shareholders*, 17 December 1997, and Canada, CRTC, Industry Analysis Division, chart/organigramme #107, "CTV Television."

63. CRTC, Public Hearing, 15 July 1997, *Supplementary Brief*: "Baton Broadcasting Incorporated/CHUM Limited Transactions: Transfer of CHUM Interest in the CTV Television Network Ltd. (CTV)," 1, 4.

64. Ibid., 20–21.

12 The New CTV: 1997–2001

1. Interview, Fredrik Eaton, 19 December 2000.

2. Douglas Bassett interview.

3. Canada, Canadian Radio-television and Telecommunications Commission, Decision CRTC 2001–457, 2 August 2001, paragraph 7. With reference to the CRTC hearing into licence renewals of TV stations controlled by CTV in April 2001, the Commission noted in its decision of 2 August 2001: "At the time of the public hearing, CKY-TV Winnipeg, CFCF-TV Montreal, and CJON-TV St. John's were affiliates, were owned by other parties and were not considered for renewal as part of this proceeding. In Decision CRTC 2001–460 released today, the Commission has approved an application by CTV to purchase CKY-TV Winnipeg. The Commission notes that it is currently considering an application by CTV to purchase CFCF-TV Montreal (see Public Notice CRTC 2001–77)."

4. *The Globe and Mail,* 26 February 1997.

5. Fecan interview.

6. Ibid.

7. Ibid.

8. Ibid.

9. CRTC, Public Examination Room, CTV Television Inc., Volume 13, file, 7240–00TN09–X/00, BBS Incorporated Application to acquire the assets of ASN, *Biographies of Directors and Officers, BBS Incorporated*, Mar. 30/97.

10. Eaton interview.

11. Ibid.

12. Beattie interview.

13. *National Post*, 18 December 1999.

14. McQueen interview.

15. Fecan interview.

16. Interview, Peter O'Neill, 29 October 1999.

17. Interview, Ray Hazzan, 1 November 2000.

18. Baton Broadcasting Incorporated (Scarborough), CTV Oral Presentation on the CRTC's Canadian Television Policy Review (Public Notice CRTC 1998–44), 14 October 1998, 4, 2–3.

19. Ibid.

20. Anthony Wilson-Smith, "The perils of CBC," *Maclean's*, 15 March 1999, 48.

21. "The Mail," *Maclean's*, 29 March 1999, 4.

22. "Repositioning: Year One, English TV Vice-President Ivan Fecan in conversation with Andrew Borkowski," *Scan* (May/June, 1993): 8.

23. McQueen interview.

24. Fecan interview.

25. Ibid.

26. Ibid.

27. Peters interview.

28. Fecan interview.

29. Baton Broadcasting Incorporated (Scarborough), Supplementary Brief, "Baton Broadcasting Incorporated/ CHUM Limited Transactions," 15 July 1997, CRTC hearing, 18.

30. Fecan interview.

31. Baton Broadcasting Incorporated, 1997 Annual Report, 7.

32. *The Globe and Mail*, 28 January 1998, and CRTC documents sent to the author "Re: Baton Broadcasting Incorporated ("Baton") corporate reorganization and ownership changes, Applications No: 199800371 and 199800389," Laura M. Talbot-Allan to Mrs. Kathryn Robinson, 23 January 1998.

33. Interview, James Hinds, 27 October 1999.

34. *The Globe and Mail*, 20 November 1999 and Eaton interview.

35. Eaton interview.

36. Ibid.

37. Beattie interview.

38. Matthew Bassett interview.

39. Isabel Bassett interview.

40. McQueen interview.

41. Ibid.

42. CTV Inc. 1999 Annual Report, 3, 5, and *The Globe and Mail*, 11 April 1998.

43. *The Globe and Mail*, 6 March 1998.

44. CRTC Documentation Centre (Toronto), Specialty Programming Undertaking Securities...Across Canada, CA.... 199910899, Volume 8, examination file, CTV on behalf of The Sports Network Inc. (TSN)...Hull Hearing, 6 December 1999, Schedule 10: Supplementary Brief, "CTV Acquisition of a Majority

Interest in NetStar Communications," 10, and CRTC, Decision 2000–86, Ottawa 24 March 2000, paragraph 5.

45. CTV Inc., Schedule 10: Supplementary Brief, "CTV Acquisition," 10, 6–7.

46. CRTC, Decision 2000–86, summary, paragraph 33.

47. Interview, Tim Casey, 31 October 2000.

48. *The Globe and Mail*, 19 January 2000.

49. *National Post*, 19 January 2000.

50. *The Globe and Mail*, 19 January 2000.

51. *National Post*, 19 January 2000.

52. McQueen interview.

53. *National Post*, 26 January 2000.

54. McQueen interview.

55. *The Globe and Mail*, 15 December 1999.

56. Cassaday interview, 16 December 1999.

57. Eaton interview.

58. CTV Inc. Toronto, Transcript of BCE-CTV Oral Presentation to the CRTC "Introductions and Opening Remarks" Jean Monty, 18 September 2000, 1.

59. Ibid., 4.

60. CRTC Public Examination Room, Public Hearing, Multiple Broadcasting and Ownership Applications, Volume 1, file 5440 00TR86XV100, Application by BCE to acquire CTV Inc., *Transcript of Proceedings*, 18 September 2000, 42.

61. Ibid., 42–45.

62. Ibid., 46.

63. Canada, CRTC Decision 2000–747, 7 December 2000, paragraph 39.

64. Canada, CRTC Decision 2000–221, Ottawa, 6 July 2000.

65. Canada, Canadian Radio-television and Telecommunications Commission, Public Notice CRTC 1999–97, *Building on Success: A policy framework for Canadian Television* (Ottawa, 11 June 1999).

66. Ibid., 8.

67. Ibid., 1.

68. CRTC Public Examination Room, Public Hearing, Broadcasting Applications TV Renewals—CTV/Global Across Canada, Volume 1, file 5440 00TR 93X, *Transcript of Proceedings*, 17 April 2001, 14.

69. Ibid., 15, 18–19.

70. Ibid., 20–21, 61.

71. CRTC, Decision CRTC 2001–384, Quebecor Média Inc. on behalf of Groupe TVA Inc., Ottawa, 5 July 2001, Appendix V.

72. CRTC Public Examination Room, Public Hearing, Broadcasting Applications TV Renewals—CTV/Global Across Canada, Volume 7, file 5440 00TR 93X, *Transcript of Proceedings*, 25 April 2001, 2140.

73. Ibid., 2139.

74. Ibid., 2141–42.

75. CTV News Facsimile, 20 March 2001, "CTV Station Group 2001 Licence Renewals—Deficiency Responses," *Transcript of Response* to Question 5 on cross-media ownership, page 15 of 47.

76. Canada, CRTC News release, "CRTC Renews CTV and Global's Licences—More Quality Programming and Services, Ottawa-Hull," 2 August 2001, 1–3. The *Statement of Principles and Practices* had three components: "Management of the broadcast newsrooms must be kept separate from the newspaper newsrooms. An independent neutral monitoring committee will be created to receive and handle complaints pertaining to the *Statement*. This committee will report annually to Commission on all complaints received and how they were dealt with. CTV and Global will each spend $1 million per year on promoting the committee and the *Statement of Principles and Practices.*"

77. Canada, Canadian Radio-television and Telecommunications Commission, Decision CRTC 2001–457, Ottawa, 2 August 2001, paragraph 113.

78. Casey interview.

Epilogue

1. CRTC Documentation Centre (Toronto), Specialty Programming Undertaking Securities...Across Canada, CA...199910899, Volume 8, Examination file, CTV on behalf of The Sports Network Inc. (TSN)...Hull Hearing, 6 December, 1999, Schedule 10: Supplementary Brief, "CTV Acquisition of a Majority Interest in NetStar Communications," 18, 8–9.

2. McQueen interview.

3. Fecan interview.

Appendix

1. Canada, *Report of the Committee on Broadcasting 1965* (Ottawa: Queen's Printer, 1965), 375.

2. NAC, RG 100, B49, Microfilm (Mf), M-3087, Board of Broadcast Governors hearing, CTV Television Network Ownership Transfer, Ottawa, *Transcript of Evidence*, 23 February 1966, 4.

3. Canada, CRTC Public Examination Room (Ottawa-Hull), CTV Licence Renewal Application, April 1970, Volume 4, File 6–113–340, dated 22/3/68 to 22/9/69, *Licence Renewal Application*, "Mr. Chairman—Members of the Commission." 1.

4. John Travers Coleman, "Canadian Television: 'Game Scenarios' for the nineties," A Private Perspective developed by John Travers Coleman, 17, and John Coleman Papers, JTC: CTV Corp. Docs., *CTV Television Network Ltd. And its Full Affiliates and Affiliates: Affiliation Agreement for the Period Commencing October 1, 1973*, Revised 3 November 1972, Schedule 1, *Share Capital Reorganization*, 26 September 1972.

5. *Financial Post*, 1 May 1976 and "ATV: From an alternative to number 1," *Marketing* (21 November 1977), 47.

6. Coleman Papers, JTC: CTV Corp. Docs., "Re: CTV Affiliation Agreement" 30 June 1986, 82.

7. Ibid.

8. Canada, *The Economic Status of Canadian Television: Report of the Task*

Force (Ottawa: Minister of Supply and Services, 1991), 24–25.

9. Ibid.

10. Coleman Papers, "CTV Television Network Rebroadcasting Outlets," April 1989.

11. Canada, *The Economic Status*, 25.

12. *The Globe and Mail*, 28 January 1993 and Canada, *Decision CRTC 94–33*, Ottawa, 9 February 1994; Canada, CRTC Public Examination Room (Ottawa-Hull), CTV Television Network Ltd., licence renewal 930682000, Volume 10, file 7240–00TN09, 27/09/93 to 06/10/94, Peter O'Neill to Allan Darling, 6 October 1994;

13. Ibid.

14. Canada, *Decision CRTC 97–527*.

15. Ibid.

16. *The Globe and Mail*, 5 September 1996 and Canada, *Decision CRTC 2000–86*, Ottawa, 24 March 2000.

17. Canada, *Decision CRTC 97–527*.

18. Ibid.

19. Ibid.

20. BCE, News Release, Toronto, 9 January 2001. Bell Globemedia Backgrounder, "Broadcasting: Owned CTV affiliates (18)" and *The Globe and Mail*, 16 April 2001.

21. Ibid.

22. Canada, CRTC (Ottawa-Hull), News Release, 2 August 2001, 1.

23. BCE, News Release, Toronto, 9 January 2001. Bell Globemedia Backgrounder, "Broadcasting: Owned CTV affiliates (18)" and *The Globe and Mail*, 16 April 2001.

24. Ibid.

25. *The Globe and Mail*, 7 July 2001.

26. Ibid.

27. Canada, *Decision CRTC 2001–460*, Ottawa, 2 August 2001 and Bell Globemedia, e-mail from Leah Anne Cameron to the author, 9 August 2001.

28. Ibid.

SELECTED BIBLIOGRAPHY

The main primary sources for this study have been the Spencer Caldwell papers at the National Archives of Canada, transcripts of public regulatory hearings, private collections, unpublished manuscripts, CTV corporate records and CTV files, the latter examined mostly at the CRTC's public examination room in Ottawa-Hull. In addition, the interviews listed in the Acknowledgements were most helpful. Other sources and materials used in the study are contained in the notes to each chapter.

Privately Held Sources

Robert Henry Black Papers, Ottawa
Nancy Caldwell Papers, Edmonton
John Travers Coleman Papers, Toronto
Johnny Esaw Manuscript, Toronto
Michael Hind-Smith Papers, Niagara-on-the-Lake
Gordon Keeble Papers, Niagara-on-the-Lake
Peter Rehak, "Notes on W5," Toronto

Royal Commissions, Committees and Task Force Reports

Canada. Royal Commission on Broadcasting. *Report*. Ottawa: Queen's Printer, 1957.
Canada. Royal Commission on National Development in the Arts, Letters and Sciences. *Report*. Ottawa: Queen's Printer, 1951.
Canada. Royal Commission on Radio Broadcasting. *Report*. Ottawa: King's Printer, 1929.

Canada. Making Our Voices Heard: Canadian Broadcasting and Film for the
21st Century. *Report.* Hull: Department of Canadian Heritage, 1996.
Canada. Standing Committee on Canadian Heritage, 1995. *Report.* Ottawa:
Public Works and Government Services Canada, 1995.
Canada. Federal Cultural Policy Review Committee. *Report.* Ottawa: Informa-
tion Services, Department of Communications, 1982.
Canada. Committee on Broadcasting, 1965. *Report.* Ottawa: Queen's Printer,
1965.
Canada. Task Force on Broadcasting Policy. *Report.* Ottawa: Supply and Ser-
vices Canada, 1986.

Books and Journal Articles

Allard, T.J. *Straight Up, Private Broadcasting in Canada: 1918–1958.* Ottawa:
Canadian Communications Foundation, 1979.
Babe, Robert E. "Regulation of Private Television Broadcasting by the Canadian
Radio-Television Commission: A Critique of Ends and Means." *Canadian
Public Administration* 19 (Winter 1976): 552–86.
Collins, Richard. *Culture, Communication & National Identity: The Case of
Canadian Television.* Toronto: University of Toronto Press, 1990.
Dewar, K.C. "The Origins of Public Broadcasting in Comparative Perspective."
Canadian Journal of Communication 8 (January 1982): 26–45.
Ellis, David. In collaboration with Julia Johnston. *Split/Screen: Home Enter-
tainment and the New Technologies.* Toronto: Friends of Canadian Broad-
casting, 1992.
———. *Networking: How Are Canada's English TV Networks Performing?*
Toronto: Friends of Canadian Broadcasting, 1991.
Foster, Frank. *Broadcasting Policy Development.* Ottawa: Franfost Communi-
cations Ltd., 1982.
Fraser, Matthew. *Free-For-All: The Struggle for Dominance on the Digital Fron-
tier.* Toronto: Stoddart, 1999.
Gittins, Susan. *CTV: The Television Wars.* Toronto: Stoddart, 1999.
Hull, W.H.N. "Captive or Victim? The Board of Broadcast Governors and
Berstein's Law, 1958–68." *Canadian Public Administration* 26 (Winter
1983): 544–62.
Kirck, Harvey and Wade Rowland. *Nobody Calls Me Mr. Kirck.* Toronto:
Collins, 1985.
Nash, Knowlton. *Prime Time At Ten: Behind-the-Camera Battles of Canadian
TV Journalism.* Toronto: McClelland and Stewart, 1987.
———. *The Microphone Wars: A History of Triumph and Betrayal at the CBC.*
Toronto: McClelland & Stewart, 1994.
Nolan, Michael. "Case Study in Regulation: CTV and Canadian Broadcast Pol-
icy" in Martin W. Westmacott and Hugh P. Mellon, eds., *Public Administra-
tion and Policy: Governing in Challenging Times.* Scarborough: Prentice Hall
Allyn and Bacon Canada, 1999, 126–35.

————. " An Infant Industry: Canadian Private Radio 1919–36." *Canadian Historical Review* LXX (December 1989): 496–518.

Peers, Frank W., *The Politics of Canadian Broadcasting, 1920–1951*. Toronto: University of Toronto Press, 1969.

————. *The Public Eye: Television and the Politics of Canadian Broadcasting, 1952–1968*. Toronto: University of Toronto Press, 1979.

Prang, Margaret. " The Origins of Public Broadcasting in Canada." *Canadian Historical Review* 46 (March 1965): 1–31.

Raboy, Marc. *Missed Opportunities: The Story of Canada's Broadcasting Policy*. Montreal and Kingston: McGill-Queen's University Press, 1990.

Rutherford, Paul. *When Television Was Young: Primetime Canada 1952–1967*. Toronto: University of Toronto Press, 1990.

Spry, Graham. "The Decline and Fall of Canadian Broadcasting." *Queen's Quarterly* 68 (Summer, 1961): 213–25.

Stewart, Andrew and William H.N. Hull, *Canadian Television Policy and the Board of Broadcast Governors, 1958–1968*. Edmonton: University of Alberta Press, 1994.

Stewart, Sandy. *Here's Looking at Us: A Personal History of Television in Canada*. Toronto: CBC Enterprises, 1986.

Stursberg, Peter. *Mister Broadcasting: The Ernie Bushnell Story*. Toronto: Peter Martin Associates, 1971.

Vipond, Mary. *Listening In: The First Decade of Canadian Broadcasting, 1922–1932*. Montreal and Kingston: McGill-Queen's University Press, 1992.

Weir, E. Austin. *The Struggle for National Broadcasting in Canada*. Toronto: McClelland and Stewart, 1965.

INDEX

Page numbers in italics indicate photographs.